BELIZE GUIDE

YOUR PASSPORT TO GREAT TRAVEL!

CRITICAL ACCLAIM FOR OPEN ROAD PUBLISHING'S CENTRAL AMERICA TRAVEL GUIDES

"**Belize Guide** is *the* book you need. Don't leave home without it. Invaluable."
- *International Travel News*

"If a visiting tourist had to limit himself to one book, the **Costa Rica Guide** would certainly be my recommendation... As accurate, detailed and practically oriented as any I have seen...this book is a pleasure to read."
The Tico Times (Costa Rica's weekly English language newspaper)

"If you have to choose one guidebook, Paul Glassman's **Costa Rica Guide** provides a wealth of practical information, with a sharp eye and a sense of humor."
Travel and Leisure

"... full of well-researched information on hotels, restaurants, sightseeing, history, and culture ... Selections for lodging and food cover a wide range of prices with plenty of inexpensive and moderate choices. Glassman's practical information tips are worth the price of the book alone ... definitely recommended." -
Series Reviews (Reviews of Travel Guide Series)

Guatemala Guide is "filled with useful information ... thoroughly explores the territory and subject."
Booklist

ABOUT THE AUTHORS

Paul Glassman is the foremost authority on Central American travel, and has been writing best-selling travel guides to the area since 1977. His **Costa Rica Guide**, **Belize Guide**, **Guatemala Guide**, **Honduras & Bay Islands Guide** and **Central America Guide** are the best sources for accurate, comprehensive, inside travel information to these beautiful and exciting lands. His research and attention to detail is unsurpassed, his style lively and literate. These books are widely considered to be the classic guides to Central America.

Ron Charles, the updater of this edition, is a professional travel journalist and author of Open Road guides to Spain, Portugal, and Bermuda.

HIT THE OPEN ROAD - WITH OPEN ROAD PUBLISHING!

Open Road Publishing now has guide books to exciting, fun destinations on four continents, but, oddly enough, some people out there still don't know who we are! We're old college pals and veteran travelers who decided to join forces to bring you the best travel guides available anywhere!

No small task, but here's what we offer:

• All Open Road publications are written by authors, authors with a distinct, opinionated point of view – not some sterile committee or team of writers. Our authors are experts in the areas covered and are polished writers.

• Our guides are geared to people who want great vacations, great value, and great tips for both standard tourist sites *and* fun, unique alternatives.

• We're strong on the basics, but we also provide terrific choices for those looking to get off the beaten path and *experience* the country or city – not just *see* it or pass through it.

• We give you the best, but we also tell you about the worst and what to avoid. Nobody should waste their time and money on their hard-earned vacation because of bad or inadequate travel advice.

• Our guides assume nothing. We tell you everything you need to know to have the trip of a lifetime – presented in a fun, literate, no-nonsense style.

• And, above all, we welcome your input, ideas, and suggestions to help us put out the best travel guides possible.

BELIZE GUIDE

YOUR PASSPORT TO GREAT TRAVEL!

PAUL GLASSMAN

OPEN ROAD PUBLISHING

OPEN ROAD PUBLISHING

We offer travel guides to American and foreign locales. Our books tell it like it is, often with an opinionated edge, and our experienced authors always give you all the information you need to have the trip of a lifetime. Write for your free catalog of all our titles, including our golf and restaurant guides.

Catalog Department, Open Road Publishing
P.O. Box 20226, Columbus Circle Station, New York, NY 10023

7th Edition

Library of Congress Catalog Card No. 95-70239
ISBN 1-883323-25-8

Front cover photo and inside photos by Ron Charles; back cover photos courtesy of Belize Tourist Board.

TABLE OF CONTENTS

MAPS & SIDEBARS

MAPS

SIDEBARS

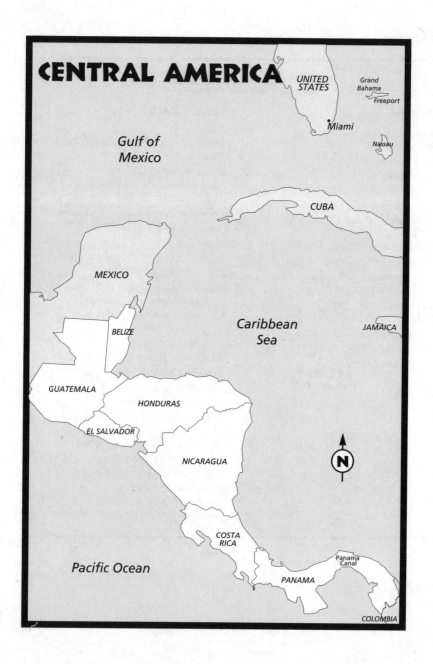

1. INTRODUCTION

Belize fills every adventure fantasy. It is is nearby, spectacular, and virtually unknown.

Coral atolls recall the South Seas. A submarine fantasy world thrives along a great barrier reef. Lush rain forests conceal ancient Mayan temples. The people come in every color, speak a dozen languages, yet number fewer than 200,000.

The obvious attractions of a warm climate and idyllic islands, little-exploited fishing, and spectacular submarine scenery along the barrier reef has not been spoiled by mass tourism with its potentially clumsy impact. No charter flights arrive with hundreds of vacationers, no streets are lined end to end with shops selling tourist trinkets, no tours depart on schedule for made-up attractions.

But natural wonders abound. A visit to Belize can still be an adventure, or it can be totally relaxing.

There are islets dotted with palm trees — and no people. There is deep-sea fishing, and bonefishing in the flats. There are rivers rushing down through granite boulders into jungles populated by monkeys and jaguars. There are insects yet to be named. There are watering holes with characters out of another century and another way of life. There are resorts that recall the days when travel was not for the masses.

In **BELIZE GUIDE**, you'll discover fascinating places and how to visit them; where to find a comfortable bed; a decent meal; beautiful coral in every shape and color; caves of unknown dimensions and hidden mysteries; fish of astounding size to catch and amazing colors to see; and miles of pristine beaches.

I hope that you enjoy your visit to the intriguing little country of Belize!

The Author's Reflections

My first time in Belize, I stumbled into a wonderland of strange peoples and things. The country was still called British Honduras then — that was in 1967 — and I had expected it to be a little bit British and somewhat Honduran. It was not.

The first Belizeans I met were border officials. Tall, slim blacks in starched shirts and shorts, and peaked caps, they were a sharp contrast to the pot-bellied officials slouching on the Mexican side. To me they spoke English, but what they spoke to each other I could not decipher, though it sounded vaguely African.

My traveling companions on the battered minibus that ran to Belize City were a severe-faced couple with straw hats and straw-colored hair. He in blue coveralls and she in a simple print dress looked as if they belonged to rural Iowa or Nebraska, but their German conversation suggested otherwise. In fact, I shortly learned, they were Mennonites and Belizeans.

Along the road, huts were of the whitewashed, thatched Mayan type. The first town of any size had a Spanish name — Corozal — Spanish-speaking Mestizo inhabitants, and clapboard and concrete-block buildings. It looked as if I had boomeranged back to Mexico. At Orange Walk, my Mennonite traveling companions disembarked and were driven away in a horse-drawn cart on dusty streets that were straight out of the Old West. Not too many miles, but long hours and numerous wrenching bumps later, I sighted Belize City, a shanty Creole town that might have been offloaded from one of the Caribbean islands. Already there were many Belizes.

Still surprised by the human geography of the country, I soon discovered that the territorial limits of Belize included not only limestone plains covered with scrub vegetation, tropical forest, coastal wetlands and piney mountains, but also a rather generous section of paradise. This was offshore Belize, where a chain of coral-and-sand islands, dotted with palm trees and cooled by sea breezes, nestled along the world's second-longest barrier reef. A few native fishermen made an easy living from the bounty of the shallow waters. Fewer still were the visitors who came to enjoy the sport fishing and diving, or to do nothing but relax and appreciate beauty.

Lesser wonders and curiosities abounded. There were places with names like Gallon Jug, Double Head Cabbage and Monkey River; unfamiliar Australian and British and Dutch products on the store shelves in the smallest settlements; and arcane forms of the English language. To my naive eye, the norm in Belize was out of the ordinary, and I would have been only mildly surprised had the Mad Hatter approached me on the street for directions.

That all I saw was new and surprising is, in retrospect, really no surprise. As Aldous Huxley once observed, *"If the world had any ends,*

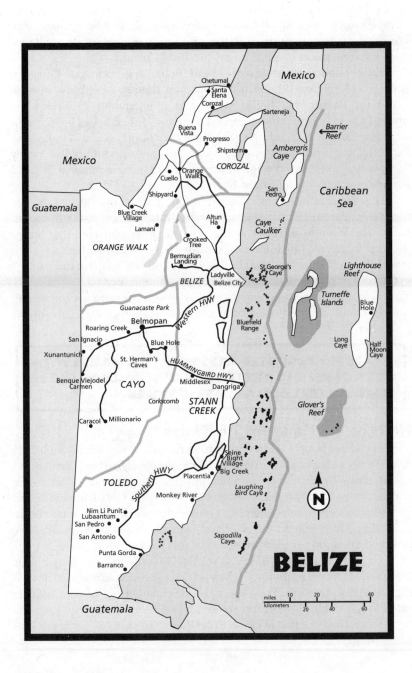

Mexico

Barrier Reef →

Chetumal
Santa Elena
Corozal
Sarteneja
Buena Vista
Progresso
Shipstern
Ambergris Caye
COROZAL
Orange Walk
Cuello
Shipyard
San Pedro
Caribbean Sea

Mexico

Guatemala

Blue Creek Village
Lamani
Altun Ha
Caye Caulker
ORANGE WALK
Crooked Tree
Bermudian Landing
BELIZE
Ladyville
Belize City
St George's Caye
Lighthouse Reef

Guanacaste Park
Roaring Creek
Belmopan
San Ignacio
Blue Hole
Xunantunich
St. Herman's Caves
Western HWY
Bluefield Range
Turneffe Islands
Blue Hole
Long Caye
Half Moon Caye

HUMMINGBIRD HWY
Benque Viejo del Carmen
CAYO
Middlesex
Dangriga
Corkscomb
STANN CREEK
Glover's Reef
Caracol
Millionario

Seine Bight Village
Big Creek
TOLEDO
Southern HWY
Placentia
Laughing Bird Caye
Monkey River

Nim Li Punit
Lubaantum
San Pedro
San Antonio
Sapodilla Caye
Punta Gorda
Barranco

N

BELIZE

Guatemala

miles   10   20   40
kilometers   20   40   60

British Honduras would certainly be one of them. It is not on the way from anywhere to anywhere else. It has no strategic value. It is all but uninhabited." For most people, mention of Belize calls up no mental image at all, not even a stereotypical tropical scene, but only a blank.

Since Huxley wrote, much about Belize has changed. Once an isolated colony dependent on tenuous maritime links with the outside world for its survival, Belize is now an independent nation with a diversifying economy, easily reached from the United States by frequent air service and good roads. Nevertheless, the country remains unknown. Peaceful and non-meddlesome, blissfully unimportant, Belize rarely merits attention in any foreign newspaper. And the new name of the land sounds even less familiar than British Honduras.

That Belize is little known, little developed, is part of its attraction. For the visitor, the land is unspoiled in ways both charming and inconvenient. Comfortable hotels and good restaurants remain hard to come by, except in a few locations, but some of the hostelries recall an earlier era when travel was not for the masses. The inhabitants do not grasp for the visitor's every cent, but they do not cater to every whim, either.

If you find something missing, or discover in your travels something that you want to share with others, please write to me in care of my publisher.

ALL PRICES QUOTED ARE SUBJECT TO CHANGE WITH-OUT NOTICE, AND ARE LISTED IN U.S. DOLLARS, UNLESS BELIZEAN (BZ) DOLLARS ARE SPECIFIED.

Notes on this Expanded 7th Edition

If you have bought earlier editions of this book, you will undoubtedly notice a few changes and additions. I have been assigned to enhance and update *Belize Guide*, and create a new approach to our hotel reviews. The special photo-filled chapter, *Most Memorable Inns & Hotels,* has been added to assist travelers in selecting places to stay that will make their trip more enjoyable. These hotels (and all other businesses listed in this book) have not paid anything for their inclusion in this publication.

I have read hundreds of letters sent to Open Road Publishing by our past readers, and have followed their advice in picking properties deserving of special mention. We hope to include even more of your highest rated lodging selections in future editions of *Belize Guide*.

Please drop us a line at Open Road Publishing with your suggestions and comments.

Ron Charles
International Travel Journalists

TAX ALERT -
NEW V.A.T. ON THE WAY!

Please note that a new Value Added Tax (V.A.T.) is scheduled to take effect by April of 1996. This new tax will most likely be added to the price of goods and services such as hotel rooms, meals, excursions, and most products sold in Belize.

Although the full details and tax rate (rumored to be in the range of 15%) have not been made available at press time, the probability is that all rates quoted in this book may suddenly rise significantly to cover the mandate of this new tax. We wish we had more details to give you, but even the government is still trying to figure the tax out!

2. EXCITING BELIZE!
- OVERVIEW

INTRODUCTION

Travel is getting away from it all and enjoying the sun. Travel is adventure and enlightenment and personal enrichment, and seeing and doing things in ways quite out of the ordinary. Travel is about doing what you like to do, in new places and new ways. Travel is about contributing to the places you visit, as well as appreciating what they have to offer you.

Travel in Belize requires more preparation than for many other destinations, for the country is relatively unknown and facilities are few. It's all too easy to miss the nicer resort areas on the cayes, or to stop only in Belize City and consider the country no more than "interesting." But with some preparation and advice, you'll experience only the best.

Getting around Belize is relatively easy: scheduled flights in small planes provide convenient ways to get around coastal and offshore Belize. Caye Caulker, Caye Chapel, and Corozal in the north, and Dangriga, Placencia, Big Creek (Independence), and Punta Gorda in the south, are served several times daily by flights from Belize City. A virtual air bridge connects Belize City to San Pedro, on Ambergris Caye. There is also fairly reliable daily boat service between various points. Please keep in mind that there are few roads in the whole country that have been paved, so a jeep will be needed to drive around in.

So, aside from getting off the plane, checking into a hotel, and trying the restaurants, what can you do in Belize? Plenty!

Here's a quick preview of what Belize has in store for you:

THE CAYES

Spread out in a 200-mile-long chain parallel to the mainland of Belize are the **cayes**, the little islands that are, for most visitors, the main stopping-points in the country.

For divers, the cayes are bases for exploring the wonders of the nearby barrier reef, second in length only to the Great Barrier Reef of Australia. For fishermen, they are the gateway to teeming, barely exploited waters.

And for just about everyone, they are idyllic locales for relaxation, where palm trees wave in gentle breezes along barely frequented beaches, people go about their business in tiny settlements with sand streets and small-town ways, and the cares of the world have no place.

NORTH FROM BELIZE CITY

The **Northern Highway** is now one of the easier routes for the traveler who wants to visit archaeological sites, experience some of the tropical vegetation zones from coastal swamp to pine barren to limestone scrub to luxuriant semi-rain forest, observe wildlife in the **Crooked Tree** sanctuary, or look in on the small-town Mestizos, rural Mayans, and Mennonites of the north.

Handily, the road provides a gateway to Mexico as well.

BEAUTIFUL AMBERGRIS CAYE

WEST FROM BELIZE CITY

Visit the Spanish-speaking towns of **San Ignacio** and **Benque Viejo**, and the major Mayan ruins of **Xunantunich**. A branch road off the **Western Highway** provides access to **Mountain Pine Ridge**, a beautiful area of pine and hardwood forests in the foothills of the **Maya Mountains**, much of it held as a government reserve for controlled logging.

TRAVEL TO GUATEMALA

In the remote jungle of Guatemala's **Petén** department, removed from any significant settlement of the last several centuries, the jungle reveals temples and palaces over a hundred feet tall, the greatest monuments erected anywhere in the world at the time, bespeaking a civilization intricately organized, conquering in war, yet prizing artistic expression, and scientifically advanced.

You can see the old ceremonial centers of the Maya at Petén, some of them cleared of jungle growth, but many still remaining to be explored, and of course, you can travel onward from **Tikal** to the rest of Guatemala, with its vibrant indigenous culture, colonial monuments, spectacular volcanic scenery and unsurpassed crafts and shopping.

SOUTHERN BELIZE

From **Belmopan**, the **Hummingbird Highway** is paved for about twelve miles through flat country of low bush, much of it once forest that has been logged out, to Caves Branch. The road then rises and runs along the northeastern skirt of the Maya Mountains, through an area of eroded limestone hills.

Here the earth is honeycombed with caves – many of which still contain ancient Mayan altars and offerings – and underground streams, and topped with misty tropical hardwood forest dense with orchids, bromeliads and ferns. There are enchanting areas, with mist and sunlight filtering through ferns and trees, and jungle vegetation tumbling down the limestone face.

REJUVENATING

There is a refuge of pampering in northern Belize, just beyond the ruins of **Altun Ha**, and off the tracks that most visitors follow. The furnishings seem to grow from the jungle floor along with the palms and ferns, suites share the forest canopy with macaws and monkeys, the creatures of the vicinity gather at a pond.

Beauty is the environment of **Maruba Resort** (see the full review), rejuvenation is the theme, attained through full body massage; tropical herbal wrap; seaweed body wrap; aromatherapy massage; mineral baths.

The exotic ingredients are drawn from petals and leaves and seeds and bark – all locally available in Belize.

BICYCLING

Highways are easy going, even for beginning cycle tourists. Distances between overnight stopping points make for practical daily runs of fifty miles or so. A side trip to Altun Ha is possible on a mountain bike, while Xunantunich can be reached on a regular touring bicycle.

FISHING

Spectacular variety and quantity of fish, and a relative scarcity of sports fishermen, make the waters of Belize an angler's dream. Fish is so abundant in Belize that hardly anybody bothers to sell certain species – they're given away. On the cayes, hotel menus groan with seafood specialties. Lovers of fish as well as fishermen come away sated.

FOOD & DRINK

While the food in Belize is usually none too elegant and none too cheap, some of the makings of memorable eating experiences are available. Fish, lobster, shrimp, and many other forms of seafood are fresh, abundant, and relatively cheap. Beef is plentiful, and a number of tropical fruits and vegetables are available. The fact that so much food is imported to Belize in dry or preserved form makes it easy for backpackers and budget travelers to picnic.

Belize produces a number of brands of rum, all of them quite good, with Dutch, German, and American brands of beer also widely available.

KAYAKING

The waters are calm and reef-protected, the day is clear, dolphins arc offshore, waiting to escort you to your immediate destination, three palms on the horizon. Start paddling!

HORSEBACK RIDING

Horses are available in western Belize, in **Mountain Pine Ridge** and near San Ignacio, and even in **San Pedro** out on Ambergris Caye.

RIDING THE RAPIDS, CANOEING, & FLOATING THE LAZY RIVER

The rivers that rush down from the **Maya Mountains** are navigable all year. Macaws, monkeys, and an occasional Maya are sighted along the way on the riverbanks, along with dense forest trailing vines, granite boulders, and even remains of ancient cities. And the water is anything but cold.

SPELUNKING

The **Chiquibul** cave system under the Maya Mountains could be the largest system of caverns in the Western Hemisphere. Over 100 miles of passageways have been surveyed. Rivers flow through caves, emerge, and drop back down again. Recent explorations have yielded fossils of extinct species of insects and crustaceans previously unknown.

TAKING THE KIDS

Belize is for kids, too. After passing favorably on the theoretical concept of pre-adult travel in Belize, I finally took along my three children, then aged 6, 8, and 12. They can't wait to go back.

You can do it all in Belize. Read on!

3. LAND & PEOPLE

LAND

With an area of only 8,866 square miles (22,700 square kilometers), Belize is slightly larger than Massachusetts, Wales, or nearby El Salvador. From the western land border with Guatemala to the Caribbean edge is never a distance of more than 75 miles. From the Rio Hondo at the Mexican frontier to the short southern border with Guatemala along the Sarstoon River, Belize stretches a total of 180 miles.

These are the dimensions of a mini-state, and yet Belize is a land of physical variety, from humid coastal swamp to coral islets to pleasant upland plateaus.

THE NORTH

The northern half of Belize is a plain that was once the bed of a sea. Over thousands of years the waters receded, eventually to be covered by a thin layer of soil, scrub vegetation, and dense tropical hardwood forest. But the ripples of the old sea bottom remain in the shallow north-south valleys, water-filled depressions, and low ridges of today's landscape. Where the forest has been cleared — mainly near the Mexican border — the land is productive. Northern Belize yields almost all the country's sugar, the main export, as well as the subsistence crops of corn and beans. But large parts of the north have been undisturbed by farming and settlement since the Classic Mayan era, more than a thousand years ago.

In the north, the coastal area is neither land nor sea, but a sodden, swampy transition between the two, thick with mangrove and grasses, and bordered by tussock grasses, cypress, and sycamore where the land truly separates from water, more than ten miles inland. This fringe is suitable to waterfowl, a paradise for bird-watchers, but hardly fit for agriculture, and less so for human settlement. And yet, by historical circumstance, Belize City and a number of lesser settlements sit squarely and uncomfortably in the swamps.

CENTRAL BELIZE

Toward the center of Belize, the landscape gradually wrinkles. Great inland stretches are covered by sandy soil. Barrens of southern pine — "pine ridge" in local parlance — alternate with stretches of savanna. Throughout the central region run river valleys, carpeted with soil washed down in floods from higher elevations to the south and west.

Their fertility attracted the Maya of the Classic period, who erected one of their greatest ceremonial centers at **Xunantunich**, along the Belize River. Today, farming in the valleys is expanding again, along with cattle grazing.

THE SOUTH

In southwestern Belize, the land rises dramatically to the granite plateaus and peaks of the Maya Mountains. **Victoria Peak**, in the Cockscomb range, is Belize's highest point, at 3,800 feet. Abundant rainfall runs off to the northwest from the highlands in a number of streams that eventually join the Belize River. To the southeast, short rivers rush through a slope combed with overhanging ledges and caves, carrying sand, clay, and silt that over the years have enriched the coastal belt and created beaches.

Southern Belize is a true tropical rain forest, low-lying and wet, with a dense cover of palms, ferns, lianas, and tropical cedar. It rains through most of the year in the south, and annual precipitation can total 150 inches or more, while the north of the country receives less than 60 inches of rainfall, and is dry from November to May.

BELIZE'S GREAT BARRIER REEF

Offshore of mainland Belize, a shallow submarine valley and ridge run parallel to the coast. The visible peaks of the ridge, ranging from ephemeral pinpricks to substantial stretches of sand, coral, and swamp, are the islets that Belizeans call the *cayes*.

Parallel to them, and just beyond, is the 200-mile-long coral barrier reef, second in extent only to Australia's, with its abundant marine life. Together, the cayes and barrier reef are what attracts most visitors to Belize.

OPEN SPACES

Most outstanding about the Belizean landscape is that its native flora and fauna, and not people, are dominant. Centuries after buccaneers first turned from plundering ships offshore to plundering inland forests, Belize is still mostly empty of human settlement, in part even unexplored. Despite all the swamp and granite mountains and pine barrens, a good portion of the country — nearly 30 percent by one estimate — consists of river valleys and plains suitable for agriculture. And yet, only a small fraction of agricultural land is used in a country that imports much of its food.

The carrying-off of the land's resources is, in large part, the history of British Honduras. The settling of the countryside and the exploitation of the land in a rational manner are major preoccupations of a new generation of Belizeans.

PEOPLE

Belize is small, but its population of less than 200,000 is minuscule, even for a country of its size. With all the available elbow room, and the lack of roads and other communications, several ethnic groups have been able to maintain their separate identities. The different peoples of Belize eat and think and dress in their own ways. Even the houses of one group differ from those of another.

How did they all get here? The ancestors of some of today's Belizeans inhabited the country for thousands of years. Others came as slaves. But Belize has also been a haven for the oppressed and the outcast. The forebears of many a Belizean arrived as refugees from war, servitude, and laws that encroached on their ways. If they found no riches, they were at least able to live unmolested.

African heritage predominates among Belizeans, followed by American Indian and European. According to the 1980 census, 40% of Belizeans are Creoles, 33% are Mestizos, about 10% are American Indian, or Mayan, 8% are Garifuna, and 4% are white. The remainder are of some other descent, including East Indian, Lebanese, and Chinese. But cultural groups in Belize transcend racial lines, and with intermarriage, and occasional crossovers in cultural identity, the picture is even more complicated than the figures indicate.

THE CREOLES

Creoles are the dominant ethnic group in Belize. They make up more than half the population, and are the people who most think of themselves as Belizean. Though predominantly African in origin, Creoles come in all shades, and it's perfectly possible to be a blond, blue-eyed Creole, for the term also denotes a way of life.

Most Creoles are descended from the first Scottish buccaneers and wood merchants, and their slaves. Social relations in the early days of the Bay Settlement were remarkably easy for the times. Labor was in short supply, and masters could not afford to mistreat their slaves. The racial prejudices of strait-laced society and of the plantation had no place, and interracial unions were never anything but the norm. Racial distinctions between black and white soon blurred, and social distinctions as well.

Creoles dominate the commerce and administration of Belize. For the most part, they live in Belize City and the larger towns. Traditionally class-conscious, they have always spurned farming as beneath their dignity, a heritage from the boom days when logging was lucrative and nobody worked the land.

The Creole language is mellifluous, picturesque, and hardly intelligible to outsiders who speak English. Archaic usages and phrases abound. A **backra** is a white man, the term deriving from the raw backs of whites who stayed in the sun too long. A meal is tea, as it still is in Ireland. Syllables are stressed as if to maximize rhythm. No social stigma attaches to speaking Creole, as it does in some of the former British islands; all classes converse in the lingua franca. Fortunately for outsiders, Creole Belizeans are also adept at a more standard and equally charming form of English.

It is not a racial stereotype or a prejudice to say that Creoles love partying and good times. In the old days, workers spent their advances at the start of the logging season on liquor. Other wild times were seen at the end of the season, and throughout the idle time when the forests were too wet to be worked. The carousing tradition has been carried to the present. Labor is not the only part of life; there's love and liquor when the work is done, and dancing and music. The Creole *brukdown*, recognizably Caribbean, is Belize's national music.

The Creole diet is another legacy of the logging life. Rice and beans, easily stored and carried to lumber camps, are still staples. Though spiced up with fish or meat and fruits at home, Creole food, as served to outsiders, is usually bland.

A few African values survive among Creoles: some believe in spirits, charms, and black magic. Drinking gatherings, with communal stews of game, take place at holidays in rural areas. But, despite the traditional distance between cultures in Belize, practices have been inevitably exchanged. Anthropologists have noted Creoles in the western Cayo district seeking cures from Mayan prayer men; and Catholicism, once the religion only of the Mayans and Mestizos, now counts many adherents among the Creole population.

THE BLACK CARIBS

In central and southern Belize live the **Black Caribs**, also known as **Garífunas**, or **Garinagu**, a people unique to the eastern shore of Central America. To outsiders, a Black Carib may be indistinguishable from a Creole Belizean. But Caribs jealously guard their separate identity and language. Though less than eight percent of the population, they play an important part in national life.

The origin of the Caribs lies in an obscure bit of colonial history. The Carib Indians of South America had, by the seventeenth century, conquered a number of islands in the Lesser Antilles. After Europeans arrived in the Caribbean, escaped and shipwrecked slaves found refuge among the Caribs. Intermarriage resulted in a people predominantly African in racial makeup, but speaking an Indian language, and with a culture that combined African and Red Carib customs.

The conflicting paths of the Caribs and British eventually led to armed conflict. Caribs on the island of St. Vincent rebelled against British authority in 1795. They were subdued and deported to the island of Roatan, off the coast of Honduras, and from there, traded and settled along the coast of Central America. By the 1820s, several thousand were living in southern Belize.

For outsiders, Carib culture is fairly impenetrable, and that is the way the proud Caribs prefer it. Legends about the Caribs abound. Some speak of dark religious practices, or a secret royalty. With or without legends, however, they are a fascinating people.

Caribs are gifted linguists. Many are fluent in the Spanish of nearby Guatemala and Honduras, and some speak the Mayan Indian tongues of the interior, as well as Creole English.

When a Carib dies, days of chanting follow the burial. On festive occasions, Caribs celebrate with street dancing and processions, often in masks and costumes. John-Canoe (or *Yankunu*) dancers perform before Christmas for money, drink, or homemade candies. A conch shell is blown at midnight on December 24th. But other ceremonies are kept by the Caribs to themselves. The religious practices of the Caribs combine African and Indian ceremonies with the Catholicism brought by Europeans.

Many Caribs are fishermen and traders, and the group is well represented among Belize's schoolteachers. Unlike most Creoles, Caribs also work the land. The staple of their diet is cassava, a root that requires laborious processing to remove harmful acids.

Among visitors, and maybe even among Belizeans, Caribs are best known, perhaps, for their music. *Cungo* is a local offshoot of Jamaican reggae. *Punta rock*, most notably performed by Andy Palacio and Children of the Most High, is machine music with the syncopations of the islands, appended through maracas, drums and turtle shells.

Caribs often have Hispanic surnames which, for outsiders, serve as a clue to ethnic identity when other signs are confusing.

MESTIZOS

Mestizos are the second-largest cultural group in Belize. Most are descended from refugees from the Caste War in Yucatan in the nineteenth century. Others migrated to the western Cayo district from Guatemala, and more recently, refugees from El Salvador have made their way to Belize.

Mestizos speak English in commerce and when dealing with outsiders, but Spanish is their language at home. Spanish has official status in Belize, and many non-Hispanic Belizeans can get along in the language, which is becoming increasingly important as trade links with Mexico and Central America develop. In the north and in Belize City, the accent is Mexican; in the west and south, Guatemalan.

The Mestizo areas of Belize have much in common with neighboring Yucatan and Guatemala. Towns center on a main square, and social life focuses on the Catholic church built on one side of it. The humdrum of small-town existence is punctuated throughout the year by fiestas — religious celebrations — at Christmas, Good Friday, and Easter, and on the day of a town's patron saint.

For many years, Mestizo towns were virtually independent of Belize City. The colonial administration, with few services to offer, kept out of strictly local matters. Law and order were in the hands of an *alcalde*, or headman, selected by consensus of the more important townspeople. This system lived on in Belize after it had been discarded in neighboring lands. Local government in Mestizo towns, as elsewhere, in now in the hands of elected councils and courts.

Mestizo food is, of course, mainly Mexican food. Black beans and tortillas — pancakes made from ground, lime-soaked corn — are staples. The diet includes squash and plantains, peppers and spices. Nowadays, Mexican food is as popular with non-Hispanic Belizeans as it is with gringos in the States: nearly everybody in Belize enjoys tamales and tacos.

Many mestizos are farmers, raising corn and beans and sometimes pigs for themselves, along with a few cash crops. The principal of these is sugar cane, the source of Belize's main export, refined sugar.

MAYANS

Mayans were the earliest inhabitants of Belize. Even after the collapse of Classic Mayan civilization, Mayans continued to live in what is now Belize. By the time Europeans arrived, the population was semi-permanent, moving from time to time as *milpas* — corn fields — were burned, cleared, planted and abandoned.

All of the indigenous people of Belize today are called Maya, though they belong to three distinct ethnic groups, and are only partly descended from the original inhabitants. Their languages are related, but different enough from each other that members of one group cannot understand those of another. Though they live mostly apart from each other, they have come to share a common identity as Indians.

Yucatecan Maya

Yucatecan-speaking Maya have inhabited the north of Belize for hundreds of years. Their numbers were bolstered by immigration during the Caste War in Yucatan in the nineteenth century. The Yucatecan Maya are almost entirely a rural people. Many still move periodically to burn off and plant new corn patches. Now, they sometimes must pay a rental fee to a private owner or the government for the use of land.

Living among Mestizos as they do, many Yucatecan Maya speak Spanish as well as their own language. Most live in distinctive huts of plastered limestone with steep thatched roofs, though modern concrete houses are becoming more common.

Kekchi Maya

The Kekchi Indian inhabitants of the southern Toledo district first came to Belize from Guatemala in the nineteenth century to labor on sugar plantations. When the plantations were abandoned, some returned to Guatemala, but others turned to subsistence agriculture. Paradoxically, the Kekchi immigrants included descendants of the Chol Indians who originally populated the south, but were deported by the Spaniards hundreds of years before. When forced labor was introduced on coffee plantations in Guatemala in the late nineteenth century, more Kekchis migrated to the forests of southern Belize, away from interfering authority.

The Kekchis settled San Pedro Columbia and a few nearby villages, where for years they lived virtually independent of the rest of Belize. They built their houses entirely of rough-hewn planks and palm thatch from the surrounding forests, and made their own utensils and furniture. Their trading links were with distant Cobán in Guatemala, from where merchants brought cloth by forest trail.

Kekchi isolation has lessened in recent years, as roads and teachers have reached their settlements. Government-guaranteed prices have brought the Kekchis into the market economy: some grow rice and red beans to sell in the Carib towns on the coast. Others have worked at times in the forests or as agricultural laborers to earn money to buy radios and other consumer items.

Mopan Maya

The third group of Mayas, the Mopan, live in the western part of the Cayo district at Succotz, near Benque Viejo, and in the south, at San Antonio and in smaller settlements. Despite their proximity, the Mopan and Kekchi in the south have mostly kept to their separate villages.

All three Indian groups of Belize have a rich cultural heritage. Their religion is a combination of the Catholicism brought by early missionaries, and the native practices that continued to flourish despite church teachings. The traditional native gods of the harvest and rain and thunder and of the other key elements of Indian life were retained after the conquest, though some were given the names of Catholic saints.

Prayer men, who were able to cure illness with chants and charms, and communicate with the powers of the universe, and herbal healers, continue to function in the absence of priests and doctors. The oral tradition of the Indians tells of demons who inhabit the forests and must be avoided or tricked, of clever animals with human attributes, of spirits who must be appeased with incense and prayers before a corn plot is cleared.

These old practices and beliefs are slowly being lost as radios, satellite television, roads, churches, teachers and clinics bring in the ways of the outside world.

MENNONITES

Some of the most visible of the recent immigrants are **Mennonites**, members of an Anabaptist religious sect who trace their origin to sixteenth-century Switzerland. Over the years, the Mennonites have wandered to Russia, Canada, the United States, Mexico and Paraguay, closing themselves into tight-knit communities, refusing military service, preserving their archaic Low German dialect, and shunning as flamboyant and ungodly any but the simplest clothing and decoration. Most Mennonite sects reject mechanization, and employ only human and animal labor.

In 1959, 3000 Mennonites from Chihuahua — members of a community that had fled to Mexico from encroaching modernity in Canada thirty years before — settled in the Orange Walk area. Their pact with the government exempted them from military service and compulsory insurance programs. Later immigration increased the Mennonite population.

The Mennonites faced great difficulties in adapting their traditional grain cultivation to the tropical climate, and some natives were initially hostile. But gradually, they have transformed themselves into Belize's premier market gardeners, and are now the major producers of poultry and eggs, as well as suppliers of fruits and vegetables.

As they have entered more and more into the world of commerce, some Belizean Mennonites have become less strict about adhering to the old ways. The most conservative have emigrated to more isolated communities in Bolivia. Mennonite men and women, in denim coveralls and simple print frocks, are now seen not only near their settlements in the Orange Walk district and in the west, but wherever in Belize their business takes them.

FLORA

This subject could fill a few books — there are well over 5,000 species of plants in Belize, with many waiting to be classified — but here are some plants that are typical of the climatic zones and agricultural areas of Belize:

Along the swamp coast of northern Belize: mangrove, grasses, ferns and sedges.

In sandy coastal areas and on the cayes: palms, including coconut palms; and the cohune palm, which yields an edible oil, and the nut of which burns nicely as charcoal.

Inland from the swamps: cypress, sycamore, bamboo, sedges and tussock grasses, giving way to scrub vegetation, palmetto and scattered taller trees, such as the Santa Maria (used in construction for its termite resistance).

Farther inland, and along river valleys: logwood, also known as Campeche wood, Belize's original export, found along river banks; mahogany, which has a more scattered growth pattern; rosewood; zericote; Spanish cedar; sapodilla (the chewing-gum tree); ironwood (practically indestructible, and still surviving as lintels in some Mayan temples); amate (wild fig); ceiba (kapok, or silk-cotton); bullet tree; allspice; breadnut; strangler fig; and all kinds of orchids, bromeliads and lianas occupying the available air space. Much of the hardwood forest of Belize may be second growth that appeared after corn patches were abandoned by the Maya. The forests of a few thousand years ago were possibly quite different from those seen today.

In the sandy and poorer soils: pine, with some growth of oak.

Major commercial crops: sugarcane, oranges, grapefruit, rice, red kidney beans, bananas, corn, pasture grasses, cacao.

Garden crops (most as noted by Eric S. Thompson, the ethnologist and archaeologist, around the Indian village of San Antonio in the 1920s): avocados, black beans, bread-nut, cacao, sweet cassava, bitter cassava, chaya (a spinach-like plant), chillies, cotton, custard apple (anona), vine and tree gourds, guava, hemp, jicama ("Mexican potato"), corn, mamey (zapote, or marmalade fruit, or mammee apple), nance, papaya, pine-apple, hog plum (jocote), squash, sweet potato, tobacco, tomato, banana, breadfruit, coconut palm, dwarf royal palm, grapefruit, okra, onion, orange, plantain, rice and yams. Though grown in small home plots, many of these fruits and vegetables are rarely marketed.

CREATURES OF BELIZE

The cast of Belizean characters is not limited to Mayans, Mennonites, Creoles, Garifuna, and White Men. There are kinkajou and King John Crow, wari and jaguars, by these and other names. I once ran into a fellow

RANDOM FLORA OF BELIZE

Here are the names of a few species jotted down over several minutes during a walk through Suzi's garden at Maya Mountain Lodge - with random notes:

achiote in Guatemala, (used as food coloring)
aloe vera
annatto (called ricado in Belize
anona, or custard apple (sweetsop)
Arabian jasmine
areca palm
aurelia
avocado
baboon cap tree
banana
begonia
bird's-nest fern
Boston fern
bougainvillea
cacao
caladium
camellia
cashew
cassia
Century
chaya, callalou (amaranth) and other edible greens
chenille plant (monkey tail)
coconut palms
coffee
coleus
cow's foot, a large-leafed plant used to treat stomach problems
cowfoot (piper petatum)
crabbu (nance)
crimson ixora
croton

crown of thorns
cup of gold (chalice vine)
diefenbacchia
dwarf bird of paradise
dwarf poinciana (blooms all year)
elephant ear or macal, which has an edible tuber
episcia
fan palm
ficus
fig
four o'clock
ginger lily
golden shower tree
guava; jackfruit
heliconia
hibiscus
Indian almond (used for shade)
ixora
kalanchoe
lace fern
lemongrass
life plant
lobster-claw heliconia
maiden hair fern
Malay or "molly" apple
mango; anthurium (flamingo flower)
milk and wine lily
night-blooming cereus
nutmeg
orange-colored Jamaican lime
orchids (at least 24 varieties)

ornamental ginger
papaya
pathos (climbing taro)
periwinkle
philodendron
pineapple
plumaria (locally called "frangipani")
poinciana (or flame tree, blooms once a year)
poinsettia
prayer plant
sapote
sensitive plant
sky vine
snake plant
sorosi
soursop
Spanish thyme
spider plant
star jasmine
Surinam cherry
tamarind (loved by cutter ants)
the butterfly or orchid tree
ti plant
trumpet tree
velvet apple.
walking iris
zericote

at the Maya Mountain Lodge whose sole activity was to classify insects in the Mountain Pine Ridge Reserve. He daily discovered species that had never before been "described in the literature."

For most of the history of Belize, and British Honduras before it, creatures were part of what was "out there," in the sometimes-dangerous hinterland that was entered for farming and hunting.

But an extraordinary turnabout has been accomplished in only a decade or so, and the jaguars that were once hunted have now been taken into the Belizean family.

The patter of a guide at the old Belize Zoo expresses that affection:

There's a jaguar. Did you know it was born at the zoo in 1984? It won't attack you unless you go out of your way to bother it, or threaten its food supply. Hiding in that log is a gibnut. (A what?) A gibnut (pronounced ghibnut – tepezcuintle in Guatemala, paca in the dictionary). I'll toss a banana to make it come out. (It does – cute little thing.)

Did you know that when the Queen of England visited from London, she asked to dine on something typically Belizean, and they gave her gibnut, which is a rodent? That's an injured white hawk. It was shot by people who didn't know any better. They thought it would eat their chickens, but it only eats snakes. We keep it so people will learn. The puma and the jaguar respect each other – they'll pass in the forest without fighting. This is the thorny caxba tree. It lives in peace with the ants that are all over it. That tropical rat snake is harmless, as are the wowla (wowla?) – you call it a boa – and 45 of the 54 species of snake. The ones with the diamond skin pattern are dangerous.

Forest Animals

Forest animals include: opossum (six kinds), howler monkey (baboon), spider monkey, anteater, armadillo, squirrel, skunk, otter, porcupine, agouti, coati, bats, paca (gibnut), fox, raccoon, kinkajou (nightwalker), kuashi, jaguar (tiger in local parlance), margay, jaguarundi, puma, tapir (mountain cow, actually related to the horse), the ferret-like tayra, or *bushdog*, peccary (*wari*), deer, antelope, ocelot, crocodiles, sloth, and assorted others, from lizards, iguanas, boas (wowla), fer de lance and other poisonous snakes down to toads, frogs, snails and the lowly and destructive parasol (wee-wee) ant.

Fish

Fish are mentioned elsewhere, with regard to sport fishing. Among the additional species found in rivers are bass and trout (the latter stocked in the Mountain Pine Ridge Reserve). Cichlids, banded tetras, mollies and toothcarps will be familiar to some visitors as aquarium fish.

Turtles

Offshore on the cayes, turtles were once a staple of the diet of buccaneers and pirates. Green turtles, named for the shade of their fat, are a traditional delicacy, growing to well over 600 pounds. Loggerheads, *lagra* in Belize, have large heads and heart-shaped shells, and grow to 300 pounds. Hawksbills have pointed faces and a hooked beak, and overlapping scales, prized for combs and jewelry.

The nesting grounds of all turtles are threatened by resort development, and pollution of the sea with traps and garbage starves, chokes, strangles, and poisons them.

Birds

Over 500 bird species in Belize include ducks, geese, kites, kingfishers, quail, pheasant, partridge, turkey, crane, pigeon, the great curassow, crested guan, curlew, snipe, ibis, stork (including the rare jabiru, illustrated on paper currency), heron, pelican, grampus, frigate bird, seagull, grackle, egrets, buzzards, nightjar, hawks, osprey, spoonbill, vultures, hummingbirds, owls (spectacled, great-horned and others), toucans (billbirds), macaws, and many other members of the parrot family. Birdwatching areas abound in the many habitats of Belize, but one of the most notable is the Crooked Tree Wildlife Sanctuary.

A comprehensive *Checklist of the Birds of Belize* lists over 500 species, with information about where and when each is most likely to be sighted. There's also space for your own field observations. To obtain a copy, send $3 for Special Publication No. 12 to the **Carnegie Museum of Natural History**, *Publications Secretary, Division of Education, 4400 Forbes Ave., Pittsburgh, PA 15213*. Substantial discounts are available for ten or more copies. The **Belize Audubon Society**, *P. O. Box 1001, Belize City*, also has a checklist, and, especially valuable in the field, a glossary giving "translations" of bird names from Creole to English.

Government Reserves

While the government is encouraging agricultural expansion, with the land-clearing it entails, it is also setting aside national parks to preserve native plants and animals. Reserves include Guanacaste Park near Belmopan, the extensive Mountain Pine Ridge, and the Cockscomb Basin Wildlife Sanctuary in the south.

National Symbols

National symbols of Belize are the black orchid (Encyclia Cochleatum, the national flower); the mahogany tree (Swietenia Macrophilla, the national tree); the keel-billed toucan (Ramphastos Solfuratus, the national bird); and the tapir, or mountain cow (Tapirella Bairdii, the national animal).

PLACE NAMES

Strange and picturesque as are some of the place names in Belize, they have a historical and functional logic. Places called **Boom** (as in Burrel Boom), are located where a chain was placed across a river to catch floating logs. **Walk** (as in Orange Walk) indicates a farm. **Pen** is a cattle farm or enclosure. **Bank** is a log-loading ramp.

Similar interesting tidbits are available in the guide to the Bermudian Landing Baboon Sanctuary, or if you talk to old forest hands, such as the owner of Native Guide Systems: **Never Delay** is a peninsula; walk across its neck to avoid waiting half a day for a boat. **More Force** is a bog; you need more force to get through. **Pulltrouser** is a swamp: "You better get off your dreaded pants or you'll mess them up to get through there.".

MOSQUITO COAST

Myself, I could care less that *The Mosquito Coast* was filmed in Belize, and in previous editions of this book, I have not thought this passing bit of trivia worthy of mention. But it just won't go away. Years after the fact, Harrison Ford remains an inescapable presence for Belizeans, and through them, for all visitors.

You're looking for spectacular fish at Hol Chan, but your guide turns you in the opposite direction: "There's the beach where the hurricane scene was shot."

You're on your way to the Belize Zoo, but your driver wants to turn off to Gracy Rock. "That's where they built the ice machine."

Macy's restaurant is noted for Belizean vittles good and quick, but what you hear is that the star ate there.

The seascape, the coral, the parrotfish, the gibnut, the waterfalls and Mayan ruins of Belize will touch the visitor; but it is the visit of Hollywood that has touched the heart and soul of Belize.

4. A SHORT HISTORY

PRE-COLUMBIAN BELIZE

Long before white men came to the New World, Belize was inhabited by a people called the **Maya**. Dozens of ruined cities in fertile river valleys and throughout the northern plain show that in Mayan times, Belize was far more densely populated than it is today. The Mayan way of life was a stable one: at least one settlement, Cuello, was continuously inhabited for more than 2,500 years. And the Maya were in some ways more advanced than the Europeans of the Middle Ages, for they practiced mathematics and astronomy with astonishing facility.

The ancestors of the Maya probably came to Belize some 4,000 years ago, as part of the great migration of peoples over the Bering Strait from Asia. They were hunters and seed gatherers; but gradually, they developed a settled way of life based on the cultivation of food crops, the most important of which was corn. Abundant corn harvests eventually allowed the formation of larger communities, as labor was freed to create permanent buildings and to administer laws.

As settlements developed, simple thatched structures took on religious use, were set apart from common houses on low platforms, and eventually evolved into temples raised on pyramids. Utensils were manufactured that were beautiful as well as utilitarian. Clay was worked into simple figurines, and later baked to form longer-lasting sculptures.

The early communities probably differed in their ways from each other. But as trade developed, as new peoples migrated into the area and mingled with or conquered their predecessors, a more or less common Mayan way of life came to prevail throughout the lowlands of Belize and adjacent lands. Cities were built with basically similar structures and styles over a wide area. While those of present-day lowland Belize never reached the height and extent of cities in Yucatan and the Petén, they appear to be older, indicating that Mayan culture might have penetrated to the interior of Central America from the Belizean coast.

THE MAYAN CITIES

The more important Mayan cities, such as **Xunantunich**, in western Belize, and **Lubaantun**, in the south, consisted of a main plaza and several lesser plazas, each surrounded by temples set atop mounds, or pyramids, and such smaller structures as palaces with interconnecting rooms, ball courts, and sweat baths. Massive as they sometimes were, these structures were built by the most rudimentary, labor-intensive techniques.

Not knowing the practical use of the wheel, the Maya carried tons of rubble for pyramids and platforms on the backs of humans. This fill was faced with limestone blocks joined by lime mortar. Not having the true arch, the Maya used a primitive version, called the *corbel*. Successive stones on each side of a doorway or hall projected inward, until they could be capped by a single stone. The corbelled arch, with its limited span, resulted in interior spaces that now seem claustrophobically small.

In the cities, carved stones (or stelae) and altars, were set in paved plazas, carved with glyphs that recorded dates, names of rulers, births, deaths, and other significant events. As well, the Maya sculpted the landscape. When a hilltop got in the way of a city plan, it was leveled. When water supply was undependable, plazas were sloped to catch runoff in reservoirs. Throughout the Mayan area, cities were built and rebuilt, reaching their greatest development during the Classic period, from about 300 to 800 A.D.

The centers of the Mayan cities were probably ceremonial precincts, populated by nobles and priests, for there was only limited interior space in Mayan stone buildings. Commoners lived in simpler houses on the outskirts, judging by the remains of many small platforms that could have been house foundations. Daily and occasional activities included ceremonial ball games, sacrificial decapitation (evidenced by finds of skulls), and, of course, building, carving, decorating, and making art objects for the elite.

At Xunantunich, archaeologists discovered a complete jeweler's workshop. Trade must have been carried on with other areas, for jade from highland Guatemala, beads of gold from southern Central America, and Pacific seashells have all been found at Mayan cities in Belize. Raised limestone causeways cut through the jungle, and cargoes were carried along them on the backs of men, for there is no evidence in the murals of Mayan temples or the scenes painted on pottery that the Maya used pack animals.

Trade also followed the rivers of the Petén and the Gulf and Caribbean coasts. Cacao grown in Belize and elsewhere along the coast served as the currency of the Mayan world.

MAYAN AGRICULTURE

Outside of the city centers, agriculture flourished. The Maya took seemingly dreadful swamps, with their store of water, and reworked them into resources that supported large population centers. Raised fields, laboriously created, were drained and irrigated by man-made canals, which might also have served as transport routes. Corn and possibly cassava and yams were cultivated intensively, to provide a nutritious diet, along with breadnuts and forest fruits.

THE MAYAN CALENDAR

While much of the way of life of the Maya remains mysterious, their mathematical and calendrical system is fairly well understood. The Maya used a zero long before the Europeans, and a system of dots and bars to represent the digits from zero to nineteen.

It often seems that the Maya were obsessed with time, but that impression could result from a hazy understanding of most other aspects of their way of life. As a farming people, they needed a reliable way to measure time, though they refined their system to an accuracy unsurpassed in the ancient world. The Yucatán Maya, for example, figured out that the planet Venus passes between the earth and the sun every 584 days. Modern astronomers, using precise instruments, put the figure at 583.92 days.

The basic Mayan year, sometimes called the *vague year*, was made up of 360 days, along with an extra period of five days. A shorter, sacred year, sometimes called the *tzolkin*, consisted of 260 days, each tagged with one of the 260 possible combinations of twenty day names and thirteen day numbers. Any one day would have a name composed of its position in each of the two years (for example, 4 Ahau 2 Cumku), and any such compound name would be repeated only once every 52 solar years.

The Mayan calendar system, and the 52-year cycle, or calendar round, were also used by the other peoples of Mesoamerica. But the Maya had a third calendar as well, the *Long Count*, which kept track of the number of days elapsed since a date equivalent to 3113 B.C. This date was used in much the same way that we now use the birth of Christ as a starting point for reckoning time. Long-count dates inscribed on stelae give the most reliable information about the development of Mayan cities.

The Maya had the most advanced native system of writing in the Americas. It was once generally accepted that each symbol, taken from nature, represented a single word or idea or number, as in Chinese. For decades, only numbers, dates, names, places, and glyphs recording significant milestones in the lives of rulers were understood. But in the last few years, scholars have made new discoveries about Mayan writing, in some cases by finding links between contemporary Maya-related languages and the ancient texts.

It is now known that some glyphs are phonetic syllables that spell out words — there can even be different symbols for the same syllable. Two-thirds of the 800 or so known glyphs, and a third of the phonetic syllables, have been deciphered. And with rapid progress in decoding the remainder, along with the structure of the Mayan language, more and more inscriptions are making sense to modern observers.

THE DECLINE OF THE MAYA

Despite its grandeur, the Classic civilization of the Maya went through a sudden and swift decay, starting in the ninth century A.D., when all city building in Belize and the adjacent lowlands came to a halt, to judge by the lack of later inscribed dates. What disaster took place at that time can only be imagined, but speculation brings up war, revolt, drought, epidemic, and exhaustion of the land as possibilities.

Reduced populations lived in and around the decaying ceremonial centers for some hundreds of years, as Mayan civilization moved northward to the Yucatan. But the settled existence of large groups had all but disappeared by the time the first Europeans came to Belize.

ALTUN HA RUINS

THE EUROPEANS ARRIVE

From the arrival of the Europeans almost to the present, the history of Belize is one of neglect and plunder. This, of course, is the story of many a colony. But in Belize, the neglect was made worse by the territory's uncertain legal status. The plunder of resources went on unbalanced by any concern for the future of the land.

Belize was at first under Spanish dominion. The explorers Vicente Yáñez Pinzón and Juan Díaz de Solís passed through in 1506 or 1508 on their way from Honduras to Yucatan, which gave Spain title by right of discovery, at least in European eyes. But in the subjugations of native empires, Belize was bypassed. There were few inhabitants, no obvious treasures, and no harbors, and a treacherous reef obstructed the maritime approach.

Later in the colonial period, the boundary between Yucatan and Guatemala in what is now Belize was never clearly defined, and officials in neither colony took responsibility for the remote area at the outer reaches of their authority. There was some missionary effort on the western fringes of Belize in the seventeenth century, and in the south, the recalcitrant Chol Indians were deported to lands more accessible to colonial administrators in Guatemala. But the Spaniards, who elsewhere sought to re-create the society of their homeland, left in Belize hardly a dent.

PIRATES, WOODCUTTERS, & SLAVES

Britain's reluctant acquisition of Belize traces back to the early seventeenth century, when Puritan settlers from Providence Island, off Nicaragua, set up trading outposts along the coast of Central America. The Spanish chased away the Puritans in 1641, but other, less peaceful Britishers were more difficult to uproot.

These were the English and Scottish buccaneers who preyed upon the Spanish ships that carried gold and the raw materials whose trade Spain sought to monopolize. Many a Spanish cargo of logwood, a source of dyes, was brought to market by buccaneer capitalists. Belize, with many rivers along which to shelter, and a barrier reef to snag the larger ships of the Spaniards, became a buccaneer haven. A Scottish captain, Peter Wallace, set up a camp at the mouth of one of the rivers, and some say that his name was corrupted into "Belize," the name of the river and country.

Unable to rid its territories of the intruders by force, Spain sought a diplomatic solution. A 1670 treaty provided for English cooperation in the suppression of buccaneering and piracy. The adaptable buccaneers, however, turned to cutting logwood themselves in the forests of Campeche and Belize. Britain wavered between cooperating with the Spanish and supporting the woodcutters in areas that Spain had not settled. Meanwhile, intermittent Spanish attacks on the Belize camps resulted in only temporary evacuations.

By the latter half of the eighteenth century, the British government became more amenable to helping out the woodcutters in what came to be called the **Bay Settlement**. Britain's presence in the Caribbean was increasing. A protectorate was established along a part of the Central American coast called the **Mosquito Shore**, where the Indian population remained unconquered by the Spanish. The treaty that ended the Seven Years' War affirmed Spanish sovereignty in Belize, but granted the British permission to cut wood in the north, and a 1783 treaty extended the woodcutting concession to the Belize River. In fact, that area had already been cut over, and the logwood entrepreneurs were by then operating to the south.

Attempting to catch up with fact, English and Spanish diplomats in 1786 extended the woodcutting concession to the Sibun River in the center of present-day Belize. This last treaty allowed the British to export logwood and mahogany, but prohibited the cultivation of crops – a sign of permanent settlement – and the formation of a government. The settlers ignored the treaty, and soon codified their own laws.

Spain's last efforts to recover Belize came in 1798. When the Spanish fleet appeared off St. George's Caye, the **Baymen**, as the resident woodcutters had come to be called, were ready. The larger Spanish force was driven off on September 10, still celebrated as Belize's national day.

BOOM ◆ ◆ ◆

The population of the Bay Settlement at this time was probably no more than a couple of thousand, most of whom lived in the town of Belize, when they were not off cutting wood. The entrepreneurs of the wood trade were mainly Scottish, but their laborers were black slaves, brought over from Jamaica. Slavery in Belize, however, was not the harsh system that it was in other locales. Slave and master worked side by side, ate the same food, slept in the same rude huts in forest camps. Few slaves took up the Spanish offer of freedom for runaways, and many joined in the defense of the settlement against the Spanish in 1798.

Even after slavery was abolished in the Bay Settlement in 1838, most blacks continued to labor in the forests. At the beginning of the timber season, in December, they were given an advance on their wages. The money was intended for provisions, but in practice, the funds financed a drinking orgy. In the forests, the laborers cut logs and dragged them to rivers, to be floated down to the coast. In May or June, logs were loaded aboard ship for export, and rum was unloaded for another round of the spreeing that, in only slightly subdued form, is still a Belizean tradition.

The commitment to the wood trade in the Bay Settlement was total, and agriculture never had a chance. The swamps around the town of Belize were unsuitable for cultivation, and with a small, transient population, the local market was limited. Agricultural labor was unavailable, for the best money was to be made from the timber merchants, to whom laborers were under exclusive contract.

The settlement grew slowly, without really developing. Beans and rice to feed the populace were imported, along with rum for amusement. Logs moved by river, so no roads were cut to the interior. Formal education was useless for woodcutters, so schools were not built. Town life had a temporary quality, and the population lived in tumbledown shacks that might have been abandoned at any moment.

Nevertheless, with some good luck, the Bay Settlement prospered for many years. The logwood market became glutted at the end of the eighteenth century, and later collapsed, when synthetic dyes were developed. But fortunately for the woodcutters, a new market was opening for mahogany, which was coming into use in fine furniture and cabinetry, and in ships and railroad coaches. Mahogany grew more sparsely and farther from the river banks than logwood, and had to be cut over a greater area. By 1826, the timber harvesting area had expanded to the Sarstoon River, the present-day southern boundary of Belize.

The independence of Central America also gave an economic boost to Belize. British manufactured goods were transshipped from Belize along the coast to the new republics, which lacked their own ports and fleets for the transoceanic trade.

♦ ♦ ♦ AND BUST

Eventually, luck ran out, and boom times in the Bay came to an end. The Central American nations developed direct trading links with the United States and Europe, and coastal shipping declined. The cost of removing mahogany rose dramatically, and supply fell, as woodcutters ventured farther from the rivers.

Meanwhile, African mahogany entered the European market, and steel replaced wood in railroad coaches and ships. Prices tumbled. Exports fell from 13 million board feet in 1846 to 3 million in 1900. With no new bonanzas to exploit, Belize became a backwater.

Over the years, the status of the settlement was regularized. Spain stopped protesting the British presence after losing her American colonies. An 1859 treaty confirmed the boundaries that still exist between Belize and Guatemala.

Meanwhile, the United States recognized British claims in Belize in return for the termination of the British protectorate over the Mosquito

Shore and the Bay Islands, off Honduras. In 1862, British Honduras formally became a colony at the request of its inhabitants, although Britain did not take over administration until 1871.

NEW ARRIVALS

Throughout the nineteenth century, the population of Belize was transformed. The original British and blacks intermarried and formed the **Creole** class that still dominates Belize. On the fringes of the colony, immigrants appeared in what had been unpopulated territory.

Between 1848 and 1858, a race war raged in the Yucatan peninsula of Mexico, to the north. Indians rose up and slaughtered their **Mestizo** and white masters, and all central administration broke down. Those Mestizos who could, fled across the Hondo River into British territory. Later, it was the turn of the Indians to flee from the avenging Mestizos. The battles spilled over into northern Belize, while the merchants of Belize City, ever with an eye toward opportunity, went into the arms trade.

The lasting result of the turmoil was the settlement of the north of the colony. By 1850, the north had a population of about 5,000 people, four-fifths of them recently arrived. Most importantly, they were farmers, who produced both subsistence and market crops.

In the south, the population grew with immigration from neighboring lands. **Black Caribs**, a people of mixed African and American Indian ancestry, entered the south of British Honduras from Guatemala and Honduras, starting in 1802. **Kekchi** and **Mopan** Indians found refuge in the south from forced labor on coffee plantations in Guatemala. A curious addition to the region were refugee Southerners who left the United States after the Civil War, rather than submit to Reconstruction. Their Toledo settlement, near Punta Gorda, flourished for a number of years.

Others came in small numbers from distant lands. **Sepoys** deported from India after the 1857 rebellion, and a few Chinese, worked on sugar plantations in the north. Nevertheless, after the immigration of West Indian plantation laborers and retired soldiers toward the end of the nineteenth century, Creoles were firmly established as the majority.

Efforts to diversify the economy of Belize started and stopped over the years. Bananas and sugar cane were planted in the Stann Creek valley of central Belize, and *chicle* (gum) was bled from sapodilla trees in the forests. But high costs, transportation difficulties and disease brought these and other developments to grief.

British Honduras stumbled along, seeing only occasional prosperity when the price of mahogany temporarily recovered, or when war created work opportunities abroad. The introduction of mechanical equipment cut forest employment even in the good times, and a series of hurricanes in the 1930s and 1940s caused severe damage and left the colony increasingly dependent on British subsidies.

INDEPENDENCE

It was the continuing economic crisis that spurred Belize's independence movement. The colonial administration devalued the currency in 1949, bringing on a sudden increase in the cost of living. Belizeans protested vehemently and without effect, but the People's Committee formed at that time turned into a political party that agitated for independence. Gradually, a democratic system took shape, and by 1965, Belize had full internal self-government.

The only obstacle to complete independence was Guatemala. When the boundaries between Belize and Guatemala were set in 1859, Britain promised to help construct a road from Guatemala City to the Caribbean. Britain helped plan the road, but it was never completed, and a renegotiated treaty that defined British obligations more clearly was never ratified by Guatemala.

The matter was largely forgotten until the 1930s, when Guatemala claimed compensation from Britain to dispose of the road issue. Later, Guatemala demanded that Britain hand over Belize.

As Belizeans began to demand independence, Guatemala became at times histrionic about its claims, and threatened to invade. The matter was negotiated, and even conditionally settled, with Britain offering Guatemala at various times money, a veto over Belizean foreign policy, and chunks of Belizean territory and seabed that might contain oil. Belizeans, wary of a traditionally anti-black Guatemalan government, rejected all agreements.

In the end, Belizean independence was proclaimed on September 21, 1981. Despite some trepidation and a closed border, no Guatemalan invasion took place. British troops remained in Belize to defend the new nation for as long as necessary. In 1988, Belize and Guatemala reached a tentative agreement to normalize relations, but distrust between the two countries continues.

BELIZE TODAY

Government

Belize has a parliamentary form of government. The legislature, called the National Assembly, consists of the House of Representatives, with 28 elected members, and the Senate, with five members named by the prime minister, two by the opposition leader, and one by the governor general.

Internal self-rule was achieved in 1965, under Prime Minister George Price, whose Peoples United Party held firm control of the house of

Representatives for almost twenty years. In 1984, in a stunning turnabout, Belizeans voted into power the United Democratic Party, headed by Manuel Esquivel, whose policies were somewhat more pro-Western and business-oriented than those of his predecessor. Price and the Peoples United Party returned to power by a small margin in September 1989, under such slogans as "Belizeans First," "Belize for Belizeans," and "Belize is not for sale."

Local government is in the hands of elected councils.

The judicial system operates on the basis of statutes enacted in Belize, as well as English common law.

In politics, Belizeans are particularly fortunate in comparison with their Central American neighbors. In Belize, violence in politics is generally confined to vicious verbiage.

Education

School attendance is compulsory between the ages of 6 and 14. There are nearly 200 primary schools, 22 secondary schools, and a teacher's college. Most are church-affiliated, but receive some form of government aid, and all schools are regulated by the government.

More than 90 percent of Belizeans are able to read and write at a minimum level, an extraordinary rate of literacy for a developing country.

Religion

About 60 percent of Belizeans are Catholic, at least nominally. The high proportion derives from the Hispanic heritage of much of the population, and the missionary efforts of American Jesuits. Anglicans form the second-largest denomination, with somewhat more than a fifth of the population as adherents. Other important Protestant sects are Methodists, Baptist and Presbyterian. There are a few Hindu and Moslem Belizeans as well.

The Economy

Independent Belize, like the colony of British Honduras, is dependent on foreign aid, and unable to feed itself without imports. But Belize is also a land without sharp contrast between rich and poor, where social tensions are lacking despite the mixture of ethnic groups, where life is benign, if not bountiful, for most of the inhabitants.

Belizeans are better off than many peoples in the developing areas of the world, though they lag far behind Americans and Europeans. In towns, tumbledown houses without running water are the norm. Gastro-intestinal ailments are a major public health problem. But public sanitation is improving, and the malaria, smallpox, and yellow fever that once scourged the populace have now been wiped out or brought under control.

Over the years, the economic base of Belize has broadened. Sugar, cultivated largely in the northern, Spanish-speaking region, is the major export, followed by citrus fruit, grown in the Stann Creek valley. Lumber remains an important business, though much of the export trade is now in pine, rather than hardwood, and in the form of sawn lumber, not logs. Bananas and fish are also important earners of foreign exchange. Unofficially, marijuana has been a big export, but the government is making a serious effort to hinder the trade.

Export revenues, however, don't pay all the bills for the food that Belize imports, let alone the petroleum products, machinery, radios, and just about every modern product that a tiny country cannot make for itself. The difference has been financed for years by British loans and grants, and by remittances from Belizeans working abroad.

One of the major goals of the government of Belize is to increase local production of food, and to find markets for it in an economy geared to imports. More than 80 percent of cultivable land is idle, much of it held privately in large tracts, a legacy of the amassing of great timber reserves. Taxes on unused land have encouraged private owners to sell off their holdings, while the government makes its own land available for farming, and guarantees prices for staple crops.

The other major national task is diversification of the economy. Poor roads, lack of port facilities, distance from markets, insufficient local demand, lack of a mobile labor supply and high costs have held back foreign investment. Nevertheless, those who bring some capital to Belize and provide regular employment receive encouragement and tax concessions.

5. PLANNING YOUR TRIP

WHEN TO GO - CLIMATE & WEATHER

Dry Season

The record is clear. Most visitors arrive in Belize during the dry season, the northern winter and spring. It coincides with the driest, coolest, most pleasant time in Belize, generally from late November to April. And for divers, the waters offshore are clearest in March and April.

The dry season in the extreme south lasts only from February to April, and is punctuated by storms.

Wet Season

There are also a few good words to be said for what's known as the wet season, which in northern Belize runs from May or June to October, with light rains into December or January. But it never (well, hardly ever), rains all day, because weather forms in a different way than in the temperate latitudes, where a mass of clouds could stay in one place for days.

Most rains are daily revolving storms, which blow in from sea and blow away, leaving plenty of time on any day for hiking, fishing, and generally being outdoors.

Since the rainy season roughly coincides with summer in the north, it's more lightly traveled. Some hotels lower their rates. The downside is that temperatures can get unpleasantly hot.

Some storms, of course, develop into hurricanes, and blast away at anything in their path, but the severe ones occur at intervals that are measured in decades. August brings a two-week dry period of dog days, known as the *mauger*, when the hot, dense air stands still and weighs heavily on the inhabitants. Relief comes in the form of renewed rains, usually blowing in from the west. Toward November, northers blow along the coast, but it no longer rains every day. By January, the rains in the north are gone, and the plateau turns dry and dusty.

Rainfall

Rainfall averages about 50 inches a year (1,250 mm) in the north of Belize, at Corozal, but increases sharply toward the South. At Belize City, annual rainfall is about 74 inches (1,900 mm); at Cayo, in the west, about 70 inches (1,800 mm); at Dangriga, 95 inches (2,400 mm); at Punta Gorda, rainfall can total 160 inches (4,060 mm) in the year.

Temperatures

Temperatures are highest from March to September, and the air is often uncomfortably humid on the mainland, though sea breezes provide some relief along the coast. The temperature in Belize City is usually in the 80s or 90s Fahrenheit (27 to 35 Centigrade), dropping to the 60s or 70s (18 to 24 Centigrade) at night. It's cooler from November to March, with highs in the 70s or 80s, and lows generally in the 60s (15 Centigrade).

In the highlands, nighttime temperatures can even drop to near freezing. Average annual temperature at Belize City is about 80 degrees (27 Centigrade).

BELIZEAN HOLIDAYS

It's annoying to find that businesses are closed down when you were planning to change money, go shopping, and arrange for your flight home. Take a quick look at the list of public holidays below. If any occur while you'll be in Belize, don't plan on getting anything done on that day except relaxing.

January 1	New Year's Day
March 9	Baron Bliss Day
(Moveable)	Good Friday
	Holy Saturday
	Easter Monday
April 21	Queen's Birthday
May 1	Labour Day
May 24	Commonwealth Day
September 10	National Day
September 21	Independence Day
October 12	Columbus Day
November 19	Garifuna Settlement Day
December 25	Christmas
December 26	Boxing Day

Note also that Sunday is still observed quite seriously as a day of rest in Belize. Bus and air service are curtailed. No businesses are open. The churches are full, the bars are empty. Go back to the beach.

ENTRANCE REQUIREMENTS

All visitors need a passport and onward or round-trip ticket in order to enter Belize.

No visa is required for visitors from the United States, Canada, or the United Kingdom, nor for citizens of most countries of Western Europe, the Commonwealth, Central and South America, and U.S. dependencies.

A visa *is* required to be issued before arrival for citizens of China, Colombia, Cuba, India, Libya, Pakistan, Peru, South Africa, and Taiwan. Contact the **Immigration and Nationality Service**, Belmopan, Belize, for issuance.

If in doubt, contact one of the consulates or embassies listed at the end of this chapter, or a British consulate in countries where Belize is not represented.

A visitor's permit will be stamped into your passport at your point of entry. Permits are usually valid for thirty days. However, if your funds are short, or if your appearance is unsavory, you could be allowed a shorter stay, or turned away altogether. Be prepared to show about $50 for each day you plan to stay in Belize, if asked. And try to look presentable, even if it's not your normal style.

For an extension of your permit to stay in Belize, apply at a police station in one of the major towns, or to the immigration department in Belize City, 115 Barrack Rd, and pay the fee of about $15.

Land borders are open around the clock. The exit tax is $12 at the airport (about $2 for children).

USING TRAVEL SPECIALISTS

For many travelers, it's worthwhile to have everything set out in advance, in order to fully use vacation time, find like-minded companions, and obtain counsel from specialists who know the territory.

Because of Belize's dismally low recognition factor, until recently your local travel agent might have been unable or unwilling to assist you with your travel plans. Now that Belize is finally becoming better known to the rest of the world, it is rather easy to book your vacation here through most big city travel agents. Most local travel agencies have access to dozens of package tours to this destination that are now aggressively marketed to them by tour operators and travel wholesalers.

The best way to plan a great trip here is to deal directly with someone who has visited Belize, and can help you to design a slightly more customized itinary (known in the business as an **F.I.T.**). If you have any trouble finding an agent who has been here, one good alternative (that can sometimes save you serious money!) is to get in touch with a specialized tour operator who deals mainly with Belize and not dozens of other resort destinations. Although many of these firms do not sell packages directly to the public, I have listed a few companies who do.

Fortunately, there are a few serious tour operators in the United States and Canada (and now Germany too) that specialize in travel to Belize. Throughout this book I mention local travel agents and excursion operators who can all help tailor a trip or provide you with experiences you can't easily arrange without help (like exploring a cave filled with thousand-year-old Mayan sculptures, or finding a sailboat to charter).

Make sure you read the fine print (some packages require payment of additional tax and service charges upon departure, and leavy stiff cancellation and revision penalties) and compare prices (which can vary considerably for essentially similar packages). Some of these agencies sell travel and Belizean real estate in tandem. In general, meals included with a package are usually no bargain unless you're going into remote and isolated areas.

Always compare prices. Many travel packages for Belize are outrageously overpriced, and without reason, other than that Belize has been at times an "in" destination. Keep in mind that all of these companies will insist on full pre-payment of any and all services you book with them. Most accept checks and major credit cards.

Suggested Specialized Tour Operators

• **Magnum's Belize**, *710 Washington Ave., P. O. Box 1560, Detroit Lakes, MN 56502, tel.218-847-3012, fax 218-847-0334, toll free from the USA and Canada 800-447-2931.* I have found this company to provide excellant prices and advice on selecting a vast selection of better quality hotels and lodges in Belize. The staff knows Belize quite well, and in fact the company owns the well-reviewed Captain Morgan's Retreat on Ambergris Caye. They will also be glad to arrange customized (FIT) programs for individuals and groups with or without excursions, transfers, meals, and airfare. We have never recieved anything but praise from our readers for this company.

• **Belize Resorts**, *c/o J. C. Travel, 10127 Sunset Dr., Miami, FL 33173, tel. or 305-595-3459, fax 305-595-2003.* This is another good selection for finding good packages to Belize. They offer discounted rates on all types of hotels and services that run the full range of the price spectrum. Their staff visits Belize regularly, and has good first hand knowledge of all regions of the country. They also offer cheap airfare add ons from several major US cities.

• **Great Trips**, *P. O. Box 1320, Detroit Lakes, MN 56501, tel. 800-552-3419 or 218-847-4441, 218-847-4442.* The folks at Great Trips know as much as anyone about Belize. A strong point is that they sell Belize as it is, with no illusions about what you'll be getting.

Great Trips also issues a number of comprehensive brochures and booklets with information about travel services in Belize, as well as general background.

- **Triton Tours**, *1111 Veterans Blvd., Suite 5, Kenner, LA 70062-4103, tel. 800-426-0226 or 504-464-7964, fax 504-44-7965.* Long-standing Belize specialists.
- **Ocean Connection**, *16734 El Camino Real, Houston, TX 77062, tel. 800-365-6232.*
- **Belize Tradewinds**, *8715 West North Avenue, Wauwatosa, WI 53226, tel. 800-451-7776 or 414-258-6687.*
- **Best of Belize**, *672 Las Gallinas Ave., San Rafael, CA 94903, tel. 800-735-9520 or 479-2378, fax 800-758-2378.*
- **Travel Belize Ltd.**, *637-B South Broadway, Boulder, CO 80303, tel. 303-494-7797, 800-626-3483.*
- **Le Grand Travel**, *211 Pearl St., Monterey, CA 93940, tel. 408-646-1621.*
- *Island Expeditions Co., 368 - 916 W. Broadway, Vancouver, B.C., Canada V5Z 1K7, tel. 604-687-2428.*
- **Sea Belize & Land Tours**, *10051 S. W. 48 St., Miami, FL 33165-6379, tel. 800-322-1202 or 305-559-0439, fax 305-551-9154.*
- **Vacation Representatives**, *3355 W. Alabama, Suite 750, Houston, TX 77098, tel. 713-526-2262 or 800-444-2992.*
- **Sea & Explore**, *1809 Carol Sue Ave., Gretna, LA 70056, tel. 800-345-9786 or 504-366-9985, fax 504-366-9986.*
- **Toucan Travel**, *32 Traminer Dr., Kenner, LA 70065, tel. 800-747-1381, 504-465-0769, fax 504-464-0325.*
- **Voyagers International**, *P. O. Box 915, Ithaca, NY 14851, tel. 607- 257-3091 or 800-633-0299, fax 607-257-3699.* Wildlife, eco-tourism.

Nature Tours

Some of these agencies have space reserved at remote lodges, which are difficult to book on your own:

- **Victor Emmanuel Nature Tours**, *P. O. Box 33008, Austin, TX 78764, tel. 800-328-VENT, 512-328-5221.*
- **International Zoological Expeditions**, *210 Washington St., Sherborn, MA 01770, tel. 508-655-1461, fax 508-655-4445.* Highly recommended.
- **Worldwide Adventures/Quest Nature Tours**, *920 Yonge St., Toronto, Ontario, M4W 9Z9, tel. 800-387-1483*, specializes in birding trips.

Belize-Based Tour Operators

If your plans call for more intensive planning, or you have a specific interest (remote scuba locations, deep jungle touring, overnight horseback riding trips, cave exploring, ect.) it may well be worth sending a fax to one of the leading tour operators in Belize itself. Most will accept credit cards to book packages, and can create a trip using locations, guides, boats, and properties that many of the big US companies can't match.

You can also get in touch with most tour operators and travel agencies based in Belize by letter or by phone. Most expect you to dial at the drop of a hat. Expect to pay about $1 per minute for nighttime faxes and calls to Belize ($2 to $3 from Canada) if you're having problems in making arrangements. See the Tours and Travel Agencies section in the *Belize City* chapter of this book for extended listings.

- **S & L Travel Services & Tours**, *91 North Front St. (P. O. Box 700), tel. (02) 77593 or (02) 75145, fax (02) 77594*, is run by Lascelle Tillett and his wife Sarita Tillett, two of the most experienced guides in Belize.
- **Discovery Expeditions Belize**, *126 Freetown Road (P. O. Box 1217), tel. (02) 30748, fax (02) 30750*, additional offices at the International Airport and Ramada Royal Reef hotel.
- **Mayaland Tours and Travel**, *67 Eve St., tel. 30515, fax 32242*.

If You Don't Pre-Reserve Your Accommodations

It's always best to try to call at least a day before your intended arrival, in order to make sure that your room is clean and ready. Use toll-free numbers, when available, to contact a hotel's agent in the States, or call Belize direct. Some resorts will request a follow-up check or a credit-card authorization to hold your space when you call well in advance.

When in Belize, call ahead to the next place where you'll be stopping. (Yes, the phones work!) While you're on the line, or when you get to the front desk, *ask for a discount*. Many hotels will give you credit for the 20 percent that would normally go to a travel agent or wholesaler, especially during the rainy season.

You can write, as well, but Belizeans, like their Latin neighbors, push written communication to the bottom of a handy pile. They prefer to deal with a voice or a person. A fax has a better chance of being answered than a letter, especially if your arrival with dollars is imminent.

Some hotels, for various reasons, just do not respond to inquiries from individuals. Often, they're remote facilities that take groups only, or well-established and don't go out of their way for new business. Where you see the words "book through travel agents" as part of a hotel description in this book, you're probably wasting your time and money if you attempt to contact the hotel directly.

GETTING TO BELIZE

By Air From North America

Most visitors will reach Belize by connecting with daily flights from Miami, Houston, or New Orleans. From one of these gateways, the regular round trip fare to Belize City is usually between $330 and $440.

However, as any traveler knows, it's not a matter of what you're supposed to pay, but what fare you can get. Reductions are sometimes available in combination with even a limited ground package. Frequent-flyer credits can be used on Continental and American airlines. Seasonal specials are often available just after Easter, or in the fall. Special 14 and 30-day advance purchase excursion fares can reduce what you have to pay, but they usually come with nonrefundable restrictions. Some tour operators can sell special tickets (know as Net Rate or Bulk Fare) that may be much less expensive than the above mentioned excursion fares offered directly by the same airline, but don't expect to get any frequent flyer points for this type of reservation.

Other airlines serving Belize City from the United States are **TACA**, from Miami, New Orleans and Houston, *tel. 800-535-8780*; **Continental** *tel. 800-231-0856 or 800-525-028*, from New Orleans via Houston and Honduras; and **American Airlines**, *tel. 800-624-6262*. All of these airlines can quote through fares from most U.S. and Canadian cities, even those that they don't service directly.

Be aware that since many flights leave from U.S. gateways early in the afternoon, you might not be able to make it all the way to Belize in one day.

By Other Air Routes

Aerovías and **Aviateca**, *tel. 800-327-9832*, fly several times a week from Belize City to Flores and Guatemala City, Guatemala. Taca flights continue to San Salvador. **Tropic Air**, *tel. 800-422-3435*, operates a tour flight from Belize City to Flores, Guatemala, for bus connections to the Mayan ruins at Tikal.

By Charter Flight

Charter flights travel at least once a week during the high season from several major North American cities and usually go direct to Belize (although some also stop in Costa Rica). These are currently operated from the American cities of Chicago and Minneapolis, and Canadian cities such as Toronto and Vancouver. These so-called Charter Flight Operators sell tickets only through travel agencies, and will not take phone calls or inquires from passengers.

The biggest of these companies are **Pleasure Holidays** in Chicago and **Adventure Tours** in Toronto. Information and schedules on charter flights is available only at most major local travel agencies, not from the company that organizes the charter. Prices vary according to where and when you make your reservation, so check around before you pay. There are some bargains available as little as $900 for your ticket, including a week at hotels in Belize City and perhaps San Pedro. The laws governing charter operators mean that the planes can leave several days late in either direction, and the settlements for lost luggage (a common problem) are painfully limited.

If you want to save a few bucks and don't mind running the risk of arriving totally off schedule (perhaps sleeping at the airport departure lounge for a night or two), they provide a decent alternative to scheduled normal airline service.

By Way of Cancún

A charter flight to Cancún will eliminate several landings and takeoffs and changes of plane from most departure points in the United States and Canada, not to mention slashing your costs. Reasonably priced private transfers can be arranged in advance by calling **S & L Travel Services** in Belize City *at (02) 77593*. Buses to Chetumal, on the border with Belize, run about every hour from Cancún, a trip of five to six hours, connecting with hourly buses for Belize City.

By Car

The 1,350 miles from Brownsville, Texas, through Mexico to the border of Belize can be covered in as little as three days. The shortest route on paved, all-weather highways through Mexico is by way of Tampico, Veracruz, Villahermosa, Escarcega and Chetumal. Burros and pedestrians in the roadway may slow you down at times, but the route is eminently driveable. For vehicle recommendations, driving tips, and possible drawbacks of auto travel in Belize, see the *Getting Around Belize* section of this chapter, a few pages ahead.

By Bus & Train

Bus travel to Belize is easy and cheap. Fast, comfortable, first-class coaches operate from all U.S. border points to Mexico City. Buses for Chetumal, near the Belize border, leave several times a day from the southern inter-city bus terminal in Mexico City. Seats are reserved, so buy tickets as early as possible.

It costs less than $75 to go from Laredo, Texas, to the border of Belize. Travel time is 35 hours, or less by the Gulf Coast route via Veracruz (which might involve midnight bus changes). Buses leave Chetumal hourly for Belize City, from 4 a.m. to 6:30 p.m., passing through Corozal.

Express trains with sleeper cars operate through Mexico as far as Merida, where connections may be made for buses to Chetumal on the Belize border. First-class fares are as economical as those on buses, and second-class Mexican train travel is quite cheap.

By Private Boat & Plane

Maritime ports of entry are Belize City, Corozal, Dangriga, San Pedro (Ambergris Caye), Barranco and Punta Gorda. Report your presence to the police or immigration authorities at one of these ports as soon as possible after entering Belizean territory. No special advance permits are required. You'll need to present the documents of the vessel, a clearance from the last port of call, three copies of the crew and passenger manifest, and three copies of a list of stores or cargo.

Philip Goldson International Airport at Belize City is the only authorized entry point for private planes. Permission to land must be obtained if arriving from Colombia. Belizean airspace is open during daylight hours only. Landing fees are about $5 plus $1.60 per ton of aircraft weight above three tons.

Radio frequencies are: airport control tower, 121 MHz; aerodrome, 118 MHz; VOR-DME, 114.3 MHz.

CUSTOMS ALLOWANCES - ENTERING BELIZE

Visitors are allowed to bring anything they will reasonably need, including fishing and diving equipment. Twenty imperial ounces of liquor (57 cl), 200 cigarettes, and one bottle of perfume may be entered duty-free. Don't bring any firearms for hunting unless you've arranged for clearance in advance.

Pets can be brought to Belize only with written permission obtained in advance from the Ministry of Agriculture. Proof of inoculation against rabies, and a veterinarian's certification of good health, are required. *For information, call 02-45230 in Belize City.*

Citizens' band radios will be held by customs until a license is obtained from the Belize Telecommunications Authority.

CUSTOMS ALLOWANCES - RETURNING HOME

U.S. customs allows an exemption of $400 in goods for each U.S. resident, including one quart of liquor and 200 cigarettes.

Canadian residents may use their once-yearly $300 exemption, or their $100 quarterly exemption for goods brought home, with a limit of 1.1 liters for liquor, and 200 cigarettes.

These specifics are academic, since you probably won't buy much in Belize. Whatever you take home, don't include pre-Columbian artifacts, coral, fish, or shells, including anything made from turtles. These could be confiscated on your way out of Belize, in your home country, and/or land you in jail or delayed with a court case.

Departure Tax

Those flying out of Belize will be subject to a $22.50 (BZ) departure tax that is not included on your airplane ticket. Make sure you have enough US or BZ currency at the end of your trip to cover this tax!

WHAT TO TAKE

The warm climate and informality of Belize make packing easy. Casual clothes are the norm everywhere. On the other hand, you don't want to leave behind any essentials.

Keep your luggage as light as practical, tag your bags inside and out, and pack your indispensable items in your carry-on. And remember that if you don't take it, you might not find it, or you might not want to pay the price.

Before you pack, consider what your trip will be like. If you'll be at one hotel, take as many changes of clothes as you feel you'll need (as long as it all fits in a couple of suitcases), and do the laundry when you get home.

The other extreme is incessant travel, a single change of clothes in a carry-on bag, and laundry in the hotel sink every night. For a vacation on the cayes, bring reading material.

Essentials
• passport
• travelers checks
• tickets
• some U.S. cash in small-denomination bills

Which Clothes?

Take lightweight all-cotton clothing, or loose-fitting, easy-care cotton blends. T-shirts are available at reasonable prices in Belize, but don't count on finding beach wear at reasonable prices. Include:
• hat with ample brim
• a bathing suit
• a few shirts or blouses
• shorts
• comfortable walking shoes. Running shoes will suffice for most purposes, even for jungle walks.
• socks, underclothes
• sandals or surf shoes
• at least one lightweight, long-sleeved top and slacks, in case you overexpose yourself to the sun, and for evenings, when mosquitoes might lurk.
• a light sweater or jacket for cool mornings and evenings, though a

heavier one or a jacket will do if you're going into the Maya Mountains in the dry season.
- a raincoat or umbrella if you travel during the rainy months (late spring through fall in the north).

For the Business Traveler

Businessmen may take a light suit or jacket, though a *guayabera* — a light shirt worn outside the pants, and without a tie — is the more usual "formal" attire in the tropics.

Fishing & Diving

Fishing and diving equipment are available, but the selection is sometimes limited, so you're often better off with your own gear. If you have them, take:
- mask, snorkel and fins
- regulator, buoyancy compensator, certification card, wet suit(optional)
- preferred fishing equipment

Packing for Other Sports

Take equipment for other sports that you practice, as it is unlikely to be found easily in the country. You may want to bring:
- a day bag for carrying purchases, sunscreen, whatever. I prefer a see-through mesh bag — it shows that you have nothing worth stealing. Fanny packs are insecure and undesirable in towns, but fine for the countryside.
- a pen or two, including a felt-tip pen (ballpoints clog up) and paper
- cosmetics, toiletries, and small personal items, including sunglasses, sunscreen, and your favorite personal kit of aspirin or substitute, sunburn cream, malaria pills, spare prescription glasses, mosquito repellent (most convenient in stick form), etc.

Habits, Hobbies, & Vices

- camera and waterproof bag, film (more than you think you'll need), batteries
- camping equipment and flashlights (but note that camping is illegal in public places)
- personal stereo
- favorite cigarettes
- duty-free liquor
- snacks. If you're going to be staying in one place, consider taking a suitcase full of snacks and convenience foods. These are available in Belize City and on Ambergris Caye, but prices are high and selection

is limited. The owners of the Caribbean Villas in San Pedro suggest pancake mix, cold cuts, crackers, and peanut butter.

TRAVELING ON YOUR OWN

Can you travel in a little-known country like Belize, book your own hotels or show up unannounced, find good food and fun things to do? Can you change your plans to stay longer in a nifty place, take off with new friends, or follow your whims?

Of course you can. After all, flexibility and changing plans can be part of the fun and enrichment of travel. And you've picked the right book to show you exactly how to do it!

Space is available almost everywhere. Hotel occupancy in Belize has been running under 40 percent in the last few years. Except at the busiest times — Christmas, New Year's, Easter, and local holidays, such as Garifuna Settlement Day in Dangriga — you can almost always find a place to sleep, room on a diving boat, a seat on the bus, with no advance notice.

Just try to have an idea of a few possible hotels that suit your taste and pocketbook, in order not to be steered to a joint beneath (or above) your dignity; sketch out your itineraries, taking into account your time and available transport; and figure out how much diving and fishing you can afford.

GETTING AROUND BELIZE
By Air

Scheduled flights in small planes provide the most convenient way to get around coastal and offshore Belize. Caye Caulker, Caye Chapel, and Corozal, in the north, and Dangriga, Big Creek (Independence) and Punta Gorda, in the south, are served several times daily by **Maya Airways** and **Tropic Air** from Belize City. A virtual air bridge connects Belize City to San Pedro, on Ambergris Caye. Charter service to all points is available from both the municipal airstrip and the international airport. The frequency of service makes it easy to connect with international flights and avoid having to spend a night in Belize City.

Fares are quite reasonable. It currently costs $22 each way to fly to or from Belize City Municipal Airport to Ambergris Caye, or $38 one way to fly between San Pedro and Belize's main International Airport. To Punta Gorda, otherwise an all-day trip by road, the fare is $63 per direction. Over to Placencia you can expect to shell out about $47 in either direction. Children under 12 can get up to 30% off the above fares when accompanying adults. Maya Airways has just put out a low season 10% cash discount on all adult round-trip fares; call them for details.

Small planes afford an unsurpassable sightseeing opportunity. The sparkling tranquility of Caribbean waters, the scattered dots and irregular masses of land that are the cayes, the barrier reef evidenced by a long line of breaking waves and a sudden change from deep to pale-blue waters, can be no better appreciated than from a plane flying at low altitude.

Details of air service are given in the sections of this book covering Belize City and the towns.

By Bus

Buses run hourly between Belize City and the major towns to the north and west, as well as to Chetumal in Mexico. Service to Dangriga, south of Belize City, is limited to four runs in each direction daily, and on most days, there are only two buses all the way to Punta Gorda. Service is curtailed on Sundays on most routes. Fares are low: the longest bus trip, from Belize City to Punta Gorda, costs about $13.

Belizean buses bear a strong resemblance to American school buses, which is what some of them once were. With adults crowded into kiddie-sized seats, assorted poultry on overhead racks, and leg room so ungenerous that knees are bruised against the back of the next seat at every pothole, the buses are somewhat less than comfortable. They are, however, a significant improvement on the mixed passenger-and-cargo trucks that provided much rougher service only a few years back. And now that roads in the north and west are well surfaced, and distances are short, you need not dread relying on buses to get around. A few of the buses on the northern route are Greyhound-type units. Catch one of these if you're large or fussy.

All bus companies sell reserved seats in advance. It's not a bad idea to show up early and try to get a seat toward the front, which is generally more comfortable. Recent bus schedules are given for most towns mentioned in this book.

A new special service that includes daily door to door shuttle service from anywhere in Belize City (including the airports), to anywhere in San Ignacio in the Cayo district, can be arranged by calling **Discovery Expeditions Belize** *at (02) 30748*. The fare is a bargain at only $29 each way, and the brand new air-conditioned vans are much more comfortable than typical long-range buses.

By Boat

Caye Caulker and Ambergris Caye are served by scheduled passenger boats from Belize City. The fare is about $12.50 per person each way to San Pedro, and about $7.50 each way to Caye Caulker. Boat operators can drop passengers at other islands on the way, such as Caye Chapel, Long Caye, and St. George's Caye, but pickup will be chancy.

There is also fairly reliable daily service between Dangriga and Tobacco Caye, and weekly to Glover's Reef.

Otherwise, getting to an island offshore will be arranged as part of a fishing and diving package; or you'll have to charter a boat to fit your own schedule. Figure $130 as a bare minimum from a coastal town to a nearby caye by the barrier reef; more to distant cayes; and up to several hundred dollars to one of the atolls, such as the Turneffe Islands or Lighthouse Reef.

Boat service between Belize City and coastal towns has all but disappeared in favor of road transport.

Cruising on a Houseboat

Weigh anchor and set off for your cruise on inland waters where few visitors penetrate. Enter the Burdon Canal, constructed long ago to connect Belize City with the south, in response to the plaints of Sibun farmers whose produce boats were swamped at sea, since bypassed by the newer roads running inland. Onward, through the Northern and Southern lagoons, the majestic Maya Mountains to the west, howler monkeys and toucans and jabirus in the scrub and forest along the way. Drop anchor at whimsy and jump over the side, or troll for fish as you explore.

But pay attention, first, at your obligatory captain's training course where you'll learn the ins and outs of being a jungle pilot.

River Haven proposes this unique adventure from its river port at Freetown Sibun, southwest of Belize City. The houseboats are not luxurious in Kashmiri style, but trim 10- by 15-foot floating cottages, with accommodations for four in two separate sleeping areas, full bathroom, 12-volt lighting system, CB and AM/FM radio, kitchenette, fresh-water tank, and four-foot-deep rear deck.

The rate is $670 by the week, or you can get a day cruise with pilot and lunch for $230 for up to eight persons (with stops for fishing, snorkeling, swimming, birding, crocodile-watching) and shorter mid-week and weekend rentals.

Follow the signs to River Haven's port, three miles from the junction at Mile 16 on the Western Highway. *For information, write to River Haven, P. O. Box 78, Belize City, fax 02-32742. Visa, Master Card accepted.*

By Car - The Roads

There are two driving experiences in Belize; the Northern and Western highways, along with improved sections of the Hummingbird and Southern highways - and everywhere else. Most roads are not paved, so a rental Jeep will be a wise choice for those who wish to drive themselves. Taxi drivers and tour guides may also be hired from $100 and up per day (plus hotel and meal expenses) to chauffeur you around the country.

The main roads running from Belize City to the Mexican and Guatemalan borders are two lanes wide, and paved in their entirety. The Northern Highway is almost totally flat, while the Western Highway has some gentle grades and ascents in the rolling countryside past Belmopan. If you stick to these roads — which will get you to or near much of what there is to see in Belize — you need have no worries about driving down in the family car.

Elsewhere, roads in Belize are generally narrow, bumpy, and a challenge to vehicle and driver. Unpaved roads become seas of mud after heavy rains; and are dusty, choking, and rock-strewn at other times. A number of forest and swamp tracks are passable only in the driest of times. Absolutely the worst roads in Belize are those that received a narrow strip of asphalt in the center many years ago, and have seen little repair. The potholes are permanent, and wise drivers stay to the side, off the asphalt altogether. The old loop of the Northern Highway via Maskall is a prime example.

It will be apparent that the family sedan is not the best vehicle for travel off the main roads, unless you are indifferent to its return in one piece. In the right vehicle, however, a motoring trip to Belize can be a safe adventure. Drive what the Belizeans drive: a four-wheel-traction Jeep or Land Rover, a minibus with a high clearance, or a sturdy pickup truck. These vehicles are suitable, too, if you're planning to continue to Guatemala, where there are also long stretches of poorly maintained dirt roads.

SOME DRIVING POINTERS

Watch out for the other guy. With the improvement in roads over the past few years, car ownership has increased, but driving skills have not kept pace. Drivers pass on curves, park in the right of way, and drink while at the wheel.

Be prepared to disconnect your catalytic converter, since unleaded gasoline is not available in Belize.

Make sure your vehicle is in good condition. If you have mechanical problems, you might not find spare parts, and your trip will be in ruins.

Take along a couple of spare tires, extra gasoline, water for you and the radiator, points, plugs, electrical tape, belts, and whatever else might bust or foul up on bumpy, dusty, or muddy roads.

Regular gasoline currently costs about $2.25 per U.S. gallon in Belize.

Liability Insurance

Liability insurance coverage, required in Belize, is available at booths just inside the borders from Mexico and Guatemala. It is not advisable to enter Belize on Saturday or Sunday, when the insurance agencies are closed. You'll need your driver's license and registration to get your vehicle into Belize. You'll be required to obtain a temporary 90-day driver's license unless you show an international license.

Road Maps

Maps of Central America that include Belize are available from your local auto club, and from travel bookstores. A map of Belize is available from the Belize Tourist Board, and a detailed topographical map from the Ministry of Natural Resources.

Automobile Rental

No doubt about it, car and jeep rentals are overpriced in Belize. With a bit of advance planning, you can save plenty of money by reserving and prepaying a discounted rate from several major car rental outfits in North America. You can save over 60% per booking in this manner, and can get better cars with unlimited milage ready at the airport when you arriv. I would suggest first calling Budget, National, and Avis to get their prices.

To save even more money, give a call over to **Auto Europe's** staff in the US *at (800) 223-5555*. They will beat any published price, and provide fully refundable vouchers that are accepted with no hassel at the major rental companies' (usually Budget) pick up locations.

Four-wheel-drive Isuzus, Suzukis, and Jeeps are available for rent (see Belize City listings), and are highly recommended for visits to some of the Mayan ruins, or the Mountain Pine Ridge forest reserve.

The prices, however, can be astounding. National Car Rental quotes a rate of $88 daily for a Jeep Cherokee plus 55 cents a mile after the first 75 miles. For that price, you don't get insurance or a drop of gas, or even a firm reservation. Avis quotes a rate of $520 for a small, four-wheel drive Suzuki Samurai, $590 per week for an Isuzu Trooper.

These prices, hard as it is to believe, are lower than they were a couple of years ago, and with increasing competition, there is every chance that they will approach the affordable at some future date.

You can sometimes find older vehicles for rent at reduced rates, though the mechanical condition will be chancy.

You will be substantially responsible for any damage to a rented vehicle.

It's also possible to rent a car in Mexico and drive it into Belize, if you don't tell the agency where you're going. But don't blame me if you have a breakdown or accident, and the car has to be towed back to Mexico for lack of parts. Pay the high cost of a Belizean car rental, or take a taxi, or use public transport.

By Tour

The travel agencies listed at the beginning of this chapter offer packages which include air travel, and accommodations in Belize City, on one of the cayes, or in the Cayo area. Most will arrange for tours that take in archaeological sites and natural points of interest.

Otherwise, any Belize City travel agency can make arrangements. See the *Locally Based Tour Operators & Guides* section of the *Belize City* chapter for more information.

HANG OUT & RELAX IN BELIZE!

6. BASIC INFORMATION

Listed here, in alphabetical order by topic, are practical information and recommendations for your trip to Belize.

BUSINESS HOURS

Most stores are open from 8 a.m. to noon and from 1 to 4 p.m. Many stores are open during morning hours only on Wednesday and Saturday. Some businesses are open from 7 to 9 p.m. as well. Banks are generally open from 8 a.m. to 1 p.m. with afternoon hours on Friday.

COST OF LIVING & TRAVEL

For Central America, Belize is expensive, but for the Caribbean, it is not. High import duties, a limited local market and lack of competition make many items more pricey in Belize than in the United States and Canada. This doesn't mean, however, that a vacation in Belize will carry a high price tag. Here are a few specifics:

Hotel Prices

Hotels are not cheap, but some provide very good value. A good resort hotel in or near San Pedro, on Ambergris Caye, will charges about $170 to $220 double. This includes a basic to comfortable room, all meals, and a seaside location. There are no extras except drinks, tax, service charges in some cases, and rental of diving or fishing equipment. Costs can be reduced considerably if you eat in the village. The rate can be higher – as much as $510 for a double in one somewhat snobby small luxury hotel a few miles north of the village. A more modest hotel in San Pedro, still comfortable but without a seaside location, charges $45 to $70 a night double, without meals.

In Belize City, hotels give you less for your money. A good air conditioned hotel in the best part of town will cost $90 to $160 double without meals (though heavily discounted out of season), while a room for two in the medium range might cost $60 or more with air conditioning, often in unattractive surroundings. There are a few – a very few – budget places that give you better value.

Elsewhere in the countryside on the mainland, and on Caye Caulker, hotel prices are generally lower, though, with the growing popularity of Belize, the middle range is being squeezed out. Pleasant hotels in or near Corozal charge about $55 double. Prices are higher at most country lodges in the western Cayo district. But there are still a number of clean budget hotels in Corozal, San Ignacio, and on Caye Caulker that charge $25 double, or less.

Boat & Diving Rentals

A small fishing boat with outboard motor rents for about $150 to $175 for a full day at one of the larger hotels on Ambergris Caye, with a guide included. Large deep-sea fishing boats rent for $350 per day or more. Lower prices may be negotiated at smaller hotels or with private boat owners on Caye Caulker and in Placencia, especially during the slow season, from May to October.

Diving costs per person range from $35 for a one-tank dive to as much as $125 for a full day, depending on where you're diving and the number of tanks of air. A 3 to 4 day PADI scuba ccertification averages about $350, although during the off season it could be found for as little as $250 if you shop around.

Transport Costs

Costs for public transport and a number of other services are reasonable. The bus fare from Belize City to the Mexican border is about $6. Taxi fares within a town, fixed by the local taxi association, can be more than you might expect. In Belize City, expect to pay $2.50 per tavi ride for a short trip in the central area. But a taxi hired for a day-long outing will cost at least $100. And if you rent a car, you will pay well over $100 for the day.

Food

Meals eaten in restaurants on the mainland cost about $5 as a minimum for the simplest food, such as a piece of fried chicken with rice and beans. On the cayes, prices can be double. Drinking follows a two-tier price system. Belizean beer and rum are inexpensive in bars and hotels, at about $1 to $1.50, while imported beer and drinks cost at least twice as much.

Miscellaneous

In general, anything that's pre-packaged or manufactured and imported will carry a high price in Belize – usually double the American price at least. This includes many food items (e.g., $1.25 for a 10-ounce can of juice), American cigarettes ($2 a pack, versus $1 for Belizean brands) and foreign liquors ($16 for Scotch, $4 for Belizean rum). Exceptions are subsidized European cheeses and powdered milk. Fruits and vegetables in season are lower-priced than similar produce at home, at least on the mainland.

Prices mentioned above and elsewhere in this book were valid at publication.

As in other countries with limited infrastructure and public services, if you hurry from place to place in Belize, or stray from what is easily available, you can bleed, money-wise. Scenarios:

• You're disappointed with the beds at your country lodge near Cayo, and look for a room elsewhere. Extra taxi cost: $60.
• You miss the scheduled flight or boat (boats often leave up tp 30 minutes early) to or from one of the cayes, or the last bus from an inland town, charter an air taxi to make your flight home, and are out of pocket for several hundred dollars.
• You innocently order a glass of California wine, which comes in at $6. Always inquire about the price of goods or services, and plan carefully if you're on a tight budget.

ELECTRICITY

Electricity is supplied at 110 volts, alternating current. American and Canadian appliances should work without any adapters, but ask about the voltage in your hotel before you plug anything in. Some hotels at remote locations have electricity furnished by generators that may shut off at 10pm, or may only supply a DC current of 12 volts.

GETTING MARRIED

Love is why, marriage is what, you know with whom, Belize is where, when is now, and this is how:

• You must be in Belize 15 days to apply for a marriage license.
• Proof must be presented of divorce or death of a previous spouse, if applicable.
• Civil marriage can be performed upon 24 hours' notice and payment of $5 registry fee and a $5 license fee.

HEALTH CONCERNS

Public health standards in Belize are generally higher than elsewhere in the region. If you're travelling to the cayes to sun, swim, fish and dive, there are few health precautions to take. Your food will be safe to eat, you'll have bottled beverages or treated water to drink, and your accommodations will probably be screened to keep out troublesome mosquitoes and other insects. Your biggest problem could be overexposure to the sun. Take it in small doses at first. And remember to wear a shirt when you go snorkeling, so your back doesn't get fried.

Good sense, of course, will tell you to get your health affairs in order before you travel. Catch up on immunizations, such as those for tetanus and polio, and consult your doctor if any condition or suspected condition, such as an ear infection, might trouble you during air travel or when diving. Take along the medicines that you use regularly, and an extra pair of prescription glasses.

For extensive travel in mainland Belize, a malaria preventative, such as Aralen, is advisable. Adult dosage of Aralen is two tablets per week, preferably starting two weeks before leaving home. If you exercise normal cautions about what you eat and drink, no other special shots are needed. But if you're really roughing it, say, on an archaeological dig, your local health department or tropical disease clinic might advise a dose of immunoglobulin for protection against hepatitis, and a typhoid booster. Also, watch what you eat when you're off the beaten track, and try to avoid spreading your own germs to rustic eateries when you're ill.

THE ADVENTURE COAST!

Despite the well-promoted image of Belize as the "Adventure Coast," resist the urge to carry or use hunting knives, harpoons, spears, and other pointed objects. Wounds heal slowly in the topics, and if you do hurt yourself in some remote location, you might find medication unavailable.

Public water supplies in the major towns are generally chlorinated. In some rural areas, water for domestic use is runoff from roofs, stored in cisterns, or "catchments." It's not always safe to drink. An easy treatment is to add a couple of drops of laundry bleach (easily carried in a dropper bottle) to a quart of water. Shake and let stand a half-hour.

MONEY & BANKING

Belize's currency, the dollar, is worth about 50 cents in U.S. funds. Prices for tourists are sometimes quoted in American dollars, so always make sure which currency you're talking about. In this book, all prices are quoted in U.S. dollars, unless Belizean (Bz) dollars are specified.

Belizean paper currency comes in denominations of 1, 2, 5, 10, 20, 50 and 100 dollars, coins in units of 1, 5, 10, 25 ("shilling") and 50 cents, and one dollar.

U.S. dollars in cash are accepted everywhere in Belize, though, technically, you are supposed to change all foreign money at banks. U.S.-dollar travellers checks are accepted at most hotels, often with no commission deducted (banks make a small charge). Canadian dollars and sterling may be exchanged at banks. Other currencies will be turned down. Normal banking hours are generally from 8 a.m. to 1 p.m. weekdays, with afternoon hours on Friday, and some variation from bank to bank.

Personal checks are not accepted by hotels, except from repeat visitors. However, you may send a personal check as a deposit when reserving a room.

Credit Cards

American Express, Visa, and Master Card are now widely accepted at hotels and shops, though a surcharge of at least five percent will be added to your bill at smaller hotels, and at most shops and restaurants. The issuing company's exchange rate costs you another one or two percent.

The service agency for both Visa and Master Card is Credomatic, Hutson St. at Eyre St., Belize City, tel. 32911, fax 32912. Cash advances are available, with a service charge deducted from the proceeds, in addition to the charge imposed by your bank.

Make sure to re-convert your Belizean money to U.S. dollars before leaving the country. The airport bank will exchange Belizean currency to U.S. dollars, with a tax of 2 percent on anything over U.S. $50.

POST OFFICE

Belize's stamps, with their exquisite depictions of the nation's tropical flora and fauna, are among the most beautiful of any country's. Send plenty of cards and letters, even to friends who are not philatelists.

Post offices are located in all towns, and most hotels will accept letters. Hours are 8 a.m. to noon and 1 to 5 p.m. The air mail rate for a post card or half-ounce letter to the United States or Canada is 60¢ Belizean.

Letters may be received at the post office in Belize City or other towns if addressed to your name in care of General Delivery; or you may have your mail sent to your hotel. Documents of value should be sent by registered mail. Gifts should not be sent, except books, which pass duty-free. The Belizean mails are generally quick and reliable.

OBSERVING HER MAJESTY'S FORCES

They are present for the defense and security of the nation, to forestall any concretization of residual Guatemalan claims to the territory of the still-young republic, and to collaborate in training and civic action missions with the Belize Defence Forces. But forgive me, Prime Minister, Her Majesty's Forces also provide a certain backdrop and entertainment value to any trip to Belize.

There they are at the airport, Royal Air Force helicopters under camouflage netting, huge steel baffles against explosives, and artillery pieces ready to fire at invaders. Servicemen in t-shirts, shorts and combat boots off-load cargo planes that bear the red-and-blue bull's-eye. A helicopter unexpectedly bears down on Ambergris Caye, its mission a mystery, until three officers are disgorged for a spot of lunch at Journey's End. A Harrier jump jet roars down the coast, performs an impossible turn, and roars off, in full view of the residents of Punta Gorda, and, more importantly, of the Guatemalans.

Visitors are stuck in mud on the Southern Highway, but rescue appears as a Land Rover full of Gurkha troops in-country for training.

At the pool of the Ramada Royal Reef resort, a Royal Air Force spouse discusses the relative costs of living in Belize City and London, boarding schools, and coming out with a year's worth of cleaning supplies, and applies more sun block.

At the Adventure Inn, a mixed British-Belizean patrol on a mission for mysterious "other purposes" has accomplished its objectives and is given permission by radio to relax. They store their weapons in an empty room, take over the restaurant, string hammocks between the palms _ and incidentally rescue my son from a capsized sailboat.

In the bar of the Belize Biltmore Plaza, the troops recall the tour of duty in Belfast, toss darts, and order up Guinness.

The last time I encountered most of these characters was in a Graham Greene novel, and the only place in the hemisphere you're likely to find them is Belize.

RADIO

Radio Belize operates with English and Spanish programming at 834 cycles on the A.M. dial. A cheap walkman or transistor radio is handy for listening to local F.M. broadcasts, which are a melange of reggae and rock music, religious programming, official announcements, ads, police reports, weather, local news, and relays of the B.B.C. news from London. It all makes for an interesting window on Belizean life.

RETIRING IN BELIZE

Unlike other Central American countries, Belize has no law that specifically seeks to attract foreigners with a pension income.

But also unlike other Central American countries, Belize does not make it extraordinarily difficult for an outsider with modest means to immigrate in a legal manner.

The cost of living in Belize can be higher than for a comparable standard of living in the States, housing is below U.S. standards, and personal security might be either better or worse than where you live now.

But the attractions can be considerable: a mild climate; the availability of land with no restrictions on ownership by outsiders; cheap booze, satellite television, an excellent telephone system, and numerous other comforts lacking elsewhere in the region; a laid-back way of life.

Otherwise, the place to start your inquiries about residence is the Embassy of Belize, *2535 Massachusetts Ave. NW, Washington, DC 20008, tel. 202-332-9636, fax 202-332-6741.*

SHOP (BUT NOT 'TILL YOU DROP)

Nobody comes to Belize for the shopping. The selection of handicrafts pales in comparison to what Mexico and the rest of Central America have to offer. There are, however, a few purchaseables, along with some items to avoid.

Black coral jewelry is supposed to be sold only by authorized persons, though you'll find it everywhere. In the interests of conservation, avoid articles made from coral or turtle shell.

Among the other odds and ends for the tourist trade are jewelry made from ziricote (a hardwood) and mahogany carvings, straw hats, and t-shirts advertising the country, the cayes, the Belizean ski team, Habenero pepper hot sauce, and Belikin beer. Clothing and handicrafts from Guatemala are widely sold, and the prices are reasonable, though of course somewhat higher than in Guatemala itself.

Also, don't overlook the curiosities, foods, and utilitarian items from all over the world that find their way to Belize's shops. Do you need a can of Australian butter or a pair of scissors from China? An enameled coffee pot from Mexico? Take a few oddments home for yourself and your friends. And don't forget to buy your bottle of Belizean rum duty-free before you depart.

STAYING OUT OF TROUBLE

There are only a few possible sore points for visitors to keep in mind. Theft is a serious problem in Belize City, best dealt with by staying at a secure hotel and by not carrying valuables. Use of controlled substances is a touchy matter anywhere. Exercise caution, even if it appears that the locals smoke up with abandon. Native standards will not necessarily be applied to you, and the police might not be polite if they even suspect you of having smoked dope.

The Belize Tourist Board issues this advisory:

In an effort to preserve our resources and amenities for the enjoyment of others, the following is prohibited by law:

1. Removing and exporting of coral.

2. Hunting without a license.

3. Picking orchids in forest reserves.

4. Removing archaeological artifacts.

5. Spear-fishing (while scuba diving).

6. Overnight camping in any public place, including forest reserve (except with police permission).

Sorry campers, if you discover the most beautiful spot in the world and pitch your tent, you could be arrested. Always get permission first.

For permission to stay on public land, *call the Ministry of Natural Resources, Belmopan, tel. 08-22037 or 72232.*

Export of turtle parts is also prohibited.

TAXES

Your hotel bill for room and meals is subject to an 8-percent tax. The departure tax at the international airport is $12, $2 for children. There are no local add-on sales taxes, which mitigates somewhat the impact of high prices for imported goods.

TELEPHONES & TELECOMMUNICATIONS

A modern, automatic telephone system serves Belize City and the major towns. In fact, BTL (Belize Telecommunications Ltd.) is very much like any phone company in North America or Europe, which makes it much the exception in this part of the world.

Calling Belize

From the United States, dial 011-501, followed by the abbreviated Belizean area code (2 for Belize City, 4 for Corozal, etc.) and the local number. Rates are less than $2 for the first minute from the States during the day, and just under $1 for each additional minute. From Canada, the tab is much heftier, $3 Canadian for the first minute and $2 thereafter.

Call 800-235-1154 to place a collect call to Belize from the United States *(800-578-1154 from US Sprint phones).* From Canada, the number is *800-463-1154.*

For telephone numbers not listed in this book, ask your local operator to connect you with directory assistance in Belize. There is a charge from the United States, but the service is usually free from Canada.

Calling Home from Belize

A three-minute call to the States costs about $5, or $7 person-to-person from a private phone or a BTL office. To Europe, the direct-dial rate is about $9 for three minutes ($12 person-to-person); to other countries, $12 ($16 person-to-person).

For service, dial:
• **114**, Calls to Central America and certain other Latin American countries
• **115**, Other international calls
• **555**, AT&T USADirect (for collect and credit-card calls)

Calling Within Belize

Public telephones are available in most towns, identifiable by green booths and lineups. They accept 25¢ coins.

Calls can also be made from BTL offices. In Belize City, the telephone office at 1 Church St. is open from 8 a.m. to 9 p.m. every day. At offices in the major towns of each district, hours are 8 a.m. to noon and 1 to 4 p.m., mornings only on Saturday. Services also include telegrams (20¢ per word to the States), telex, and fax transmission and reception.

Within Belize, use the full area code with "zero" prefix for long distance: 02 for Belize City, 04 for Corozal, etc. Long-distance calls cost from 15 to 60 cents U.S. per minute during the day. Rates drop by 50% between 6 p.m. and 6 a.m.

Service numbers in Belize are:
• **90**, Fire and Ambulance
• **110/112**, Operator
• **113**, Directory Assistance
• **121**, Time of day ("Talking Clock")

Calling from Hotels

Hotels impose hefty surcharges on phone calls. Local calls in Belize City can cost as much as $1 each, even if nobody answers. In-country long-distance costs as much as $5 if placed from a hotel, against 50 cents from a pay phone. Look for a pay phone, when convenient, or place your call from the BTL office. From a hotel, verify charges first.

It will usually be cheaper to call home collect or charge the call to a telephone credit card, but some hotels still charge as much as $5 to your room bill for each one of these (supposedly free) calls.

AREA CODES IN BELIZE

	From the US	Within Belize
Belize City	011-501-2	02
Caye Caulker	011-501-22	022
Ladyville	011-501-25	025
San Pedro	011-501-26	026
Orange Walk	011-501-3	03
Corozal	011-501-4	04
Dangriga	011-501-5	05
Placencia	011-501-6	06
Punta Gorda	011-501-7	07
Belmopan	011-501-8	08
San Ignacio	011-501-92	092
Benque Viejo	011-501-93	093

TELEVISION

Television came with a whack to Belize a few years ago. Local broadcasting did not exist. Then, suddenly, dish antennas made it possible to receive and re-broadcast over 50 channels via satellite signals, and a whole new world opened. Belizeans became Chicago Cubs fans, watched the news from Atlanta, and followed soap operas from Venezuela. As elsewhere in the remote tropics, television changed small-town ways. People stayed glued to the tube, instead of chatting on the street or patronizing bars. Life suddenly seemed dull, compared to what took place on the screen.

Regulation and some order have come to televisionland in Belize. Local operators are allowed to re-broadcast signals on only two channels. In practice, they switch back and forth at will between available programs. The baseball announcer promises news after the game, but you're cut into the middle of the late-night movie from Detroit. A few locally produced Belizean news features are even allowed to interrupt American programs. Where else can you watch Knowlton Nash and the news from Toronto, fading into the reggae sound track of an ad?

The debate continues to rage over whether television is good for Belize, by opening new worlds, or bad, by bringing unrealistic and unsuitable aspirations. Overheard at a bus shelter: "I come to Dangriga, the television tower is looking down on everyone. People are watching the soaps all day, they start acting like the people in the soaps. They want $90 tennis shoes. They're making Belize into a young America. You don't got to go to New York."

Most hotels, even the most modest ones, have a television, and many have their own satellite dishes.

TIME

Belize is on Central Standard Time, equivalent to Greenwich Mean Time less six hours.

TIPPING

Well-trained service personnel are thinly stretched in Belize, so rewards for good service can be rather a moot point. Did I tell you about the time it took seven round-trips to get a room-service order straight? This was in one of Belize City's best hotels.

There is no language problem, but there is a cultural gap. Many Belizeans are well aware of a history of servitude, and it doesn't sit quite right to be waiting on outsiders. This can come across as brusqueness or an I-don't-care attitude, but it's nothing personal. On the other hand, Belizeans have no tradition of extorting baksheesh for every service and non-service, and usually won't hold out their hands, nor will they be excessively servile or ingratiating.

In Belize, if somebody waits on you with a smile and gives you exactly what you want or explains something in detail or extends a special kindness, by all means, express your satisfaction, and not only with a tip. Tell the waiter you appreciate his service. Shake his hand. Thank the woman who cleans your room and brings you towels. You don't have to jump up and perform a jig (although you may well feel like doing so), but let Belizeans know that you are dealing with them as equals.

Tipping at Hotels & Restaurants

Service charges of up to 15% are added to room as well as meal charges at many establishments. This is an unsubtle way to underquote the real rate (when was the last time you tipped the chambermaid fifteen percent?) but at least it relieves you of any additional obligation. It still may be a good idea to leave an additional few dollars to the people who have helped you far above the call of duty.

In hotel restaurants, a 10-15% tip is adequate for good service. In small, family-run diners, tipping is optional, but something extra is always welcome. Give the doorman or porter at your hotel a dollar or two for carrying your bags.

Tipping Guides

Diving and fishing guides should be rewarded with at least a few dollars by each person in a group. If your out on a private tour or excursion, you might want to tip the guide as much as 15% of the total cost if he does a great job. Be more generous if your guide has led you to a good haul of underwater scenery or fish.

Tipping Cabbies

Taxi fares are standardized within towns, and no tip is required unless the driver handles your luggage. In that case, tip as you would a porter. For day trips by taxi, you'll have to negotiate the rate.

WEIGHTS & MEASURES

You'll find the English system of pounds, ounces, inches, yards and miles in use in Belize, though gasoline is sold by the American gallon. And since so much of what Belizeans use is imported, packages are often labeled in the metric system.

In this book, I follow local usage, and give distances in miles and yards.

WHERE TO FIND INFORMATION ABOUT BELIZE

· **Belize Tourist Board**, *421 Seventh Ave., New York, NY 10001, tel. 212-563-6011, 800-624-0686; Fax 212-695-3018.* Contact the Tourist Board's New York representative for exquisite brochures, and a Vacation Planner with listings of hotels and services. For specific information about prices, tours, etc., you'll have to contact the travel agency or hotel directly.

· **Belize Tourist Board**, *Box 325, Belize City, Belize.* The Tourist Board will send a packet of information on request, but will not respond to specific inquiries. For a quick answer, you're better off to contact their New York representative.

· **Embassy of Belize**, *2535 Massachusetts Ave. NW, Washington, DC, 20008, Tel. 202-332-9636, fax 202-332-6741*

· **Belize High Commission**, *112 Kent St., Suite 2005, Ottawa, Ontario K1P 5P2*

· **Belize High Commission**, *10 Harcourt House, 19A Cavendish Square, London W1M 9AD*

· **Belize Tourist Industry Association**, *99 Albert St., Belize City, Belize, Tel. 02-75717 (Call or drop in only).*

· **Belize Tourist Office**, *Calle 58 No. 488, Mérida, Yucatan, Mexico*

· **Belize Tourist Office**, *Lobby, Hotel Parador, Av. Tulum No. 26, Cancun, Mexico*

Publications

An excellent book covering the history, geography and economy of the country is *Formerly British Honduras: A Profile of the New Nation of Belize*, by William D. Setzekorn. Order it from Ohio University Press, Athens, Ohio 45701. Older British publications on various aspects of Belize may sometimes be found in the larger public and university libraries.

The best magazine piece I have seen about Belize is "Wild and Weird in Central America," by Ronald Wright, which appeared in the Summer 1987 edition of *Destinations*, the travel magazine of the Toronto Globe and Mail. Another article, about Lamanai, ran in the November-December 1985 edition of *Equinox*, another Canadian magazine. Mr. Wright's *Time Among the Maya*, published by Weidenfeld & Nicolson (Penguin in Canada) has several chapters describing parts of Belize.

For a highly entertaining fictionalized account of life and things Belizean, read *High Adventure*, a novel by Donald Westlake, published by the Mysterious Press. For more realistic adventure, Alan Rabinowitz' *Jaguar: Struggle and Triumph in the Jungle of Belize* tells about the establishment of the world's first jaguar reserve.

Belize Review, an environmentally conscientious magazine that covers tourism developments, is available on newsstands in Belize, or for $36 per year from Box 1234, Belize City.

Within Belize, Cubola Productions publishes an assortment of titles ranging from history to archaeology to geography to fiction. Among current titles are *The Sinner's Bossanova*, by Glenn Godfrey, an adventure novel set in Belize and New Orleans; *A History of Belize*; *Heart Drum: Spirit Possession in the Garifuna Communities of Belize*; *Atlas of Belize*; and *Warlords and Maize Men: A Guide to the Mayan Sites of Belize*. All volumes are attractively produced, and will be found on sale at major hotels in Belize City, among other places. Or, write for an order form and catalogue to Cubola Productions, 35B Elizabeth Street, Benque Viejo del Carmen, Belize, *or call 093-2083 (011-501-93-2083 from the United States), fax 2240.*

Belize Adventure, a fast-moving fifteen-minute video travelogue covering virtually every type of attraction in the country, is available from Great Belize Productions, Box 679, Belize City. And out in the dumpster behind your video store, you might find a copy of *Caribe* (S C Entertainment Corp.), a forgettable 1989 adventure film with stunning exteriors shot in Belize. *Mosquito Coast*, though filmed in Belize, tells as much about the country as a Spaghetti Western does about Italy.

Skin Diver magazine publishes classified ads for hotels and travel services in Belize.

For detailed topographical maps, write to the Lands and Surveys Department, Ministry of Natural Resources, Belmopan, Belize. There are two maps, one covering the north of the country, one the south. Each costs $7 by mail, including postage. Send a money order. In Belize City, maps are available above the main post office.

Other Sources of Information

- **Chief Information Officer**, Government Information Service, Belmopan, Belize. This office distributes a free monthly publication, *Belize Today*, which covers official activities and, to a certain extent, events and places of interest to tourists.
- **Belize Chamber of Commerce and Industry**, *63 Regent St., Belize City, tel. 73148 (tel. 75108 for the chamber's Export and Investment Promotion Unit)*
- **Comptroller of Customs**, *Customs House, Fort St., Belize City, tel. 77405*
- **Central Bank of Belize**, *Treasury Building, Belmopan (or P. O. Box 852, tel. 77216, Belize City)*
- **Economic Development Office**, *P. O. Box 42, Belmopan, tel. 08-22526*
- **Chief Education Officer**, *West Block, Belmopan*
- **Belize Newspaper Association**, *P. O. Box 707, Belize City*
- **Principal Immigration Officer**, *East Block, Belmopan*
- **Investment Promotion Office**, *Investment Centre, Belmopan*

7. SPORTS & RECREATION

FISHING

Spectacular variety and quantity of fish, and a relative scarcity of sports fishermen, make the waters of Belize an angler's dream. Fish is so abundant in Belize that hardly anybody bothers to sell certain species — they're given away. On the cayes, hotel menus groan with seafood specialties. Lovers of fish as well as fishermen come away sated.

Flats Fishing

In the flats, bonefish is abundant all year. Average weight is about two to six pounds, but they come larger. Permit are also found throughout the year, while tarpon are usually fished from March to July, and average 40 pounds in weight. Other common species are barracuda, snook, jacks, several types of grouper, and varieties of snapper, including mutton, mangrove, black, yellowtail and red.

Ocean Fishing

On the ocean side of the great reef just off the cayes, fishing is said to be excellent for king mackerel, Spanish mackerel, grouper, barracuda, snapper, bonito, blackfin tuna and wahoo. Farther out, deep sea fish include swordfish and tuna. White and blue marlin and sailfish pass through Belizean waters from February through April and September through November.

River Fishing

Belize's rivers and estuaries are good for snook, tarpon, bonefish, snappers, and jack-crevalles. Catfish abound off Belize City, but they're a garbage fish that thrives on sewage. Other marine life includes dolphins and sharks. Commercial fishermen catch shrimp, conch (sea snail) and spiny lobster (or "crawfish"), most of it exported to the United States. Lobster season is from July 14 to March 15. Conch season is from October 1 through June 30.

Preparation

Hotels in the cayes rent out boats and fishing tackle. Guides will steer you to the best-known fishing grounds. But the waters are still so unexploited that you're likely to find a few good spots on your own.

Many of the offshore resorts mentioned elsewhere in this book have week-long fishing packages at an inclusive rate, or you can book such packages through the travel agencies mentioned above. Live-aboard fishing expeditions are also available on the boats mentioned above, in the diving section.

Fishing tackle and rods and reels available at hotels may be of limited variety. Experienced sportsmen will want to bring their own equipment, including a variety of rods, perhaps one each of a light and medium spinning, or fly rod, and one heavier spinning, fly, or baitcasting rod.

Equipment Recommendations

The **Paradise Resort Hotel** on Ambergris Caye makes these recommendations:

- **for bonefish and the flats**, a light, open-face spinning rod, seven feet long, very light lures, four- to six-pound test line, minimum capacity 200 yards
- **for baitcasting**, six- to seven-foot rods, light lures, small reels, capacity 200 yards of 6-pound test line
- **for fly casting**, light rods up to nine feet, WF5- to WF8-size line, floating lines, reel capacity 200 yards of 12- to 20-pound Dacron line, leaders at least as long as the rod.
- **for shoreline and mangrove**, heavier spinning and baitcasting tackle to suit the close quarters — 10- to 20-pound test, 150-yard capacity reels.
- **for fly tackle**, reels with capacity of 150 to 200 yards of 20- to 30-pound-test Dacron-backed line, smooth drag, on rods that handle WF9-WF11 lines.
- **for offshore jigging and trolling**, stiff rods as for along shore, 15-pound test line, 20- to 50-pound test for heavier tackle.

Lures should be varied:
- **for bonefishing**, lightweight skimmers for baitcasting and spinning, small inverted flies for flycasting.
- **for shoreline fishing**, surface-darting plugs, underwater swimming plugs, jigs and spoons for spinning and baitcasting; floating and sinking lines, streamer flies in red and light colors for flycasting. Live bait is not always available, though frozen shrimp can be substituted, according to one experienced fisherman.

What Will It Cost?

A lot of fishing travel is sold as a package that includes room, meals, travel from Belize City to your hotel, and morning and afternoon fishing on six days from a skiff either along the reef or in the flats. The price generally runs from $1,200 to $1,500 based on double occupancy. And despite Belize's reputation for high prices, this is less than you'll spend at fishing lodges elsewhere in Central America.

To book your fishing on-site for only part of your stay, you'll pay about $175 to $200 for a full-day excursion in the flats or along the reef in a small boat for three people, less (but not much less) for half a day. Deep-sea fishing costs about $400 for a full day, $250 for a half day, or more, depending on the boat.

Specialists in arranging fishing in Belize include:
· **Action Belize**, *c/o Van Every, 425 Pine Lake Dr., Naples, FL 33962, tel. 813-775-2079*. Many satisfied clients.
· **PanAngling Travel**, *180 N. Michigan Ave., Chicago, IL 60601, tel. 800-533-4353 or 312-263-0328, fax 312-263-5246.*
· **World Wide Sportsman**, *Box 787, Islamorada, FL 343036, tel. 800-327-2880, 305-664-3692.*

There are many fishing operators within Belize, mentioned throughout this book.

Resorts that specialize in fishing include:
· **El Pescador**, Ambergris Caye
· **Turneffe Flats**
· **Turneffe Island Lodge**
· **Manta Reef Resort**
· **Belize River Lodge**

SPELUNKING - EXPLORE THE NETHERWORLD

Limestone underlies a good part of Belize, and much of it is perforated by caves.

The **Chiquibul** cave system under the Maya Mountains could be the largest system of caverns in the Western Hemisphere. Over 100 miles of passageways have been surveyed, some as much as 100 yards wide. The Belize Chamber is one of the five largest natural caverns in the world. Near the Caves Branch River, south of Belmopan, rivers flow through caves, emerge, and drop back down again. Inland from Punta Gorda, cliffs are combed with smaller caverns.

Recent explorations have yielded fossils of extinct species of insects and crustaceans previously unknown. Mayan sculptures remain in place in many locations. Ancient skeletons, ghoulishly intertwined over the years with stalactites formed by dripping, mineral-rich water, are encrusted with limestone crystal that sparkles in the beam of headlamps.

The caves are not open to casual visitors, but in the last couple of years, it has become possible to explore some of the caves in a safe and organized fashion. The best time to explore is in the dry season — the underground rivers that helped create the caves can flood them during wet periods.

Adventurous Belize *(Box 233, Belize City, tel. 02-33903, fax 02-33966)*, operated by Ian Anderson, offers caving, among many available capers, on a 60,000-acre leased plot near Belmopan, perforated by hundreds of caves. Mr. Anderson is not your typical tour operator. When you accompany him into the jungle and down into caves, you go *his* way, which is to leave sites as if you had never been there. Cigarettes are bagged and removed. Footprints are washed off crystal.

Some of the caves visited by Adventurous Belize are of the walk-in type, others require a rappel down ropes from surface openings. Many are considered archaeologically sensitive, with fossilized Mayan footprints, ancient sculptures, and crystallized skeletons in place. Some caves hold waterfalls. The waters of the inland Blue Hole re-surface on the site, then disappear again. Camping and day trips range from "soft" to "hard" in difficulty.

An underground river tubing trip, suitable even for timid folk, runs from light shaft to light shaft, up to the surface and down under again, around pillars several feet thick carved with Mayan images, with breaks to walk through the jungle where logs have floated through and jammed the thoroughfare. Trips to remote sites last as long as a week.

The price for these excursions runs about $30 per day, more if you're not staying on-site or need to be picked up. A bed with meals in hostel-type rooms in a couple of farm houses off the Hummingbird Highway costs about $60 per person daily for bed and meals, less if you stay in a tent. There is no electricity, and no running water but for a basic cold shower. There are also walking trails on the site, lined with native flora transplanted from the vicinity. Observation decks are being constructed at canopy level.

Mountain Equestrian Trails, *at Mile 8 on the road into Mountain Pine Ridge (Central Farm P.O., 92-3310 or fax 082-3361,* offers caving and underground river trips on the edges of the Chiquibul system, along with horseback excursions.

Whenever you go underground, with whomever, remember that:
• you are (probably) in an unfamiliar environment, and unfamiliar with the dangers
• step only where told to by your guide
• touch nothing that you do not have to touch
• remove nothing

JOURNEY IN THE JUNGLE

Mr. Anderson of the caving trips also offers a subsistence course, a sort of jungle-style Outward Bound, in which participants set off without tents, build shelters of cohune palms, extract water from vines, dig latrines, and live among unexcavated Mayan ruins on breadnuts and whatever game they can track. With global positioning system equipment and cooperation from Her Majesty's Forces in case of urgency, you can't get too lost, but that's the least of potential contretemps. Making it in the wild could well involve clobbering a fer-de-lance that lies in your path. (There's a limit to leaving things as you found them.)

Review your medical insurance before you even think about signing the detailed waiver of liability. If you have your doubts, consider one of the less pure excursions in the wild offered by some of the lodges near San Ignacio-Chaa Creek *(tel. 092-2188)*, **duPlooy's** *(tel. 092-3301)*, or **Red Rooster Inn**, *tel. 092-3016*, among others.

HUNTING

I used to have more to say in this category, but times and laws have changed. Specifically, jaguar-hunting, which used to be a drawing card for some sportsmen, is now prohibited, as is the hunting of wild turkeys, Baird's tapirs, jabiru storks, boobies, alligators, manatee, monkeys, otter (water dogs), young animals, and hunting at night.

Hunting of unprotected species by visitors is not currently encouraged, as Belize builds its reputation as a conservation-minded nation. But hunting for plentiful game, such as the gibnut (paca) and deer, is part of the Belizean way of life. If you are thinking about hunting, make arrangements in advance through a travel agent so that you will be accompanied by a licensed guide in Belize. You'll also need your own license, obtainable from the Forestry Department, Ministry of Natural Resources, Belmopan, for a small fee. Weapons must be registered with the police.

KAYAKING THE SEA FROM CAYE TO CAYE

Put on your t-shirt, sunblock, dark glasses, and hat. You had your training session yesterday and your own sea kayak is on the beach. The waters are calm and reef-protected, the day is clear, dolphins arc offshore, waiting to escort you to your immediate destination, three palms on the horizon. Start paddling!

Turtles race — yes, *race* — out of your way. It's only a few miles to the deserted caye. Schools of 'cuda, rays and parrotfish zip below. You make landfall, set up camp, catch your dinner, snorkel offshore. Tomorrow is another caye, a new mini ecosystem, mangrove or reef or atoll, sand or sea grape or palm.

Exercise this is, strenuous it isn't. You need to be in shape for crossings that range up to six miles and four hours, but you don't need to be a competition athlete. Week-long kayaking trips include time for reading and relaxing. Your kayak is a means to see the offshore, as much as an end. Emergency contact is maintained by radio in case of weather problems or injury.

Operators of kayaking trips include:

- **Slickrock Adventures**, *P. O. Box 1400, Moab, Utah 84532, tel. and fax 801-259-6996*. Oldest operator of kayak trips in Belize, from a base at Glover's Reef, with transfer from the mainland by sailboat.
- **Laughing Heart Adventures**, *P. O. Box 669, Willow Creek, CA 95573, tel. 800-541-1256 or 916-629-3516*, regularly runs kayaking trips.
- **Ecosummer Expeditions**, *1516 Duranleau St., Vancouver B.C., Canada, tel. 604-669-7741, fax 669-3244 or 936 Peace Portal Dr., Blaine WA 98230, tel. 206-332-1000 or 800-688-8605*.
- **Laughing Bird Adventures**, *P. O. Box 131, Olga, WA 98279*, is a new company, operating trips of from five to eleven days from Placencia.
- **Baboon River Canoe Rentals** *in Burrell Boom, Belize, tel. 028-2101*, can set you up with a canoe or kayak for paddling along the Belize River. They're only 20 miles from Belize City, but the area is a jungle, alive with iguanas, toucans, and macaws along the banks.

REJUVENATING

There is a refuge of pampering in northern Belize, just beyond the ruins of Altun Ha, and off the tracks that most visitors follow. The furnishings seem to grow from the jungle floor along with the palms and ferns, suites share the forest canopy with macaws and monkeys, the creatures of the vicinity gather at a pond.

Beauty is the environment of Maruba, rejuvenation is the theme, attained through full body massage; tropical herbal wrap; seaweed body wrap; aromatherapy massage; mineral baths. The exotic ingredients are drawn from petals and leaves and seeds and bark — all locally available in Belize.

Maruba has an a la carte menu for body treatments ($45 to $60), or, if you've been roughing it underwater or on a boat, you can be picked up for lunch, a visit to Altun Ha, and a choice of treatment, at about $150. It's also a fine hotel.

Maruba Resort, *Maskall, tel. 03-22199; or P. O. Box 300703, Houston, TX 77230, tel. 800-627-8227 or 713-799-2031, fax 713-795-8573*.

BICYCLE RIDING

Jean-Pierre Panet, author of *Latin America on Bicycle*, reports that the Northern and Western highways are easy going, even for beginning cycle tourists. Distances between overnight stopping points make for practical daily runs of fifty miles or so. A side trip to Altun Ha is possible on a mountain bike, while Xunantunich can be reached on a regular touring bicycle. Panet took his bicycle with him on the boat to Caye Caulker, and put it on top of a bus when he didn't want to re-trace his route. He found cycling to be an eminently practical way to get around in the dry season.

Panet's book gives useful general information for bicycle touring in the hemisphere, as well as descriptions of trips in several countries. An account of the Belize trip is promised for the next edition.

Riding a bike through Belize is a straightforward affair, with J. P. Panet's advice, but if you're looking for companions, try **Tour de Caña**, *P. O. Box 7293, Philadelphia, PA 19101, tel. 215-222-1253*; or **The Touring Exchange**, *P. O. Box 265, Port Townsend, WA 98368, tel. 206-385-0667*.

In Belize City, mountain bicycles are available for rent at **Bike Belize**, *in the Bakadeer Inn, 74 Cleghorn St. (off Douglas Jones St.), tel. 31400*. A day's usage runs about $10, and the rate drops quickly for multi-day rentals.

In western Belize, **Red Rooster Inn**, *2 Far West St., San Ignacio, tel. 092-3016, fax 2057*, has a fleet of mountain bikes and runs biking/rafting tours at $30 to $50 per day.

On Caye Caulker, the gift shop across from Mad Annies offers new mountain bikes for $2.50 per hour and $12.50 per day.

HORSEBACK RIDING

Horses are available in western Belize, in Mountain Pine Ridge and near San Ignacio, and even in San Pedro out on Ambergris Caye. While horses elsewhere in Latin America can be criollos (economy breeds that get a job done without consuming excess feed) Belizean horses, like Belizean cars, run toward the ample. They eat a lot, and consequently can be pricey to hire. Rates vary wildly, from about $20 for a day on your own to $75 on a guided ride.

Mountain Equestrian Trails, *at Mile 8 on the road into Mountain Pine Ridge (Central Farm P.O., 92-3310 or fax 082-3361*, pioneered horseback travel in Belize. Their full- and half-day trips take visitors over trails and along rivers to waterfalls and canyons that can't be seen from roads. Cost is $45 to $65 per person, excellent box lunch included. They also have multi-day packages that alternate days of riding with motorized visits to ruins, and caving trips.

Guacamallo Treks, *Mile 4-1/2, Pine Ridge Rd. (P. O. Box 198, Belmopan), tel. 092-2188, fax 2060, at Maya Ranch*. Guacamallo offers rides to the vast

Caracol archaeological site, a shorter ride to Pacbitun, and a wagon trip to the Barton Creek Mennonite community. Costs range from $35 for a short ride with breakfast to $280 for the Caracol ride with a night's lodging before and after.

Banana Bank Ranch, n*ear Belmopan, (P. O. Box 48, Belmopan, tel. 08-23180, fax 22366)*, is an American-owned beef farm where 25 saddle horses are kept.

Other lodges and establishments that keep horses or regularly arrange riding are:

• **Warrie Head Lodge**, *Mile 56.5, Western Highway, Teakettle Village.* Information through *Belize Global Travel Services, 41 Albert St. (P. O. Box 244), Belize City, tel. 02-77363, fax 75213.*
• **Maya Mountain Lodge**, **duPlooy's**, **The Grove**, **Chaa Creek**, **Nabitunich**, and **Easy Rider Stables**, *all in or near San Ignacio.*
• **Isla Equestrian**, *in San Pedro, Ambergris Caye.*
• **FITS Equestrian Tours**, *2011 Alamo Pintado Rd., Solvang, CA 93463, tel. 800-666-FITS, 805-688-9494, fax 805-688-2943*, arranges horseback trips in west-central Belize.

RIDING THE RAPIDS, CANOEING, FLOATING THE LAZY RIVER

Rafting is relatively new to Belize, but the practicalities are indisputable: the rivers that rush down from the Maya Mountains are navigable all year. Macaws, monkeys and an occasional Maya are sighted along the way on the riverbanks, along with dense forest trailing vines, granite boulders, and even remains of ancient cities. And the water is anything but cold.

You can arrange canoe trips and rafting, at the **Red Rooster Inn**, *2 Far West St., San Ignacio, tel. 092-3016, fax 2057*. A full-day float trip on the Mopan River (Class I and II rapids) costs from $30 to $50 per person, depending on the number in the group. Included are lunch, snacks and equipment. Half-day biking/rafting tours cost the same or slightly more, again depending on numbers.

For more adventure, Red Rooster also has river trips extending over two, three and four days, at about $40 per day.

Unaccompanied float and canoeing trips down the Macal, Mopan and Belize rivers are offered by the Red Rooster Inn, Float Belize and others in San Ignacio. An all-day trip, unaccompanied by guide, costs $30 and up, depending on where you arrange to be retrieved, and there are hourly and half-day rates.

Organizers provide raft, paddles, helmet, and life jacket. Wear a bathing suit and tennis or surf shoes, and take a change of clothing.

CRUISING THE COAST

For those who spend their vacations cruising, provisions are available at mainland fishing villages and at resorts on the cayes. Here are a few possibilities, starting with sailing down to Belize on your own:

Sailing Down in Your Own Boat

The definitive handbook is *Cruising Guide to Belize and Mexico's Caribbean Coast*, by Freya Rauscher. It's available from *Westcott Cove Publishing Company, P. O. Box 130, Stamford, CT 06904, for $34.95*, and includes numerous maps, charts, and customs information that will get you safely to, through, and out of Belizean waters.

Chartering a Sailboat

To have a sailboat waiting for you, contact a travel agency that specializes in Belize, or one of these sailing services:
- **Associated Mystic Yacht Charters**, *9 Navyaug Rd., Mystic, CT 06355, tel. 800-873-2692, fax 203-536-6081.*
- **Belize Charter Services**, *P. O. Box 743, Belize City, tel. 02-31138.*
- **Belize Marine Enterprises**, *P. O. Box 997, Belize City, tel. 02-45798, fax 30263*, offers sail charters from a base on Moho Caye, less than a mile out from Belize City. Weekly rates range upward from $1,400 "crude" for a 31-foot Irwin, to $7,000 for a boat that sleeps six, with crew and food. Look over the boat *carefully* before you set out and, preferably, before you put down any money.
- **Fanta-Sea Charters**, *Box 768, Belize City, tel. 44396*, operates with a Stingray sailboat out of the Ramada Royal Reef Resort.
- **Caye Caulker Sailboats**, *Caye Caulker, tel. 022-2196.*
- **Seaing is Belizing**, *Caye Caulker, tel. 022-2234.*

Chartering a Motor Boat

Motor vessels without sails can also be secured. **Barothy Belizean Enterprises**, *P. O. Box 1076, Belize City, tel. 025-2017*, operates the 36-foot *M. V. Lucretia B.* for customized cruising.

Taking a Cruise

The ship *Caribbean Prince* sails regularly during the winter from Belize City to Ambergris, Chapel, Caulker, Laughing Bird, Sapodilla and Tobacco cayes, as well as Placencia and Punta Gorda, and continues on up the jungle-lined Río Dulce to Lake Izabal in Guatemala. That's a lot of Belize in twelve days. Prices run from $1,700 to $2,300 per person.

For information, contact **American Canadian Caribbean Line**, *P. O. Box 368, Warren, RI 02885, tel. 800-556-7450.*

The Ukrainian-registered *Gruziya* sails regularly from St. Petersburg, Florida, to Belize, and onward to Honduras. The five-deck vessel has two restaurants, a casino, pool, disco, and a crew offering an unusual Russian and Ukrainian experience in the Caribbean. Contact **Odessa America Cruise Company**, *170 Old Country Rd., Mineola, NY 11501, tel. 800-221-3254.*

Special Expeditions, *720 Fifth Ave., New York, NY 10019, tel. 800-762-0003, 212-765-7740,* also regularly runs seaborne adventures through Belizean waters.

8. SCUBA DIVING

Belize, of course, is the country that was made for diving.

The water is warm, usually about 80 degrees Fahrenheit. A wet suit is needed only as protection against sharp outcroppings. Visibility is superb — often over 100 feet. Waters are calm and practically free of currents in the lee of the reef. Accommodations on the cayes are within a few minutes' ride of major dive sites.

And the diving sites are spectacular.

ONE INCREDIBLE REEF!

The barrier reef, alive with coral and resident fish in every color on the artist's palette, runs for 174 miles parallel to the coast, and, mostly, just a few feet under water, making for easy dives and efficient use of oxygen.

Toward the open sea, steep walls drop off a hundred feet or more. Three atolls rise up from the ocean depths, offering shallow lagoons and a ring of submarine ramparts in waters thousands of feet deep. There are patch reefs and caves. And the Blue Hole of the Lighthouse Reef Lagoon, dropping hundreds of feet under the ocean floor, is comparable to no other diving spot anywhere.

What do you see when you dive in Belize?

Almost all Caribbean corals can be found: brain, elkhorn, lettuce and star coral; pillar coral, several feet long, on patch reefs; undulating sea fans; bouquets of sponges; coral canyons, ledges and caves; orange tube sponges on walls; black coral trees.

There are caves with stalactites that once lay underground, but were flooded in prehistoric time. There are canyons and walls and ledges and cracks and clefts.

And there are schools of rainbow-colored fish — parrotfish, grunts, blue chromis, butterfly fish, indigo hamlets, angelfish, and rock hinds that favor the reef, as well as eels, snappers, tarpon, jacks, groupers and stingrays passing through, all glimmering and shimmering in shafts of light. And dozens of manta rays and turtles; dolphins; nurse sharks that you can pet, if you trust your guide; and sharks from which you are best advised to flee.

This other-world lies only several hundred yards from any hotel on the cayes; in some cases, you can wade from your room by the beach to the drop-off and spectacular wall sites. The truly exceptional is only a little bit farther out.

WHEN TO DIVE

Visibility is always greater than 50 feet, and well over 100 feet during the driest months, from December to April.

Fleeting storms can churn the bottom near the reef and kill visibility for short periods at any time of year, but diving operators claim that there is no difference when you're 80 feet down.

So, according to your skill and diving level, you're likely to find superb conditions most of the time. And during the less-trafficked periods, when rains are more frequent, you can often negotiate lower rates with dive resorts and dive shops.

MAKING ARRANGEMENTS

Escorted dives are easily arranged from most hotels on the cayes and coast. Typical rates on Ambergris Caye range upward from $35 for a single-tank dive, $50 for a two-tank dive, higher for an expedition to outlying sites, such as the Blue Hole. At Caye Chapel, the rate for a close-in dive is about $50. Add $5 to $10 per day for items of personal equipment: mask and fins, buoyancy compensator, and regulator with octopus.

You must bring your PADI certification card to show when you rent scuba equipment or go on non-instructional ocean dives. Those participating in multiple day scuba packages may to be asked to take a checkout dive so that the dive master can determine your skill level. Most operators will also handle free or reduced rate transfers to and from your hotel.

A well maintained decompression chamber is available in San Pedro on Ambergris Caye. If your dive master offers the $1 per tank emergency insurance, I would strongly suggest signing up for it!

DIVE INSTRUCTION

The shallow waters off the cayes, protected by the barrier reef from the turbulence of the open sea beyond, are as tranquil as a huge swimming pool, and are ideal for beginning scuba divers and snorkelers. Resort and certification courses are widely available on Ambergris Caye, and at most island resorts.

Typically, a short 3 hour beginner's resort diving course costs about $125 and includes all equipment and an ocean dive; a PADI certification course over three or four days, $350. If you're booking a week-long diving package at an offshore resort, inquire as to whether instruction is included in the price. If you find a great instructor, you may wish to consider tipping him (an extra $10 per person for each day is the average).

SNORKELING TRIPS

For those of you who want to experience an inexpensive alternative to scuba diving, snorkeling trips can be easily arranged. While several seaside hotels will provide their guests with free snorkeling gear to view the adjacent shallow beaches, your best bet is check out the abundant marine life in the reefs.

From the Cayes, a typical snorkeling excursion by small boat to the reef will set you back between $10 and $35 per person including the use of a mask, fin, and snorkel. The least expensive trips run about an hour or so and depart from Caye Caulker and San Pedro, while mainland departures and half day multiple sight snorkeling trips tend to cost more. You can check with your hotel for details, or walk to the small boat piers and check with the locals for better prices.

Make sure to put some waterproof sunblock on your back since the UV rays penetrate the sea. A disposable waterproof camera with high speed (ASA 400) film would be a wise item to bring with you from home, as they are rather epensive if bought here.

DIVE OPERATORS

Here are some operators or representatives of diving services:
• **Rum Point Divers** in the Placencia area has been offering Belize's most comprehensive (and uniquely educational) scuba programs at their inn since the 1970's. Under the direction of it's legendary owner George Bevier, Rum Point remains the top place to go for those who are serious about exploring the underwater environmentIt's also a superb location for beginners who wish to learn from the absolute finest instructors. The flagship of their extensive fleet of boats is the powerful 42 foot Auriga jet boat. *Give them a call at 06-23239* and get ready for a real ocean adventure. Highly Recommended!
• **Out Island Divers** on Ambergris Caye offers one-day excursions by a combination of plane and dive boat to the Blue Hole of Light House Reef, as well as shorter outings, with guaranteed departures. Two of their boats are live-aboards. *Contact them at P. O. Box 7, San Pedro, tel. 026-2151, fax 2810, or P.O. Box 3455, Estes Park, CO 80517, tel. 800-258-3465 or 303-586-6020)*

· **Indigo Belize**, *P. O. Box 450987, Sunrise, FL 33345, tel.* 800-468-0123, operates the *M/V Manta IV* diving boat, complete with shark cage and video equipment. In San Pedro, inquire at the Belize Yacht Club, or call 026-2130, fax 2834. Their overnight trip to Lighthouse Reef, with five dives and five meals, costs about $230 per person. A three-dive day trip to the Turneffe Islands costs about $110 per person
· **Fantasea Watersports**, *tel. and fax 026-2576*; **Amigos del Mar**, *tel. 026-2706*; **Bottom Time Dive Shop**, *tel. 026-2348*; **The Dive Shop, Ltd.**, *tel. 026-2437*; **Reef Divers**, *tel. 026-2371, fax 2028*; **Hustler Tours**, *tel. 026-2279 (all on Ambergris Caye)*. These guys do so many different scuba, snorkeling, and sea-based excursions that on any given day they have something special to offer.
· **Belize Diving Services**, *Caye Caulker, tel. 022-2175*
· **Blackline Dive Shop**, *P. O. Box 332, Belize City, tel. 33187, fax 31975*
· **Dive In**, *Ramada Royal Reef Resort, Belize City, tel. 30265*
· **Adventure Coast Divers**, *Mile 3, Northern Highway, Belize City, tel. 33185*
· **Belize Diving Service**, *P. O. Box 667, Belize City, tel. 22143*
· **Caribbean Charter Service**, *P. O. Box 752, Belize City, tel. 45814*
· **Maya Landings Marina**, *P. O. Box 997, Belize City, tel. 45798, fax 30263*
· **Placencia Dive Shop**, *Placencia, tel. 06-22017*
· **Boulder Scuba Tours**, *1737 15th St., Boulder, CO 80302, tel. and fax 303-449-8617*
· **A B W Travel**, *2413 N E 53rd St., Kansas City, MO 64118, tel.* 800-678-6871. Representing St. George's Lodge, the most serene diving lodge in Belize, and others
· **Go Diving**, *5610 Rowland Rd., Minnetonka, MN 55343, tel.* 800-328-5285, fax 612-931-0209
· **Hot Dive International**, *P. O. Box 790027, San Antonio, TX 78279, tel.* 800-346-8348
· **Oceanic Society Expeditions**, *Fort Mason Center, Building E, San Francisco, CA 94123*
· **See & Sea Travel Service**, *50 Francisco St., San Francisco, CA 94133, tel.* 415-434-3400, 800-DIV-XPRT
· **Tropical Adventures**, *111 Second North, Seattle, WA 98109, tel.* 800-247-3483, 206-441-3483, fax 206-441-5431

Most travel agencies specializing in Belize can also make arrangements. Look in *Skin Diving* magazines for ads for additional diving services.

Snorkeling equipment is available for rent on Ambergris Caye and Caye Caulker for just a few dollars.

DIVE RESORTS

In addition to the resorts on Ambergris Caye and hotels in Belize City that arrange diving, the offshore waters are dotted with lodges, some of them one-to-an-island, that specialize in diving with no distractions, often in barely touched locales. Among them are:

• **St. George's Lodge**, *St. George's Caye*
• **Spanish Bay Resort**, *Spanish Lookout Caye*
• **Turneffe Islands Lodge**, *Turneffe Flats*, and **Blackbird Caye Resort**, *Turneffe Islands*
• **Lighthouse Reef Resort**
• **Blue Marlin Lodge**, *South Water Caye*
• **Manta Reef Resort**, *Glover's Reef*

LIVE-ABOARDS

Terrific diving is within easy reach of almost any hotel on the cayes, and even of those on the mainland. Absolutely superb diving at the Blue Hole of Lighthouse Reef, or where the sea creatures are not yet accustomed to seeing masked humans, is a little farther out. To reach a number of such sites requires dragging your gear to the dock every morning, setting out for a long ride, returning for lunch, setting out again, and returning to your hotel, followed by repeated packing up and unpacking as you move on to your next diving base.

Or, you can live aboard your dive boat, and roll off the dive platform shortly after you roll out of bed.

Live-aboards come at a price. A week-long trip, with six days of diving, runs from $1,200 to $1,500, based on double occupancy. And the diving can be tougher. You'll spend more time in the water, probably at greater depths than if you dive from a shore base, sometimes in uncharted seas. Medical help in an emergency is *not* at hand.

But live-aboards also come with amenities: sundecks, video libraries for evening entertainment, good-sized rooms, and often photo-processing facilities. And since the diving is usually limited only by decompression tables and safety considerations, the cost per dive can turn out to be even more reasonable than from a land base. As many as five daily dives are scheduled.

Here are some of the live-aboards currently operating in Belizean waters:

• The 120-foot *Wave Dancer* carries 20 passengers in ten large suites, and provides hot towels, mints on your pillow, and similar necessities. Week-long diving trips run $1,500 to $1,600 per person. *Contact Peter Hughes Diving, 1390 S. Dixie Highway, Coral Gables, FL 33146, tel. 800-932-6237.*

• The *Belize Aggressor,* 110 feet, also carries 20 passengers in air-conditioned cabins, and has underwater cameras for rent, and slide processing. The rate is about $1,400 per person for a weekly trip with five-and-a-half days of diving at Lighthouse Reef, the Turneffe Islands, and Glover's Reef. Resort and certification courses are available on board. *Contact Aggressor Fleet, P O Drawer K, Morgan City, LA 70381, tel. 800-348-2628 or 504-385-2416, fax 504-384-0817, 45798 in Belize City.*

• **Barothy Belizean Enterprises**, *P. O. Box 1076, Belize City, tel. 025-2017, operates the 36-foot M. V. Lucretia B.* with customized live-aboard diving.

• The *Manta IV* sails to the Blue Hole three times weekly. *Contact Indigo Belize, P. O. Box 450987, Sunrise, FL 33345, tel. 800-468-0123, 305-473-1956, fax 305-473-6011.*

• *Off-Shore Express* operates from Ambergris Caye. *Contact Coral Beach Hotel, San Pedro, Belize, tel. 026-2001.*

• *Reef Roamer II* sails once or twice weekly to diving spots at Lighthouse Reef, including the Blue Hole. Visitors to Ambergris Caye can fly out to Lighthouse Reef to join the ship, or take the smaller *Reef Roamer I. Contact Out Island Divers, P. O. Box 7, San Pedro, Belize, tel. 026-2151, fax 2180, or P.O. Box 3455, Estes Park, CO 80517, tel. 800-258-3465 or 303-586-6020).*

All of the agencies mentioned above can also book these and other live-aboards.

SCUBA SAFETY

A decompression chamber is maintained at the airstrip at San Pedro, Ambergris Caye, supported by a surcharge on all air-tank rentals in Belize. Additional facilities at Cozumel, Mexico, are available. In a pinch, the Royal Air Force has been known to transport divers needing assistance.

*Most Belize operators are in touch with the **Divers Alert Network**, an association of medical doctors based at Duke University (P. O. Box 3823, Duke University Medical Center, Durham, NC 27710). The number for emergency medical referral is 919-684-8111.*

Insurance tailored for divers is available from P.B.A., P. O. Box 907, Minneapolis, MN 55440, tel. 800-446-2671 or 612-588-2731.

But these facilities are no substitute for your own precautions. You should:
- *Never dive alone*
- *Tell your guide when you last dived*
- *Inquire about unusual conditions*
- *Never dive if you don't feel alert and well*
- *Never drink and dive*
- *Never dive where you can't easily get out*
- *Never dive while on medication, unless you first consult a doctor*
- *Never feed fish while diving – you could attract sharks and barracudas*
- *Never dive beyond your physical capabilities*
- *Avoid diving if you have asthma, diabetes, or are subject to seizures*
- *Dive with a partner you can trust; your life depends on your buddy*
- *Do not touch coral or unfamiliar sea plants or fish. You could suffer painful injury*
- *If confused or unsure, get out of the water*
- *Inspect your diving equipment carefully*
- *If unsure of your divemaster, ask for a referral from a recent client. Otherwise, look elsewhere.*

9. TAKING THE KIDS!

Belize for kids? You're putting me on, dude! Belize is the Adventure Coast, where aspiring Indiana Joneses dive the coral reef, climb temples, and tube through caves dotted with Mayan sculptures.

Well, move over, yuppie adventurers. I hate to burst your balloon, but Belize is for kids, too. After passing favorably on the theoretical concept of pre-adult travel in Belize, I finally took along my three children, then aged 6, 8 and 12.

They can't wait to go back. This chapter will tell you why.

KIDS LOVE BELIZE

At Spanish Bay Resort, my kids spotted dolphins, woke up and jumped from their room into the sea, called the fish into the lagoon, examined starfish, and played Robinson Crusoe on a four-palm tropic isle. But they had to leave several bucketsful of shells behind.

At the **Belize Biltmore Plaza**, they suckered local kids into swimming races, chased crabs along the walkways, and stared down a lizard on a concrete pillar. And after enough sun, the cable TV offerings were excellent.

At **Victoria House**, they took snorkeling trips to the reef, played volleyball, ate free popcorn at the bar, and had a sleepover with other kids. The food was not their style, but at least you could get a good hamburger and pizza up in San Pedro Town.

At the **Adventure Inn**, there were sailboats and a long dock and pirate ghosts. They learned that some of their local counterparts had Super Nintendo. At **Maya Mountain Lodge**, they ate B.L.T. sandwiches and got to sleep in bunks. The **Río On** pools were more fun than a water park. British Army community action units gave them candy. Not to mention climbing ruins and canoeing on a jungle river at **duPlooys'**.

Belizeans welcome kids, and they're not surprised when they turn up. Maybe it's because the way has been prepared by the children of British forces, regularly over on holiday from boarding school. When base accommodations are lacking, the lucky little ones sometimes spend a few weeks at places like the Adventure Inn — several notches above summer camp.

HEALTH PRECAUTIONS

If you're only going to the cayes, there are few special health concerns for children. Limit exposure to the sun, and apply sun block regularly and generously. Make sure that your child gets plenty to drink. For extensive travel on the mainland of Belize, see the general health precautions given later on.

PLAN AHEAD

Pack the same clothing items for children as for adults. Take a few books and toys, including a pail and shovel for the beach. Take snorkeling gear for the kids even if you plan to rent your own. Kid-sized items are difficult to find. Take baby wipes for quick cleanups of any child.

TRAVELING WITH INFANTS

For babies, take changing supplies and bottle-feeding equipment, if needed. Disposable diapers are available in Belize, but not always in every size, and they're expensive. Ultra Pampers won't take up much room in your luggage. A cloth carrier or back pack is preferable to a stroller on the sandy cayes and bumpy streets. Cribs are not widely available, but you should be able to improvise at the better hotels.

Readily available food items for babies include powdered whole milk, canned condensed milk, dry cereals that must be cooked, canned processed cheese, fruits, and jars of baby food (about 75¢ each in Belize City). It would be wise to bring a small stock of food items from home to supplement the limited local fare. Suggestions of what to take: crackers, cookies, instant cereals.

DINING OUT WITH KIDS

I haven't yet found a restaurant or resort in Belize that is too formal to enter with children. At a budget level, in hotels and local restaurants, you're likely to find hamburgers and pancakes for kids with no sense of culinary adventure. But food can easily run $200 a day for a family of five at a resort hotel — yes, $200! — and for that price, the kids will probably leave the lobster and salad untouched.

You can slash this by asking for a kids' rate on meals. Better yet, if you have a choice, take the kids to local eateries, where towns exist, for hamburgers and sandwiches, or bring along non-perishables for their fussy palates. Only a few upscale hotels, such as the Biltmore Plaza in Belize City, have a menu of items to kids' tastes.

Room service can be a boon when you don't all feel like trotting off to a restaurant, and plates of food can be shared more discreetly in the privacy of your room.

When reserving hotel space, find out exactly how much you'll be charged for children, especially if you're under a plan that includes meals. Consider staying at a place with cooking facilities (mainly in San Pedro), as late hotel meal hours might not suit kids' hunger pangs.

SWIMMING

Though there are few swimming pools in Belize, the reef-protected waters are calm and relatively safe. You'll still have to keep an eye on the kids, of course — there are no lifeguards. Snorkeling, sailing, and other water activities can be enjoyed by kids as much as by adults, and nobody will throw the kids out if you bring them along to the local watering hole.

REMEMBER ♦ ♦ ♦

Children need their own identification for immigration purposes.

Kids generally pay only half the adult fare on international airline routings, which can make it cheaper to take them to Belize than to domestic destinations. And many hotels will let the kids stay for free, or only charge for an extra bed.

10. ECO-TOURISM & TRAVEL ALTERNATIVES

BE AN ECOTOURIST

No doubt about it, Belize is one of the world's ecotourism centers. Trouble is, nobody is quite sure what ecotourism is.

For some, eco-tourism means getting close to nature, rather than just getting away. It means learning about natural systems, and how they interact. But it doesn't necessarily have any benefit for nature (a fact I learned when my son's Boy Scout troop raised money to clean up after trekking eco-tourists in Nepal.)

For others, ecotourism is travel that enhances or preserves the natural environment. It applies the visitor's money to good ends. It can involve:
• composting and recycling of waste generated by tourists;
• employing the resources of local communities without turning them from traditional ways;
• reducing the pillage of native species of plants and animals;
• encouraging sustainable use of resources and respect for local people, rather than cultural change and imposition of foreign ways.

This is tourism that doesn't necessarily put the whims of the visitor first. When you book an ecologically-oriented excursion, consider its impact both on you and your surroundings.

ECOTOUR POSSIBILITIES - THREE ADVENTURES

Here are some typical adventures of the type booked by nature-oriented visitors.

Adventure A: You spend several days in a cabin in the rain forest near a Mayan ruin. You've arrived in a chartered plane that burns fossil fuels, along with beer, liquor, tinned food, and paper products. A diesel generator provides power. Non-compostable garbage disappears mysteriously, either buried or carried to an off-site dump. Animal-watching excursions are taken in Jeeps and motorboats, a generator smashes any hint of bird songs until well after sunset. After a hard day getting to know nature, iced drinks are always available. Were it not for the lodge, the Mayan ruin would surely have been looted, and the forest burned over for farmland.

Adventure B: You take a bus from Belize City, and are met at a roadside marker. You hike to a clearing, carrying all your food, cooking equipment, and sleeping gear. You spend a weekend birding, hiking, spotting snakes and small mammals, listening to branches crack and trees fall, and watching bromeliads and ferns renew life from the decay of the old. Mostly, you try to keep dry or get used to being rained on. Muddy and exhausted, you finally emerge enlightened about the interactions of natural systems. But you are one of the last to take the trip. The land has changed hands, and will soon be cleared and planted in orange trees.

Adventure C: You join a snorkeling trip to an underwater reserve, where fish and coral are protected from commercial exploitation, and visitors are controlled. But you find that vigilance is inadequate to keep the hordes from stepping on and breaking off coral, or feeding the fish. The reserve has attracted the kind of attention and visitor traffic that is likely to do in the coral, rather than save it.

THE REALITY OF ECO-TOURISM

What is eco-tourism in Belize? At its best, it is the serious effort of a few operators to acquaint visitors with tropical life systems, while doing as little damage to them as possible, and perhaps even protecting and enhancing them.

But eco-tourism can also be nothing more than the folklore of travel in Belize, corresponding to handicrafts and colonial monuments in Guatemala, and schnitzel in Vienna. It can be a superficial walk through a zoo, overcrowded reserves where footsteps scare away the animals, squandered resources and new sources of trash, uninformed pattering guides, restaurants with good and bad food and hotels with or without cable television and friendly management. Eco-tourism can be like tourism anywhere.

But we're dealing with the real world here, and the inescapable fact is that outsiders want to see a part of the world still relatively unaffected by population pressures and human alterations. And Belize would like to see some economic benefit from letting outsiders in.

PROTECT THE ENVIRONMENT

So what can you do to keep your depredations to a minimum?

• Touch *nothing* if you can possibly avoid it. Touching kills coral. Touching unfamiliar plants in the forest could kill *you.*

• Buy *nothing* that appears to come from the ocean or the forest or ancient cities, unless you are assured by an authority (not the seller) that commerce in the product is legal. This means not buying coral jewelry or tropical birds or Mayan artifacts. Hardwood carvings are all right.

• Eat *nothing* that is out of season. Lobster season is July to March. Forget the beast the rest of the year, no matter the temptation.

• Keep *nothing* that you catch from the sea, unless you plan to eat it.

• Leave *nothing* on the land that wasn't there before you arrived, unless it will decompose.

I could go on and on, but you get my point. When we visit foreign countries, what results is not always what we anticipate, or what we want. Let's recognize the problem, and try to keep things under control.

Can you be an eco-tourist in Belize? It depends on you, and the choices that you make.

EARN COLLEGE CREDITS

Check the listings on the department bulletin boards at local universities for possibilities. Archaeological digs are one way to run up credits, independent studies another.

Maya Mountain Lodge, *P. O. Box 46, San Ignacio, tel. 092-2164, fax 092-2029*, offers a summer workshop in rain forest ceramics and a course on developing rain forest-related curricula for schools. Planned future course offerings include rain forest biology, botany in Belize, tropical cooking, and tropical gardening. Fees are $500 to $750 per week, including course fees, room and board, depending on accommodations. These courses are intended for degree credit, at one unit per week.

The Institute for Central American Development Studies in San José, Costa Rica, sponsors internships in Belize and other Central American countries, structured to provide a recommended 15 credits for a semester program, or 8 credits for the summer. Themes are agriculture, women's studies, the environment, public health, and journalism.

Fees are hefty — about $6,000! For information, write to: *ICADS, P. O. Box 025216-826, Miami, FL 33102-5216, or call their office in Costa Rica, tel. 506-250508, fax 506-341337.*

STAY WITH A MAYAN FAMILY

There's an unusual program afoot in Punta Gorda, in southern Belize, that arranges for visitors to stay with families in the interior, instead of in formal hotels.

It involves spending hundreds of dollars for your ticket, taking time off from work, and ending up somewhere in the bush to sleep on a hard bed or in a hammock in a thatch-roofed hut with a dirt floor, stumble in the dark through the scratching chickens to an outhouse, eat rice and beans, and wash with cold water. If you see it strictly in these terms, skip to the next section.

So what's in it for you?

Meeting local people as people, who go about their daily business and farm and survive and enjoy life on their own, not as servants to outsiders. Learning how corn is soaked in lime water and ground and formed into tortillas; how wild herbs are used in cooking, and to cure illness; how local materials are harvested from the forest to build houses; how crops are grown with a minimum of chemicals; tilling corn and beans along with your hosts; splitting firewood; beating clothes on rocks in a river; hiking to caves.

It's also visiting ancient cities in the company of the descendants of those who built them; seeing how it's possible to live without cars and piped gas and electricity, and also how radios and satellite TV have made their way to some of the more remote places on earth. It's giving indigenous peoples the assurance that they have something to contribute to the rest of the world, as well as allowing them to share the cash that normally flows to more go-getter types in the tourist trade.

If you're interested in staying with a Mayan family, contact **Toledo Visitors Information Center**, *P. O. Box 73, Punta Gorda, tel. 07-22470.* Since this is a shoestring operation, send an international reply coupon, or a check for $2, to cover reply costs.

The price of lodging is under $20 per person per night, meals are less than $6 each, and there is a registration fee of about $12.

More formal guest houses are being organized in participating villages, with western-style toilets.

11. FOOD & DRINK

Lower your sights. The food in Belize is usually none too elegant and none too cheap, the service is none too good. An expanding hospitality industry is sorely pressed to come up with the kind of food visitors appreciate. The few notably good cooks are hired away every few months.

Some of the makings of memorable eating experiences are available in Belize. Fish, lobster, shrimp and many other forms of seafood are fresh, abundant, and relatively cheap. Beef is plentiful, and a number of tropical fruits and vegetables are available. But preparation and presentation can be down at the heels, or at least inconsistent. In one of the better restaurants in Belize City, a succulent, inch-thick steak might be served with greasy fried potatoes, and nothing else. A delicious boiled lobster may be married to lukewarm spinach fresh from the can, and paper-textured white bread.

One problem is that Belizeans themselves have no tradition of dining out for pleasure. Belize's ethnic groups have a variety of staple foods and cuisines, but they enjoy them at home. Eating out is a relatively recent phenomenon. The demand for creative cooking comes almost exclusively from visitors, foreign residents, and from the small but growing class of bourgeois Belizeans.

TRADITIONAL & LOCAL CUISINES

This doesn't mean you can't eat well in Belize. Some marvelous food is available, if you look for it.

Creole cuisine dominates, of course. The most typically Belizean dish is rice and beans, a holdover from the times when these foods, in dry form, were carried to logging camps in the interior. Rice and beans can be prepared with vegetables, coconut milk, and spices, with lobster, chicken, or beef, ending up as a tasty melding of flavors. But in a small-town eatery, they might be nothing more than what the name says. Ask before you order.

Game meat – gibnut (paca), armadillo and brocket deer – is traditionally stewed in pots over open fires. You can occasionally find game meat
on the menu at hotels in Belize City, to please curious visitors, and at
country lodges. But most Belizeans no longer hunt their own food, and
what gets distributed commercially is beef, chicken, and imported ham.
On small-town menus, you'll generally find fried chicken and steak (a thin,
somewhat tough piece of meat), usually served with rice, sometimes with
French fries, almost never with a green vegetable. This isn't typically
Creole, it's just what is served to hungry stomachs until they can get home.

More traditional is "stew chicken" and "stew beans," exactly what they
sound like, slow-cooked in dark sauce, and tasty. Conch fritters, meat pies,
cow foot soup, and fruit pastries are also Creole staples that are available
in some Belize City eateries.

For breakfast, you may find fry jacks (corn cakes), Johnny cakes
(biscuits), and, in genuinely Belizean homes, fried fish and Creole bread.

A hamburger is often the best choice on the menu in Belize, if you're
not familiar with an eatery – it's likely to be large and tasty. But specify
what you want on it – you'll sometimes find the most unpredictable
dressings pre-applied.

If you want something other than a bottled soft drink or beer to go
with your meal, you're generally out of luck. Canned fruit juices and fruit
drinks from Mexico, of all places, are sometimes available. Places with
good taste offer fresh-squeezed orange juice, or limeade ("lime water").

FOREIGN CUISINE

Other cuisines carry better to restaurants. Hispanic food – tamales,
salbutes (something like the tostadas of central and northern Mexico),
beef seared over the coals or cooked in sauces, and eggs with tortillas and
beans are served in restaurants everywhere in Belize, and not just to
Hispanics. Where else but in Belize would you find Gilhooly's tortilla
factory?

Most noticeable, though, are Belize's Chinese restaurants, many
founded in the last ten years by new immigrants. In a small town where
not long ago you couldn't find a place to eat, there are now two or three
Chinese diners.

But even if you like Chinese food, be warned that the version in Belize
is not *haute cuisine*, and you could overdose quickly. Almost all Chinese
restaurants have the same menu: chow mein, chop suey, egg foo young,
and one or two house specialties, along with rice and beans, steak, and
sandwiches. You can usually have a meal for $6 or less, though sometimes
the tab is surprisingly high. Decor is limited or non-existent, you get a
paper napkin, your special house chicken comes on big pieces of bone,

and the sweet-and-sour sauce is mostly sugar. A couple of hotels and restaurants in Belize City serve something more elegantly Chinese.

FOOD AROUND THE COUNTRY

In Belize City, the food scene is generally better than elsewhere in the country, though there are still rough spots. The curried shrimp surrounded by condiments, attractively served, turns out to be mushy. Nevertheless, it's obvious that people are making an effort. In hotels here and there, on the cayes, in Placencia, and around Cayo, there are some pleasant surprises, and standards are getting higher. If you limit your expectations, ask about what you're getting, and choose carefully, you won't be disappointed. Just don't trust that the food is good unless some reliable recent visitor has reported it to be so. And even then, the cook could well have gone off.

The fact that so much food is imported to Belize in dry or preserved form makes it easy for backpackers and budget travelers to picnic. Even in the smallest settlements, stores offer tinned powdered milk, Australian butter, and Dutch cheese, all at reasonable prices. (There are also cans of peas and carrots for $3, but you can pass these up.) Don't forget your can opener. Fresh oranges and grapefruits as well as tomatoes, onions, and a few other vegetables are available everywhere on the mainland.

RUM, BEER, & WINE

Belize produces a number of brands of rum, all of them quite good, as well as Belikin and Crown beers, which come in a small bottle, and may or may not agree with your tastes. Dutch, German and American brands of beer are also widely available, at about double the price of domestic brew, hence the Belikin slogan, "the only beer worth drinking."

A premium version of Belikin tastes something like American beer, comes in a larger bottle, and carries an American price. There is also Belikin stout, which I prefer to all of the above. Wines made from cashew fruit and berries are a traditional product of Belize, though they're getting hard to find, as American and French wines take over the market.

YOUR AVERAGE BELIZEAN RESTAURANT
"We serve the best food in Belize"

BILL OF FARE

Breakfast
Eggs any style
Huevos Rancheros
(Eggs in a tomato and pepper sauce)
One egg with fried beans
Two eggs with fried beans
All our breakfasts are served with fry jacks, our crisp Belizean breakfast cakes.

Our appetizers
Conch cocktail
("Conk" is our budget seafood, a.k.a. sea snail)

Our soups
Conch soup
Campbell's soup *du jour*

Our main courses
Stew chicken
Fry chicken
Baked chicken with rice
Pork chops
Rice and beans
(Our national dish)
Rice and beans with stew chicken
Rice and beans with meat balls
White rice with stew beans
(Variations on our national dish)

Our Regional Specialties
Escabech *(Chicken in pickling)*
Relleno
Garnachas *(Think of a tostada)*
Tamales
Empanadas
Salbutes *(Think of a tostada, without the toasting)*

Our seafood
(Available in season, and sometimes beyond)
Fried fish
Fried lobster
Fried shrimp
Rice and beans with lobster
Rice and beans with conch

Lunch
Hamburger
Cheeseburger
(All our sandwiches are served with imported Pringles. You may substitute French fries at an extra charge)
Ham sandwich

Our Beverages
Lime juice
(You know it as lemonade)
Coke, Sprite, Pepsi, Coffee, Tea

Our Desserts
Lemon pie
Bread pudding
Rice pudding

Our condiments
Salt
Pepper
Melinda's Habanero Pepper Hot Sauce
Habanero Pepper Extra Hot Sauce
(The Belizean versions of a West Indian sauce, a secret blend of peppers, carrots, vinegar, and the finest fresh ingredients)

12. MOST MEMORABLE HOTELS & INNS

MARUBA RESORT & JUNGLE SPA

Mile 40.5, Old Northern Highway, Maskall Village, Tel. (03) 22199, Fax. (713) 799-2031 (Texas), US & Canada Bookings toll free at (800) MARUBA-7 (Belize It Tours), Year round Rack Rates from $130 per double room per night (EP), Full Spa, Adventure, and Special Interest packages are available, Meal Plan with Breakfast & Dinner is $34.50 per person, Meal Plan with Breakfast, Lunch, & Dinner is $46.50 per person.

Maruba is one of the most exotic properties anywhere in the world! The Nicholsons have spent the last 9 years creating this deluxe jungle resort just a few miles away from the Mayan temple of Altun Ha. Comfortably spread out over two thousand acres of private jungle reserve landscaped with hibiscus, orchids, mangroves, birds, wild animals, you can't help but feel like you have finally found paradise the moment you arrive here.

The resort consists of 15 individually designed tropical rooms and rustic thatched roofed casitas that are cooled by either ceiling fans or air conditioning. All of the rooms show a strong Mayan and African inspiration in their furnishing, with textiles creatively designed to give a rustic but elegant flare. They all have private bathrooms, tile or mosaic floors, hand-made furnishings, great big beds, a selection of the highest quality natural hair and skin care products, original artwork, and local carvings.

The independent cabanas are the perfect choice for romantic honeymooners, especially the magic Chapel Room with its sloped ceiling and stained glass window, or the tree house styled Jungle Suite. All of the units face out onto unforgettable gardens lined with Coconut Palms and birds.

Guests are truly pampered with personalized service offered by the friendliest staff in Belize. Besides being encouraged to take advantage of the lush garden-lined swimming pool (with its own waterfall) and mineral baths, guests should not even think about leaving here without experiencing at least one spa treatment. Located in huts infused with relaxing tropical music, the resort's excellent full spa is a perfect introduction to the wonders of natural healing and uses only natural oils and skin care products made right here at Maruba from common fruits and plants found in the nearby rainforest.

Among the treatments available are invigorating full body massages, tropical herbal wraps, aromatherapy, body scrubs, facials, seaweed body wraps, and manicures. Other noteworthy services and facilities here include transfers to and from Belize International Airport, snorkeling and scuba excursions to the Cayes, jungle boat trips to the Mayan ruins at Lamani, guided tours to Altun Ha, and of course jungle wildlife safaris by horseback and foot with expert guides who will stop to point out medicinal herbs, and even prepare a fruit salad from ingredients that you'll pass alongside.

Dining here is a delightful experience, with a superb casual open air gourmet restaurant featuring breakfasts, lunches, and dinners. Their native executive chef (Vilma) prepares a daily assortment of beautifully presented multiple course menus featuring locally caught fish, fine cuts of steak, seasonal wild game, delicious fruits and vegetables grown right on the resort, and mouth watering desserts.

Special meals can be custom designed to fit specific dietary concerns. For those of you who are rather adventurous, I strongly suggest asking for a glass of Viper Rum (with a real snake in each bottle), or Scorpion tonic (guess what's inside that one!)

Maruba gets my highest recommendation, and it should not be missed!

DU PLOOY'S

10 miles West of San Ignacio, Cayo District, Tel. (092) 3101, Fax. (092) 3301, US & Canada Bookings at (803) 722-3301 (Belize Bound), Rack Rates from $32 per double guest house room per night (EP), Rack Rates from $76 per double lodge room per nights (EP), Meal Plan with Breakfast & Dinner is $21.00 per person, Meal Plan with Breakfast, Lunch, & Dinner is $30.00 per person.

DuPlooy's, a surprisingly affordable Cayo district property, is located in one of the most beautiful sites in western Belize on the pristine Macal River. There are a multitude of enchanting attractions that can be visited nearby including Mayan temples, Mountain Pine Ridge, ancient caves, and countless acres of peaceful nature trails. Owners Ken and Judy duPlooy will be glad to arrange unforgettable guided excursions via boat, horseback, or van to extraordinary Mayan temples, natural parks, jungle sights, waterfalls, and traditional villages. The congenial ambiance here makes it easy to meet new friends and plan trips together.

Accommodations at duPlooy's are provided in 3 different categories. For romantic couples I suggest staying in one of their brand new luxury Jungle Bungalows that feature King-sized beds, refrigerators, private patios with hammocks, coffee makers, huge private bathrooms, and excellent ceiling fans. The moderately priced Lodge Rooms offer private bathrooms, screened-in porches, and rather comfortable furnishings (two of these units can connect for family use). Last, but not least, are the budget-priced quarters in the Pink House guest house with its six nice bedrooms and 2 bathrooms that make it possible for everyone to afford a stay in the jungle (also perfect for small groups!).

DuPlooy's is well known by birders, and early most mornings you can find Ken pointing out exotic birds like Trogans, Emerald Toucanets, Parrots, and Tetyras to mention only a few. While you are birding with Ken, be sure to ask him to take you on one of his special unadvertised jungle adventures.

Dining here takes place in a rustic jungle view restaurant that serves up hearty cooked to order breakfasts (a bargain at only $5 each!), delicious lunches, and 4 course dinners with homemade breads, exotic tropical fruits and vegetables from their own gardens, and a choice of regular or vegetarian entrees.

If you're looking for a great family-owned and operated place to stay with an abundance of nature and historical day trip possibilities, this is a superb choice. Highly Recommended for singles, couples, families, and people of all ages.

RADISSON FORT GEORGE HOTEL

2 Marine Parade, (P.O. Box 321), Belize City, Tel. (02) 33333, Fax. (02) 73820, US & Canada Bookings toll free at (800) 333-3333 (Radisson), Low Season Rack Rates from $74 to $124 per double room per night (EP), High Season Rack Rates from $89 to $139 per double room per night (EP).

The Radisson is usually the first hotel that I pull into after arriving from an international flight to Belize. This seaside deluxe hotel caters to the heads of multinational corporations and visiting tourists that are looking for the most luxurious accommodations in all of Belize City.

What they get is one of 100 superbly-designed rooms that feature every deluxe amenity and facility you can think of, including freezing cold air conditioning, huge modern private bathrooms (some with marble floors and antique-style fixtures), imported designer fabrics, fine furnishings, large picture windows looking out onto the pools or the waterfront, direct dial telephones, the best beds in town, mini-bars, large closets, and in some cases even private patios.

Since most guests eventually depart the relaxing environment of their spacious rooms, the extensive array of hotel facilities added after a $2 million renovation are sure to satisfy all guests. For businessmen there are secretarial services, a fully equipped business center with computers and fax machines, special meeting rooms, conference facilities, and VIP rooms with a private elevator in the unique Club Tower wing.

Vacationers and executives alike will be pleased to find a gift shop and newsstand, a brand new bar and adjacent sea view restaurant serving up 3 tasty meals a day (including a huge cooked to order American breakfast), available baby-sitting services, smoke free rooms, 2 nice outdoor pools with sun decks and snack bars, a private marina and fishing pier with service to the Cayes upon request, free parking, 24 hour security, a taxi stand in front of the hotel, and abundant excursions and car rental possibilities at the guest services area.

If you are looking for the best that money can buy in town, this is the place for you. Highly Recommended.

CAPTAIN MORGAN'S RETREAT

Ambergris Caye - 3.5 miles North of San Pedro, Tel. (026) 2567, Fax. (026) 2398, US & Canada Bookings toll free at (800) 447-2931(Magnum Belize), Low Season Rack Rates from $120.00 per double cabana per night (EP), High Season Rack Rates from $170.00 per double cabana per night (EP), Meal Plan with Breakfast & Dinner is $26.00 per person, Meal Plan with Breakfast, Lunch, & Dinner is $35.00 per person.

This wonderful seaside property is certainly my favorite place to stay on Ambergris Caye. From the moment that Baldi (the resort's charming sight manager) personally greets you at the San Pedro airport or ferry dock, you know that you are in for a special experience. The ambiance here is decidedly casual and friendly, with many of the clientele wearing shorts and a T-shirt throughout their stay.

The hotel is setup as a series of 21 delightful self-standing beach front casita-style cabanas, each with thatched roofs, modern private bathrooms, tile flooring, ceiling fans, comfortable king or double beds, terraced porches, local wooden furnishings, and plenty of cool breezes. There are no telephones or televisions to distract guests from the perfect stress-free vacation.

Facilities here include a large outdoor swimming pool, outdoor snack bar, dining room, bar and grill, free canoe rental, complimentary fishing and snorkeling gear, a gift shop, daily water ferry service to and from San Pedro (at only $5 round-trip!), volleyball nets, excellent white sandy beaches, boat docks, and lots of hammocks.

Among the optional services that guests can enjoy daily are the island's best scuba diving trips guided by Patojo Paz, snorkeling excursions, sailing trips, parasailing, and guided boat trips and coach tours to attractions such as Mayan ruins and wildlife preserves.

Dining at Captain Morgan's is an equally impressive experience, with a rustic sea-view restaurant complete with long wooden tables that encourage guests to socialize with each other. The set menu changes daily and may include twin grilled lobster tails, farm fresh meats, locally caught fish, and regional specialties. During the high season, a "Fiesta del Maya" beach-side pig roast and barbecue takes place on Tuesday nights with live Mariachi music. For those of you with special dietary concerns, the cooks will be glad to prepare special customized meals to suit your needs.

This is a not-to-be-missed hotel for those of you who want to stay on a beautiful island, and do as much or as little as you want. Highly recommended.

RAMADA ROYAL REEF RESORT & MARINA

King's Park, Belize City, Tel. (02) 32670, Fax. (02) 32660, US & Canada Bookings toll free at (800) 854-7854 (Ramada Renaissance), Year Round Rack Rates from $127.00 per double room per night (EP), Meal Plan with Breakfast & Dinner is $34.00 per person, Meal Plan with Breakfast, Lunch, & Dinner is $50.00 per person.

This modern four-story waterfront hotel is located in the safest section of Belize City. The Ramada offers 114 newly renovated sea-view rooms that all feature air conditioning, 40 channel satellite television, full private bathrooms, tasteful tropical rattan furnishings, either one or two beds, ceiling fans, and plenty of interior space. Four additional suites (about 40% more expensive) even offer mini-bars, fax machines, and in some cases private patios. Popular among visiting businessmen and more deluxe vacationers, the Royal Reef is an oasis of tranquillity.

Among the many features offered is a great outdoor swimming pool with both a swim-up snack bar and a large sun deck, surrounded by gardens and palm trees. Although not exactly a beach, the private sunning area on the property's north edge has been covered with fine sand and includes beach chairs and thatched sun umbrellas just in front of the sea.

They have even installed some sand topped volleyball courts nearby. Other facilities include a full service private marina, direct ferry service to the Cayes, on sight snorkeling and scuba trips, a Budget rental car desk, excursion desk, 2 bars, business meeting rooms, available secretarial services, taxi stand, ice machines, ping pong room, art gallery, boutique, 24 hour security, free parking, room service, and lots of terraces where you can sit and enjoy the view.

There is also an abundance of dining and nightlife choices. To start off with, there are the Friday night (high season) outdoor barbecues, and the weekly Manager's cocktail party on Wednesday where you can enjoy free drinks and hors d'oevvres while chatting with Mark Espat, the hotel's friendly resident manager. Full meals can also be enjoyed at the bright and airy Reef Restaurant during normal dining hours, while more youthful clients and locals gather at the fantastic Calypso club to munch and drink while watching the country's hottest live bands nightly.

The Ramada is fine place to stay before venturing further into Belize's islands and vast interior, or to stay while sampling day trips to the outlying areas. Highly Recommended.

HIDDEN VALLEY INN

Cooma Carin Road, Mountain Pine Ridge, Tel. (08) 23320, Fax. (08) 23334, US & Canada Bookings at (800) 334-7942 (C.W. Maryland), Year Round Rack Rates from $105 per double cottage per night (BP), Meal Plan with Dinner is $17.50 per person, Meal Plan with Lunch, & Dinner is $25.00 per person.

Hidden Valley Inn sits comfortably amidst an 18,000-acre private estate in the breathtaking Mountain Pine Ridge preserve in the Cayo district. With its beautiful grounds attracting over 150 species of wild birds and animals (including a recently spotted Jaguar), the property has become the favorite inn for repeat visitors to this area.

All 12 of the bright and airy rooms are set in a series of 6 independent adobe style cottages, each with large private bathrooms, working fireplaces, extremely comfortable bedding, and large screened-in windows with views of the grounds. Registered guests can even spend a night at the inn's fully equipped Bull's Point camp-out sight with its isolated location, perfect for avid birders.

Facilities in the main house include several living rooms, screened-in patios with telescopes for viewing shy wildlife, a large library, a game room, and a bar area. In the same building is the dining room where 3 delicious meals are prepared daily, and served by some of the most delightful staff in the country.

The days at Hidden Valley generally start off with a cheerful greeting from resident managers Laurie & Virginia Furnell over a complimentary full breakfast with a cup of the best coffee I have ever tasted (grown and roasted right here). Through the course of the day guests can just relax or partake in numerous activities, including hikes on their 90 miles of nature trails, horseback riding trips, visits to unforgettable waterfalls and caves, canoe rides, excursions to the mystical Mayan temples with delightful picnic lunches, and much more.

As time for dinner approaches, the dining room fills up with guests of all ages and backgrounds who look forward to hearing more captivating tales from Mr. Bull Headly (the gentleman who owns the inn) who lives here during much of the year. This is a great place to base yourself while exploring the natural beauty of Mountain Pine Ridge and the Mayan sights. Highly Recommended.

RUM POINT INN

Rum Point, Placencia, Tel. (06) 23239, Fax. (06) 23240, US & Canada Bookings at (800) 747-1381 (Toucan Turs), Low Season Rack Rates from $130 per double room per night (EP), High Season Rack Rates from $150 per double room per night (EP), Meal Plans, Special Scuba Programs, and Fishing Packages Available.

The fantastic Rum Point Inn is situated on a gorgeous palm lined beach, just 2.5 miles up the road from Placencia. Owned and operated by the Bevier family since its inception in 1974, this one of a kind windswept inn has become one of the most unforgettable properties in all of Belize.

All accommodations here are based in a series of 10 private self-standing ferro-cement cabanas, and are surrounded by lush tropical gardens. Each spacious unit has a large private bathroom, beautiful furnishings, ceiling fans, lots of windows, and fantastic sea views.

The inn's casual main house features an outstanding open-air dining room serving up 3 meals a day, a great little bar with music, a gift shop, and even a living room-style library with countless books and entertaining videos about the history, culture, and wildlife of Belize.

As the country's only R.E.E.F. marine education station, visitors here get a chance to learn much more about the underwater environment. Special multiple-day scuba packages include daily 2 tank dives aboard one of Rum Point's well-appointed dive boats, 3 meals daily, transfers from Placencia airstrip, and available next-day film developing. Intensive instruction ranging from a beginner's resort course, to full (and advanced) PADI and NAUI certifications are also available. Those who prefer to snorkel the day away can take advantage of guided adventures above the reef.

Among the many complementary activities and services offered onsite are bicycles, kayaks, wind surfers, snorkeling gear, sunfish sail boats, and they will even do your laundry. While you're wandering the grounds, be sure to keep your eyes open for the hundreds of wild birds (including flocks of Pelicans) that love to stay here too. Don't miss this place! Highly Recommended.

SERENITY RESORT

Placencia Road, Placencia, Tel. (06) 23232, Fax. (06) 23231, Low Season Rack Rates from $50 per double room per night (EP), High Season Rack Rates from $60 per double room per night (EP), Meal Plan with Breakfast & Dinner is $22.50 per person, Meal Plan with Breakfast, Lunch, & Dinner is $30.00 per person.

This peaceful and relaxing seaside property rests on 1,000 feet of prime beachfront only 2.5 miles from the village of Placencia. The gentle sounds of the rolling surf combine with the singing of rare tropical birds to create a uniquely serene environment.

Guests can choose to stay in one of 12 independant cabanas, or in the 10 brand new air conditioned double rooms. All accommodations contain private bathrooms, refrigerators, coffee machines, ceiling fans, and verandas with sea or lagoon views. After enjoying a swim, or snorkeling, in the crystal clear waters just of the sandy beach, guests have the option of experiencing a a variety of tours and excursions led by guides like Cirilo Chun.

These include boat rides to the nearby Cayes, one and two tank scuba dives, wildlife Safaris, hikes within the famed Jaguar Reserve, and tours by air conditioned van to the Mayan sights of Nim Li Punit and Lubantuum. Complimentary bicycles are provied if you want to visit the charming Garifuna village of Seine Bight, or the Creole village of Placencia.

At the ocean-front restaurant you can enjoy the freshest locally caught seafood, traditional Belizean specialties, and vegetarian entrees. Dinners here are especially enchanting, as the moon rises over the crashing waves.

13. THE CAYES

INTRODUCTION

Spread out in a 200-mile-long chain parallel to the mainland of Belize are the cayes, the little islands that are, for most visitors, the main stopping-points in the country. For divers, the cayes are bases for exploring the wonders of the nearby barrier reef, second in length only to the Great Barrier Reef of Australia. For fishermen, they are the gateway to teeming, barely exploited waters. And for just about everyone, they are idyllic locales for relaxation, where palm trees wave in gentle breezes along barely frequented beaches, people go about their business in tiny settlements with sand streets and small-town ways, and the cares of the world have no place.

Numbering in the scores, the cayes are the visible tips of a submarine geography of undulating ridges and trenches, plateaus, and coral reef. They range from mangrove-entangled spots that poke out of the water at low tide to coral specks to uninhabited sandy islets with a few palm trees to islands with sufficient dry land to sustain a varied vegetation as well as fishing villages. Most of the cayes are tucked behind the protection of the barrier reef, surrounded by waters multi-toned in blues and greens, the visible seabed speckled with coral and seaweed clusters. Farther from shore, four atolls — rings of coral enclosing shallow lagoons amid deep waters — transplant a bit of the South Seas to the Caribbean.

Archaeologists have found evidence of Mayan fishing and hunting camps on the cayes. In colonial times, the islets were the lair of buccaneers who preyed on the galleons that carried the treasures of the New World to Spain. Protected by a maze of shallow passages from the heavy ships of the Spaniards, the buccaneers rested up on the cayes between depredations, divided their booty, and dried turtle meat for provisions. Divers still occasionally come up with old Spanish coins dropped by those earlier inhabitants. The term for these islands reflects the Spanish presence. *Caye* (pronounced *key*) derives from the Spanish *cayo*.

As British adventurers shifted their attention from the plunder of ships to the plunder of the forests, the cayes were bypassed. Coconuts were planted on a large scale at one time, but hurricanes knocked down many of the trees, and in some cases wiped entire cayes from the map. In recent years, however, the islands have prospered. Commercial fishing has become a big business, and tourism has provided new jobs while fueling a real estate and construction boom.

The main cayes of interest to visitors are described below, followed by mention of a few mainland resorts with facilities and attractions similar to those found on the cayes.

AMBERGRIS CAYE

Largest of the cayes, **Ambergris** (pronounced by locals with the accent on the second syllable) is 25 miles long, separated from the Yucatan mainland of Mexico only by a narrow channel. The island, in fact, was once claimed by Mexico. On a map, the elongated land mass with its several peninsulas and sea inlets is clear enough, but up close, most of Ambergris is mangrove swamp, that amorphous bordering condition that seems to belong to neither land nor sea. The limited dry land, and most of the coconut trees and people, are concentrated toward the island's narrow southern tip.

In Mayan times, Ambergris Caye was a trading post — ruins have been excavated at the Marco Gonzales site. Buccaneering and whaling are part of the past of Ambergris — the name testifies to the latter. Today's inhabitants are mostly fishermen. The tourist business and attendant real-estate speculation and construction are in second place and increasingly important. Ambergris boasts a premier location for exploring the barrier reef, and its hotels, fishing, and diving facilities are the best in the country.

SAN PEDRO

San Pedro is the major settlement on Ambergris, a little town of colorfully painted, mostly wooden, tin-roofed houses, criss-crossed by a half-dozen sandy streets. It is the only place in the cayes that has a number of motor vehicles, but this does not bespeak a bustling air. The island's fleet of pickup trucks carries visitors from the airstrip on the southern end of town to hotels and lodging houses, and odd bits of cargo from the docks. Four-wheel all-terrain vehicles service outlying hotels. But mostly, the streets belong to strollers.

The adjectives usually attached to San Pedro are "delightful" and "charming." The houses are huddled close one upon another, and much

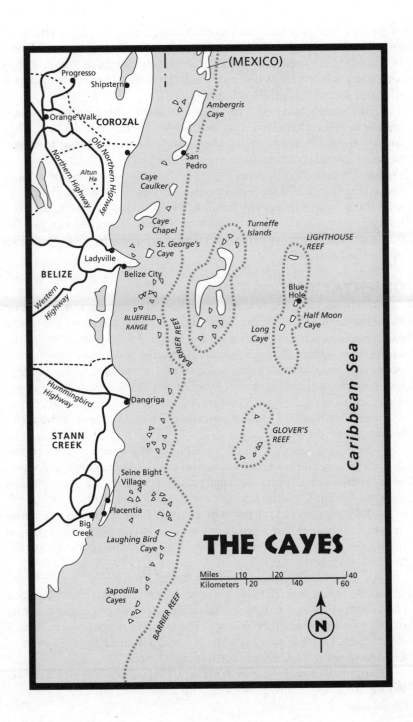

THE CAYES

of the foot traffic of the place moves through narrow alleys. The same houses in Belize City would constitute just another shanty town, but in San Pedro, they are well maintained, the streets are fairly clean, and a refreshing breeze usually blows through. The effect of the close quarters is one of sociability and friendliness.

The charm of San Pedro also comes from the townspeople. Numbering about fifteen hundred, they are mostly of Mexican descent. They speak a formal Spanish among themselves, and a somewhat fractured Belizean English with outsiders.

San Pedranos are approachable and friendly, never distant or surly toward the visitor. The feeling of easiness and equality on both sides owes something to the prosperity brought by fishing. San Pedro is rather bourgeois, in a Belizean way. The stores are well stocked not just for tourists, who find the prices for Kraft dinners and Spaghetti-O's appalling, but for locals as well.

ORIENTATION

Before deciding where to stay, it's essential to understand something about the layout of San Pedro, and the advantages and disadvantages of each hotel's location. To start with, the beach in San Pedro town is little wider than a sidewalk for most of its length, and serves mainly as a pedestrian thoroughfare and a place to pull up smaller boats. There is little room for sunbathing at any of the hotels in town, except the Paradise, where the sand of the hotel's compound is more than ample. Of course, any beachside hotel, in town or out, will offer superb views of the waves breaking over the reef.

Guests who stay in San Pedro are closer to a variety of restaurants, dive shops and places to rent boats, and to the late-evening spots where visitors and locals eat, dance, exchange tales, and engage in beer-drinking contests. Sociability is the key element in San Pedro, and the gift of gab in any language goes a long way. On the other hand, if getting away from people and noise is part of what you seek, or if you simply want a good night's sleep, you'll do better to stay on the edge of town, or at one of the hotels to the north or south.

For accommodations right in San Pedro, from the best to the worst, almost all rooms are relatively bare. Most hotels are standard huddled clapboard or concrete structures. The difference from the top of the scale to the bottom is whether you get more or less light, a sea view, a comfortable bed, hot water at all hours, and perhaps a few decorations. Outside of town, pickings are considerably better.

Captain Morgan's, the **Belize Yacht Club**, **Ramon's**, and **Victoria House** are in especially good taste, and most other lodging places are casual and comfortable.

AT THE SHORE, SAN PEDRO

Air conditioning is a benefit in the dog days of April and later in San Pedro, until the rains come, or at any time of year near the airstrip and the noise of planes taking off. Otherwise, you probably won't need it.

Almost all hotels in the town are along or just off the five blocks of Barrier Reef Drive (Front St.), the street that runs north-south on the reef (east) side of San Pedro.

GETTING AROUND TOWN

Along the seaside in San Pedro, everything is boats, from skiffs to cabin cruisers to rusting fishing boats, tied up to docks in stages of repair from serviceable to caved in. Life for residents and visitors alike focuses on the water, of course, but if you want a change from fishing and diving, turn to bird-watching on the swampy, lagoon side of the island. No expertise is needed to spot flamingoes, pelicans, egrets, and those great diving frigate birds. Other favorite activities are shelling and general beachcombing. But be aware that much of what washes up is plastic containers of one sort or another which, with no use to anyone, remain as permanent eyesores.

As a Hispanic town, San Pedro has its share of traditional fiestas tied to the Catholic faith of most of the inhabitants. Christmas and Easter are celebrated with processions and church services. The town's particular fiesta is June 29, the day of Saint Peter, which coincides with the blessing of the fleet. A more secular celebration takes place on November 27, the anniversary of San Pedro's formal incorporation as a township, in 1985.

Time was, not long ago, when the only fuel needed in San Pedro was for boats, the electrical generator, and a couple of pickup trucks. But four-wheel all-terrain vehicles have begun to kick up sand in the coconut groves, golf carts buzz back and forth, and there are even some beat-up private cars, used as taxis and for general cruising on San Pedro's two-mile road network. Planes drone over town on takeoff, regularly breaking the peace. Though still essentially small-townish and friendly, San Pedro is not immune to pretense as it develops into an international resort.

The Front Street of a few years ago is now Barrier Reef Drive (though you can't drive very far on it), and Middle St. is Pescador ("fisherman") Drive. And don't take my map all that seriously. Every time I visit San Pedro, shops, restaurants and travel agencies have shuffled and settled into new locales. But you won't have any trouble finding things in the few square blocks.

San Pedro Style

The entrepreneurs of the commuter airlines, fishing boats, diving services, restaurants, and other businesses in San Pedro have their own particular style, shared by all, whether of American, Creole, Hispanic, or some other origin. Call it outback efficiency. None go anywhere, to eat, drink, or chat, without a VHF radio strapped to their belts, ready to spring into action when the call comes.

This hands-on-the-job appearance is more show than substance, however. You could stay for days and not see one of these radios used. And if you walk into a travel agency through its open door, you will wait and wait, and find that it is unattended. Posted restaurant hours are observed indifferently. Your boat might not show up. Things really aren't too different from elsewhere in Belize.

ARRIVALS & DEPARTURES
Arriving By Air

San Pedro is about 35 miles from Belize City. The dirt airstrip is just south of San Pedro, a walk of a hundred yards or so. A virtual air bridge operates from both the Belize City municipal airstrip (fare $21.00) and **Philip Goldson International Airport** (fare $38.50). Flights are added as needed to accommodate waiting passengers. There is no need to enter Belize City if your destination is San Pedro.

Airlines serving San Pedro are: **Island Air**, *tel. 31140 in Belize City, 2484 in San Pedro*. Eight flights daily, and charters. (Call **Maya Airways** first as they sometimes have a special round-trip cash fare during slow periods); **Tropic Air**, *tel. 45671 in Belize City, 2012 in San Pedro*; operates 11 flights daily from Belize City.

Maya Airways, *tel. 77215 or 72312 in Belize City*; operates eight daily flights in 6-passenger planes from the Belize City airstrip, from 7 a.m. to 4:30 p.m. From Corozal, near the Mexican border, Maya Airways planes leave for San Pedro at 8:25 a.m. and 4:25 p.m, Tropic Air at 8:50 a.m. and 2:50 p.m.

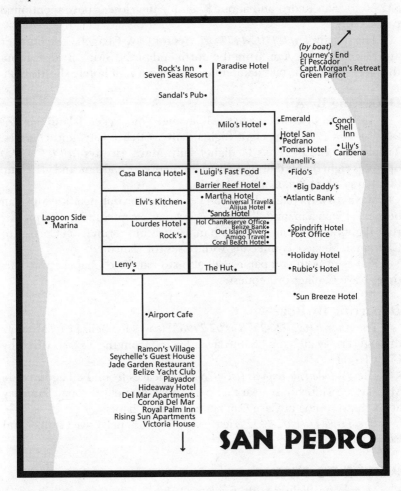

Arriving By Boat

Several boat services are currently available between downtown San Pedro and Belize City. These 8 to 24 passenger speed boats are known to depart as much as 30 minutes before schedule if they are already full, so arrive early! The 1 hour and 40 minute ride costs $12.50 each way.

Details of boat transportation may change slightly from year to year and
season to season, so please ask your hotel for the current schedules.

The *Andrea* (tel. *026-2578 or 02-74988)* departs from in front of the
Bellevue Hotel in Belize City at about 3 p.m. during the week, 7 p.m. on
Saturday. The *Thunderbolt Express*, a speedboat (tel. *026-2217),* departs
from the Swing Bridge in Belize City at 4 p.m. Monday through Friday,
1 p.m. on Saturday, stopping at Caye Caulker and Caye Chapel. Fare is
$12.50 for San Redro and about $7.50 for the closer above mentioned
cayes.

The speedy *Triple J (02-44375)* leaves for Caye Chapel, Caye Caulker
and San Pedro at 9 a.m. from the north end of the Swing Bridge. From
the pier, either walk, take a water taxi, or hop on your hotel's shuttle boat.

Departing By Air

Any hotel or travel agency will arrange your ticket. **Island Air** *(tel.
2484 in San Pedro)* has eight flights daily to Belize City, and charters.
Tropic Air *(tel. 2012)* has 11 flights daily. **Maya Airways** *(tel. 02-77215)*
operates eight flights daily to Belize City, between 7:30 a.m. and 5:15 p.m.
(Sundays only at 8 a.m. and 5:15 p.m.)

Maya Airways planes leave San Pedro for Corozal, near the Mexican
border, at 7:55 a.m. and 3:55 p.m. every day except Sunday. **Tropic Air**
runs flights at 9:30 a.m. and 3:20 p.m. Hourly buses run from Corozal to
Chetumal, Mexico, connecting with buses for Cancun.

Planes of both companies will also stop at Caye Chapel and sometimes Caye Caulker on request.

Departing By Boat

The *Andrea (tel. 026-2578 or 02-74988)* leaves for Belize City Monday
through Friday at 7 a.m., Saturday at 8 a.m., from the Texaco wharf by
Lily's Hotel.

The *Thunderbolt Express (tel. 026-2217)* leaves from the Lagoon Side
Marina (the white house near the soccer field) Monday through Saturday
at 7 a.m., stopping at Caye Caulker and Caye Chapel.

The *Triple J (tel. 02-44375)* leaves for Caye Chapel, Caye Caulker and
Belize City at 3 p.m.

WHERE TO STAY

Telephone dialing code for San Pedro is *026* from elsewhere in
Belize, *011-501-26* from the U.S.

In & Around Town

RAMON'S VILLAGE, *tel. 026-2071. 61 rooms, including cabanas and
suites. $105 to $135 double, up to $225 in suites, extra person $10, plus 10%*

service plus tax. Meals additional. Summer discounts avai' tions: P. O. Drawer 4407, Laurel, MS 39441. tel. 800-624-421⁊, ⌣ fax 649-1996.

A minute's walk south of the village of San Pedro, Ramon's is known among repeat visitors as well-managed and carefree. Recently renovated, it consists of a main dining pavilion and individual cane cabanas crowded onto the site, each with private bath and ceiling fan. The grounds are nicely landscaped, and the salt-water swimming pool is a rare feature on the island. "Suites" are efficiency apartments with kitchenettes. Full fishing and diving facilities, windsurfers, sailboats, bicycles and motor scooters for rent, excellent food, and one of the nicer beaches close to town.

MAYAN PRINCESS RESORT HOTEL, *tel. 026-2778, fax 2784. 23 One bedroom apartments. $75 to $115 single/$85 to $125 double plus 5% service and 6% tax. $10 for third person, children under 12 free in same room. Visa and Mastercard.*

This modern pink seafront apart-hotel represents a good selection for those who want the modern facilites and ammenties of a condo style unit and wish to prepare at least some of their own meals. The property boasts comfortable one bedroom ocean view apartments featuring air conditioning, tile flooring, satellite color television, full kitchens with microwave ovens, ceiling fans, white ratan furnishings, large private bathrooms, large beds, and windswept balconies. With a great location in the heart of downtown San Pedro, this is a great location to base yourself during a long or short stay on the Cayes.

PARADISE RESORT HOTEL, *tel. 026-2083, fax 2232. 41 rooms and cabanas. $50 to $100 single/$70 to $150 double (about $20 less May through October) plus 5% service plus tax. $20 for third person, children $10. Visa, Master Card, American Express. U.S. reservations: Paradise Tours, Box 42809-400, Houston, TX 77242 tel. 800-537-1431 or 713-850-1664, fax 713-785-9528.*

Located on the northern fringe of San Pedro, Paradise Resort is an exception among town hotels in that it has an extensive, private sandy beach. The accommodations are offered in a series of wooden and thatched roof cabanas, cement semi-detached villas, and a wooden central 2 story side wing. Some of the more expensive units have air conditioning. Most rooms are wood-panelled, with pastel bedspreads, vanity, a shower, and one large and one small bed. Facilities include a bar and gift shop, rental of diving and fishing equipment, and travel services. There is a deli and a snack bar by the beach.

SAN PEDRO HOLIDAY HOTEL, *tel. 026-2014, fax 2295. 16 rooms. $75 with fan, $85 air-conditioned, single or double, plus 10% service plus tax. Apartments, $120 double. Rates about $20 lower out of season. American* *xpress, Visa, Master Card. Reservations: P. O. Box 1140, tel. 44632 in Belize City.*

The Holiday Hotel is a series of interconnecting, well-maintained wooden and concrete buildings. There's only a small sign, but the entrance is marked by the figure of a seagull swinging overhead. There's more beach here than at most other in-town hotels, an advantage, as is the adjacent Celi's Restaurant, one of the better eating spots in San Pedro. Outboard motorboats are available through local guides, and there's a dive shop and travel service.

SANDS HOTEL, *tel. 026-2040. 11 rooms. $75/$85.*

A balconied concrete structure with private sundeck up top. There's also a large sandy-grassy lawn, with thatched shelters. Most rooms have compact cooking facilities and television. One very large room goes for a higher rate. There's a homey sort of disorder about this place, and the beds could be better. Bicycles are available for rent.

CORAL BEACH HOTEL, *P. O. Box 16, tel. 026-2031, fax 026-2834. 11 rooms. $30 single/$45 double with fan, $45/$65 with air conditioning, plus $30 for three meals, plus 10% service plus tax.*

This hotel is a homey little place with its front porch on San Pedro's main street, with no sand, no grounds, no pretense to being other than a base for divers. Food is good and plentiful. The hotel's Tackle Box Bar is detached, located a block away, over the water, attached to a little "sea-quarium", a pen in the sea; and the dive shop is there as well. Fishing boats are available for rent, but the emphasis is on diving for people of all skill levels. Packages available (example: three nights with diving and meals, $350 per person).

SPINDRIFT HOTEL, *tel. 026-2174, fax 2251. 30 rooms. $50 double with fan, $80 to $125 double with air conditioning, no service charge. One- and two-bedroom apartments with kitchenette available. Visa, Master Card, American Express. Lower rates may be available in off-season.*

An attractive new concrete building, and something of a town center, with the post office, pharmacy and travel agency on its ground floor. Seafront rooms are air-conditioned.

HOTEL ALIJUA, *tel. 2791, fax 2362. 8 apartments. $94 double, $125 for four with tax in high season, $88 and $110 in low season. Credit cards accepted.*

Though not furnished in the best of taste, nor situated in a quiet location, these are comfortable and spotless apartments with kitchenette, sitting room with sleep sofa, and large bedroom with one king and one queen bed. Rates are lower by the week and month.

HOTEL SAN PEDRANO, *tel. 026-2054. 7 rooms. $18/$28.*

This is one of several smaller, clean hotels in town. Meals are provided for guests on request. Private bath, good for the price.

LILY'S CARIBEÑA, *tel. 026-2059. 11 rooms. $35/$45, lower May-October.*

A bare-bones little place right on the water. The best rooms open onto a veranda with good sea views. All rooms have fans, and have been freshened up recently with new panelling and linoleum and lighting.

CONCH SHELL INN, *tel. 026-2062. 8 rooms, $25/$35.*

Simple, breezy rooms facing the sea, some with kitchenette.

SUN BREEZE HOTEL, *P. O. Box 14, San Pedro, tel. 026-2345, 800-327-3573 in the U.S., 32302 in Belize City. 34 rooms. $90 single/$100 double plus 10% service plus tax. Add $40 for three meals. Visa, Master Card, American Express.*

By the airstrip (but still only a few minutes' walk from town), an attractive, substantial, low-lying building in Mexican style, with covered archways, and an extensive sandy compound. Unusually, all rooms are air-conditioned, which disguises intermittent airplane noise, besides keeping things cool. Rooms are rather plain, with a tiled bath area. Dive shop with lessons, certification, equipment rentals. A pool is to be installed soon. Golf carts are available for rent, at about $25 for the day.

BARRIER REEF, *tel. 026-2075, fax 2719. 10 rooms. $48 single/$65 double.*

Located in one of the oldest houses in San Pedro, and an adjacent extension. Rooms in the original building have verandas for watching town life, and the sea nearby. Boat available for guests. Subject to late-night noise since across the street is Big Daddy's disco.

Other lodging places in San Pedro are the **TOMAS HOTEL** ($35 double), **RUBIE'S HOTEL**, and **MILO'S HOTEL**, in both of which the charge is about $15 per person sharing bath, or less. Rubie's has some rooms with private bath at $25 to $35 double, with the higher rates on the upper floor. None have any special features, but all are acceptably clean.

MARTHA'S HOTEL, *tel. 2053, two blocks back from the sea near the Sands,* has plain accommodations at $23 single/$35 double with private bath, less during the rainy season. The **CASA BLANCA HOTEL** *(tel. 2924, 9 rooms, $10 double shared bath, $25 double with private both)* has bare rooms a few blocks back from the sea and main street, but with a disco downstairs, that's no advantage.

Out-of-Town

The hotels described below are located from a few hundred yards to several miles from town. The facilities are in general more substantial and attractive than at hotels in town:

North of San Pedro

ROCK'S INN, *14 units. $95 to $125 double, $10 per additional person, plus 10% service, slightly lower May through October. Phone 026-2336, fax 2349, or 800-331-2458 in the States.*

There are two stories of apartments here in a white building in old Miami-Cozumel style, with balcony and concrete balustrade facing the sea. It's all fairly new, and each room has a kitchenette with microwave and utensils, a main room and bedroom, tiled shower, air conditioning and ceiling fan. Clients here bubble with satisfaction over the value. Located just past the Paradise Resort and a condominium project.

SEVEN SEAS RESORT, *tel. 2382, fax 2472. 12 units, $95 per night.*

About a half-mile north of San Pedro, these apartments with kitchenettes are in a three-story building covered with wood shakes. There are no services or pool.

Vehicle travel comes to an end at a waterway about three-quarters of a mile north of San Pedro. There is talk of extending the road some day, even all the way to Mexico – unlikely, but then, the most unlikely deals have already come to pass in San Pedro, despite a stretched supply of fresh water and the difficulties of transporting construction materials.

Hotels on Ambergris Caye Accessible Only By Boat

The following hotels are reached by boat only. With the exception of guests at Journey's End (which provides a courtesy water taxi), and Captain Morgan's (who only charges $5 roundtrip on their private launch), you'll most likely have to pay around $40 (per boat-not per person) for every trip to town after your arrival. If you would rather walk into town, a path can take you there in about 45 minutes, but bring a powerful flashlight if returning after dark!

CAPTAIN MORGAN'S RETREAT, *tel. 026-2567, fax 2398. 21 units. $130 single/$170 double high season, $95/$120 low season plus 5% service plus tax, $35 for three meals. Rates higher at holidays. Master Card, Visa, American Express. U.S. reservations: Magnum Americas, Box 763, Detroit Lakes, MN 56501, tel. 800-447-2931.*

Captain Morgan's has a comfortable beachcomber's atmosphere. Each thatched-roof cabana, named for a pirate captain, comes with double beds, cross ventilation, porch, fan, and tiled shower. The grounds are well shaded. Facilities include a fresh-water pool and 40-foot-high crow's nest. Fishing, sailing, snorkeling and diving available, as well as diving and fishing packages. One transfer each way from San Pedro is included.

The sand-floored grill serves sandwiches, and the upstairs dining room offers great multiple course meals, with treetop-level views out to sea. Non-guests are welcome to dinner by advance reservation.

JOURNEY'S END CARIBBEAN CLUB, *P. O. Box 13, San Pedro, tel. 026-2173, fax 2028. 70 units. From $137 single/$184 double, $45 additional for three meals, no service charge. Rates higher at holidays. American Express, Visa, Master Card. U.S. reservations: tel. 800-447-0474 or 305-456-8708.*

Strewn over an expanse four miles north of San Pedro, Journey's End has comprehensive resort facilities: Olympic pool, whirlpool, billiards, lighted tennis courts, sundeck for naturists, basketball, sailboats, windsurfers, multiple bars and restaurants, and even slot and poker machines.

Accommodations are provided in small cabanas that are attractively furnished. Stucco cabanas away from the beach are larger but sun-baked. Most comfortable are the lower-priced Lagoon View rooms, with tile floors and terrace.

All on-site facilities and sporting equipment are included, but not fishing, scuba diving or snorkeling. Air-conditioning is included in Lagoon View rooms, extra in cabanas. Television and phones are not available in beach cabanas, included in other units. The beach bar opens at 8 a.m., and non-guests are welcome to stop by for a drink, or one of the regular beach barbecues (currently Tuesday and Friday evenings and Sunday at noon) for $27.

EL PESCADOR, *tel. 026-2975, fax 026-2398. 12 rooms, all with private bath. $110 single/$180 double with three meals, plus 15% service plus tax. No credit cards. Weekly fishing package $1,375 with transport from Belize City. Reservations: P. O. Box 793 in Belize City.*

Located three miles north of San Pedro, El Pescador is a self-contained light-tackle fishing camp/resort, specializing in bonefish, tarpon, and permit. Rooms are in a large plantation-style house built by two German brothers, one of whom is the manager. Meals are buffet-style, mostly fish. Airport transfers and diving and fishing packages available on request.

GREEN PARROT RESORT, *P. O. Box 36, San Pedro, tel. 026-2331. 7 units. $65 single/$80 double; or $100 single/$150 double/$180 triple with three meals. No credit cards. U.S. reservations: Morrison Travel, 2401 N. Federal Highway, Boca Raton, FL 33431, tel. 800-328-1005 or 800-432-2069.*

Green Parrot is a small resort of wooden beachside guest cottages with private facilities, six miles north of San Pedro, and five minutes from the Mexico Rocks snorkeling site. The central three-story tower that houses the restaurant and bar provides excellent views seaward. Boat from San Pedro arranged with reservation. Food is served family- or buffet-style, with a rotating menu that includes Italian, Mexican, and Belizean specialties, as well as lots of seafood. Divers will be picked up at the resorts dock for outings arranged through San Pedro dive shops.

South of San Pedro

VICTORIA HOUSE, *tel. 026-2067. 31 rooms, all with private bath. $95 single/$110 double in standard rooms, $120/$150 in cottages, $125/$170 in deluxe rooms with air conditioning, plus 10% service plus tax. Low-season rate $68 single/$80 double. Suite and beach house available. Small charge for additional person or children. Add $40 plus 10% service for three meals (children half price). Major credit cards accepted. Reservations: P. O. Box 20785, Houston, TX 77030, tel. 800-247-5159 or 713-529-6800, fax 713-661-4025.*

This classy hotel consists of a lovely old plantation house and thatched-roof Mexican-style cottages, along the nicest beach on the island, about a mile south of San Pedro. The cottage units have tile floors, hardwood vanities and shutters, two large beds with floral bedspreads, art prints on the walls, a desk, mini-refrigerator, shower stall, and high thatched roof, as well as a porch – altogether, several cuts above what you'll find elsewhere in San Pedro. Other rooms, in row units and the main house, are also quite large, with wicker furnishings and pastel decor. Meals are fixed-menu with plain, plentiful fare. Service is top-notch.

The grounds at Victoria House ramble on, with plenty of hammocks on shaded porches and between the palms, expanses of grass, and flower beds – landscaping details which are absent elsewhere on the island. The beach compound includes a volleyball area, and a three-sided bar in a separate pavilion, with free popcorn. Bicycles are provided at no charge for commuting up the sand lane to town, and the hotel van and boat make regular runs at no charge. There are also golf carts ($10 per hour), kayaks and windsurfers for rent. Diving and fishing are available at Fantasea Watersports right on the hotel dock.

BELIZE YACHT CLUB, *P. O. Box 1, San Pedro, tel. 026-2777, fax 2768. 44 units. $125 to $150 double plus tax and 10% service charge.*

The Yacht Club is a condominium boat-and-apartment complex a quarter-mile south of San Pedro, with some of the most attractive accommodations in Belize. The architecture is Spanish-colonial, with red tile roofs and archways everywhere. On-site are a gym, fresh-water pool, extensive gardens, and artificial reef. Furnishings and detailings are in excellent taste, including wicker furniture, overhead fans, full kitchen with appliances, Mexican tile counter, and wooden trim throughout. All units have a terrace and sea view. The marina supplies water and fuel, and can take boats with up to a seven-foot draft. All that's missing is a restaurant.

CARIBBEAN VILLAS HOTEL, *P. O. Box 71, San Pedro, tel. 2715, fax 2885. 8 suites, 2 rooms. $85 to $180 ($65 to $120 June through October, higher at holidays), no service charge.*

One of the more attractive lodging places in San Pedro, a Mediterranean-style building with archways and red roof, and comfortable accommodations in an assortment of sizes, with archways, wicker furnishings, tiled floors, large bathroom-dressing room, both ceiling fan and air conditioning, cross ventilation, and full cooking facilities, including microwave oven. Three can sleep in most units, and a deluxe unit has a huge loft with a second bath.

The beach is large, and outdoor facilities include two hot tubs, showers, and a 30-foot "people perch," a tower with one bird-viewing level at treetop level, and a second with a view to the lagoon side and to the sea. Grounds are intentionally kept much as they were when the land was acquired by the friendly owners. The rate includes daily maid service with dishwashing, pickup at the airstrip, and use of bikes.

MATA ROCKS SOUTH, *tel. 026-2336, fax 2349, or 800-331-2458 in the States. 9 apartments, $65 to $75 per night, plus 15% service plus tax, $55 to $65 May through October.*

A mile south of town, these are wood-sided units with steep roofs, furnished with the works, including microwaves. The large downstairs units, air conditioned, with king-sized bed and sleep sofa, go for $75 plus 15% service charge. Smaller upstairs units with double beds and sofas are $55 and $65. These are also available by the month. If you book directly, ask for a discount equivalent to the usual 20% travel agency commission. The owners (who also operate the Rock's Inn apartments) will also make diving and fishing arrangements.

ROYAL PALM INN, *P. O. Box 18, tel. 026-2148, fax 2329.*

These units have recently been totally refurbished as condominiums, and will can be rented as one-bedroom apartments with kitchens, and a pool on the grounds.

CORONA DEL MAR APARTMENT HOTEL, *tel. 026-2055, fax 2461. $85 double plus 15% service plus tax, $10 per extra person, more at holidays. Low-season rate (May through October), $75 plus service and tax.*

Half a mile south of San Pedro, these are apartments in a concrete building on a white beach a few feet from the water. Furnishings, strictly home-style, include two double beds with frilly spreads, and sleep sofa in living room. Also: full kitchen, bathroom with tub and carpeted seat, and fan and air conditioning. Upstairs units have nice views.

HOTEL PLAYADOR, *tel. 026-2870, fax 2871. 20 units. $95 double in cabanas, $105 double in air-conditioned rooms, $125 in air-conditioned cabana ($75, $85, $105 in summer).*

Just south of the airstrip, convenient to town. Accommodation is in basic thatch-roofed cabanas, and in air-conditioned concrete rooms. Restaurant, bar, attractive beach.

HIDEAWAY HOTEL, *tel. 026-2141. 29 rooms. $50 per person with two meals plus 10% service plus tax. In summer, the rate drops to about $30 double without meals.*

Located about 3/4 mile south of San Pedro, the Hideaway is not directly on the beach, but provides access to facilities for its guests. With a fresh-water pool, this hotel is a very good value. The bar has some relatively inexpensive sandwiches, and breakfast items at a couple of dollars each.

Apartments

"Apartment" is a loose term here – sometimes it means a hotel room with a hot plate, sometimes two bedrooms and a separate kitchen and dining room. The **DEL MAR** apartments *(tel. 2695)*, south of the airstrip, are single rooms with a stove and refrigerator stuck in. The rate is about $40 a day.

Farther south, **CORONA DEL MAR** and **HOUSE OF THE RISING SUN APARTMENTS**, and **ROCK'S INN**, north of town (all mentioned above), are more like hotel suites. Smaller apartments are available in town, and attached to several hotels mentioned above. The **TOMAS HOTEL** has one for $30 a day. And real estate agents will be happy to set you up in a condominium unit or private homes when these are available.

WHERE TO EAT

Prices for food in San Pedro are not inconsiderable. When you see the basket of carrots strapped into a seat on the plane, you'll understand something about the cost structure. Nevertheless, some eating places provide good value, and you can choose from a variety of cuisines that includes Creole-Belizean, Mexican, Italian, Chinese, and unadorned American.

ELVI'S KITCHEN remains the current trendy eating spot in San Pedro. You can't miss the huge thatched roof. Inside, a tree sprouts in the middle of the sand floor of the main cavern, and not in a pot either. There is another, step-up level to the side. White walls with dark wood trim are decorated with assorted bottles. And aside from all this island atmosphere, the food is generally better than you'll find elsewhere in San Pedro, and prices are reasonable. Choices range from rice and beans with chicken ($4) through hamburgers and fishburgers, club sandwiches, fish in garlic and wine, t-bone steak and sautéed lobster ($15). $5 gets a daily blue plate special that could be Mexican grilled beef. Breakfast offerings for $6 or less include Yucatecan-style eggs.

JADE GARDEN, *about half a mile south of the airstrip*, is one of the better eating places in town, and certainly the most distinguished, setting-wise. It's in an elevated, South Seas-style building with wood siding and cathedral ceiling. You sit on wicker chairs inside, or dine on the porch with sea view. The menu is Cantonese, with chops and American-style seafood as well. Curry, sweet-and-sour, chow mein and foo young main courses are available with fish or shellfish or beef, and there are fried lobster, conch and fish with French fries, and assorted large salads as well. $12 and up for a full meal, $5 and up for sandwiches with French fries. If you've reached that point, *phone 2126 or 2506*, and they'll even deliver to your lodgings.

South of town, **MICKEY'S PLACE**, *in the Hotel Playador*, has a mixed menu that includes a Mexican assortment, lobster, Veracruz-style fish. $10 and up for a main course, less for sandwiches or breakfast.

THE HUT, *at the south end of town where you turn from the main street to go to the airport*, serves bar food with a Tex-Mex flavor in a room with a low ceiling hung with macramé planters and electric lanterns. A nacho and salad plate, or chicken with rice and beans, along with breakfasts, go for under $8; and there are pricier fish and surf and turf plates and seafood kabobs available on a rotating basis.

LILY'S RESTAURANT, *snuggled along the passageway right under Lily's Hotel*, is unpretentious but pleasant, dark-wood-panelled, with wicker chairs under fluorescent lights. The owner-cook has a reputation for doing up seafood properly. A meal with broiled fish, fried conch fritters or chicken runs under $14, and breakfast is available.

At Fido's shopping complex in the central part of town, **THE GRILL** chalks up the menu daily. Recently: B.L.T. or hamburger with fries, $4, grilled grouper or chicken with fries, $7, hot dogs or burritos for $2. You eat on a wooden deck, and, as at most San Pedro eateries, your serving does not include bread or butter or salad or any other extra on the side. At the Pizza Place, take your choice of a whole pizza for up to $16, or hamburgers or deli-style sandwiches (Reuben, club) with fries for up to $5.

In the Sunbreeze Hotel at the south end of town, the **COCO PALM RRESTAURANT** serves breakfasts for $4 to $6, sandwiches, and Mexican combination plates for up to $12. That's comparable to what you'll pay elsewhere, but the atmosphere is more pleasant with wicker chairs, pastel tablecloths, white walls with dark wood wainscoting.

CELI'S RESTAURANT *is adjacent to the Holiday Hotel* – go through or alongside the hotel, then left along the beach. There are no secrets: the kitchen is open to the dining area with its white walls, dark beams and carved posts and wicker chairs. The regular menu includes hamburger platters, fried fish, shrimp and lobster main courses (Creole, fried, Parmesan, stuffed – you name it) for $6 to $20; but you should take a look at the special of the day, such as fish with stir-fried vegetables for $10 or so. Key lime pie or cheese cake are extra, but you won't want to pass them up. They open for breakfast at 7 a.m. (ranchero eggs, waffles, omelettes $3 and up), not for lunch. **THE DELI**, *on the main street side of the Holiday Hotel*, has BLT, turkey, chicken and other sandwiches to go at $3 and up.

One of the better values for light fare is the **COFFEE SHOP** *by the airport*. Breakfasts, waffles, burritos, tostadas, chile con carne, hamburgers and sandwiches go for about $3 to $4. Open from 6:30 a.m. to 3 p.m., and air-conditioned.

Several eateries will serve you local food bare of pretense. One is **LENY'S PLACE**, *near the turn from town to the airport*. Beef with onions, fried shrimp, and rice and beans with chicken range from $3 to $7.

For snacks, there are several ice-cream-cone outlets. At **MANELLY'S**, *on Barrier Reef Drive (Front St.)*, the ice cream is gummy but comes in yummy flavors such as Oreo, for 50¢ to a dollar for a cone, and there are hamburgers as well. **Scoop's** ice cream, the Ben and Jerry's of Belize, is sold at **ALICE'S STORE**, *a block west of the Coral Beach*. The restaurant under the Barrier Reef Hotel has pizzas in assorted sizes for $9 to $15, and interesting sandwiches for $4.

NIGHTLIFE

Drinking spots are abundant, in hotels, in restaurants, and as free-standing establishments. **Sandal's** *is near the north end of the main street*, **Fido's** *is in the thatched shopping center in the central part of the seafront*, and **Big Daddy's** *is a block to the south*. Big Daddy's is also a disco, and the action goes on late into the night. The **Tackle Box Bar** *is on a pier over the water*. Butts and crumbs accumulate on the sand floor, which is renewed as necessary. The **Mayan Xtasis** disco and bar, recently inaugurated *in the Casa Blanca hotel*, brings the noise over to the other side of town.

For a uniquely Belizean entertainment, attend the Wednesday-night chicken drop at the bar of the **Spindrift Hotel**. Patrons bet on where a chicken ends up doing his business on something like an oversized bingo board.

EXCURSIONS: AMBERGRIS ALTERNATIVES

Ambergris, of course, is an island, and can give a closed-in feeling. If you want to get off, but don't feel like going home, try a mainland excursion. The larger hotels will arrange flights to **Belize City**, and connecting transport to the ruins of **Altun Ha** or the highlands of the **Mountain Pine Ridge** forest reserve. Or you can fly on your own to Belize City and hire a taxi to **Altun Ha**. Now you can even take a flying day tour to the ruins of **Tikal** in Guatemala for about $200. Any travel agency in San Pedro can make the arrangements, or contact Island Air.

An alternative mainland destination is **Corozal**, a pleasant little seaside town for wandering about, but facilities hardly compare with those of San Pedro.

You might also wish to do as so many Belizeans are doing these days: go shopping in the duty-free town of **Chetumal** just over the border in

Mexico. The selection of French clothing, perfumes, radios and household gadgets is rather uneven, but prices are fair. Take a taxi or bus from Corozal. Border formalities are minimal, but remember to bring your passport.

You can spend a few hours at the stores in the morning (most close for the afternoon), or stay over and return to Ambergris the next day.

SPORTS & RECREATION
Diving

Almost every hotel offers scuba diving, either with their own boats and equipment, or through local dive shops. If you call around to the divemasters listed below, you can often negiotiate the prices down by 25%.

Typically, a short resort diving course for beginners featuring an exciting ocean dive costs about $125 USD; a 3 day PADI certification course is only $350; a 35 to 50 minute 1 tank ocean dive for certified divers diving is $25 to $35, a 2 tank dive goes for $40 to $55, or $30 to $40 for a 1 tank night dive. Rates may be higher when booked through your hotel rather than in town, or lower, especially between May and October.

Rental rates for equipment vary considerably. Figure a minimum of $7 daily for either a regulator or buoyancy compensator, $5 for mask, snorkel and fins. If you haven't pre-arranged diving, these dive shops offer good rates and quality service with typical Belizean charm:

- **Patojos Dive Shop** *(Patojos Paz), Boca de Rio area in San Pedro, tel. 026-2283.* This native expert diver guides the islands' best resort (almost 3 hours in the sea!) and most memorable ocean dives in conjuction with Captain Morgan's Resort.
- **Hustler Tours**, *Hustler pier (north of San Pedro)tel. 2279, fax 2719*; long and short range scuba and snorkeling trips.
- **Amigos del Mar**, *in front of Lilly's Hotel,(Changa Paz Owner) tel. 026-2706.* They oofer all sorts of diving trips at good prices.
- **Fantasea Watersports** *(Chris Berlin and Rebecca McDonald, PADI instructors), Victoria House, tel. and fax 2576, 2615 evenings.*
- **Bottom Time Dive Shop**, *Sun Breeze Hotel, tel. 2348*

Overnight Dive Programs
- **Out Island Divers**, *opposite the Sprindrift Hotel, tel. 2151, fax 2810, (reservations to P.O. Box 3455, Estes Park, CO 80517, tel. 800-258-3465 or 303-586-6020)* has diving boats with live-aboard accommodations. Their star attraction is a Saturday excursion to Lighthouse Reef. Divers fly out to Northern Caye early in the morning and board the Reef Roamer II for a brief dive into the singular Blue Hole, followed by a wall dive at Half Moon Caye, a visit to the Booby Bird Sanctuary,

and a wall dive on Long Caye. The cost is about $200, or up to $300 for a two-night trip with seven dives. Mid-week trips can be arranged, and they have other multi-dive packages to the Turneffe Islands, as well as a less-expensive Blue Hole trip by water direct from San Pedro. Departures are guaranteed.

• **Indigo Belize** *(P. O. Box 450987, Sunrise, FL 33345, tel. 800-468-0123), operates the M/V Manta IV diving boat, complete with shark cage and video equipment. In San Pedro, inquire at the Belize Yacht Club, or call 2130, fax 2834.* Their overnight trip to Lighthouse Reef, with five dives and five meals, costs about $230 per person. A three-dive day trip to the Turneffe Islands costs about $110 per person; and they have daily diving along the reef as well.

Fishing

Fishing in the flats and along the reef costs $175 to $200 for a full-day excursion in a small boat for three people, less (but not much less) for half a day, while deep-sea fishing costs about $400 for a full day, $250 for a half day, or more, depending on the boat.

If your hotel can't help you with fishing, here are some contacts: Francis Leslie, *tel. 2128*; Roberto Bradly, *tel. 2116*; Melanie Paz, *tel. 2437*, Romel Gómez, *tel. 2034*.

Snorkeling

Scuba diving takes some training and some dollars and some time. For the casual visitor, a first acquaintance with the underwater world off San Pedro is often through snorkeling.

A snorkeling trip from San Pedro, if booked through a travel agency, runs $15 to $20, usually to **Hol Chan Marine Reserve** (see below), Mexico Rocks, or Coral Garden.

All-day snorkeling trips with a stop at Caye Caulker are run by Tony Eiler on his boat, *The Rum Punch*, from the Tackle Box pier. The $35 fee includes drinks, but lunch is $5 extra (such are priorities in Belize). On some days, a beach barbecue-snorkeling trip is operated for $40 per person.

Snorkeling trips are a hotly competitive item from time to time, and some operators are offering discounts on the above. At **Rubie's Hotel**, you can currently book a place on a snorkeling excursion to Hol Chan Marine Reserve for $12.50 ($5 for children); a Caye Caulker trip for $25; or just rent snorkeling gear for $5 for the day and go out on your own. Look around and ask around. There are snorkeling boats everywhere, and you might even find a better rate.

• **Hustler Tours**, *tel. 2279, at the pier just north of San Pedro*, runs a jungle river trip a couple of days a week that takes you across to the Northern

River on the mainland, for about $65 per person. They also have morning and afternoon glass-bottom boat rides for about $12, and run the catamaran *Mee Too* on snorkeling trips to Caye Caulker ($40), and a snorkeling-and-barbecue trip to Rocky Point, north of San Pedro, for $45 per person.

· **Fido Badillo**, *tel. 2286, in Fido's courtyard*, also runs a boat trip across the channel to the New River and Altun Ha. **Island Adventures**, also at Fido's, has a Caye Caulker trip, and a sunset cruise that calls at Journey's End and then heads through a channel to the lagoon side to watch the orb descend. Pay $15 to get aboard.

HOL CHAN RESERVE

At the southern tip of Ambergris is **Hol Chan Marine Reserve**, *a national park that includes part of the barrier reef, as well as mangroves, and a stretch of seabed with its own sinkhole and underlying cave – a smaller version of the famed Blue Hole of Lighthouse Reef. The three sections are ecologically related – species spend different parts of their lives in each of the three zones.*

Snorkeling tours often stop in the reserve, which is named for a cut in the reef (Hol Chan means "little channel" in Mayan). The walls of the channel are lined with coral, and the cave is home to green moray eels. The channel serves as a throughway for fish commuting to feeding areas.

Hol Chan Reef Rules:
1. Plants and wildlife are not to be touched or disturbed.
2. Fishing and collecting are prohibited.
3. Boats must tie up at buoys.
4. Entry fee of $3 must be paid.
5. Stepping on coral is prohibited. Look for sandy or grassy footings, and only when absolutely necessary.
6. Stay horizontal. Clouds of sand deteriorate coral.
Hol Chan Realities:
1. There is no effective patrol, or supervision of visitors.
2. Snorkelers often step on coral, and intentionally break it off.
3. The establishment of the reserve has served to channel visitors to a small and fragile part of the reef, and threatens the destruction of the very habitat under protection.
4. Boat traffic at the reserve is heavy, and snorkeling and scuba diving are dangerous at peak periods.
Do your part. Follow the rules for visiting Hol Chan (which apply to the coral reef in general), or you could be one of the last visitors.

Boat Trips

There are also **glass-bottomed boat** excursions. $15 will get you a ride of a couple of hours with a stop of about a half-hour for snorkeling (if you don't insist on staying dry).

Pilots are adept at spotting sharks and barracudas and sting rays and schools of grunts and parrotfish and angelfish, and repeatedly maneuvering into position above them, so you can combine random views as a snorkeler with extended observation of the really interesting stuff. Look near the Salty Dog pier.

Underwater Photography Rentals

Although those disposable $14 plastic underwater cameras are fine for quick snorkeling snapshots, scuba divers may require more sophisitcated camera gear and strobe lights.

The best place to rent Nikonos, Sea & Sea, or Sony underwater cameras and video recorders is over at **Joe Miller Photography** *in Fido's Courtyard in San Padro*. Give Joe a call *at 026-2577* and ask him what he suggests for your specific needs. Expect to spend between $25 and $50 a day for a camera, and at least $35 for a video system.

More Water Fun

Water skiing runs about $55 per hour for two people. **Beach cookouts ... party boats ... night snorkeling ... water taxis ...** you name it, one of the above will provide it for a fee.

Charters

Charter trips to Caye Caulker and Belize City are available at the **Lagoon Side Marina** (the two-story white house adjacent to the soccer field on the lower west side of San Pedro), *tel. 026-2488*. They also have canoe rentals, and can arrange other water sports.

At **Bottom Time Dive Shop**, *tel. 2348*, a 35-foot Bristol is available for $50 per person, minimum three persons.

Sailing

The *Winnie Estelle*, a 66-foot island trader sailboat, is operated from the **Paradise Hotel** dock most days on a cruise that includes snorkeling stops, lunch, and drinks, for $45, $20 for children. *Call 2394 for information.*

Otherwise, look around the **Tackle Box Bar** for sailboats on day trips from Caye Caulker. They'll take you back for about $10.

Horseback Riding

Isla Equestrian, by the airstrip, has horses available for exploration of the byways of Ambergris Caye.

Travel Agencies

Universal Travel *(tel. 2137)* and **Amigo Travel** *(tel.2180)*, opposite the Spindrift Hotel, will sell you airplane tickets, arrange tours, and even rent out bicycles and scooters.

Travel and Tour Belize Limited is at the airstrip.

PRACTICAL INFORMATION

A branch of the **Atlantic Bank** is located on Barrier Reef Drive, not that you'll need it, as travelers checks are accepted at most establishments.

There are several groceries in town with stocks of Pringles, Cheese-Whiz and liquors, most notably **Rock's**, a block west of the Coral Beach Hotel.

CAYE CAULKER

Located south of Ambergris Caye, about twenty miles from Belize City, **Caye Caulker** has been described as a slightly enlarged version of Gilligan's Island. Like Ambergris, Caulker is partly swamp, and has only a limited settled area. But the island and town are much smaller — it measures a half-mile by about five miles, with fewer than 750 inhabitants.

Facilities for visitors are fewer in number, but recent expansion and development threatens to soon destroy it's peacefulness. In recent years the local police have put somewhat of a damper on formerly accepted activities such as openly smoking marijuana, and topless bathing.

Once a pirate lair, Caye Caulker is now a relatively prosperous community of fishermen. Lobsters and conch are the main catch. Some of the residents are also skilled at boat-building. The island is called *Cayo Hicaco* in Spanish — hicaco is a species of palm, the coco plum — whence comes the English name, which is also spelled Corker.

For years, Caye Caulker was *the* place in Belize for hanging out and watching the sea. Backpackers from all over came to examine the scene, and ended up staying for indefinite periods at Belize's low-key, un-crowded, and unluxurious People's Resort.

Times have changed, and with the inauguration of a landing strip and an air shuttle to Belize City, accommodations are in a state of flux. Prices have begun to rise, several hotels have changed hands, and new restaurants, excursion providers, and souvenir shops have begun to pop up.

Alas, Caye Caulker . . .

ORIENTATION

Caye Caulker village is a square of sandy lanes under the palms, facing the gentle sea to both east and west. On the reef side are docks and docks and docks. This is genuinely a fishing village, and you are a bystander. The beach is no more than 11 inches of sand, meandering down the shoreline. There is said to be a pickup truck somewhere, and several golf carts sneak up and down the lanes, but sleeping dogs occupy the right of way at all hours. Outlying clusters of houses are reached by trails through the palms.

Almost all of the buildings on Caye Caulker, for guests and residents, are raised on posts, or more spindly stilts. This keeps you above the level of the sand flies (another reason development is limited) and more squarely in the breeze. When the wind is strong, your room has a noticeable sway — something like that caused by a mild earthquake.

To the north, the village comes to a halt at the Cut, where Hurricane Hattie blew through the island in 1961. It's a popular swimming spot. The water is shallow and fast-moving. Many of the structures on the island look like they would not survive another good storm.

The southern tip of Caye Caulker and part of the offshore extending out to the reef comprise **Siwa-Ban**, a nature reserve in development. As at the better-known Hol Chan Reserve off Ambergris Caye, Siwa-Ban has three zones.

The forest includes stands of coco plum, sea grape and mangrove; a sea grass section extends to the reef; and the reef section includes two channels that are throughways for roaming schools of fish. The black catbird (*siwa-ban* in Yucatec Mayan) nests only in the forest on Caye Caulker and in the rapidly disappearing stands of trees on Ambergris Caye.

The establishment of the reserve, during a period of frenzied building, could help save the black catbird, as well as provide a sanctuary for other species, including the American crocodile. For more information on the reserve, send a request (and donation) to **Siwa-ban**, *47 Caye Caulker, tel. 022-2178.*

ARRIVALS & DEPARTURES
Arriving By Air
A ticket to Caye Caulker on **Island Air** *(tel. 31140 in Belize City)* costs about $40 round trip from the Belize City municipal airport, $58 from the international airport.

Arriving By Boat
Most boats for Caye Caulker leave from **A&R's Texaco** station on the north side of Haulover Creek in Belize City, near the Swing Bridge. Departure is at about 11 a.m., fare about $7.50 per person, or more if one

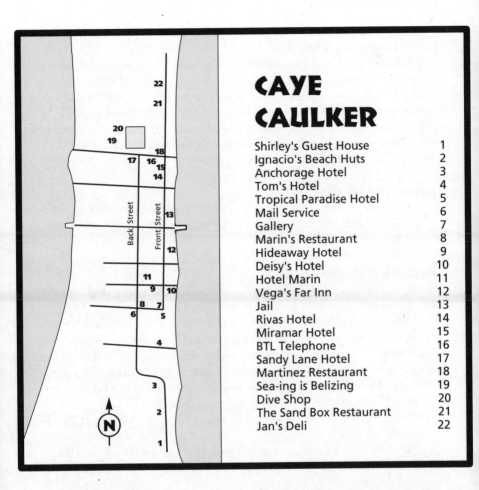

CAYE CAULKER

Shirley's Guest House	1
Ignacio's Beach Huts	2
Anchorage Hotel	3
Tom's Hotel	4
Tropical Paradise Hotel	5
Mail Service	6
Gallery	7
Marin's Restaurant	8
Hideaway Hotel	9
Deisy's Hotel	10
Hotel Marin	11
Vega's Far Inn	12
Jail	13
Rivas Hotel	14
Miramar Hotel	15
BTL Telephone	16
Sandy Lane Hotel	17
Martinez Restaurant	18
Sea-ing is Belizing	19
Dive Shop	20
The Sand Box Restaurant	21
Jan's Deli	22

of the local touts claims a commission for allegedly having brought you (usually the case). Later boats will make the run for a higher price. The hour-long trip out is a tour of the cayes in itself, a zig-zag route following the path of least resistance, zipping through mangrove-lined passages, thwack-thwacking in open water, speeding over a flat surface in the lee of Caye Chapel.

Most boats are double-outboard skiffs, some are tiny single-outboards. Take the largest boat available for a more comfortable passage. Various sources will advise you to take **Chocolate's boat**, though there must ten persons of all shades who claim to be Chocolate. The *real* Chocolate is available at **Mom's Restaurant**, or you can call him on Caye Caulker *at 022-2151*.

Capt. Jim Novelo, like Chocolate, has good reason to understand gringos. His boat, *Sunrise*, can also be booked in advance *(tel. 022-2195, fax 2239).* If possible, try to share a boat with local people, and pay only upon arrival at Caye Caulker.

Another boat, the *Thunderbolt Express*, leaves from the south side of the Swing Bridge for Caye Caulker and Ambergris Caye Monday through Friday at 3:30 p.m., Saturday at 1 p.m. Phone San Pedro *(026-2488)* to confirm that the boat is running and to inquire for additional departures. The *Triple J* leaves for Caye Chapel, Caye Caulker and San Pedro at 9 a.m. from the north end of the Swing Bridge in Belize City. *Call 02-44375 to verify the latest schedule.*

Departing By Air

You can go back to Belize City, or, on **Island Air**, to Caye Chapel or Ambergris Caye, but make sure to call at least 3 hours in advance to confirm a stop here is scheduled.

Departing By Boat

Speak to the captain who brought you out (if you were satisfied with the service) to arrange your return to Belize City.

Otherwise, tell somebody at your hotel of your travel plans. **Deisy's Hotel** can book your trip the day before, and there are others who will make advance arrangements for slightly less than what you paid to get out to Caye Caulker. Or be out by the dock near the **Martínez Restaurant** at 6:30 a.m. Unusually, departure is prompt, at 7 a.m. One boat usually leaves at 8 a.m. and another at 3p.m., from Deisy's.

The *Thunderbolt Express* from Ambergris Caye touches Caye Caulker at about 7:45 a.m.

For Ambergris Caye or Caye Chapel, look for the *Triple J* at 10 a.m. or the Thunderbolt Express at about 4:30 p.m., or arrange a dropoff from a sailboat headed that way.

GETTING AROUND CAYE CAULKER

Most of the island's larger southern section can be accessed by foot. For those who are a bit lazy, golf carts can be found at shops along front street for $10 per hour and $60 per day. Mountain bikes can also be rented for $3 per hour and $13 a day.

WHERE TO STAY

For booking purposes, you should know that the telephone dialing code for Caye Caulker is *022* from elsewhere in Belize, *011-501-22* from the U.S.

Caye Caulker is small enough that you can look over a few places before settling on one that suits you and that has a room available. If you're traveling at an unusually busy period, you can call **Dolphin Bay Travel** *(tel. 022-2214)* from the mainland to book your room.

THE TROPICAL PARADISE HOTEL, *toward the south end of the village on the reef (east) side*, next to the old island cemetery, is the most substantial lodging place in Caye Caulker, a neat compound of golden clapboard buildings. Three new luxury cabanas, with air conditioning, refrigerator and television, go for $60 double, $70 triple, plus tax. Five other cabanas, and the ten clean, light, plain rooms with fan and private bath, go for $37 to $45 for one or two persons. The hotel has a fair-sized sandy compound with lounge chairs, and full-time hot water. *For reservations, call 022-2124, fax 2225, or write to P. O. Box 1573, Belize City.*

At the northern end of the village, by the Cut, is the OUT ISLAND BEACH CLUB, a palm-shaded beach village of nine clapboard cottages. With ample sand and water on three sides, it is one of the more desirable locations on the island. The rate is about $35 double, $45 for four persons, less during the rainy period. *Call 022-2041 for current prices and reservations.*

THE SEA BEEZZZ, *just next to the Tropical Paradise on the far side from the village,* has some high-security rooms. The cost is about $20 per person.

TOM'S HOTEL *(27 rooms, tel. 2102)* is a neat, white building about 100 yards south of the Paradise. Rooms in the main building go for $12 with two beds and $18 with three beds. They're neat and clean, with shared bath. There are also four small cabanas with one double and one single bed each, and private tiled bath, for $35 per night, a good buy.

THE ANCHORAGE, *next after Tom's (tel. 45937 in Belize City),* consists of Mayan-style thatched cottages.

Next door are IGNACIO'S BEACH HUTS, little multicolored units that look like a takeoff on roadside motor courts of the early days of the automobile era. At less than $10 per person (minimum two persons) with private shower, they're a bargain.

SHIRLEY'S GUEST HOUSE *(tel. 2145)*, next down the coast, has nice but small rooms, some sharing bath ($20 double), some with private bath ($30 double). It's not your best deal money-wise, unless you take into account the relative privacy, with an extensive sandy area and well-tended plants, and then it starts to look very good indeed.

In the Heart of Town

Clustered near the water on the reef side, in the middle part of the village near where boats dock, are: DEISY'S HOTEL *(6 rooms, tel. 2123)*; LENA'S HOTEL, behind Deisy's *(11 rooms, tel. 2106)*; and VEGA'S FAR INN *(7 rooms, tel. 2142)*. To the north are the RIVAS GUEST HOUSE *(6 rooms, tel. 2127)* and the MIRAMAR. Back from the beach are the HIDEAWAY *(6 rooms, tel. 2103)*; Edith's, with quite small rooms; the SANDY LANE, *on the sandy lane that cuts across the island from the Martínez*

Restaurant, with hot water; and the **HOTEL MARÍN**. All have mostly basic rooms for $12 per person, or less. But being by the sea under the palms relieves what might be dismal accommodations in a mainland town. The Marín also has some units with private bath for $20 double.

Two new concrete rooms at Vega's Far Inn are an exception to the above general description. These have air conditioning, private bath and all modern conveniences, at a rate of $50 double.

THE REEF HOTEL, *just north of the Miramar* and looking out to sea, is more substantial than its neighbors, a concrete structure downstairs and wood-clad on the upper level, painted white with red trim. Rooms have private showers, and the rate is $20 single/$25 double, slightly less during the low season from May through October.

Next door, the **RAINBOW HOTEL**, the light-blue and green building, has 16 rooms with private showers for $32 double downstairs, $36 upstairs. There are at least a dozen other places where you can rent a room inexpensively by the week or month, either on the beach, or set back in the village. One, **M & N FURNISHED APARTMENTS**, *tel. 2111, is just behind the Martínez Restaurant.* Chocolate's gift shop, where Mr. Lionel Heredia and Mrs. Annie Heredia stock t-shirts and the like, has one room for rent at $50. *Call 022-2151 to reserve, or write to P. O. Box 332, Belize City.*

WHERE TO EAT

You are served in Caye Caulker's eateries strictly in island style. In one place, a man in fedora who looks like he hasn't slept in days sidles up, slips you a menu, gives you a conspiratorial glance, and hunches to write down your order out of view of anyone nearby. In another eatery, you sit down, study the menu posted on the wall, and are ignored. You ask the man behind the counter if the restaurant is open, and are still ignored. In another, you comment that there are a lot of mosquitoes. The owner agrees.

Lobster is the best buy on Caye Caulker, when it's in season, from mid-July to mid-March. Boiled or broiled, it costs $9 or less as a main course. By the time lobster gets to Belize City, the price has more than doubled. Most restaurants here open for lunch and dinner, and close their kitchens at 9pm sharp!

Follow the crowds to the **SAND BOX** restaurant for one of the most reasonably priced menus in Belize, and the best home cooking on the island. Look over the large menu posted outside and choose from dozens of gourmet offerings, and don't worry about the spelling. A filling bowl of chili con carne (with chili!) is just $3, and they also have lasagne, snapper filet, barbecued chicken, stroganoff, and other pleasant surprises for $6 and less. On the higher priced side there is shrimp with garlic and rice, loster with mushrooms, and daily specials that average about $8 for a complete dinner. Most eateries on the island are dark and dreary, but the Sand Box is light and airy, with high ceiling and plenty of windows, sand floors, and an ooudoor dining area.

MAD ANNIES *on Front Street* offers the best value of any area restaurant. Here they serve breakfast, lunch, and dinner without interruption from 8am until 10pm. They make huge portions of great omlettes, veggi burritos, burgers, curried lobster, pasta, and freshly caught fish. After dining on onre of their casual open air sections, be sure to have the island's coldest beer. Expect to pay between $4 and $11 for a complete meal. Highly recommended.

THE TROPICAL PARADISE HOTEL has what comes closest to being a real restaurant. It's clean, well-lit, has artificial flowers in vases and superimposed blue and red tablecloths on the tables, and keeps regular hours. Banks of ceiling fans put out a breeze to lift the roof. Main courses such as curried shrimp or steak with beans or plantain and rice go for $5 to $7, sandwiches and breakfasts for less.

MARÍN'S RESTAURANT, in the southwest part of the village, and the **MARTÍNEZ RESTAURANT**, offer similar fare less attractively, at slightly lower prices. **SOBRE LAS OLAS**, *located to the north of the cluster of hotels at the long pier*, has a menu of Mexican and seafood items. **JAN'S DELI** has grocery items and a tour menu.

The **ABERDEEN CHINESE** restaurant *in the Rivas Guest House* serves foo youngs and chow meins and curries, as well as rice and beans with lobster and steak sandwiches. About $5 to $7 for a meal. And there is any number of home-based eating rooms. **GLENDA'S**, *one street back from the sea*, has been recently popular, especially during breakfast hours.

SPORTS & RECREATION
Snorkeling & Boat Excursions

Prices for excursions from Caye Caulker are generally lower than elsewhere in Belize. A snorkeling trip out to the reef in a sailboat or a small motorboat, with stops in two or three places with different types of coral formations, will cost under $10.

A run to Ambergris Caye and back, again in either a sailboat or motorboat, or a snorkeling trip to Hol Chan Marine Reserve, will cost under $15 per person.

Talk to the boat owners any morning, in the vicinity of the Martínez Restaurant, where they get groups together, or inquire at Seahawk Sailing, to the north near The Cut, or try one of these operators with fixed abodes:

Island Sun offers daily sailing trips to the reef for about $10 with rental of snorkeling equipment, $15 for a trip to Hol Chan reserve off Ambergris Caye.

Sunrise Boat Tours *(Jim and Cindy Novelo, tel. 022-2195, fax 2239)*, has a fixed-price menu of trips: $13 to San Pedro and Hol Chan Reserve, $12 to $25 to cayes to the north or south, $35 to the Turneffe Islands. All prices are per person based on ten passengers. Get aboard for a Robinson Crusoe adventure.

Snorkeling equipment can be rented at a number of places — one is next to the police station (which is usually locked up) — for less than $5.

SUGGESTED CAYE CAULKER ITINERARY

The daily round of events on Caye Caulker runs something like this:
- **7 am**: *Skiffs leave for Belize City.*
- **8 am**: *Restaurants are scheduled to open.*
- **9 am**: *One or two restaurants open.*
- **9:30 am**: *Owners of sailboats and skiffs meet with visitors on the reef side of the village to organize the day's trips.*
- **10 am**: *Boats are supposed to leave. Boat owners look for a few more passengers.*
- **10:30 am**: *Maybe now the boat gets going.*
- **11 am**: *Or now.*
- **Noon**: *Snorkeling without a shirt.*
- **3 pm**: *Application of sunburn cream. (Residents call the gumbo limbo tree, with its continuously peeling bark, the tourist tree.)*
- **Sunset**: *Sand flies and mosquitoes swarm to the village for dinner. Visitors who have already spent an evening as victuals cover up, apply insect repellent generously, or head for the water.*

Diving

The island's dive shop, **Belize Diving Services** *(tel. 022-2143)*, at the northwest corner of the village, by the soccer field, offers two-tank dives for $35 to $50, night dives, a four-day entry-level course for $300, and full equipment rental. Inspect your equipment carefully before you go out. *Write to P. O. Box 667, Belize City, to make advance arrangements.*

Underwater Photo Adventures

Sea-ing is Belizing is an unpretentious gift shop and photo studio, toward the north end of the village, by the soccer field. Owner James Beveridge offers underwater photo safaris to all offshore areas of interest, and underwater photography courses, as well as books, photos, slides and film for sale.

Call 022-2189, or write to P. O. Box 374, Belize City, for advance arrangements.

PRACTICAL INFORMATION

The **post office** is at **Celi's store and bar,** which is inland from the Tropical Paradise Hotel.

Chocolate, the boat operator of local renown, has a **gift shop** well stocked with t-shirts and post cards, toward the north end of the village, reef side.

Dolphin Bay Travel, *tel. 022-2214,* just south of the piers, arranges air tickets.

CariSearch *(postal address: 47 Caye Caulker)*, run by a marine biologist, offers marine tours and lectures, and also operates Galería Hicaco, an art gallery and gift shop, near the Tropical Paradise Hotel.

CAYE CHAPEL

Caye Chapel measures only one by three miles. Most of it is covered by coconut plantations and beaches. The island boasts a location just off the barrier reef only fifteen miles from Belize City, and has its own landing strip.

ARRIVALS & DEPARTURES

By Air

Maya Airways and **Tropic Air** flights between Belize City and Ambergris Caye.

By Boat

The *Triple J* boat *(tel. 02-44375)* leaves for Caye Chapel, Caye Caulker, and San Pedro at 9 a.m. from the north end of the Swing Bridge in Belize City, from Ambergris Caye at 3 p.m.

The *Thunderbolt Express (tel. 026-2217)* leaves from the Lagoon Side Marina on Ambergris Caye at 7 a.m., stopping at Caye Chapel on the way to Belize City. Departure from the Swing Bridge in Belize City is at 4 p.m. Monday through Friday, 1 p.m. on Saturday. Sometimes, other boats for Ambergris Caye, will stop at Caye Chapel on request.

WHERE TO STAY

PYRAMID ISLAND RESORT, *32 rooms and two beach houses. $60 single/$96 double, plus 10% service plus tax. Add $30 per person for three meals. Low-season rate $40/$60. Master Card, Visa, American Express. Reservations: Box 192, Belize City, tel. 02-44409, fax 32405. U.S. reservations tel. 800-458-8281.*

This resort owns all of Caye Chapel. Accommodations are in a long row of die-of-depression fifties-motel-style plywood rooms with plastic

panelling, linoleum, and cheap furniture. But they're slowly being renovated, they all face seaward and are air-conditioned, and the beach is long
and sandy and beautiful.

The central bar-common room rises to a pyramid roof, visible by any
navigator. In addition to the dive shop, gift shop, and fishing and diving
boats found at most of the better hotels on the cayes, Pyramid Island has
a fresh-water pond, tennis and volleyball courts (at no charge) and a golf
driving range, as well as a full-service marina — and a beach party on the
last Sunday of every month.

Fishing in small boats is available at $125 for two persons, diving for
$50 per person, snorkeling at $15 per person.

NORTHERN LONG CAYE

CASTAWAYS LODGE is the only outpost on this mostly grassy and
denuded caye, a wooden building with a large deck. The six rooms are
bare but adequate and light, without cross ventilation, each with a toilet
and shower. Everything is painted in cheery white with turquoise trim,
and the awnings of the common room and bar open up to the sea air.
Diving and fishing are the main guest activities. A sea wall protects the
beach. Castaways is pretty and has a sense of isolation, though it is an easy
hop by boat from Caye Caulker.

This lodge is still being refurbished. Inquire at the tourist office in
Belize City for more information. Access is by hiring a boat at Belize City,
or by persuading a boat for Caye Caulker to drop you off. How you get
back is between you and the owners.

ST. GEORGE'S CAYE

Nine miles out from Belize City, St. George's Caye was the site of the
major settlement and informal capital of Belize from about 1650 to 1784.
A Spanish fleet was driven away just off the island in 1798, an incident that
secured Britain's hold on the territory. An old graveyard from the early
settlement remains at the southern tip of the island.

St. George's Caye suffered badly in 1961 when Hurricane Hattie
washed away a good part of the island, but rebuilding has proceeded over
the years. Today, it is a little slice of paradise, with at least two windmills,
a venerable cemetery, a dozen private cottages with neat lawns on island-
wide lots, several docks, and a rest-and-recreation base for British forces.
There are no facilities for the public, and unless you're staying at one of
the two lodging places, the island is basically not visitable.

WHERE TO STAY

ST. GEORGE'S LODGE, *10 rooms and 6 cottages. $228 to $257 per day per person, including airport transfers, meals, two dives daily, tanks, and weights. 25% reduction for non-divers, 50% for children. American Express, Master Card. Reservations: Box 625, Belize City, tel. 02-44190 (radio patch to lodge), fax 30461; tel. 800-678-6871 in the U.S.*

St. George's is the most serene of the diving lodges I have encountered in Belize, a state that results from the nature of the island — a non-commercialized getaway — and the seemingly imperturbable personality of the owner, Mr. Fred Goode.

The main building is a shipshape roundhouse, hardwood-panelled, shuttered, and set above the grassy ground on piers. Guest rooms in this part are like cabins aboard ship, each with a full bathroom. Over-water cottage units are larger, with thatched roofs, and air circulation over, under, around and through. Waves lap underneath the clefts in the floorboards. Electricity is provided full-time by windmills and batteries. Meals are mainly seafood, plain but copious, served family style. Bring your own bottle of liquor. Coffee is brought right to your door at 6:30 a.m.

There are a sun deck and a palm-shaded beach, and a solar-heated hot tub, but most guests come to enjoy diving with no distractions, and ratings of St. George's Lodge are consistently high. The reef is a half-mile out, and varied sites for divers of all levels are no more than twenty minutes away. Equipment includes three compressors and four dive boats. Instructors and a divemaster on site can complete dive training started elsewhere, or certify from scratch. Fishing, too, can be arranged, and there have been numerous perfectly contented guests who were out doing not much at all.

COTTAGE COLONY is a set of cute guest units with porches and cut-out trim, built in rows close to one another. Floors are of polished wood, furniture is wicker, the bathrooms are motel-standard with showers. Two units in front, near the beach, are larger, with kitchens. The arrangement of the cottages across a sandy-gritty compound affords little breeze, and there is no cross-ventilation, but the air conditioning cools things off. Barbecues and picnic tables are provided. There is a dive shop on site.

Cottage Colony affords an opportunity to stay on a pleasant and little-visited island with easy access from Belize City. The rate is about $100 single or double, $1000 for a week-long dive package, $1400 for a fishing package. *For information, contact the Bellevue Hotel, 5 Southern Foreshore, Belize City, tel. 77051, fax 73253.*

GALLOWS POINT CAYE

Gallows Point is almost due east of Belize City, and just seven miles away. Even in the wide-open Bay Settlement, justice sometimes caught up with miscreants, and Gallows Point in the otherwise tranquil Cayes is where that justice was meted out.

WHERE TO STAY

GALLOWS POINT RESORT, *6 rooms with private bath. $87 single/ $120 double/$50 per extra person, plus 15% service plus tax, including three meals and transport from Belize City. Also rustic shared-bath accommodations with bunk beds for under $15 per person. Reservations in Belize City c/o Hotel Belcove, 9 Regent St. West, tel. 02-73054, fax 77600.*

Hotel rooms are all on the second floor, off a sea-view veranda, each with cold-water shower. Activities here are snorkeling, scuba and fishing. Anchorage available for yachts. This resort also offers day trips to the caye from Belize City for about $45, including a light snack; and diving trips, for about $60. Weekend excursions, including one meal and two nights of lodging, are about $140.

SPANISH LOOKOUT CAYE

This 234-acre mangrove island is just ten miles east-southeast of Belize City.

WHERE TO STAY

SPANISH BAY RESORT, *71 North Front St., tel. 72725, fax 72797 in Belize City. 10 units. From $160 daily including meals, diving and tax, from $100 daily non-diving. Credit cards with surcharge.*

Spanish Bay is a divers' resort, two miles from the barrier reef, affording easy access to a number of southern sites less frequented than those near Ambergris Caye and Caye Caulker, some of them uncharted.

A powerful dive barge takes groups out in short order to reef, walls, and as far as the Turneffe Islands; and compressors, air tanks, belts and weights are sufficient for as many divers as the lodge can sleep. The central roundhouse bar-dining pavilion sits over the water and is almost encircled by a deck. Inside, it's spacious and airy, hung with maps and charts, and stocked with board games for evening amusement. Guests stay in individual over-water cottages, each with two double beds, with hot water, fans, and hardwood panelling. Price includes transport from Belize City. Only drinks at the bar are extra. And since Spanish Bay is just a jump from Belize City, it can be a base for inland travel as well.

Hold onto your false teeth! The boat to Spanish Bay Resort hesitates not for swells or wakes. In ten miles and thirty minutes, it chatters through shipping channels and past police patrol skiffs and stray islands, from the heat and hustle and hassles of Belize City, toward an enlarging tangle of mangrove and palms, around the point of **Spanish Lookout Caye**, into harbor.

The entire resort settlement lies within a hundred yards or so of the dock. A central roundhouse office-bar-dining room, as at virtually every offshore resort in Belize, is a workaday structure with no architectural distinction or exterior adornment to face the weather, save a solidly anchored wraparound deck.

All the character resides inside: decorations of ships' wheels, umbrella ceiling, kerosene lamps to light board games and card games and conversations at night, a floor fan turning constantly, propelled not by electricity, but by a ceaseless breeze that also encourages bugs to move on.

The masterwork of Spanish Lookout is comprised of its five double cottages, set on stilts directly over the shallows, facing into the prevailing easterly breeze. Forget air conditioning. When the sun pulps a standing person into a sweat — and it can, all year, anywhere in offshore Belize—step *inside*. The wind skips off the Caribbean, cools to sea-water temperature, slides through screening and opened louvers, and exits toward the mangrove: all-natural cooling.

Spanish Lookout is a modified mangrove islet. The sand and shells of the lodge grounds were deposited by dredging a channel with shovels and wheelbarrow, and only sticks appear to hold it all together. There is no topsoil, the beach is minimal. But the compost of the island's vegetation — "mangrove peat" — blooms with tomatoes and watermelons and radishes and carrots, bananas and soursops and avocados and watermelons, papayas and peppers and herbs. The same substance, with a top coating of sand, underlies the other-worldly Air-pillo trails through the property. A channel crosses the island, along with a plank walkway.

Drinking water comes from rain caught off the roofs of caye-standard plywood workaday outbuildings, and a small desalination operation. Here, away from everything in the world, the staff cottage has satellite television, powered by solar panels and the generator that runs the compressors. Beyond the lodge area, the island is as it was built up by colonizing plants, and carved by winds and rains and tides and storms. Red and black and white mangroves dominate, along with buttonwoods.

Ecology is the folklore of Belizean tourism, and every offshore resort proposes an eco-menu: trails through mangrove inhabited by rare bird species; swimming with dolphins in a protected lagoon; on a lucky day, a manatee waddling-swimming just off the dock. Remoteness from the modern world.

Spanish Bay is all this, except that remoteness is a state of mind, a matter of where you aim your gaze. Follow the plank walkway over the mangrove and channels to the western edge of the caye, and watch the sunset over the mainland, and, at a quarter-turn, the lights of Belize City.

Light your torch, cross back above the black waters to your porch, and the other world, a moonlit sea, a swell of waves, and phosphorescence.

Though scuba diving is the mission for most visitors to Spanish Bay, I was on a non-diving visit with my wife and three children one August. What do you do at a diving resort when you are not diving? Plenty. You take it as you would any South Seas isle where you have the good fortune to be marooned. You plow through the stack of novels that was piling up at home unread, with a break when absolutely necessary to fetch a piña colada.

The kids have the run of the island while the divers are out: they pile up shells in mounds and more mounds, which will wait to be fetched on our next visit. They jump into the sea out the back door of our room, swim around to the beach, and repeat the process in numberless iterations. They go through all the board games. They chase teeny fiddler crabs, play peekaboo with fish that blend into sea grass, drop bread crumbs into an empty spot of water and watch the tarpon swarm and churn. They imagine perils aplenty, but there are no dangerous animals, not even deep water or undertow or crashing surf.

Nearby is Little Offshore Belize: Sargeant's Caye, Goff's Caye, English Caye and Rendezvous Caye, various specks of sand or mangrove on which to make landfall and explore for ancient remains, or shells, or bottles from afar.

One day we pulled a Robinson Crusoe. On its way to the reef, the diving barge, skippered by Karen Pasquariello, once a church administrator in Texas, stranded us with a hamper and cooler at Sergeant's Caye, a half-acre, three-palm-and-sand remnant of the larger island that was blown apart one hurricane year. What remains of a settlement is snorkelable: a miniature lost world of post anchors, a concrete block, a bathtub, scattered among brain and fan and elkhorn coral.

We moved from submarine archaeology back to our South Seas fantasy on the beach, sandwiches and fruit and drinks, touched with specks of sand, which is not a plentiful substance in Belize.

Food is a touchy point when traveling anywhere with kids, who abhor novelty. And it is a touchy point where last-minute shopping for finicky tastes is not possible. It was not a touchy point at Spanish Bay, where replenishment of the freezer from Belize City is less of a problem than elsewhere. We all enjoyed hamburgers at lunch, and my kids amazed me by slurping up an okra soup that initially looked yukky. But one evening, they cringed at a platter of lobster. I could have creamed them. But Elda Ceballos, lodge manager, cook, and accommodating hostess, had chicken ready in minutes. The employees were lucky that evening.

Rains descend on a vulnerable island in instant rage. When blinds flapped and papers flew up, we scurried to batten down our tempest-tossed room, sealing shutters and securing doors, making a snug haven a rock on stilts in the lashing, roaring wind. But only for minutes, till the weather moved on.

This is Spanish Bay, and to some degree, it is any lodge off the mainland of Belize. The food will be more plentiful or less so. A longer-than-usual rain might limit diving and muddy the view under the water. You will almost certainly be more removed from Belize City in nautical miles, if not in ways that matter. And when it is time to leave, you could hope for another weather delay, or, as we did, ask the boat driver to slow down.

MIDDLE LONG CAYE

This island, southeast of Belize City, is about 45 minutes away by boat.
MOONLIGHT SHADOWS LODGE has just two thatch-roofed cabanas on the island, going for about $50 per day. Fishing can be arranged, but there is no diving equipment, and you'll come out here just to be away from *everything*. Food can be prepared according to your preferences, or you can do your own cooking. *Call 08-23665 to discuss everything.*

BLUEFIELD RANGE

These are small cayes 20 miles south of Belize City, inside the barrier reef. A commercial fishing camp is located here; otherwise, there are no inhabitants.

WHERE TO STAY

RICARDO'S BEACH HUTS, Father and son Eterio and Ricardo Castillo have constructed five simple, over-the-water guest cabanas at their lobster and fishing camp in the Bluefield Range, 21 miles south of Belize City. Visitors may birdwatch, snorkel, or fish from dugout canoes. They also have an unusual opportunity to look in on the lives of the fishermen. There's lots of sand here — more than at many a formal beach resor t— and unspoiled, unlittered mangrove and palms, as well as the usual aquatic attractions.

The minimum charge for a stay at Ricardo's is about $150 for two persons for two nights and three days. This includes meals and transportation, and for additional days, the charge is about $30. *For information, speak to Anna Lara at the Mira Río Hotel, 59 North Front St. (P. O. Box 55, tel. 02-44970) in Belize City.*

TURNEFFE ISLANDS

Twenty-five miles east of Belize City, the **Turneffe Islands** form a large ring surrounding a shallow lagoon — an atoll. Most of the cayes are swampy, but a few contain enough sand to support coconut trees, and are used as fishing camps.

The main attraction for visitors is the fishing. The flats within the island group are said to contain one of the largest concentrations of bonefish in the world. Permit frequent the deeper waters and, like bonefish, are present all year, while tarpon run in the spring in large numbers.

For divers, there are sharp dropoffs, coral varieties and sponges on the ocean side, while snorkeling is good in the relatively shallow waters of the Central Lagoon and inside the reef. Bird sightings regularly include great numbers of blackbirds, brown pelicans, frigate birds, sandpipers, terns, and cormorants.

WHERE TO STAY

TURNEFFE FLATS, *6 individual cabins. About $1,800 per week of fishing, including transfer from Belize City; $1,300 diving; $950 non-fishing. The fishing rate includes a guide and skiff for every two fishermen. No additional service charge. Reservations: Box 36, Deadwood, SD 57732, tel. 605-578-1304, fax 605-578-7540. Open all year.*

A fishing and diving camp situated on the northeast side of the island group. Despite the remote location, the cabins are wood-panelled and attractively furnished, and provided with private baths. The camp chef serves up meals with seafood, of course, as well as fruit and fresh-baked pastries. The package price includes a stay of one night in Belize City, and a two-hour boat trip to the island on a 31-foot Ocean Master.

TURNEFFE ISLAND LODGE, *9 rooms. U.S. address: 11904 Hidden Hills Dr., Jacksonville FL 32225, tel. 800-338-8149. One-week package $1200 diving, $1600 fishing, $900 relaxing, including meals and transport from Belize City.*

On 12-acre Caye Bokel, this is a village of houses on tall stilts with screened porches, standard-issue catch-the-breeze structures. The lodge has a 38-foot dive boat; the main attractions are diving where relatively few divers go, and fishing for bonefish and permit in the flats surrounded by the islands. Diving packages generally include three dives daily.

BLACKBIRD CAYE RESORT, *P. O. Box 888, Belize City, tel. 77670, or 800-537-1431 in the U.S. $1,100 weekly, or $1,350 for diving, or $1,550 for fishing, including boat from Belize City, meals, tax and service charges.*

This is a sports resort with an ecological theme, on mangrove-covered Blackbird Caye, one of the major islands of the Turneffe group. Visitors are invited to swim with bottlenose dolphins (the subjects of ongoing studies) and view alligators, turtles, and manatees from fairly close up. For scientists — and maybe for you — an attraction is that local species live largely without mainland influences, and some of the resident birds have flourished, while becoming virtually extinct on the mainland.

Guests stay in single-room thatch-roofed cottages on stilts, each with private bath. No liquor is available except for what you tote along. Fishing packages include two sorties daily. Diving packages include three dives daily.

LIGHTHOUSE REEF

Sixty miles east of Belize City is the **Lighthouse Reef Lagoon**, its shallow waters surrounded by a reef and the open sea. Lighthouse Reef is barely populated, but not unvisited, for it is home to some rare wildlife, and its waters hold the **Blue Hole**, one of the natural wonders of Belize.

WHERE TO STAY

LIGHTHOUSE REEF RESORT, *tel. 800-423-3114. 9 cabins. $1100 weekly; $1200 weekly with diving; $1500 weekly with fishing, meals and transport included.*

Convenient to the Blue Hole, this resort is a luxury getaway even without the diving. Guest rooms are air-conditioned, and there is lots of lonely beach. Unlike most offshore lodges, Lighthouse Reef Resort has an airstrip, and divers on week-long packages get out here in less than a half-hour from Belize City.

SEEING THE SIGHTS

Half Moon Caye Natural Monument, *near the southern end of the 30-mile-long, 8-mile-wide lagoon*, is Belize's first national park, a bird sanctuary for the nearly extinct red-footed booby. White boobies predominate on Half Moon Caye. Elsewhere, most adult boobies are brown. Other species that make their home on the sandy caye include the magnificent frigate bird, ospreys, mangrove warblers, and white-crowned pigeons, as well as nearly a hundred others. Iguanas also live here, and hawksbill and loggerhead turtles lay their eggs on the beaches. Vegetation is sparse, mostly coconut palms, along with a few ziricote and wild fig trees. The waters off Half Moon Caye are said to be among the clearest in Belize, with visibility of 200 feet. The solar-powered lighthouse on the island, and the one on Sandbore Caye, to the north, give the reef its name.

Camping is permitted on Half Moon Caye. Visitors should check in first at the Audubon Society in Belize City.

The **Half Moon Caye dropoff** is rated unbeatable by many divers, plunging from a coral ridge 25 feet under the surface down, down, down, several thousand feet, broken by caves and canyons, bridges and tunnels.

More than 400 feet across, the **Blue Hole** is a shaft that drops from the ten-foot-deep lagoon, and opens into a series of elaborate, stalactite-filled caverns, starting at a depth of about 90 feet, and continuing down to 400 feet. The caves were formed in another geological age by underground rivers. In a more recent time, the ocean crashed through the ceiling of the cavern, creating the Blue Hole. Locals say it is the lair of a sea monster. Tilting stalactites indicate that earthquakes have shifted the formation from its original alignment.

The tunnels and chambers of the Blue Hole system were explored intensively by Jacques Cousteau in the early seventies, and may be visited by divers based on larger chartered boats (see Diving, page 46), which usually anchor at Lighthouse Reef. Long day excursions are available from most of the cayes, and shorter excursions from the Turneffe Islands. Fish species are not especially plentiful in the Hole, but for divers, it's a seemingly bottomless wall.

From the air, the Blue Hole is recognized by a change in the color of waters, from the light blue of the open sea to the darker blue of the Lighthouse Reef Lagoon to the deep blue of the shadowy Blue Hole.

Out Island Divers, *at San Pedro on Ambergris Caye (tel. 026-2151),* offers a one-day excursion to Lighthouse Reef, with a brief dive into the Blue Hole, followed by two wall dives and a visit to the Booby Bird Sanctuary. **Indigo Belize** *in San Pedro (tel. 026-2130)* operates overnight diving trips to the reef on the *M/V Manta IV*, including five dives.

SOUTH WATER CAYE

South Water Caye is a 12-acre island east of Dangriga, with just one real hotel, and assorted cottages and rooms for rent.

WHERE TO STAY

BLUE MARLIN LODGE, *P.O. Box 21, Dangriga, tel. 05-22243 (radio patch), fax 22296, 800-798-1558 in U.S. 14 rooms. $110 single/$175 double with meals, plus $125 round-trip for boat transfer, or $1195 per person for a one-week diving package, including meals and two daily boat dives (Saturday arrival). Fishing, $1650 per week, non-divers, $975 per week. Surcharge for credit cards, travelers checks.*

Blue Marlin is a private island getaway that has been expanded to take a few guests. Diving is the main activity here. Introductory and certification courses are available. The diving package includes day trips to outlying sites, such as the Blue Hole and Glover's Reef. Videos are taken on request. And, as you might guess from the name, marlin fishing is excellent (from March through May), though only limited fishing equipment can be provided.

All rooms have attached bath, hot shower, and fans. The lodge dining pavilion hangs out right over the water. Additional amusements include billiards, wind-surfing, volleyball and horseshoes, and inland trips to the jaguar reserve and along a river. In Dangriga, ask at the Riverside Hotel for information about shorter stays.

PELICAN BEACH RESORT *on the mainland in Dangriga (P. O. Box 14, tel. 05-22044, fax 22570)* has two wooden vacation houses on stilts available for rent at about $100 per day. Each sleeps six, and includes linens and cooking facilities. Meals can be arranged for an additional $30 per person.

At **PELICAN INN** *on the western side of the island,* five bedrooms of assorted sizes, each with toilet and shower, are available at $55 per person daily with three meals.

TOBACCO CAYE

Southeast of Dangriga, **Tobacco Caye**, consisting of a few acres of sand and coconut palms, is developing as an informal resort island. You can do nothing here without a guilty conscience, or enjoy snorkeling—the reef is within wading distance — or pitch in with lobstering and fishing.

Tobacco Caye is in the process of opening up, like Caye Caulker several years ago. Costs are moderate, but for the trip out, which can run as much as $125 for a charter from Dangriga or Placencia if you can't find space on a boat that's already going. Campsites with cooking facilities and modest rental cabins are available. Meals can be taken in private homes.

ARRIVALS & DEPARTURES
By Bus & Boat

To make it in one day to Tobacco Caye from Belize City, take the 10 a.m. Z-Line bus to Dangriga. There are usually several boat owners waiting at Riverside where the bus terminates, and they will organize transport out for about $15 per person.

Otherwise, *call 05-22171 in Dangriga* (the number for Reef's End) to hook up with a scheduled departure, or hire a boat at Riverside for a special run.

WHERE TO STAY

REEF'S END *(P. O. Box 10, Dangriga), one of the better accommodations, is a row of four rooms, each with private bath, going for $40 single/$65 double, and there are two cabanas, each with two double beds, at a higher rate. The eatery-bar is positioned over the water. Call 05-22171 in Dangriga to reserve and arrange transport.*

Mr. Elwood Fairweather is a boat owner who can arrange stays on the island. He runs regular trips from Dangriga on Tuesdays and Fridays for about $15 each way, and has rooms with meals for about $25 per person, as well as camping. Ask for Mr. Fairweather (and inquire about new facilities) at the Río Mar Inn in Dangriga.

LAUGHING BIRD CAYE

Laughing Bird is a *faro*, an atoll-like island rising steeply from the sea floor and enclosing a central lagoon, and so unusual in Belize that it is a protected area. Located about 20 miles east-southeast of Placencia, the island is home to the laughing gull, as well as pelicans, green herons, swifts, and melodious blackbirds.

CARRIE BOW CAYE

This little island is the site of a Smithsonian Institution field laboratory. Some of the resorts of southern Belize arrange visits during island-hopping tours; or you can check in with the Pelican Beach Hotel in Dangriga.

GLOVER'S REEF

Seventy miles southeast of Belize City, **Glover's Reef National Park** is a circular stretch of coral surrounding a lagoon, virtually duplicating a Pacific atoll. The cayes on the southeast side of the reef were in earlier times the base of the pirate John Glover. There are no permanent inhabitants at the reef, though it is visited from time to time by commercial fishermen. Pieces of old pottery indicate that the Maya of Belize frequented the reef in pre-Columbian times.

WHERE TO STAY

MANTA REEF RESORT, *Southwest Caye. U.S. reservations: 14423 S.W. 113 Terrace, Miami, FL 33186, tel. 800-342-0053, fax 305-388-5842. 10 cabanas. About $1200 per person weekly, including meals, diving, and transport out by boat, $1500 fishing, $1000 for R&R.*

Manta Reef gives immediate access to little-explored dive sites: Spaghetti Western, Barrel Head, and Hot Fish Hollow, among others. Whale sharks are common sights, along with the manta rays that lend their name to the establishment. Divers of all skill levels are welcome, and everyone begins with a check-out dive, followed by an optional review course. Two daily boat dives and two night dives per week are included in packages, along with beach dives. Bonefishing is available right at the resort, or from skiffs in the flats of Glover's Reef Atoll. Accommodations are in panelled cabanas with wicker furnishings, more attractive than usually found offshore, and an air-conditioned house is available. Food is ample. Add about $500 single occupancy, children under 12 half price.

FISHING SEASONS AT MANTA REEF

Bonefish and permit	All year
Tarpon	March through June, November
Grouper	December and January
Billfish	March through May
Barracuda, snapper, jack, wahoo, mackerel, bonito, tuna	All year

GLOVER'S ATOLL "RESORT" AND BIOLOGICAL FIELD STATION is an isolated yet accessible colony of seven rustic cabins on 15-acre coconut-covered **Long Caye**, directly on the reef, and nearby **North East Caye**. The Lomont family, who have run things here for years, offer a Sunday trip out to Glover's Reef at 8 a.m. from Sittee River, where they also have a modest guest house (arrive by the 8 a.m. Saturday Z-Line Punta Gorda bus from Belize City, connecting with truck at Sittee River junction, or taxi).

The price is right: less than $100 per person for a week, under $150 for two weeks, including the boat ride (three to six hours, returning Saturday). And — get this — you pay only half as much to camp. Nobody tends to your every wish here, and some aspects are rather basic. But you get cooking facilities (bring, buy or catch the food, or take meals with the caretaker), well water, porch, hammock, lanterns, outhouse, and gravity shower, and can rent boats and canoes. Bring your own towels.

For divers, limited snorkeling and diving gear is available, along with a compressor. You can wade out to the dropoff, or rent a diesel boat for a longer run. Bring equipment to fish for tarpon, snapper, jacks, bonefish and barracuda.

Out at Glover's Reef, rentals and services are usually on a cash basis, to minimize overhead, though Master Card and Visa can be accepted with advance approval (a 10% surcharge will be applied). Sample charges: $50 for half-day sailboat charter, $5 daily dugout rental, $12 for an air tank plus equipment rental for a dive from shore. Scuba instruction and certification are available.

NORTH EAST CAY, *across a channel from Long Cay*, with three of the cabins, is a reserve, and use of motorboats, and certain guest activities, are limited, to avoid disturbing nesting turtles and other species.

If your needs are modest, *call the Glover's Atoll contact at 08-22149, fax 05-23505 to see if there's room. To charter a boat out and arrange a taxi, try calling Mr. Tino Tzul in Dangriga at 05-22438. For a radio patch to the island, call 092-3310. For firm reservations send $50 by cashier's check to Gilbert Lomont, Box 563, Belize City. Closed September through November.*

WIPPARI CAYE

Just eight nautical miles due east of Placencia, **WIPPARI CAYE LODGE** has four cabanas going for about $20 double, or $50 with food. For that price you get limited facilities and great snorkeling. Scuba diving is not available. *Call 06-23130 for information*, or ask around in Placencia for George Cabral or David Dial.

RANGUANA CAYE

Cabanas with cooking facilities and shared bathrooms are available at **RANGUANA REEF RESORT**, for $25 single/$35 double, plus $75 for the trip out. Bring your own groceries, scuba and fishing gear. *To make arrangements, contact Eddie Leslie at Ranguana Lodge in Placencia, tel. and manual fax 06-23112.*

COASTAL RESORTS

To a greater or lesser extent, the villages along the coast of Belize listed below have facilities comparable to those on the cayes:

· **CONSEJO SHORES**, in the north, near Corozal.
· **BELIZE RIVER LODGE**. A fishing camp upriver from Belize City, near the international airport at Ladyville. *The address is Box 459, Belize City, the telephone number is 025-2002,* but you'll do best to book through a travel agency. The rate for six nights of sleeping and fishing is about $1,300.
· **PELICAN BEACH RESORT**, Dangriga
· **THE PLACENCIA PENINSULA**
· **SAFE HAVEN LODGE**, near Punta Gorda.

14. BELIZE CITY

INTRODUCTION

An 1842 print shows a waterside view of Belize City. One- and two-story tin-roofed wooden buildings with shady verandas line the shore, backdropped by towering palms waving in the sea breeze. Sailboats and skiffs dart across the water. Black soldiers in uniforms of the era lounge in front of cannon, as if their presence is required more for decoration than for defense. It is a pleasant, idyllic, languid view. It could also, but for the period dress, be a certain view of the city today.

That is part of the charm of Belize City. Whatever the natural and man-made disadvantages of the place — and there are not a few — there is also a sense of a colonial seaport of the past living in the present. Though roads have been built in the past few decades, and patterns of commerce are slowly changing, Belize City still huddles along the shore, unsturdy, vulnerable to the ravages of nature, largely depending on ships to bring it nourishment and the practical necessities of life from far and wide.

Merchants and tradesmen, hawkers and hangers-on predominate on the streets. Though the air and light are different, the city and the texture of its life contain a whiff of early Boston or Newport.

Belize City Today

There are somewhat pleasant residential areas in Belize City, especially on the north side along the sea. Neighborhoods with names like Cinderella Town, Lake Independence, and Queen Charlotte Town suggest something picturesque.

However, it should be made clear that Belize City is mostly a shanty town. Built in a swamp and on sand dunes, allegedly on a foundation of rum bottles, its houses are falling-down affairs of decaying bare wood, propped up on stilts above the dust and dirt of the streets, and the waste that sits in drainage canals until a rainstorm washes it out to sea. The city is known to people from the countryside and remembered by some unfortunate visitors not for its historic buildings or for the bustle of its streets, but for the resourcefulness, daring, and success of its thieves.

Belize City is what the rest of Belize is not. With more than 60,000 inhabitants, it is a churning cauldron of people, while the rest of the land is almost empty. The pace of life in the countryside is relaxed, and the visitor feels inconspicuous. In Belize City, outsiders are constant targets for hucksters.

That some aspects of Belize City are not pleasant or salubrious owes itself in part to colonial history. Belize City was never intended to be a permanent settlement. If it had been, another site would surely have been chosen, for the swampy location with its attendant malaria and yellow fever, and the lack of deep-water docking facilities, were always obvious disadvantages.

For buccaneers, it was nothing more than a base camp. For Creole forest workers, it was a place to shelter in crude huts until the start of the next logging season. For merchants of the coastal trade, it was a site for warehouses. The town was evacuated on several occasions when the Spaniards asserted their rights or threatened to assert them, and it was not until Britain assumed formal colonial responsibility in 1862 that any presumption of permanence was possible.

Natural Disasters

Nature, however, made continued settlement uncertain. Hurricanes have been to Belize City what earthquakes have been to other Central American capitals. On September 10, 1931, as the city was celebrating the anniversary of the battle of St. George's Caye, the skies darkened and a hurricane swept in. Palm trees and houses were ripped away and people blown out to sea, and a flood followed to rampage over what was left. More than 2,000 people were dead or missing in the wake of the storm, and the cost of rebuilding shackled the economy for years.

On October 31, 1961, Hurricane Hattie destroyed much of Belize City once again, and blew away some of the smaller offshore cayes altogether. But the inhabitants had been warned of the approaching storm, and loss of life was minimal. The present houses of Belize City, run-down as they are, are said to be an improvement over those that existed before the storm, and some of the newer commercial buildings of reinforced concrete construction are hurricane-resistant.

The damage wrought by the 1961 hurricane was the impulse behind the relocation of the capital to Belmopan, but Belize City remains the largest settlement and commercial center of the nation.

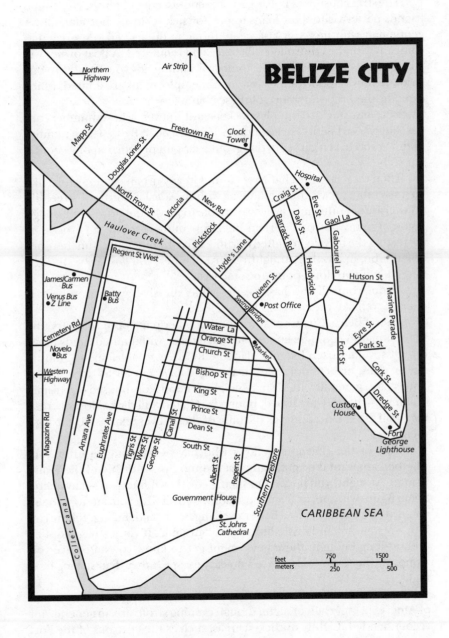

BELIZE CITY

Northern Highway
Air Strip
Mapp St
Freetown Rd
Clock Tower
Douglas Jones St
Hospital
Craig St
North Front St
Eve St
Victoria
New Rd
Daly St
Gaol La
Barrack Rd
Pickstock
Haulover Creek
Hyde's Lane
Gabourel La
Regent St West
Queen St
Handyside
Hutson St
James/Carmen Bus
Venus Bus
Z Line
Batty Bus
Post Office
Marine Parade
Cemetery Rd
Swing Bridge
Eyre St
Fort St
Park St
Novelo Bus
Water La
Orange St
Market
Western Highway
Church St
Cork St
Bishop St
Dredge St
King St
Magazine Rd
Prince St
Custom House
Amara Ave
Euphrates Ave
Tigris St
West St
George St
Canal St
Dean St
Fort George Lighthouse
South St
Albert St
Regent St
Southern Foreshore
Collet Canal
Government House
CARIBBEAN SEA
St. Johns Cathedral

feet   750   1500
meters   250   500

Be Careful!

The street hustles of Belize City are reminiscent of Cairo's. Newfound friends pester visitors for loans to pay for sick relatives' hospital bills. A gentleman who met you last week, though you arrived yesterday, has come up with the controlled substance you requested. A boat owner will take you on a tour of the cayes tomorrow, but needs your money to buy gasoline now. Opportunities for gainful employment are limited, which explains the preponderance of these characters.

Less amusing are the pickpockets and thieves, whose numbers are few, but whose talents are legendary. I have been in Belize City a number of times and haven't lost anything, but a certain proportion of visitors is not so lucky.

Then there are the characters found in any urban center, who make life miserable for visitors unfamiliar with the local patterns of street life (as well as for authorities, who are unable to prosecute once witnesses go home). On my last visit, certain Belizean youths were in the process of perfecting the bicycle-mounted daytime drive-by mugging. And there are others who, in a rather straightforward manner, will *threaten* you with a mugging, if you don't pony up some cash.

Aside from all the hassles, the generally shabby environment is enough to make the place no fun.

Even if Belize City were as tranquil as other parts of the country, the hotel situation could be enough to make those with limited funds move on. Of several dozen lodging places, only a few establishments, mostly newer ones, are comfortable, secure, and pleasant all at once. Older hotels are generally in dismal neighborhoods or housed in dismal buildings — harshly furnished, poorly ventilated and dark. Most distressing of all are the pretensions of some of these dives, expressed through their rates.

Most of the charming fellows who have something to offer you, whether you want it or not, hang out around the south end of the Swing Bridge. At night, you'll run into them — or they'll find you — anywhere. Some figure will appear from the shadows, stroll with you, attempt to sell you drugs, a tour, sex, or a better exchange rate, and, failing, follow you into a restaurant and invite himself to your table. If you manage to stick around long enough, these guys might get to know you and leave you alone. Maybe. Otherwise, there's no easy escape, other than staying in at night.

In general, avoid the side streets south of the Swing Bridge and west of Albert St., especially at night; though evening strolls are, in general, not recommended. Lightly trafficked areas, such as the environs of the Fort George Hotel, are a hangout of muggers even in the late afternoon. If you arrive by bus after dark, take a taxi to your hotel.

The Changing Face of Belize City

Slowly, ever so slowly, Belize City is changing. Wooden buildings downtown are giving way to reinforced concrete structures more typical of Central American capitals. Street hawkers of umbrellas, fruits, underwear and knick-knacks, most of them Hispanics and some of them refugees, also remind you of what region you're in. On the outskirts, concrete houses, both on the ground and on stilts, are sprouting in new subdivisions. The next big hurricane will face serious opposition.

Even the streetside drainage canals are less odiferous than they have been in the past. This is due largely to the generosity of Canada, which financed the digging up of Belize City's streets and the installation of a sewage disposal system. Canadians are great experts at moving semi-liquids below the frost line. Convincing people to connect has been quite another matter, however, so some household outflow continues to run alongside the streets.

Not that it's impossible to stay happily in Belize City. Startling improvements in accommodations have come about in just a year, and there are even a few budget establishments that provide safe havens amid the hubbub. A number of interesting restaurants serve continental, Creole, Mexican and oriental cuisine for which no excuses need be made, and at a few, the prices are even affordable. A dive shop, travel services, and a central location make the old capital a feasible base for day trips to fishing grounds, diving spots, and inland sights.

BELIZE CITY WATERFRONT

And if you're willing to confine yourself to the six blocks or so of the Fort George area, you might consider the city absolutely delightful. You'll be safe enough, as long as you don't do anything that you wouldn't do in New York. And the city has a certain fascination, once — if — you get past the street hassles. Belize City is certainly tolerable for a few days — or maybe I was just in a good mood on my last visit.

Still, if your funds are limited, or if you want an absolutely carefree, relaxing vacation, which you can find just about anywhere else in the country, you'll move on after a short stay. There is no substitute for staying in the jungle or sleeping on a tropic isle, rather than just visiting them on day trips.

ORIENTATION

Most hotels, businesses and points of interest are clustered in an area measuring about a thousand yards square, around the mouth of **Haulover Creek**, which untidily divides the city in two. Your basic reference point is the **Swing Bridge**. Since all streets bear names instead of numbers, a street map or taxi driver will come in handy when you're looking for anything. For streets beyond the central area indicated on the map on page 161, consult the map of Belize available from the Tourist Board.

Note that street numbers on one side of a street have no necessary relationship to those across the way.

Wise residents of Belize City carry umbrellas in the dry times as well as the wet, to shield themselves from the sun. Visitors, as well, should avoid unnecessary exposure. It's easy to forget that you're subject to frying as you go about doing whatever you're doing.

ARRIVALS & DEPARTURES
Arriving By Air

Yes, there are two airports. **Phillip Goldson International Airport** is about ten miles west of the city, off the Northern Highway. The modern terminal includes a duty-free shop, bar, banking and postal counters, and telephone office. There are a few rather limited hotels nearby (see hotel listings, below), handy if you'll be flying onward the next day. The pricier hotels in Belize City have courtesy phones, in case you've arrived without a reservation. Taxi fare from the airport into Belize City is about $15 for up to five people.

A local bus leaves for town at 6 and 8 a.m., noon, and 4 and 6 p.m., passing all bus stations in Belize City. The alternative way into town is to flag down a bus on the Northern Highway, just over a mile from the terminal.

Most domestic flights use the **municipal airstrip**, located about a mile north of the city center, along the Caribbean shore. Flights to San Pedro on Ambergris Caye depart from the international airport as well. Charter flights are available from both the international airport and the airstrip. Taxi fare from town to the airstrip is about $3.

Airlines

Following are the airlines that fly to and within Belize (with their Belize addresses):

International airlines
- **TACA**, *41 Albert St., tel. 77363*
- **American Airlines**, *New Road at Queen St., tel. 32168*
- **Continental**, *32 Albert St. in the Hindu temple, tel. 78309*
- **Aerovías** (Guatemala), *55 Regent St., tel. 75445*; service currently Tuesday, Saturday and Sunday to and from Guatemala City via Flores/Tikal; Wednesday and Friday to Chetumal (Mexico) and Guatemala City.

Local Airlines
- **Island Air**, tel. 31140, serves Caye Caulker and San Pedro (Ambergris Caye).
- **Maya Airways**, *6 Fort St., near the Fort George Hotel, tel. 77215*, serves Caye Chapel, San Pedro (Ambergris Caye) and coastal towns.
- **Tropic Air**, *tel. (026) 2012*, serves San Pedro (Ambergris Caye), Caye Chapel, Caye Caulker, Corozal, Flores (Guatemala), Placencia, and Punta Gorda.

In most cases, flights can be boarded at either the municipal airstrip, on the edge of downtown, or, for a higher charge, at the international airport.

All destinations are less than an hour away. There are more than a dozen flights daily for San Pedro, on Ambergris Caye, some of which continue to Corozal. The other major route is southward to Dangriga, Big Creek (opposite the Placencia Peninsula) and Punta Gorda. For recent schedules, see coverage of each town in this book, or stop in at any travel agency in Belize City.

Local airlines also offer charter service to any airstrip in the country.

Arriving By Bus

Terminals of intercity buses are along or near Collet Canal, about eight blocks west of Regent St., downtown. There are no attractive accommodations in the immediate area. If you arrive in the late afternoon or at night, take a taxi to your hotel to avoid possible undesirable encounters.

For the latest schedules, stop in at the tourist board. Schedules of buses between Belize City and the major towns, as of publication of this book, are given in individual town coverage

Departing By Air
From the International Airport
The airport bus departs at 5:30, 7:15, 8:30 and 11:15 a.m. and 3:30 p.m. and 5:30 p.m. Fare is about $1. The route is from Pound Yard Bridge along Cemetery Road and Central American Boulevard to the Northern Highway. *Call 73977 or 77811 to check the latest schedule and routing.*

Departure tax is about $12, $2 for children. A couple of duty-free shops are open for all departing flights, and their prices are excellent for liquor. The airport bank, open 8 a.m. to 11 a.m. and noon to 4 p.m., will exchange Belizean currency to U.S. dollars, with a tax of 2 percent on anything over U.S. $50.

From the Municipal Airstrip
Flights depart from the municipal airstrip, located about a mile north of the city center, along the Caribbean shore, for San Pedro on Ambergris Caye, Caye Chapel, and Caye Caulker, and for the coastal towns of Corozal (near Mexico), Big Creek (near Placencia), Dangriga, and Punta Gorda. Taxi fare from town to the airstrip is about $3.

Departing By Bus
Terminals of inter-city buses are mostly along or near Collet Canal, about eight blocks west of Regent St., downtown. Each company has its own station or parking spot, among them:
• **Batty Bus**, *15 Mosul St. at Bagdad, tel. 72025.* Northbound buses to Orange Walk and Corozal, and Chetumal, Mexico; and west to Belmopan, San Ignacio, Benque Viejo.
• **Novelo Bus**, *West Collet Canal, tel. 77372.* Westbound buses to Belmopan, San Ignacio, Benque Viejo.
• **Venus Bus**, *Magazine Rd., tel. 73354.* Northbound buses to Orange Walk and Corozal, and Chetumal, Mexico.
• **Z-Line**, *Magazine Road, tel. 73937.* To Dangriga, Punta Gorda.

Recent schedules are given in the coverage of each area served by these companies.

Departing By Boat
See "Boats — Scheduled Service" section of this chapter.

GETTING AROUND TOWN
Car Rentals

Rentals cost a fortune in Belize but, if you are smart, you can save a fortune by booking ahead from the US or Canada and prepaying a discounted rate. My last survey of US reserved rates averaged about 18% lower than local rates, and included the unusual advantage of unlimited milage. Another call to **Auto Europe's** staff in the US *at (800) 223-5555* saved me over $68 a week off all other major companies quoted rates, and included a category upgrade to a better jeep with radio and air conditioning.

Prices are inching downward as competition increases. Most vehicles can also be booked while in Belize, and are available at the international airport and downtown locations. If you did not reserve from the US or Canada, expect to pay somewhere around $75 per day/$380 per week for a small sedan, or $95 per day/$495 per week for a more useful 4 wheel drive jeep. Government tax is additional and is currrently charged at 6%.

In general, you're better off with name brand companies, including:
- **National Car Rental**, *126 Freetown Rd. tel. 31587, and at the international airport, tel. 025-2294*
- **Avis**, *Fort George Hotel, tel. 31987*
- **Budget**, *on the Northern Highway, tel. 32435*
- **Hertz**, *Mile 2-1/2, Northern Highway, tel. 32710*
- **Safari Rentals**, *11A Cork Stret, tel (02) 33504*
- **Crystal Rental**, *1-1/2 miles Northern Highway, tel. 31600*

Other operators have used vehicles at lower rates, but are unreliable, and some, according to readers, are out-and-out con artists. Alternatives to car rental include tours; taxis from Belize City; or taxis from district towns in combination with buses.

CAR INSURANCE TIPS

*An important item to consider is that the additional damage and collision insurance know as **CDW** (called **LDW** here) costs about $12 per day, and you are still responsible for a deductable of $750 or more if any accidents or damage occurs. Without taking this optional insurance, you may end up having to pay for a new car if any serious accidents occur. Take the LDW – at least it will minimize your liability to the rental company.*

Taxis

Check with the tourist board for the latest rates, and verify the price with the driver before you go anywhere. Recent fares are $2.50 for a short trip within Belize City or to the small Municipal Airport; hourly for between $7 and $12 depending on the season; $15 to the international airport. Fares to out-of-town destinations are by negotiation.

TAXI FARES

Fares in town are, in theory, fixed by the government, but for visitors, they're likely to rise between the time you enter a cab and the moment you reach your destination.

One of my kids' lasting impressions of Belize is of a beefy taxi driver dragging off a suitcase with my wife still attached to the handle, refusing to surrender baggage and mother until we paid the agreed fare plus an extortion factor. Belizean bystanders, accustomed to a residual level of brawling on their streets, could have cared less.

Just remember, growled our driver as he surrendered to my wife after a ten-minute staredown, this is my country.

It certainly is. Fortunately, this usually means showing the good side of things Belizean.

In any case, don't even think about insisting on your rights with a taxi driver at night in some unfamiliar quarter.

Taxis have green license plates. A limited number of taxi drivers are actually qualified sightseeing guides, but they will all offer daytrips at rates that can be bargained down, especially during the rainy season.

Taxi operators include **Cinderella Plaza Taxi**, *tel. 33340*; **Caribbean Taxi**, *Albert St., tel. 72888*; **City Garage**, *Queen St., tel. 45833*; **Baldemar Varella**, *73600*.

WHERE TO STAY

Good news! The hotels visitors have been waiting for are here today. Belize City's first tourist-class rooms — several hundred of them — have all come on stream in a relatively short time span. Facilities at the Belize Biltmore Plaza and the Ramada Royal Reef Resort compare with the best in the region.

Not-so-good-news: Rates at the better establishments, at over $100 a day double, are, to say the least, discouraging.

Getting Discounted Rooms

But it's not as bad as it sounds. Operating costs are high in Belize, and you could pay almost as much at less desirable hotels. And even if your pockets are not deep, you might be able to work something out. Most of the new rooms are still sitting empty, and flexibility is the order of the day.

If you don't like the rack rate quoted, ask for the special rate, the corporate rate, the weekend rate, the off-season special, or the Central American rate. You're likely to hit somewhere, either by calling a hotel's toll-free number in the U.S., or by picking up a courtesy phone at the international airport. Just by showing this book, you'll get 20 percent off the published rate at the Belize Biltmore Plaza.

If you're an experienced international traveller, I don't have to tell you that there's a downside to bargain rates at upscale hotels. You'll pay heavy surcharges for phone calls, double the going rate for drinks, and more for a taxi back from downtown. (And if you're not an experienced traveller, I've just told you.)

Rates are in US$, subject to change. Dialing code for Belize City phone numbers is *02* from elsewhere in Belize, *011-501-2* from the United States.

Away From Downtown

These hotels are away from downtown hustles, but just a short taxi ride from anything you need.

RADISSON FORT GEORGE HOTEL, *2 Marine Parade (P. O. Box 321), tel. (02) 33333, fax (02)73820, toll free in the USa and Canada (800) 333-3333, 100 rooms. $74 to $124 single/$89 to $139 double, plus 10% service plus tax.*

The Fort George has long been the most deluxe hotel in the city, a British colonial and modern establishment where everything works, and the hustle outside isn't allowed to intrude. With yet another multimillion dollar renovation, the hotel has become even more comfortable and has added several more facilities including 2 outdoor swimming pools with snackbars, private pier and marina with ferry service to the Cayes upon request, a brand new waterview restaurant and lounge, boutiques, excursion and car rental desks, business meeting rooms, free parking, 24 hour security, a small health club room, special VIP rooms in the modern Club Tower wing, available business center with personal computers and fax machines, and plenty of others as well.

All rooms are air-conditioned and contain deluxe private bathrooms, satellite color remote controlled televisions, beautiful hardwood furnishings, one or two large beds, direct dial telephone, limited or full seaviews, the city's strongest air conditioners, and available minibar, hair dryer, and non smoking rooms. With it's dedicated clientele of businessmen and high end tourists, the Radisson is among the top full service business class hotels in all of Central America.

RAMADA ROYAL REEF RESORT, *Newtown Barracks (P. O. Box 1248), tel. 32670, fax 32660. 118 rooms. $115 single/$127 double plus 10 percent service, tax. U.S. reservations tel. 800-854-7854.*

Everything about the Ramada has a cool marine feel, from the pastel blue, white and maroon of this multi-story structure rising beside the water, reflecting the sea and the reef, to the tile in the lobby, to the comfortable glassed-in air-conditioned public areas.

The Ramada's compound is dotted with thatched shelters and gardens, the courtyard with fountains and fan palms in planters; the pool is huge and there a small man made beach like area. Fishing, diving and snorkeling are all arranged at the on-site marina. Every guest room has an ocean view, and is complete with Marble vanities and furnishings from natural materials such as wicker that are all easy on the eyes.

The Reef restaurant emphasizes seafood, pastas, and meats with most main courses running about $14.00. A nice continental breakfast buffet can be ordered for another $7 a day, and it features bagels and cream cheese, English muffins, fresh fruit salad, cereals, 5 types of fruit juice, local pastries, and good coffee. Their Calypso bar and grill is also a great place to enjoy cool drinks and hot music. A good choice for relaxing accommodations in Belize City.

FORT STREET GUEST HOUSE, *4 Fort St. (P. O. Box 3), tel. 30116, fax 78808. 5 rooms with shared bathroom, $44 single/$58 double with breakfast, no service charge. Credit cards accepted. U.S. reservations contact is (800)-240-3678.*

Bed and breakfast in a picture-perfect old house with porches all around, plenty of wicker, wind chimes, wainscotting, high wood ceilings and fans, inviting sitting area. It's not all perfectly refinished, just nicely worn, and totally charming. Some of the rooms have canopied beds, antique furnishings, huge screened in windows, and plenty of sunlight. Don't miss the fabulous home cooked gourmet meals in their charming diningroom and open air patio. You can also leave notes for the staff (wake-up time, coffee requests, etc.) in a wine bottle by your door.

BELIZE BILTMORE PLAZA, *Mile 3, Northern Highway, tel. 32302, fax 32301, 90 rooms. $100 single/$110 double, no service charge. U.S. reservations: tel. 800-327-3573.*

Located in a mixed-use suburban area, the Biltmore is plain on the outside, but inside is another matter. In the best Central American tradition, the Biltmore is oriented to a courtyard, and it's past the entry that you'll find the gazebo, gardens with almond and coconut trees and banana plants and aloe (with giant crabs hiding among them), and most public facilities. You don't have to go far to appreciate Belizean wildlife. Resident turtles and even crabs lurk in the gardens. Call the architecture, with its pediments and columns eschewing excess decoration, a sort of post-modern English colonial.

Management is in the hands of the experienced Biltmore group, and service is provided with a finesse that belies the hotel's tender age. Good-sized rooms, opening either off the courtyard with its pool, or from an encircling veranda, have both quiet air conditioners and ceiling fans, easy-on-the-eyes oak-veneer furniture, pastel-floral bedspreads, and art prints of the best of old Belizean houses. The swim-up bar at the pool is open on weekends and when numbers warrant. Cuisine in the Victorian Room, with its dark wainscotting, is both continental and regional, with items such as broiled chicken, grilled snapper, and tournedos bearnaise, at about $10. The Squires Lounge is inviting (see below).

CHATEAU CARIBBEAN, *6 Marine Parade (P. O. Box 947), tel. (02) 32988, fax (02) 30900. 20 rooms. $69 single/$79 double, $95 for the deluxe penthouse units.*

A seafront colonial mansion, with attached new wing, near the Fort George. After finishing up a new round of renovations, this charming little hotel is turning into a real gem. All of the rooms are well maintained and feature private bathrooms, satellite television, powerful air conditioning, direct dial phones, and extremely comfortable furnishings. The deluxe rooms (#401 & # 402) offer 2 queen size beds, twice the space of any other hotel room in town, and private enclosed water view terraces.

There is also a seaview bar and restaurant that opens for breakfast, lunch, and dinner. A great place to stay in the best part of town, with a uniquely Carribean ambiance.

COLTON HOUSE, *9 Cork St., tel. 44666. 5 rooms. $65 single/$80 double, $75/$90 with private bath, $10 per extra person.*

This small home style inn provides charming accommodations in a smoke free environment. Housed in a restored merchant's home that dtes back to 1928, the owners invite guests to relax on sofas in their common livingroom. The inn is located on one of the safest blocks in the city (just steps from the US Embassy) and has lots of natural light, high ceilings, overhead fans, area carpets, attractive wallpaper, and many other homey details, such as old-style bankers lamps, built-in wardrobes, and hardwood furniture. Some room are air conditioned, and one even has a small kitchenette. All guest rooms are large and have outside entrances, and while 3 have private baths, two of them share a bathroom.

There is a television-lounge area, and a long outside veranda with swings and recliners. All in all, Colton House is nice alternative to the big hotels in town, although it has few real facilities and no meals are served.

BELIZE GUEST HOUSE, *2 Hutson St. at Marine Parade, tel. 77569. 4 rooms. $33 single/$44 double. Credit cards with surcharge.*

Pleasant, clean, seaside house. All rooms with shared bath and fan. Drinks available, no restaurant. Four-wheel-drive rental vehicle available.

North of the Swing Bridge

Between the Swing Bridge and the Fort George area are:

BAKADEER INN, *74 Cleghorn St. (off Douglas Jones St.), tel. 31400, fax 31963. 12 rooms. $45 single/$50 double and up.*

First of all, you've got to give the owners credit for architectural originality, with their post-modern Tudor façade. Inside, facilities are strictly U.S. style: all the rooms are carpeted and contain a full tiled bathroom, desk, dressing area, cable television, air-conditioning, mini-refrigerator, and neutral decor. The breakfast room is air-conditioned as well and serves up a great $4 American style buffet with eggs. There's nothing of interest in the area, but this will be an attractive lodging place if you're traveling by car, since protected parking is available at $5 a day.

DIBÁSEI, *26 Hydes Lane, tel. 33981, fax 32136. 9 rooms. $30 single/$40 double.*

The guest house with a cultural difference is a re-habbed, blue-painted wooden house at the corner of New Road, hosted by proud folk from Dangriga. It's all clean and modern, and each large, carpeted, plywood-panelled guest room bears the name of a bird in the Garifuna language. Most are air-conditioned, and all have individual bathroom and shower. Decorations include Garifuna fish nets and John-Canoe masks. Lectures are scheduled, and a craft shop is in the works.

GLENTHORNE MANOR, *27 Barrack Rd., tel. 44212. 6 rooms. $25 to $35 single/$35 to $45 double, plus tax and service, including breakfast.*

This historic wooden mansion, designed by a fugitive Italian archi-tect, contains the oddest combinations of hardwood detailing and mod-ern accretions. Every guest room is different, from a single with private bath to a double with recycled kitchen cabinets; a Formica-panelled single; a honeymoon suite with room-wide window, imitation-brick tile, and textured wallpaper in the bathroom. All rooms are off several large common rooms with television and piano and odds and ends of furniture. Guests may use the kitchen and, for a fee, the washing machine and dryer.

Owner Winil Grant Borg, of the distinguished Belizean family of public servants and artists that named this building after their one-time London residence, will fill you in on historical details, and see that you are well started every morning with Creole bread, Johnnycakes and fried fish. In the sitting room, among the solid mahogany furniture, is the throne used by the Queen of the Bay.

GOLDEN DRAGON, *27 Queen St., tel. 72817. $20 double.*

This hotel, facing a lot south of Queen St., is clean with plain rooms, though the cramped buildings of the neighborhood mean there will be little air circulation on hot nights. The restaurant serves Chinese food.

ROYAL ORCHID HOTEL, *New Rd. and Douglas Jones (P.O. Box 279), tel. 32783, fax 32789. 22 rooms. $45 single/$55 double plus tax. Visa, Master Card, American Express.*

A new, four-story, Chinese-run hotel. Unadorned, but somewhat modern and comfortable, with decent rooms, each with cable television, air conditioning and fan, direct dial telephone, basic furnishings, and fully vented bathroom. Secure parking is provided. The top-floor Chinese restaurant provides 270-degree views of the city, with a reasonably priced menu and good breezes.

HOTEL KISS, *Douglas Jones and Mapp streets, tel. 33916, fax 31030. $46 single/$92 double.*

A new concrete slab on the busiest street leading into town. In case you wondered about the name, yes, you can get a three-hour block of time for $20. But the rooms are not bad, with air conditioning, tea and hot water, refrigerator, television, and acceptable furnishings.

EYRE ST. GUEST HOUSE, *7 Eyre St., tel 77724. 9 rooms. $10 to $28 per person.*

An older, once-elegant building with wainscotting and built-in convection ventilation, quiet and cool, and clean. Most rooms share bathrooms, and only these are a good value. Inexpensive vegetarian meals are served.

KAHLUA GUEST HOUSE, *120 Eve St., tel. 31130, fax 31185. 12 rooms. $30 to $40 single/$35 to $45 double.*

This little hotel is in a good seafront location. All rooms are off an enclosed side porch, and all rooms, though plain, have television, telephone and air conditioning.

Budget Lodging on North Front Street

Along North Front Street, about a block up from the Swing Bridge, are three budget lodging places, with differing managements that set their tones.

At the **NORTH FRONT STREET GUEST HOUSE** *(124 N. Front St., tel. 77595)*, run by an American and a Canadian, rooms are basic and bare, going for $8 single/$13 double, less if you share a bunk room. A couple of breakfast choices are served, along with a prix-fixe evening meal. They'll also do your laundry and typing, and arrange for safe parking. Some readers have reported burglaries here.

BON AVENTURE, *122 North Front St., tel. 44248, $15/$20*, is clean, and Chinese managed. Across the way, **DIMAS' MIRA RIO**, *59 North Front St., tel. 44970*, is one of the friendliest resting spots around. $9 single or $12 double gets you one of seven small rooms with a toilet and sink right in the corner. If you're going somewhere, you can be picked up by boat at the terrace over the river – it's also a pleasant drinking spot. The owners can arrange for a stay at Ricardo's Beach Huts on a caye southeast of Belize City.

South of the Swing Bridge

BELLEVUE HOTEL, *5 Southern Foreshore, tel. 77051, fax 73253. 37 rooms. $79 single/$83 double plus 10% service plus tax. Full American plan $25* *additional. Visa, Master Card, American Express. U.S. reservations tel. 800-223-9815.*

On the seafront, the Bellevue is housed in what was once a fine old seafront home, expanded over the years into the present building. The rooms are quite large for Belize City, with carpeting, air conditioning, cable television, pastel bedspreads, bureau, small refrigerator, table and chairs, and large bathroom and dressing room. The upstairs lounge-bar has attractive sea views, and the pool and surrounding area have been totally refurbished (and can be used by non-guests for a fee). The dining room menu is certainly more elegant that what you'll generally find in Belize City. The Southern Foreshore neighborhood, in decline for a number of years, is now improving. The hotel also owns cabanas on St. George's Caye, and has an in-house travel agency.

HOTEL MOPAN, *55 Regent St., tel. 77351, fax 75383. 12 rooms. $25 single/$35 double (more with air conditioning, when available).*

Located toward the south end of Regent St., the Mopan is a large old house with screened-in porch. Though run down, it has long been a base for aspiring Indiana Joneses, and some old Belize hands swear by it. Owners Tom and Jean Shaw, distinguished in Belizean society, have as much knowledge as anyone about the country. The neighborhood, less seedy than others in the city, includes a number of historic buildings. If you're staying elsewhere, you can always crowd in at the bar and eavesdrop on what's really happening in Belize.

EL CENTRO HOTEL, *4 Bishop St., tel. 72413, fax 74533. 13 rooms. $35 to $50 single or double. No service charge.*

A modern businessman's hotel with comforts available in a minimalist fashion: small, industrial-carpeted, plywood-panelled rooms tucked under stairs, and narrow halls. Very clean, air conditioned, with private baths, in-room phones, televisions, even an ice machine (welcome on sweltering days). Good value for Belize City. A block from the central park. Only a few rooms are available at the lower rates.

BLISS HOTEL, *1 Water Lane, tel. 72552. 20 rooms, $23 single/$28 double ($33/$40 with air conditioning).*

This is an old concrete building, a bit musty, but the rooms are good-sized and clean, with television, wardrobes, desk, and tiled bath. There's even a pool in the courtyard, though you should not think that this is a resort. Friendly management.

Budget Lodging South of Swing Bridge

SEASIDE GUEST HOUSE, *3 Prince St., tel. 78339. 8 rooms. $13 single/ $19 double, or $8 per person in bunk room.*

A find for budget travelers – modest, clean, American-run, pleasant, and safe, with an occasional sea breeze and Caribbean view. Inexpensive breakfasts are served. Five blocks south of Swing Bridge, then east. Ask for Phillip.

BELCOVE HOTEL, *9 Regent St. West, tel. 73054, fax 77600. 9 rooms. $20 or less per person.*

Located along Haulover Creek on one side, and a seedy section of Regent St. on the other. Most rooms share bathrooms. The management also runs a resort on Gallows Point Caye and a travel agency specializing in services for boat owners, who are the main and perhaps only clientele.

Northern Edge of Downtown

Other acceptable lodging places are **FREDDY'S GUEST HOUSE**, *86 Eve Street, tel. 33851, on the northern edge of downtown, $20 double*, with just three rooms; and **MARIN'S TRAVELODGE**, *6 Craig St., $10/$14*, clean, small cubicles.

By The Airport

There isn't much in the way of lodging out here, but you can find a place to sleep if you have an early flight and are dead set against spending another night in Belize City. At the *(tel. 025-2049)*, just outside the international airport along the Northern Highway, rates in the 60 run-down, musty rooms are about $25 per person with air conditioning. Apartments are available.

ESTELLE'S, *across the road (inquire at Elsie's Shopping Centre)*, is another basic place, with rooms for $25 single or double. **BELIZE RIVER LODGE** *(tel. 025-2002)* and **RIVERBEND RESORT** *(tel. 025-2297, reserve through travel agents)* are mainly for fishermen, located down a side road and across the river from the airport. The setting is remote and tropical, even though you're near Belize's metropolis. Riverbend has several cabins for $55 to $65 double, each with a veranda. Call first to find if non-fishermen are being accepted, and to arrange for a boat across.

If you have a car, you can try the **RIO HAUL MOTEL** *(tel. 44859)*, at *mile 5 on the Northern Highway*, near where the Belize River empties into the sea. There's nothing much out here, but the place has been painted and improved recently, the air conditioners work, and the charge is only about $25 double.

WHERE TO EAT

Except for snack places, you'll be able to eat in Belize City mostly at standard meal hours, typically 6:30 to 10 a.m., noon to 2:30, and 6:30 to 11 p.m. Many restaurants are closed for all or part of Sunday.

Some of the best dining in the city is in the hotels. The fifth-floor, glassed-in dining room of The **RADISSON FORT GEORGE**, *13 Cork St.*, is a can't-miss experience in Belize City. Air-conditioned, with full city views, it features both Lebanese fare (kebabs, kibi, stuffed grape leaves) and more traditional steaks and chops (lobster thermidor, filet mignon, mixed grill). Main courses are $10 to $15. If the tab is past your budget, at least stop by for a drink on the open deck, and watch the people below, and the lights of the ships at sea.

Another good choice is the **REEF RESTAURANT** *of the Ramada Royal Reef Resort on Barrack Road, northeast of the town center.* What can you say about a restaurant that offers Carlo Rossi as the house wine? That it is reliable and consistent, with a genuine hotel chef on staff. That it is air-conditioned, with superb views through plate-glass windows to the marina and the sea, accompanied by soft music. That the waiters bug you for a larger tip than the service charge that is automatically added to your bill.

You'll find standard "international" hotel fare: club sandwiches, large hamburgers, and chicken breast at lunch for $6 and up, snapper in parchment, curried pork chop and steaks at dinner at $8 to $20 for the main course alone. A complete breakfast costs about $6, and there are buffets on Sunday and sometimes during the week at about $12 to $14, half-price for kids, a Belizean bargain. Limited children's menu. As at any hotel, the prices and offerings can change by the season.

The elegant upstairs dining room of the **CHATEAU CARIBBEAN**, *6 Marine Parade,* affords lovely views to the sea, anchored boats, and nearby cayes. You can have a sandwich for $4, or a complete Chinese or American meal (lobster, filet mignon, chicken with cashews) for $12 to $20. Service is good.

Across the Swing Bridge, the dining room of the **BELLEVUE HOTEL**, *5 Southern Foreshore,* has an elegant menu. Appetizers at the moment include hot cucumber à la crème and smoked marlin (a passable imitation of lox); main courses are baked stuffed lobster, shrimp primavera, and chicken florentine. With a drink, a full dinner will run $20 or more. *American Express and Visa accepted.*

THE GRILL, *164 Newtown Barrack Rd.*, is away from the downtown hustle past the Ramada, a pleasant, modern, air-conditioned dining room overlooking the sea. Many items are prepared over charcoal, but there are also shrimp creole and pepper steak for more delicate palates. $6 for the lunch special, about $10 to $15 for dinner.

MOM'S, *7145 Slaughter House Rd. (near Technical College)*, always lively, is a long-time favorite of visitors, and many Belizeans as well. Loyal patrons should note that Mom's has just moved – this is the new location. On a Sunday morning, when Belize City looks like a ghost town, walk into Mom's, and discover where everyone has been. Rice and beans with assorted accompaniments, burritos, roast beef, stew chicken, sandwiches and breakfast combinations with eggs and fry jacks, or French toast and ham, go for $4 to $8, and there are kids' portions; palates with loftier tastes will find lobster or shrimp salad. Wine is served as well as beer. They'll even accept your credit card (Master Card or Visa).

Mom's was started at the south end of the Swing Bridge by a transplanted American grandmother, who brought her favorite recipes from the old country. In its former location on Handyside Street, it was a gathering place and communication point, where you can post a message, meet travelling companions, and read posters advertising new budget hotels and services. *Open from 6 a.m. to 10 p.m., closed Saturday.*

PEARL'S FINE FOODS, *at 13 Handyside St. next to Mom's*, has just a few tables with checked cloths, and a limited selection: pizza by the slice or whole, spaghetti, and sausage and meatball heros/hoagies/submarines dripping with sauce. Reminds me of where I used to have my school-day meals, and they do, indeed, get an after-school crowd. Less than $4 for a light meal.

G G'S CAFE, *2B King St.*, is clean and cheery, and serves good Belizean food in a flash at low prices (this is not a triple oxymoron!). Dine on the patio under large parasols, or inside under a low ceiling punctuated with fans, in a room decorated with carved model ships and sconces and the works of Belizean artists. It's stew chicken/pork/beef with rice and beans and coleslaw for lunch at $4 or so, and the stew in this case is a nicely spiced dark sauce with some Mexican heritage, in which the meat is simmered to bone-softening and beyond. Hamburgers and other sandwiches are available as well. G G's is always crowded, so get there early (noon to 2 p.m. for lunch, after 5 p.m. for dinner). *Closed Sunday.*

The **FOUR FORT STREET** is a picture-perfect verandaed house hung with lanterns and plants, the tables set with lace tablecloths, fans wafting overhead. Intrigue, romance and adventure lurk. Try the mosquito toast or perhaps French toast stuffed with honey and cream cheese for breakfast, about $5. Sandwiches are served at lunch. The changing full-dinner menu offers such main courses as garlic or dilled lobster, Cajun shrimp, and grouper stuffed with spinach, at a fixed price of up to $18.

Queen Street is the site of several popular Chinese restaurants, especially **SHEN'S PEKING PANDA**, *just north of the Swing Bridge*, and upstairs. $8 or so will get you a Szechuan specialty, such as chicken and cashews. The facilities are a bit down-at-the-heels, though the terrace is a good locale for street watching, if you can make it through the gauntlet of characters who intimidate visitors outside. Other Chinese restaurants include **CHINA TOWN**, *across the street from Shen's*, and not as good; and the **GOLDEN DRAGON**, *off Queen St. opposite Barrack Rd.*, $2 to $6 for sandwiches and standard Belizean and Chinese fare.

DIT'S, *50 King Street*, light and clean and well-fanned, is popular with locals for Belizean-style rice and beans with chicken or beef, meat pies, and tamales. No main course costs more than $3. Or, just stop in for lemon pie, coconut pie, caramel cake, or another fruity dessert with tea, for less than a dollar. Service is instantaneous, and no alcoholic beverages are available.

Nearby, the **MEXICAN CORNER**, *29 King Street*, is a favorite hole in the wall of not the slightest pretension, a room of painted boards with a fan overhead. The fare is Yucatecan and Hispanic specialties, including pollo kiki (roast chicken), escabeche (chicken in pickling) and burritos. It would be hard to spend more than $5.

MACY'S restaurant, *16 Bishop*, has a daily Belizean-style menu for $5 that lets you choose from the likes of gibnut, stewed chicken, curried chicken, and whole snapper. There are just five crowded tables, so you might have to share and chat. Macy's has a take-out window.

Near the north end of the Swing Bridge, the **ARK RESTAURANT**, *109 North Front St.*, serves up stew cowfoot, stew pork, stew chicken and stuff ham (all sic) for anywhere from $2 to $4 per portion.

Nearby, **EARL'S CAFÉ**, *91 North Front St.*, offers light fare on a terrace with river view. There are Caesar and chef's salads, teriyaki chicken, and a daily special for about $6.

The restaurant of the **EL CENTRO HOTEL**, *4 Bishop St.*, is cool, clean and air-conditioned, if uninspired. Breakfast is $4, lunch up to $10, and Belizean-style food, such as stewed chicken, is often served.

Light Fare

SCOOPS, *Gaol Lane at Eve St.*, serves ice cream only, from a 50¢ cone to a $2 sundae. Look for the pathology lab – Scoops is underneath. The same ice cream is available in less haunting surroundings at several other outlets. **CELEBRATIONS**, *16 Queen St. opposite the radio tower*, and the **BLUE BIRD**, *35 Albert St.*, have ice cream, fruit juices, and burgers and sandwiches for less than $2.

Pizza by the slice is sold at the **PIZZA HOUSE**, *King St. west of Albert*. **PETE'S PASTRIES**, *41 Queen St.*, has meat pies, tamales, enchiladas, and pies and tarts made from lemon, raisins, coconut and many other fruits, cow foot soup on Saturday.

SEEING THE SIGHTS
The Fort George Area

A good place to start a tour of Belize City is the **Fort George Hotel**. Originally it was Fort George Island, and was the locale of a barracks until the 1850s. The strait separating the fort from the city was filled in, in the 1920s, and a park was laid out to honor the dead of the first World War. Nearby are the Customhouse, the tomb of the benefactor Baron Bliss, and a lighthouse.

The Fort George Hotel was built on the former island in 1952, and was until recent times the leading hotel in Belize. Its Club Wing is a skyscraper by local standards, rising to six stories, and representing Chicago architecture come to Belize: in the right light, the curving, aluminum-and-glass façade, reflecting the sky and sea and clouds, would fit in nicely on East Wacker Drive, and is quite beautiful; though, from seaward on a cloudy day, it looks like nothing so much as an oversized oil storage tank set among the two-story clapboard architecture of the neighborhood. It's all overwhelming, still, to the populace, who gawk at the glass-walled elevator clinging to the outside of the tower.

If any neighborhood has class in Belize, it is the one around the Fort George. The streets are quiet. A breeze blows in from the sea. A few large, old, plantation-style residences, hung with balconies, have been restored or otherwise spruced up to serve new functions. One is the **Chateau Caribbean Hotel**, *facing the water on Marine Parade*, another the **U.S. Consulate** at *29 Gabourel Lane*, one of the few U.S. diplomatic missions without armed guards, originally built in New England, and transported to Belize as ballast and re-erected around 1870. Still another is the Four Fort Street Guest House.

Queen & Front Streets

Fort Street leads from the Fort George neighborhood to **Queen Street**, where the offices and showrooms of the major import houses of Belize, as well as the police station and the post office, are located. Most of the buildings are the by-now-familiar one- and two-story clapboard affairs, bare or with peeling paint. Belize's merchant class is not pretentious. Gradually, newer concrete buildings are replacing some of the old structures. *At the corner of Front Street, facing Haulover Creek*, is the **Paslow Building**, several stories housing the main **post office** downstairs, and government offices upstairs.

Continue left (seaward) along North Front Street. In the modern building *at number 83, on the second floor*, you'll find the information office of the **Belize Tourist Board**. *Hours are 8 a.m. to noon and 1 to 5 p.m. (to 4:30 p.m. on Friday). For assistance, call 77213 (fax 77490).*

Across the way, *at 160 North Front Street*, is a commercial office with a world-class collection of beachcombers' bottles, ranging from inkwell- to gallon- size. Anywhere else, these gems would be on display for an entry fee, but in uncommercialized Belize, they're simply there for you to appreciate through the window.

The Swing Bridge

The **Swing Bridge** *crosses Haulover Creek at the center of Belize City*, with vehicles and pedestrians in constant motion throughout the day and into the night over its roadway and narrow walkways. The only breaks in the action come at 5:30 a.m. and 5:30 p.m., when the bridge is opened to allow boats to move up and down the river. Haulover Creek is a delta branch of the Belize River, and a major trade artery. The bridge is at the point where livestock was once "hauled over" from one bank to the other.

South of the Swing Bridge

At the southern end of the bridge is the modern **City Market**, recently rebuilt. Take a walk through for a sampler of tropical fruits and vegetables, some as colorful as the fish along the barrier reef, and equally exotic, with names like *soursop* and *mammey apple*. Here's your chance to match the real thing with the strange name. Farmers upriver used to bring their produce to town by boat in the days when roads hardly existed in Belize. Now, pickup truck are main means of transport, and many farmers avoid congested streets and unload at the Farmer's Market, a mile upriver near the Belcan Bridge.

South of the river is Belize City's Central Park, or **Market Square**, with its municipal buildings and what was once the national administration center. The **Supreme Court** is a grand old edifice, with an ironwork stairway leading up from the street to a long, second-floor veranda. Neoclassical columns and pediments lend an incongruous, pompous air to the building. The **town clock** looks out from a central tower. The original courthouse of the settlement was erected on the site in 1818. When it was demolished in 1878, the mahogany piles were found to be in perfect condition. The next courthouse burned down in 1918. The governor of the day, William Hart Bennett, was fatally injured as he helped to chop down a burning flagpole in front of the building.

In the vicinity of Market Square are the national headquarters of the major banks, all in solid concrete buildings that contrast with the prevailing architecture. Running on parallel sides of the square are **Albert Street** and **Regent Street**, once known as Back Street and Front Street. Along Regent Street are some of the oldest surviving buildings of Belize City, with brick basements where slaves were kept.

A block to the east of the square, facing the water on Southern Foreshore near Bishop Street, is the **Baron Bliss Institute**, a fiftyish building of flowing Frank Lloyd Wright-ish lines, which includes a theater, library, museum, and the National Arts Council. A Mayan stela from Caracol and two altars are on display, well documented. The legacy of Baron Bliss is one of the more curious bits of Belizeana.

The gentleman, who died aboard his yacht offshore in 1926 without ever having set foot on the mainland, directed that his worldly fortune be used for the benefit of Belizeans. The bequest was invested, and over the years has paid for not only the institute, but market buildings, roads, and other public works all over the country. The beneficence of Bliss is remembered on March 9 every year.

Farther down Regent Street is **Government House**, a plantation-style clapboard mansion on spacious, well-tended seafront grounds, with ample shuttered, screened and windowed openings. Locally reputed to have been designed by noted British architect Christopher Wren more than 150 years ago (obviously a posthumous work), the building served as the residence of the superintendent, and later the governor, of British Honduras. The official home of the Queen's representative in Belize, the governor-general, is now Belize House in Belmopan. But this most elegant of Belizean residences still serves for official functions, and as a guest house for visiting royalty. The Prime Minister maintains an office in the compound.

Across from Government House is **St. John's Cathedral**, constructed between 1812 and 1826 of red brick imported from England as ships' ballast. The style is traditionally Anglican, but more on the scale of a country church than a cathedral. A plaque commemorates the victims of yellow fever, a scourge along the swampy coast until the beginning of the century. St. John's was the first Anglican church in Central America, and, as befits a minor relative of Westminster Abbey, has seen its share of coronations. Three kings of the Mosquito Coast protectorate, puppets of Great Britain in part of what is now Honduras and Nicaragua, were crowned amid great pomp and flowing rum in the 1800s.

Farther south, *at the end of Albert Street*, is **Yarborough Cemetery**, burial site of prominent figures from 1781, and of lesser members of the community since 1870.

NEW MUSEUM OPENING ... SOON!

*North of central Belize City, a new **museum and cultural center** is being erected near the sea and the Ramada Royal Reef Resort. This is a wonderful example of regional geopolitics made concrete. In the aftermath of rapprochement with Guatemala, Belize finds itself the lucky beneficiary of competing attentions. Mexico is helping out with construction, largely to balance Guatemalan influence.*

SHOPPING

This is not a major activity for visitors, but you can try **Cottage Industries**, *26 Albert St.*, for pricey straw baskets, decorated conch shells, hardwood spoons, and necklaces of hardwood beads. The cow-horn carvings are interesting and, in a certain way, attractive. Hotel shops offer mahogany and ziricote carvings, black coral, and straw hats, as does

Burnaby's art gallery, 9 Regent St. Admiral Burnaby's also has paintings, t-shirts, and assorted gift items.

The **National Handicraft Center**, *3 Fort St.*, is a big shed with paintings, coral and slate carvings, baskets, bottled Belizean herbs, and t-shirts — altogether a one-stop shopping center for Belizean souvenirs. Among the benefits: it's air-conditioned, they take credit cards, and you can probably buy coral items without worrying about whether they're legal.

Go Tees, *23 Regent St. at Prince St.*, has many, many t-shirts, many of them works of art. They also have Guatemalan crafts and carvings in rare local hardwood.

At various shops, you'll see coral necklaces, black and otherwise. It is illegal to buy black coral from unauthorized persons, and you shouldn't buy it at all, though you'll probably be offered some on the streets.

NIGHTLIFE

For an evening of drinking and/or dancing, head for Queen St., just north of the Swing Bridge.

At the corner of Daly St., is the **Hard Rock Café**. The steak is the best in Belize, and there are also blackened fish and Cajun shrimp, at $10 to $15 for a main course. It's not New York's Hard Rock, but with air conditioning, a third-floor view, and wrought-iron decor, it's as yuppie a place as you'll find in Belize.

The Big Apple, a centrally located dance hall, *is at 67 North Front St.* Farther out, *on the Northern Highway*, and reachable by taxi, is the **Lumbaa Yaad**. *Call 31790 to see when they open.*

Back in town, budget travellers sit around over drinks and watch the river at **Dimas' Mira Rio**, *59 North Front St.*

Another favorite nightspot is the incredible **Calypso** club *on the seafront immediately behind the Ramada Royal Reef hotel.* This marina-style wooden building stands on stilts above the water, and is a great place to grab a burger while enjoying the island's best tape-recorded Rock, Soul, and Blues music. After about 10pm each night (including Sunday's) the place gets packed with locals and visitors alike enjoying cool frozen drinks and hot Latin and Reggae music bands. There is nothing else like it in the whole country!

For the best strangers' drinking spot, I recommend the **Belize Biltmore Plaza Hotel**, *a couple of miles out on the Northern Highway.* Tucked behind the restaurant is the **Squires Lounge**, a modern, homey, pub sort of place, with a tiled, U-shaped bar, polished hardwood surfaces, glasses hanging from overhead racks, and subdued lighting. The *karaoke* attracts British soldiers and talented locals, including some of the hotel's own employees. Prices are moderate as things go in Belize.

> ## BE SMART - TAKE A CAB AT NIGHT!
> *Like all busy cities in the world, Belize City is no stranger to criminal activity and crack-related violence, especially after dark. Although the new green-shirted "Tourist Police" squads can be seen walking around major hotels, the thiefs pretty much know exactly when and where the coast is clear to bother foreigners. Walking through the streets after dark is just plain stupid! Take a taxi to and from the hotels, restaurants, and nightclubs. The $2.50 taxi fare is well worth the peace of mind, and security, that it brings.*
>
> *Several nightspots downtown have run the cycle of opening, dissolving into violence, and shuttering. Be careful of where you venture after dark, re-check any recommendations to night spots that are not mentioned here, and, again, please take a taxi back to your hotel. It's a few dollars well spent, even if you're on a budget.*

EXCURSIONS FROM BELIZE CITY

Boats

Scheduled Service

Regularly scheduled boats operate to Caye Caulker, Caye Chapel and Ambergris Caye. Even if you don't have time to linger on one of these islands, the boats make for budget-class tours of offshore Belize. Fare is usually $12.50 to San Pedro, and $7.50 to Caye Caulker. Dropoffs can be arranged at other cayes that are not far off the route.

Most frequent service to Caye Caulker is from **A&R's Texaco** station, on North Front St., at 11 a.m.

- *The Andrea (tel. 026-2578 or 02-74988)* departs for San Pedro, Ambergris Caye, from in front of the Bellevue Hotel at about 3 p.m.during the week, 7 p.m. on Saturday.
- *The Thunderbolt Express*, a speedboat *(tel. 026-2217)*, departs from the Swing Bridge at 4 p.m. Monday through Friday, 1 p.m. on Saturday, for Caye Caulker, Caye Chapel and Ambergris Caye.
- *The Triple J (02-44375)* leaves for Caye Chapel, Caye Caulker and San Pedro at 9 a.m. from the north end of the Swing Bridge.

Where to Find a Boat

Let's say you want to take a day trip from Belize City to one or several cayes, and poke around the lagoons to the south. Where do you go?

- **A&R's Texaco station**, *on Front St. along Haulover Creek*, is where boat owners gather to find passengers for Caye Caulker. The operators come without recommendations, and without safety equipment, and drive hard bargains (bargains?).
- **Captain Chocolate** *(tel. 022-2151)* and **Capt. Jim Novelo** *(tel. 022-2195)* on Caye Caulker regularly pick up passengers in Belize City for day

trips to outlying cayes, at mostly fixed prices, based on a minimum group size.
• The hotels along the sea — the **Fort George**, **Ramada Royal Reef**, and **the Bellevue** — have their own boats or resident charter operations.
• Belize City marinas will charter skiffs with operator and life jackets. From **Blackline Marina** (*mile 2 on the Northern Highway, tel. 33187*), a boat for the day for three persons, with stops at two cayes and some snorkeling, will cost about $150. I've been satisfied with their services and safety.

Other boat parks are **Caribbean Charter Service**, *Mile 5, Northern Highway, tel. 45814*; and **Belize Marine Enterprises**, *tel. 45798*.
For more options, see "Chartering a Sailboat;" "Take a Cruise;" "Chartering a Motor Boat;" "Dive Operators;" and "Live-Aboards"in this chapter.

Side Trips
The country is so small that almost any place of interest can be visited in a one-day outing from Belize City. However, the jarring roads to the south will make you want to limit your speedy round trips to excursions to the following:
• **Altun Ha** ruins
• nearby cayes, and diving and fishing excursions
• **Crooked Tree Wildlife Sanctuary**
• the **Zoo**
• **Baboon Sanctuary**
• and, possibly, **Mountain Pine Ridge** and the Mayan ruins of **Xunantunich**

SPORTS & RECREATION
Diving & Dive Shops
• The **Blackline Dive Shop and Marina**, *at mile 2 on the Northern Highway* (*P. O. Box 332, tel. 33187, fax 31975*), runs diving and fishing trips from Belize City, or will outfit and drop you on an offshore caye, or just rent out equipment. Dive trips run $75 per person for the day, reef fishing $250 for a group of three, and there are assorted other river and sea excursions on offer, including a Belize River Safari for $50 per person.
• **Dive In**, *tel. 30265, at the Ramada Royal Reef Resort*, offers two-tank dives at a price of $60 per, and night dives for $50.
• **Adventure Coast Divers**, *Mile 3, Northern Highway, tel. 33185*
• **Belize Diving Service**, *P. O. Box 667, tel. 22143*
• **Caribbean Charter Service**, *Mile 5, Northern Highway, P. O. Box 752, tel. 45814*
• **Maya Landings Marina**, *P. O. Box 997, tel. 45798, fax 30263*

TOURS/TRAVEL AGENCIES

The agencies listed below will arrange excursions to various parts of the country. Similar services, including diving and fishing trips, are available through hotels and/or travel agencies in Consejo, San Pedro (Ambergris Caye), Caye Caulker, Placencia, and San Ignacio (Cayo).

Locally-Based Guides & Excursion Operators

S & L Travel Services & Tours, *91 North Front St. (P. O. Box 700), tel. (02) 77593 or (02) 75145, fax (02) 77594,* is run by Lascelle Tillett and his wife Sarita Tillett, two of the most experienced guides in Belize. This impressive locally-owned company offers the best service and prices on complete customized vacation packages, discounted hotel rates, organized overnight packages by air and land to Tikal in Guatemala, customized private guided tours with local experts on ornithology and wildlife, exciting half and full day snorkeling and fishing trips, excursions to Mayan temples and rainforest areas, car and jeep rentals, local and international airline tickets, and transfers between all sights within Belize and to international flights via Cancun in Mexico.

Rates are slightly cheaper if booked directly with their offices instead of through travel agencies and tour operators in the US and Canada.

A few of their best offerings aboard air conditioned vans include:
• a full day trip to the Mayan sight at Xunantunich with a stop at the zoo and lunch in Cayo district – $78 per person (minimum of 4 passengers);
• an exciting 2 day/1 night trip to Tikal with hotel, transport, all meals, guide, and entrance fees – $300 per person (minimum of 2 people);
• a half day tour to Altun Ha for $30 per person minimum of 4 people).

There are also several 2 to 10 night packages starting from $300 per passenger that have been created especially for visitors with specific interests of all sorts.

Discovery Expeditions Belize, *126 Freetown Road (P. O. Box 1217), tel. (02) 30748, fax (02) 30750, additional offices at the International Airport and Ramada Royal Reef hotel.* This giant of the Belize tour operator and excursion industry caters primarily to the world's largest multinational tour operators who just happen to include Belize for some of their packages. Although they tend to concentrate on large groups, if called or faxed directly they can handle more varieties of excursions and sightseeing trips than anyone else.

Among their scheduled excursion packages you will find:
• full day tours via boat to the Myan temple of Lamani for $90 per person (daily except Monday and Wednesday)
• half day tours to the famed Baboon Sanctuary for $35 per person;

• full day trips out to the Mountain Pine Ridge forest reserve at $83 per passenger (Monday and Thursday only)
• full day Island and Reef cruise aboard Bimini sailboat with optional fishing for $75 a head.

They also offer more extensive tours by airplane to destinations like the Jaguar Preserve south of Dangriga, the Mayan palace of Tikal in Guatemala, and other distant sights. Most tours include complimentary shuttle van pick up from your Belize City hotel.

Other local guides include:
• **Mayaland Tours and Travel**, *67 Eve St., tel. 30515, fax 32242.*
• **Belize Travel Adventures**, *168 North Front St. tel 33064, fax 33196.*
• **G & W Carib Holiday**, *International Airport (P. O. Box 820, Belize City), tel. 025-2461, fax 2645.*

Specialized Private Local Guides

These individuals and organizations will take you anywhere you want to go, and provide a private tour via sedan, jeep, or van. Guided by experienced local experts in natural history, Mayan culture, wildlife, and the forests, this is one of the best ways to learn about the countryside while seeing sights that ordinary tours never quite get to. Prices are negiotable, especially during the low season.

Among the best providers of these trips are the following:
• **Adventure Belize Tours**, *Western Highway-Mile 7.5, tel. (02) 31153 or (02) 71696.* Run by the charming Mr. Maurice Bernard, this one-man operation is one of the best places to call when you want a totally customized private excursion. Maurice will personally guide you just about anywhere you want to go, at prices that are a steal. He is an excellant resource for information about Mayan culture, animal and sealife, native plants, bird species, and the rainforest.
• **Native Guide Systems**, *6 Water Lane (near the Bliss Hotel), P. O. Box 1045, tel. 25819, fax 74007.* The owner is one of those knowledgeable gentlefolk who have made the transition from hunting and chicle gathering to guiding birders, divers, and archaeologists. Samples from the tour menu are a full day trip to Baboon sanctuary and Altun Ha costs $70 with lunch, an outing to Xunantunich and Mountain Pine Ridge at about $65, or a 2 tank dive off the reef for $60.
• **The Belize Audubon Society**, *12 Cork St., tel. 77369,* manages wildlife reserves in Belize in cooperation with the government and private organizations. It's a good idea to check in with the Audubon Society to inquire about the current state of facilities and seasonal conditions if you're planning a trip to the Community Baboon Sanctuary at

Bermudian Landing in the Belize District; the Cockscomb Basin Wildlife Sanctuary in southern Belize; the Crooked Tree Wildlife Sanctuary north of Belize City; and the Half Moon Caye Natural Monument. No special arrangements are needed before stopping at Guanacaste Park, near Belmopan, or the Blue Hole National Park, along the Hummingbird Highway. The Audubon Society also has a bird checklist, and, especially valuable in the field, a glossary giving "translations" of bird names from Creole to English. *The mailing address is P. O. Box 1001, Belize City.*

Note that two reserves managed by the Audubon Society are strictly for research, and are off-limits to visitors. These are **Bladen Nature Reserve** in the Maya Mountains, and **Society Hall Nature Reserve**, at the northern edge of Mountain Pine Ridge.

General travel agencies include:
- **Universal Travel**, *8 Handyside St. (opposite Mom's Restaurant), tel. 30963, fax 30964*
- **Belize Global Travel Services** *(American Express representatives), 41 Albert St., tel. 77363*
- **Belize Tours**, *115 Albert St., tel. 75443, fax 77681*
- **Belize Travel Adventures**, *168 N. Front St., tel. 33064*
- **Jal's**, *148 North Front St., tel. 45407*

If you pretty well know where you want to go and don't need a package with hotel and meals, you might get lower rates by negotiating with a taxi driver. Try the taxi stand on Albert St., south of the Swing Bridge, or call one of the operators mentioned under Taxis in the "Getting around Town" section of this chapter.

PRACTICAL INFORMATION
Banks/Money Exchange
Belize City's banks, clustered around Market Square, are: **Atlantic Bank**, *6 Albert St.* (associated with Chase Manhattan); **Bank of Nova Scotia**, *Albert and Orange Streets*; **Barclays Bank**, *on Albert St.*; and **The Belize Bank of Commerce and Industry**, formerly the Royal Bank. Catch them before 1 p.m. on weekdays (extra hours from 3 to 6 p.m. on Friday).

Most hotels and restaurants accept U.S. cash and travelers checks without charging commission, so there's little reason to change money at a bank. Some fellows on the street will offer to pay more than the going exchange rate if you follow them up a dark alley. Hmmm.

Books, Magazines, Newspapers

The **Book Center**, *144 North Front St.*, just west of the Swing Bridge, has all kinds of paperbacks at about 20 % over U.S. prices, plus writing supplies, greeting cards, and magazines. The **Cathedral Book Shop**, *on Regent St. near the tourist office*, has a similar stock of goods.

The shops at the Belize Biltmore Plaza, the Fort George, the Ramada Royal Reef Resort, Mom's Triangle Inn hotel and restaurant, and a few other outlets carry *Time, Newsweek*, and the *Miami Herald*, as well as tourist-oriented publications.

Consulates

The major consulates are:
- **United States**, *29 Gabourel Lane (Fort George area), tel. 77162, open 8 a.m. to 5 p.m. Monday through Friday*
- **Canada**, *89 North Front St., tel. 31060 or 44182*
- **Mexico**, *20 North Park St. (Fort George Area), tel. 30193*
- **Costa Rica**, *8 18th St., tel. 44796*
- **Netherlands**, *14 Central American Blvd. at Banak St., tel. 73612*
- **El Salvador**, *120 New Road, tel. 44318*
- **Guatemala**, *Northern Highway*
- **Honduras**, *91 North Front St., upstairs, tel. 45889*
- **Jamaica**, *Hyde's Lane at New Rd., tel. 45446*
- The **British High Commission** *is on Embassy Square in Belmopan, tel. 08-22146.*

Groceries

Brodie's Supermarket, *at Albert and Church streets, just south of the Central Park*, has a large selection of canned goods, local and imported liquors, wine, drugs, and sundries, mostly imported. Figure about double the American price for anything. If you're tired of eating out, go to the deli counter for sliced cold cuts and salads. They're open in the morning on Sundays, in addition to the more usual hours during the week.

Across Albert St., **Romac's** also has a large selection of packaged foods, as does the **Save-U Supermarket**, *on the north side of Haulover Creek, a mile upriver at the Belcan Bridge.*

Immigration

For an extension of your permission to stay in Belize, or other immigration problems, go to the **Immigration Department** *at 115 Barrack Rd., tel. 77237.*

Maps

The **Survey Office** *is above the Post Office*. A detailed topographical map of Belize in two sections, on a scale of 1:250,000, sells for $8, less detailed maps for $2. Be prepared to wait in line.

Office Services

Any large hotel can handle your faxes and correspondence, for a price. But to do it all without losing your shirt, check the office at **Mom's Triangle Inn**, *11 Handyside St., tel. 45523, fax 31975.* Mom's functions as home base for more than one startup enterprise.

Parking

Safe parking is a serious problem if you have a car and plan to visit the cayes. Inquire at hotels for enclosed parking, at a fee.

Post Office

Located on Queen Street, at the north end of the Swing Bridge. Hours are 8 a.m. to noon and 1 to 5 p.m., to 4:30 p.m. on Fridays. Post cards to the States or Canada cost 30¢ Belize (15¢ U.S.), lightweight letters 60¢ Belize (30¢ U.S.).

Telephones

Telephone calls from your hotel are charged at extortionate rates. Look for a pay phone, or call collect, or from the air-conditioned telephone company offices *at 1 Church St. (near the Central Park), open every day from 8 a.m. to 9 p.m.* Two USA-Direct phones are available at this location, or you can dial 555 from any phone to reach AT&T in the States.

Pay phones are located in the larger hotels, and in green booths throughout the city.

For more information about the telephone system, see pages 69-71.

Tourist Office

The **Belize Tourist Board** (or Bureau) *is located at 83 North Front St. (across the street from the post office, a couple of buildings toward the sea) on the second floor.* You can purchase a map of Belize here, and inquire about buses and current hotel rates.

For assistance by telephone, *call 77213 (fax 77490). Hours are 8 a.m. to noon and 1 to 5 p.m. (to 4:30 p.m. on Friday).*

15. NORTH FROM BELIZE CITY

INTRODUCTION

Not too long ago, the **Northern Highway** was an insult to vehicle and body. A single-car-width strip running down its center had once been paved, but the accumulated potholes of many years did so much damage to vehicles that wise drivers kept to the unpaved shoulders. On my first trip to British Honduras, the minibus in which I traveled suffered three flat tires between the Mexican border and Orange Walk. It took more than twelve body-wrenching hours to cover the hundred miles to Belize City.

Bad as the Northern Highway used to be, its construction in the 1930s was a major advance for the colony. An alternative was provided to the coastal boats that provided a sometimes shaky link between Belize City and Corozal, and a great impetus was given to the development of the sugar industry. Mayan ruins were raided for surfacing materials, a cultural loss, but a practice in keeping with the methods of the Maya themselves, who often re-used the building materials of their ancestors.

With realignment and reconstruction, the Northern Highway is less of an adventure, though the recherché thrills of extreme discomfort and uncertain arrival time can still be experienced on the southern Hummingbird Highway and such secondary roads as exist in Belize. The Northern Highway is now one of the easier routes for the traveler who wants to visit archaeological sites, experience some of the tropical vegetation zones from coastal swamp to pine barren to limestone scrub to luxuriant semi-rain forest, observe wildlife in the **Crooked Tree** sanctuary, or look in on the small-town mestizos and rural Mayans and Mennonites of the north. Handily, the road provides a gateway to Mexico as well.

Driving time from Belize City to the Mexican border, a distance of about 90 miles, is under three hours. Buses take four hours or less. The

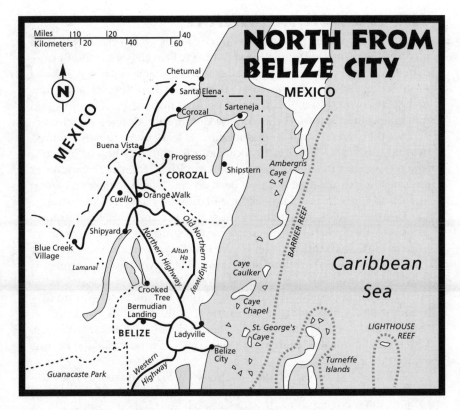

route is almost totally flat, and, now that the road is wide and in good repair, less interesting than it was when traffic was forced to move at a snail's pace.

Through the mangrove belt on the outskirts of Belize City, the roadway is banked just above the level of Haulover Creek on one side and the sea on the other. Past the swamps, the Northern Highway traverses patches of sandy soil once largely covered with pine — a few scraggly specimens remain, along with palmettos. Most of the land, though, only supports grasses and other low growth characteristic of the edges of swampy areas. Here and there are farm houses on stilts. The population is sparse, despite the proximity of Belize City.

At **Ladyville**, a community that stretches along the road *in the vicinity of Mile 9*, is **Phillip Goldson International Airport**. Ladyville is well-built and prosperous, with assorted small industry, British and Belize Defence Force barracks, and a couple of hotels (mentioned under Belize City). It is also home of **Raul's Rose Garden**, pointed out to passing tourists as the most reputed house of ill repute in Belize, though it is not the sole contender for that title.

THE BABOON SANCTUARY

At Mile 18, a branch road leads directly westward to villages with such picturesque names as Double Head Cabbage, Burrell Boom, and Bermudian Landing. All are on the **Belize River**, which once served as a meandering highway to the coast. **Bermudian Landing**, *26 miles from Belize City*, formerly a timber transfer point, is now mainly a farming and ranching center, known for its unique **Community Baboon Sanctuary**.

No, there aren't any baboons in Belize, at least, not as the word is used in other countries. *Baboon* is the local name for the black howler monkey, which flourishes in forests along the Belize River. Similar communities elsewhere are threatened by forest destruction. This sanctuary was set up in 1985 to forestall problems, as forest lands are converted to farming.

Unusually, all of the sanctuary consists of private lands. Owners have pledged to preserve food trees, riverside vegetation, and forest corridors in areas of cleared land, in order to give black spider monkeys a sufficient area in which to sustain their population. The payoff for the farmers is reduced erosion.

Trails through the sanctuary allow visitors to look in on – or up to – howler monkey family life. Howlers travel in the treetops, in groups of four to eight, feeding on leaves, flowers, and fruits, especially wild figs. Listen for the howlers' piercing, rasping call – it's more like the roar of a lion than a howl.

The lowland forest of the sanctuary varies from dense riverside tangles of trees and vines to drier pine forest and savanna, and is home to almost 200 species of birds, and many other forms of wildlife.

ARRIVALS & DEPARTURES

By Taxi

The easiest way to reach the sanctuary is to drive or take a taxi or a tour. The road is slippery clay in parts.

By Bus

Buses for Bermudian Landing leave George St. near Orange St., Belize City, at noon, 1 p.m. and 3:30 p.m.; another leaves at 12:30 p.m. from beside the Pacific store on Cemetery Rd., Belize City. Return buses are at 5 a.m. and noon. Inquire for directions and current schedules at the **Belize Audubon Society**, *12 Cork St., Belize City (tel. 77369)*, before you visit. (The Audubon Society sponsors the reserve, along with the World Wildlife Fund and the Zoological Society of Milwaukee County.)

The new route of the Northern Highway passes through stunted pines and scrub in sandy soil, gnarled, twisted trees, palmetto and savannah. There is some seasonally dry forest that loses its leaves for part of the year, and large expanses of pasture. Intermittently, a road leads off to some farming venture started up for the export trade. But as in the rest of Belize, the land is mostly empty of people.

Signs identify occasional settlements, such as **Biscayne Village**, population 268. Several miles down the road another sign wishes you a good journey upon leaving the same village — though you haven't seen more than one or two houses. Staggered irregularly along the way are 15-foot steel posts, installed to hinder small dope-smuggling planes from using the wide, straight, smooth road as an airstrip. Most of the poles have been removed, or bent aside. There are few places to stop for a drink, and no gas stations until Orange Walk.

At **Sand Hill**, the route divides into the **New Northern Highway**, and the **Old Northern Highway**. The latter meanders toward Orange Walk just inland from the coastal swamps.

WHERE TO STAY

A couple of bare rooms are available next door to the sanctuary for about $10 a double, and meals can be arranged for a few dollars each. There is also tent space.

LITTLE EDEN GUEST HOUSE (tel. 028-2052, P. O. Box 1713, Belize City) is a pottery studio with a couple of guest rooms sharing toilet facilities, on a palm-studded mini-estate. The rate is about $40 double with breakfast, and the location is convenient if you're driving and don't wish to spend the night in Belize City.

SEEING THE SIGHTS

Hours at the sanctuary are 8 a.m. to 5 p.m. A **welcome center** has maps and exhibits concerning the land-use plan, and answers the question on everybody's mind: why do howler monkeys howl?

In the company of a local guide (fee about $5 per hour), you can walk through the pretty village, with its modest houses scattered under the cashew trees and coco plums, and simply step out of the horse pastures and into dense tropical forest, sprinkled with ramrod mahogany trees, in one of the strips that make up the reserve. Your guide will point out the trumpet tree on which the howlers feed; identify the flora, and maybe a passing gibnut; and on a good day, steer your eyes toward a baboon. But be warned: though you can sometimes see whole families of monkeys crossing the cable that provides passage over the road, on other days they're stay-at-homes.

On the way to the Baboon Sanctuary, the road follows the Belize River. **Baboon River Canoe Rentals** in Burrell Boom can set you up with a canoe or kayak. *Call 028-2101 before you set out to set the rate and make sure* *somebody's there*. It's less than 20 miles from Belize City, but it really is jungle, with iguanas, toucans, and macaws giving you the once-over all along your route.

ALTUN HA

The junction for the access road to **Altun Ha** is located a*bout 28 miles north of Belize City along the poorly maintained Old Northern Highway; follow the side road for two miles to the west to reach the ruins.* The name of the site is simply a translation into Mayan of **Rockstone Pond**, a nearby settlement.

Mounds covered by trees and vines, the remains of what was once a great city, spread out over an area of more than 25 square miles at Altun Ha. Excavations have been concentrated in the central part of the city, where more than 275 structures have been found in an area about one thousand yards square.

Early Altun Ha

Altun Ha was probably first settled long before the Classic Mayan era, perhaps as many as 2000 years ago. For a Mayan city, the site was unusual. The soil is thin and poor, which has led some to speculate that Altun Ha was a trading center rather than a self-contained agricultural community.

Good evidence for this thesis comes in the form of a number of unusual green obsidian blades and figures turned up in a tomb at the site by Dr. David Pendergast, of the Royal Ontario Museum of Toronto. The objects date from about 200 A.D., and are virtually identical in style to others found at Teotihuacán, far to the north in central Mexico. This style didn't penetrate to more grandiose Mayan centers, such as Tikal in northern Guatemala, until much later, which suggests that trade and cultural influences in Middle America might have moved initially along the coast, and only later to the interior. Altun Ha is less than ten miles from the sea, and just outside the swamp zone that must have seemed unlivable even for the resourceful Maya.

Agriculture might also have been important to the inhabitants of Altun Ha, not only for staples — corn, beans and squash — but also to produce export crops, such as cacao. Other possible food sources were wild plants, game, and, unique to the Maya of Belize, seafood.

ARRIVALS & DEPARTURES

By Tour or Taxi

The most practical way to get to Altun Ha is by tour or taxi, or in a rented car. The road is narrow, lined with dense forest, and potholed, but passable at a slow pace.

Passenger-and-cargo trucks come down the old highway in the morning and return from Belize City in the evening — not very practical for a day's round trip. Otherwise, you can try to hitch a ride, though there's little traffic past the junction at Sand Hill.

Keep in mind that almost all the trees have been cut down at Altun Ha, and the site is open and bare and frankly less attractive to a casual visitor than Xunantunich, Caracol, and Cahal Pech in western Belize.

Normally I would advise you to shun stray dogs. But Altun Ha has a resident, friendly, somewhat mangy cur who obligingly leads the way on the best climbing route up each of the temples. He is certainly the least obnoxious tour guide I've ever encountered, and deserving of a bone.

The Altun Ha archaeological zone is open from 9 a.m. to 5 p.m., with a small entrance fee, with a $3 BZE entrance fee collected by an attendant near the parking lot.

WHERE TO STAY

Past the junction for Altun Ha on the old Northern Highway is:
MARUBA RESORT, *Mile 40.5, Old Northern Highway, tel. 03-22199. 16 rooms. $92 single/$116 double, plus 15% service plus tax. Add $46 for three meals. Visa, Master Card, American Express. Airport pickup, $45. In the United States: Belize It Tours, P. O. Box 300703, Houston, TX 77230, tel. 800-627-8227 or 713-799-2031, fax 713-795-8573.*

Just beyond the ruins of Altun Ha, and off the tracks that most visitors follow, Maruba is in a class by itself among the lodging places of Belize, a luxurious fantasy that blends almost seamlessly into the jungle.

Rock-paved paths lined by flowers lead through palm-shaded grounds past parrots and toucans and garden sitting areas with tables tiled in *faux* tablecloths, to a flower-bordered pool where the shower emerges from a waterfall; to a massage room wafting incense; to a central rotunda dining pavilion, where the furnishings seem to sprout from the jungle floor along with the palms and ferns. The creatures of the vicinity, morelet crocodiles and kinkajous, gather at a pond.

The guest rooms are all different, some individual cabanas, some in small outbuildings, others updated Mayan *ranchos*. One has a tub of Mexican tile, stuccoed walls, a platform bed with cane sides, and a futon as an alternative to the mattress. The jungle suite, up on the third level, shares the forest canopy with macaws and monkeys, and comes with video, whirlpool and refrigerator.

The kitchen relies on produce grown on-site including pineapple, grapefruit, limes, mangos, coconuts, fish, and game are usually on the menu. Presentation is excellent, right down to the exotic beverages served in coconut cups with hibiscus flowers on top.

Beauty is the theme of Maruba, and they have created an extensive jungle spa program. Try on a full body massage; tropical herbal wrap; seaweed body wrap; aromatherapy massage; mineral baths. The ingredients are drawn from petals and leaves and seeds and bark, in consultation with a local herbalist. These fine products are also available for sale.

Assorted packages are available. If you choose the right package for a river trip from Ambergris Caye to Lamani, you'll stop here for an unforgettable lunch.

CIRCLE K LODGE, *up the road from Maruba and 14 miles from the junction with the new Northern Highway*, offers basic summer camp-style cottages with linoleum floors and no decoration, on disorderly grounds.

The rate is about $25 double. Call the community phone, 03-22600, to make contact, and inquire if meals are available.

TOURING THE RUINS

The major structures of Altun Ha, called pyramids and palaces, surround two central plazas, which have been excavated and partially restored. ("Pyramid" is a handy designation for a massive platform of rubble faced with finished limestone blocks, surmounted by a temple. "Palaces" are more rambling structures than pyramids, with less massive bases.)

At Altun Ha, the temple bases are roughly oval in form and terraced, with staircases facing the plaza. The temples atop the bases, where they survive, are multi-roomed limestone structures, with corbelled interior arches. The *corbel*, or false arch, consists of layers of stone on each side of a room, protruding successively inward, until the two sides can be capped by a single block. The corbel can span only a narrow width, so massive Mayan structures contain claustrophobically small amounts of interior space.

Plazas A & B

Plaza A, the more northerly of the two central plazas, is surrounded by five pyramids and one palace. The visible parts of its temples are only the outermost of a series of superimposed buildings. The Maya periodically built new, more elaborate temples right on top of their old ones. The direct ancestor of all the temples was probably a simple thatched hut atop a paved platform. Both elements grew and became more complex and sturdy over the centuries.

Pyramid **A-1**, the **Temple of the Green Tomb**, on the west side of Plaza A, revealed an especially rich funeral chamber in its depths, with human remains and more than 300 jade pieces, including pendants, beads and figures, as well as earrings, obsidian rings, pearls, and the crumbling fragments of a codex, or book. Excavations in structure **A-4**, to the southeast, uncovered beads of a gold-copper alloy, pearls, and seashells from the Pacific, indicating that goods from as far away as southern Central America reached Altun Ha.

Plaza A was apparently the center of Altun Ha until about 550 A.D., when the addition of Plaza B enlarged the ceremonial precinct.

Structure B-4

On the east side of **Plaza B** is structure **B-4**, the **Sun God Temple**, named for the carvings of Kinich Ahau, the sun god, on either side of the first set of steps. At just 59 feet in height, it is the tallest structure at Altun Ha, but its importance has to do with more than its relative prominence. For in a tomb in the rectangular stone-and-mortar mass at the top of the temple was discovered the largest carved-jade piece ever found in Middle America, a squashed-looking representation of Kinich Ahau weighing more than nine pounds.

Other tombs in structure B-4 held offerings of jade pendants and beads. Charred jade fragments found near circular altars suggest that periodic reconstruction of the temple was accompanied by the destruction of valuable objects.

About 500 yards south of Plaza B is a reservoir that was fed by springs and rain runoff. A stable water supply was, of course, essential to any large settlement, and the Maya improved on the original natural pool.

Carbon-14 dating techniques place the first reconstruction of a building at Altun Ha at about 150 A.D. Building went on for several hundred years, and the center probably flourished until about 900 A.D. The desecration of tombs indicates that Altun Ha was not simply abandoned in a migration to some other location, but came to an end amidst civil turmoil and revolt.

Finds of trash from about the fourteenth and fifteenth century show that people still lived at Altun Ha, at least intermittently, but it was no longer part of the great Mayan cultural tradition that survived in the Yucatan, to the north.

CROOKED TREE WILDLIFE SANCTUARY

Astride the Northern Highway *about halfway between Belize City and Orange Walk* is the **Crooked Tree Wildlife Sanctuary**, consisting of several lagoons, and surrounding marshes and swamps. Operated by the Belize Audubon Society, the 3000-acre reserve is currently in a state of development.

Notable at Crooked Tree is the jabiru, a stork that is the largest flying bird in the hemisphere, with a wing span of up to twelve feet. Jabirus nest in the northern lowlands of Belize starting in November, during the dry season. There are also wood storks, and assorted herons, ducks, grebes, kingfishers, vultures, ospreys, kites, hawks, anhingas, egrets, and many other bird species, water-loving and otherwise. The varied habitats and plentiful food sources also attract black howler monkeys, crocodiles, coatimundis, and turtles and iguanas.

ARRIVALS & DEPARTURES

Only the western part of the reserve, taking in the Northern and adjacent lagoons, is open to casual visitors.

Arriving & Departing By Car

Take the Northern Highway to mile 33, where a branch dirt road cuts west onto a causeway over the Northern Lagoon, terminating at the old logging village of **Crooked Tree**, four miles from the highway.

About 50 miles north of Belize City, after the old and new Northern Highways reunite, is the Tower Hill toll bridge over the New River, built in 1967. If you're driving south, the old Northern Highway, following a more easterly route near the coastal wetlands, is the road to take to the Altun Ha archaeological site. Just beyond the river on the west side (going north) is **Jim's Cool Pool**, a spring-fed circle of water, with a roadside refreshment area. Buses, unfortunately, don't stop there.

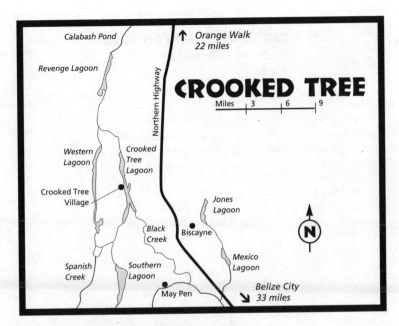

Arriving & Departing By Bus or Foot

From Belize City, the Jex bus departs for Crooked Tree at 11:55 a.m. and 4:30 and 5:30 p.m. from in front of the Habet Store, 34 Regent St.; a Batty bus leaves at 4 p.m. Departures from Crooked Tree for Belize City are usually at 5, 6 and 7 a.m. Verify schedules at the Audubon Society, 12 Cork St., if you plan to travel by bus.

Otherwise, it's a hot and dusty (or wet and muddy) walk from the junction on the Northern Highway, and there isn't enough traffic to count on hitching a ride. Residents of the village might have boats available for exploring the area. Toward the end of the dry season — April and early May — the water could be too low to launch a boat. But much can be seen on foot, from along the causeway lined with lily pads, and the shore of the long, low, lagoons, quiet and deserted except for water birds, and quite lovely.

WHERE TO STAY

CROOKED TREE RESORT *(P O Box 1453, Belize City, tel. 44101, $52 single/$65 double, 10% service)*, in an idyllic lakeside locale, has seven barely furnished, raised sapling cabanas with hot showers, on the edge of Crooked Tree village. The access road can be difficult during rainy periods, but walkways fashioned from tree stumps will keep your feet dry. The cuisine is plentiful rice and beans in the large, thatch-roofed dining room. Attractive dock and deck. Horses, guide service, tours and fishing

BIRDS OF CROOKED TREE

Source: Belize Audubon Society

Amazon kingfisher
American coot
American pygmy
  kingfisher
American white pelican
American wigeon
Anhinga
Baird's sandpiper
Bare-throated tiger-
  heron
Barn swallow
Belted kingfisher
Black vulture
Black-bellied whistling
  duck
Black-collared hawk
Black-crowned night-
  heron
Black-necked stilt
Blue-gray gnatcatcher
Blue-winged teal
Boat-billed flycatcher
Boat-billed heron
Caspian tern
Cattle egret
Common black hawk
Common moorhen
Gray-headed kite
Great blue heron
Great egret
Great kiskadee
Green kingfisher
Green-backed heron
Gull-billed tern
Jabiru
Laughing gull
Least bittern

Least grebe
Least sandpiper
Lesser scaup
Lesser yellow-headed vulture
Lesser yellowlegs
Limpkin
Little blue heron
Mangrove swallow
Muscovy duck
Northern jacana
Northern rough-winged swallow
Northern shoveler
Olivaceous Cormorant
Osprey
Peregrine falcon
Pied-billed grebe
Prothonotary warbler
Purple Gallinule
Red-winged blackbird
Ringed kingfisher
Roseate spoonbill
Ruddy crake
Snail kite
Snowy egret
Social flycatcher
Solitary sandpiper
Spotted sandpiper
Sungrebe
Tree swallow
Tricolored heron
Tropical kingbird
Turkey vulture
Vermilion flycatcher
White ibis
White-rumped sandpiper
Wood stork
Yellow-crowned night-heron

are available by advance arrangement through **Native Guide Systems**, *1 Water Lane, Belize City, tel. 25819.*

BIRD'S EYE VIEW LODGE, *tel. 72304 in Belize City; $45 single/$55 double with breakfast,* has five concrete rooms toward the south end of the village — turn left after you cross the causeway. The property is still in development, and landscaping and other details will arrive in due course. You can look right out from your room and see jabirus in the lagoon.

PARADISE INN has four cabanas to the north of the causeway, beyond Crooked Tree Resort, *at $50 single/$70 double, plus $15 for three meals.* Boat tours ($20 per person), horseback riding ($15), fishing and birding are arranged. *Call 025-2535 if you plan to stay here, before you go out.*

Farther south, birders and naturalists will find the more isolated **CHAU HIIX LODGE**, on a large tract of land that includes habitats ranging from riverside forest to pine ridge. Streams and underground springs draw a variety of wildlife, even during dry periods. The same abundant water might have attracted the builders of the nearby **Chau Hiix** (*Jaguarundi*) archaeological site. Four guest rooms are in two buildings on the shores of Sapodilla Lagoon.

Rates are $525 per person for three nights/4 days; $635 per person for 4 nights/5 days; and $935 per person for 7 nights/8 days, and include: airport transfer, meals and snacks, horses, walks on the trails that cut through the property, boats, fishing, and even excursions to ruins. Access is by boat in the rainy season, or by vehicle via the Baboon Sanctuary in the dry. *To talk to someone who's been there, and to reserve, call 800-765-2611.*

SEEING THE SIGHTS

The **visitors' center**, *on the right-hand side at the end of the causeway,* has displays that will help you identify birds and plant features, such as the logwood swamp across the water to the southeast. Three trails range from a one-hour loop on the *jacana trail* to a two-hour trek out the *limpkin trail.*

Before visiting the reserve, drop in at the **Belize Audubon Society**, *12 Cork St., tel. 77369, Belize City*, and inquire about the current state of facilities, and to pick up a folder.

ORANGE WALK

Settled by refugees from the Caste War in the Yucatan in the last century, **Orange Walk** is predominantly a town of Mestizos, people of mixed European and American Indian descent. Most noticeable in town, however, are the Mennonites who come from nearby communities to buy supplies or market their goods. With their simple denims and frocks, and their horse-drawn carts, the Mennonites are a bit of archaic rural life from the temperate zone incongruously transported to the tropics.

Aside from Mennonite undertakings, the main business in and around Orange Walk, as elsewhere in the north, is the growing, processing and transport of sugar cane. Just south of town is Belize's main sugar mill, where trucks loaded with cut cane wait in lines sometimes miles long. At times, the cultivation of cannabis has also been an important part of the economy, though it is now discouraged by the government, and many an airstrip has been shut down in an attempt to hinder clandestine exports.

With a population of about 10,000, it is one of the larger towns in Belize. But Orange Walk is hardly bustling. The unpaved streets, old mission church, straightforward, block-lettered business signs, clapboard-sided buildings with tall squared fronts, and the Mennonites with their old ways recall an earlier era. Add a couple of saloons and a sheriff, and you might think yourself in the Old West.

In fact, the remains of a couple of forts recall the wild and wooly era of Indian raids on Orange Walk in the nineteenth century. The marauders were not Apaches, but Mayas from across the border in Yucatan who attacked logging camps and held workers for ransom. In 1872, a detachment of the West India Regiment at Orange Walk held off a superior force of Icaiche Maya under Marcos Canul. The Maya leader died in battle, and the frontier settled down shortly thereafter. Some remnants of Fort Cairns remain from those troubled times, and an obelisk commemorates the battle.

Facilities in Orange Walk include a couple of bank branches and a small movie house.

ARRIVALS & DEPARTURES
Arriving & Departing By Bus

Orange Walk is about 55 miles from Belize City by road.

Buses running between Belize City and Corozal/Chetumal pass through Orange Walk about every hour. See Corozal coverage, below, for schedules.

WHERE TO STAY

Orange Walk is not a usual stopping place for visitors. There's no sea view, and the sugar-cane fields aren't all that interesting, though archaeologists and adventurers of one sort or another use the town as a base.

The best you can do for lodgings is the **HOTEL BARONS**, a concrete structure at 40 Belize-Corozal Road, the main street *(tel. 03-22518, $25 single/$35 double)*. The 31 plain rooms have private showers and are air conditioned, and there's enclosed parking and a bare patio with pool.

Comparable accommodations, without the pool or air conditioning, are available at the **CHULA VISTA HOTEL**, *at a gas station on the main*

highway in Trial Farm, a couple of miles north of Orange Walk (tel. 03-22365, about $20 single or double).
    CAMIE'S RESTAURANT AND HOTEL *(tel. 03-22266, $20 double)* has five rooms in the pink concrete building right on the square, at Park St. **THE TAISAN** is another new and plain hotel and restaurant, *one block north of Camie's.* **JANE'S HOTEL** is a big house in an attractive location, *at the east end of Bakers Street overlooking the New River,* but the rooms, singles only, are cubicles. $10 per person. The **HOTEL MI AMOR** *(tel. 03-22031), on the main street,* has better rooms but a less attractive location. About $12 per person, some rooms with private bath.

WHERE TO EAT

Orange Walk has the usual selection of Chinese restaurants. At the **GOLDEN GATE**, *36 Bakers St., two blocks west of the main street,* you can find hamburgers, chow mein, and assorted Chinese specialties to fill your stomach for anywhere from $3 to $10. Not too elegant.
    The **ORANGE WALK RESTAURANT**, *no. 27 on the main street,* also serves Chinese food in a dark, air-conditioned environment. $10 and up, no doubt to cover electricity costs. There are several other Chinese eateries.

EXCURSIONS

Jungle River Tours, *20 Lover's Lane (P. O. Box 95), tel. 03-22293,* arranges trips to Lamanai.
    Luis Godoy, *at a roadside stand in Trial Farm just north of Orange Walk (east side of the road),* can take visitors on a tour of his family orchid farm, at $20 per person. He will also take a group of four to the Lamanai ruins for about $175, including boat, lunch and beverages, and can arrange fishing for snook and tarpon in the New River. *Call 03-22969 for more information and to reserve, or ask for Mr. Godoy at Crystal Auto Rental in Belize City, tel. 31600.*

LAMANAI

The Orange Walk district abounds in archaeological sites. **Lamanai**, one of the largest Mayan cities in Belize, stretches for several miles on high ground *along the west side of the New River Lagoon.* Lamanai was occupied from the early formative period of the Maya until well after contact with Europeans — one of the longest continuing spans known for any Mayan site.
    Lamanai was probably first inhabited 3,500 years ago. The earliest permanent buildings were erected around 700 B.C. and were continually

enveloped by larger, more elaborate structures. The last stage of the major temple at Lamanai, **N10-43**, was completed around 100 B.C., and might well have been the tallest Mayan structure of its day.

Lamanai was excavated by a team of archaeologists from the Royal Ontario Museum, led by David Pendergast. More than 700 buildings were identified in the two-square-mile central section. A ghastly cache of children's bones found under one stela suggests that human sacrifice might have been practiced. A ball court marker dates from around the tenth century A.D., a time when Mayan civilization elsewhere had declined. The city's name might mean "submerged crocodile," reflecting the special esteem held by the Maya for that animal. The crocodile motif shows up on pottery and architectural decorations.

In a part of Lamanai known as Indian Church, walls still stand from a sixteenth-century mission, one of the few remaining signs of Spanish presence in Belize. An earlier church stood on the site of a Mayan temple, and might well have been sacked by unwilling converts who reverted to their traditional practices.

The people of Lamanai, who survived whatever it was that brought down Mayan civilization elsewhere in the eighth and ninth centuries A.D., fared less well in their encounters with Europeans and new diseases. By the time the British established a sugar mill at Indian Church in the nineteenth century, Chinese laborers had to be brought in to work the plantations nearby.

ARRIVALS & DEPARTURES
From Orange Walk & New River

In a four-wheel-drive vehicle, Lamanai is about 35 miles — and two hours — from Orange Walk by a track that takes a wide circle away from the New River.

Most visitors, however, arrive on a more interesting adventure excursion up the New River. Guides point out the birds along the way (red-billed hawks, northern jacanas walking on and darting over lily pads, cormorants, black-collared hawks, anhingas and flycatchers); the buttress-trunked trees and the tangled vegetation lining the banks (*hicaco*, or coco-plum; epiphytic *cactus*); and the mammals. Sometimes even a manatee will swim by. Clearings and barns and cattle mark the Mennonite settlement of Shipyard, stone embankments the sites of abandoned logging villages.

The river continually divides and rejoins through forest and grass-land and swamp, then opens up into the New River Lagoon, suddenly more than a mile wide, on the banks of which ancient Lamanai stretches. In calm weather, the glass-like surface of the water mirrors the blue of the sky and white of the clouds, and the knotted growth to either side. But don't be surprised if it rains. Operators provide ponchos, which also serve as windbreakers on what can be a surprisingly cool ride.

From Belize City

A day tour to Lamanai from Belize City is priced at about $125, but seats may be discounted out of season or on a last-minute basis. One reliable operator with guaranteed departures is **Belize Mesoamerica Tours**. In Orange Walk, inquire of **Jungle River Tours**, *20 Lover's Lane (P. O. Box 95), tel. 03-22293*.

Jim's Lamanai Experience has recently been operating daily trips to Lamanai from Jim's Cool Pool restaurant, just north of the toll bridge over the New River. Departure by boat (the *Lamanai Lady*) is at 8:30 a.m., returning to the highway at 4 p.m., tour price $28. You can also book this trip through the Batty Bus office in Belize City (Mosul St. at Bagdad, a block from East Collet Canal, *tel. 72025*) for $52, including the ride both ways on the bus.

WHERE TO STAY

Currently, there is only one possibility:

LAMANAI OUTPOST, *tel. and fax 02-33578 in Belize City, 800-537-1431 in the U.S. $70 single/$90 double.*

This new lodge is, indeed, an outpost of adventure, at Indian Church on the edge of ancient Lamanai, surrounded by dense forest alive with monkeys and macaws. You'll stay here mainly to visit the ruins, but there are additional attractions and activities: canoeing, windsurfing, horseback riding, massages, tarpon fishing, plant hunts in the jungle. Guests are charged an additional $150 for transportation, or stay on a package that costs from $125 to $150 per person per day inclusive.

TOURING THE RUINS

The ruins of Lamanai are unreconstructed and only partially cleared, with limited trails cut by archaeologists and squatters. The footing is slippery in the extreme, and the mosquitos are fearsome, even for Belize. Apply repellent before you enter the site, carry along a recall dose, and cover as much of your body as you comfortably can.

A small visitors' center focuses on wildlife and vegetation in the area, and holds some of the objects discovered at the site. Notable are eccentric flints, tripod vases in various shades of red (some with hollow legs containing pebbles for acoustic effect), and stone sculptures.

Temple of the Masks

Near the boat landing is structure **N9-56**, the **Temple of the Masks**, named for its decorations of large facial medallions, or masks. The underlying structure dates from about 200 B.C., but mostly later, outer layers of construction are visible. Its major sculpture, about nine feet high, is a realistic face, with what might be a jaguar pelt across the top section, and a basketweave motif on the upper surface and down the sides. The walls inside still retain some of the red pigment originally used to decorate the temple. Within, two tombs have been discovered. One contained a body encased in a clay shell, alongside wooden figures with jade jewelry — an odd procedure even according to standard Mayan practice of the time.

A rounded throne-like structure at the base contains curving channels. Could these have drained off the blood of sacrificed captives?

Overturned *stelae*, or inscribed stones, litter the base of the Temple of the Masks, and all of Lamanai. The figure on Stela 9 has been identified from its glyphic inscription as *Lord Smoking Shell*, a ruler of the city.

Most stelae have been left where found, face down. Some are cracked by the heat of fires that once were burned before them, probably after the decline of Lamanai. In parts of Guatemala, natives still burn incense at the ancient sites.

The High Temple

Structure N10-43, the **High Temple**, rising to 112 feet, the largest structure at Lamanai, is dated at 100 B.C. It may be climbed by a steep, intact staircase, to a perch above the jungle, swamps, and lagoon. There is no surviving superstructure, or sanctuary, at the summit, as on Mayan temples of the Classic period, such as those at Xunantunich. Most likely, whatever stood atop the High Temple was built of wood and thatch, and rotted away. Findings here include a large black-on-red bowl dated at 700 A.D., seashells, and a dish containing a bird skeleton.

Beside N10-43 is a rather eroded **Ballcourt**. In the cistern under the large central marker were found traces of mercury, which probably was mined in northern Mexico.

Other Sites & Sights

Structure N10-9, in a grouping to the south, was probably erected in the sixth century A.D., and subsequently renovated. Stairways, repeatedly modified, decorate the sides. Numerous jade objects were found here.

The **Temple of the Jaguar** is an eroded structure, with two jaguar masks, or facial medallions, one at each of the lower corners of the main face. It is one of the few structures at Lamanai with a surviving prominent central stairway. The **Acropolis** displays several successive layers of construction.

Structure N10-2 is on the west side of a small plaza in Lamanai's southern grouping. The main façade used columns, as in Postclassic construction in the Yucatan, but here they were of timber. Dozens of burials were discovered inside, some unadorned, some with clothing and decorations that identified warriors or nobility.

South of the central section of Lamanai are the remains of the **sugar mill** that operated here from 1860 to 1875, the old machinery rusting away, intertwined with strangler figs. A brick cistern was used to store molasses. The mill was steam-powered.

Farther south is **Indian Church**, one of the few remaining outposts of Spanish missionary efforts in Belize. A sixteenth-century church, built of stone from ancient Lamanai, was destroyed by Maya loyal to their traditional ways. Only the lower walls remain. A second church was erected by the persistent Christians, but it too was attacked, though more of it remains standing.

In the immediate area is the modern village of **Indian Church**, its houses of cane and split wood erected on Mayan mounds.

More Than a Ruin . . .

Lamanai is an ancient city, but it is also a botanical reserve and wildlife habitat. Troops of howler monkeys have specific territorial claims in the ruins. Oropendolas are common around the Temple of the Masks, *Aracaris*, a type of toucan, near Temple N10-9. Northern jacanas frequent the edge of the lagoon.

Trees along the trails are labeled for easy identification. The *give-and-take* tree has poisonous spines, but the sap of its roots is curative. The huge tubroose, or *guanacaste*, is often used in boatbuilding. Strangler figs, allspice and copal, with a resin used for incense, jam the jungle floor. And there are silk cottons (or *ceibas*, held sacred by the Maya), rubber trees, cedars and breadnuts (*ramón*, once a Maya staple).

CUELLO

The **Cuello** archaeological site, *four miles west of Orange Walk*, is not developed for visitors, although it has produced some of the most exciting recent discoveries in the study of the ancient Maya. Mayan civilization was once thought to have had its beginnings around 900 B.C., the earliest date of settlement previously known at any Mayan site. Excavations at Cuello have pushed that horizon all the way back to 2600 B.C.

A team led by Dr. Norman Hammond of Cambridge University studied Cuello and nearby sites in the mid-1970s. Through carbon-14 dating of wood found in what appeared to be post holes, they determined that Cuello had been occupied more than 4,000 years ago. The plastered floor in which the wood was found, together with succeeding layers of structures, demonstrated a continuity of occupation into the Classic Mayan era, and suggest that Cuello was a predecessor of Mayan culture in northern Belize, and perhaps in other areas as well.

Along with bits of old wood, Dr. Hammond's team discovered fragments of a previously unknown style of pottery. It was once thought that Mayan cultural development received a great impetus from contacts with other groups, such as the Olmecs of Mexico. The Cuello pottery predates any possible Olmec contacts, indicating, perhaps, an independent start to Mayan civilization, or other unknown cultural influences.

Artifacts from later years of the Cuello site tell something about the way of life of the inhabitants. There is evidence of a mass slaughter that took place around 400 B.C. A stingray spine, used, perhaps, in a religious ritual, shows that the sea was exploited. Blue jade and obsidian objects dating to as far back as 1200 B.C. show that extensive trade was being carried on with places hundreds of miles distant.

The higher, later levels at the Cuello excavation indicate that it was a minor center during the Classic period of Mayan civilization. The population probably lived from corn agriculture and hunting, and traded macaw feathers and animal pelts for goods from outside the area. One rather unusual discovery is that in some of the burials at Cuello, earthenware pots were placed over the heads of the deceased.

ARRIVALS & DEPARTURES
By Car or Foot
To reach the Cuello site, follow Bakers Street west from the center of Orange Walk. The ruins are behind the Cuello Distillery. Ask for permission to enter, or call the distillery first, *at 03-22141*. A taxi out this way costs about $4.

By Air
An air charter for three from Belize City to the old logging center at **Gallon Jug**, five miles away, costs about $150. The drive from Belize City via Orange Walk takes about four hours in the dry season. An alternate and rougher route is passable in the dry season from western Belize.

Southwest of Orange Walk
Farther west along the same road, and then south by southwest, about 30 miles from Orange Walk, are the Mennonite settlements clustered around **Blue Creek Village**. Farther on is an area set aside for conservation and ecological studies by the *Programme for Belize*.

WHERE TO STAY

CHAN CHICH LODGE, *12 cottages. $75 single/$90 double plus tax, meals $33 per person per day, no obligatory service charge. Master Card, Visa, American Express. Reservations in Belize: P.O. Box 37, Belize City, tel. 02-75634, fax 75635. In the United States: P.O. Box 1088, Vineyard Haven, MA 02568, tel. 800-343-8009, fax 508-693-6311.*

Almost as far from Orange Walk as Orange Walk is from Belize City, Chan Chich is one of the newest of Belize jungle resorts, one of the most comfortable, and certainly the most controversial. The thatch-roofed cottages and common buildings sit squarely in the plaza of a Mayan ceremonial center, overlooked by another, larger plaza. To some eyes, this is a desecration. To others, it's a practical way to forestall further looting (some of the temples can be entered by looters' slit trenches), while encouraging knowledge of the ancient and modern Maya, and of the tropical forest. Chan Chich (possibly "little bird" in Mayan) is part of a series of related, adjacent projects, that include farming, archaeology, and wildlife preservation and research on large tracts of privately owned former logging and chicle land.

Despite the remote location, the cabins, built largely from locally obtained thatch and hardwood, have electricity, hot showers, and ceiling fans. All have porches. The central building contains the kitchen, dining area and bar. And the surrounding forest is populated by monkeys and assorted cats and the rest of the menagerie for which Belize is famous, as well as orchids and tropical trees. Usual activities here are birding, hiking, canoeing and horseback riding.

If these, and ruin climbing (at Chan Chich itself and nearby sites), river swimming, and reading and watching the rain forest are your vacation pleasures, then you have found your place. If you crave bars and fish stories, seek elsewhere.

North of Orange Walk
NOHMUL

Nohmul is a major archaeological site a mile west of **San Pablo**, a village *eight miles north of Orange Walk on the Northern Highway.* Nohmul ("big hill") was built mainly during the pre-Classic period (before 250 A.D.), and the Late Classic Period (after 600 A.D.). The two major groups of mounds, in the middle of sugarcane fields, are connected by a raised roadway, or causeway. The main structure is about 25 feet high. Nohmul was first excavated by Thomas Gann, who carried off jewelry, shells and pottery from the site to the British Museum in London.

The area north of Orange Walk is the most agriculturally developed part of Belize, with sugar cane the main crop. Belizean cane rates with the

Cuban variety for its high sucrose content. But despite the quality of the product, the sugar industry has had its ups and downs. Once dominated by small farmers, sugar production came largely under the control of Tate and Lyle, a British firm, in the sixties. Despite the economies of large-scale cultivation and mechanization, the British company found it unprofitable to grow cane, and now most of the sugar of Belize is once again grown in small plots, though Tate and Lyle does the processing. Part of the crop goes to Jamaica, after preliminary conversion to molasses, for distillation into alcohol.

As the world price of sugar has oscillated, so have the fortunes of the northern farmers. Mostly well off in normal times, they have experienced unprecedented but short-lived prosperity when the world price of their product has skyrocketed, and disappointment and debt when it has fallen, or when smut has ravaged the crop.

COROZAL

Eighty-five miles from Belize City by road, and only about ten miles from the Mexican border, is the sleepy seaside town of **Corozal**. Founded by Mexican refugees in 1849, for many years the place was a cluster of adobe buildings. Hurricane Janet destroyed most of the old town in 1955.

Today's Corozal is part Mexican-modern, with concrete-block buildings in the center of town, and part Caribbean, with clapboard-sided houses raised on stilts to sit squarely in the refreshing sea breeze. Corozal has about 8500 inhabitants, and derives its name from a species of palm tree. Sugarcane cultivation remains the most important economic activity, though with years of low world prices, and an increasingly restricted U.S. market, the agriculture of the region is diversifying.

ORIENTATION

From the right perspective, Corozal is picturesque: palm trees fringe a lovely bay, and sailboats sometimes glide offshore in the constant, cooling breeze. North of the town center, along the water, worn wooden houses with porches atilt keep watch.

But, despite its seaside location, Corozal has no public beach. Swimmers enticed by the waters of the bay must walk along the sea front away from town and find a place among the rocks as a jumping-off point. (Along the way, perhaps they'll encounter groups of youngsters who will call out "white man!" — not in prejudice, but simply as an observation.)

Corozal is one of the more inexpensive places in which to survive in Belize, which, with town's non-commercial charm, has attracted some outsiders. As you walk around, you might run into one of the retired foreigners who lurk in the woodwork.

Like Orange Walk, Corozal was a target of Indian raids in the last century. A couple of brick piers along the central park are all that remains of the old fortifications, which were insufficient to protect the inhabitants. The town was captured a number of times by Mayan raiders from the Yucatan.

Inside Corozal's town hall is a mural by Manuel Villamor Reyes, a Belizean artist who now lives in Chetumal. Originally painted in 1953, the mural showed the settlement of Corozal by Mestizo refugees from Yucatan. When called upon to restore it in 1986, Villamor decided to repaint the whole work, taking into account his own changes as an artist.

The new mural shows the history of Corozal on a grand scale, in the tradition of the artists of the Mexican Revolution. Here are depicted the grievances of the Maya that led to their revolt, as well as the economic exploitation of northern Belize during the colonial regime. If the town hall is closed when you pass through, you can view the mural through the side windows. It's on the rear wall.

Mexican-style fiestas — called Spanish celebrations by local English-speakers — provide some break from the humdrum of small-town life in Corozal. Christmas, Carnival time, and Columbus Day — a holiday of Hispanic unity throughout Latin America — are all observed by everyone in Corozal. Particularly colorful are the *posadas* of the Christmas season, when celebrants re-enact the search of Joseph and Mary for shelter.

Though the residents of Corozal are largely bilingual, their English often lacks fine tuning. A sign at the market along the water warns that those caught riding bicycles inside "will be persecuted by law."

ARRIVALS & DEPARTURES
Arriving By Bus

Venus Bus Service operates from Belize City (Magazine Road, nine blocks west of south end of Swing Bridge, *tel. 73354*) to Corozal every hour from noon to 7 p.m. Some buses are Greyhound-type units.

Batty Bus Service departures are from Mosul St. at Bagdad (a block from East Collet Canal, *tel. 72025*) every hour from 4 a.m. to 11 a.m., with an express bus at 6 a.m. All buses continue to Chetumal.

Arriving By Air

From Belize City, Maya flights leave the municipal airstrip at 9:30 a.m. and 1 p.m., stopping at San Pedro on the way; Tropic Air at 8:40 a.m. and 2:40 p.m.

Departing By Bus

Northbound buses for Chetumal pass through about every hour, until 8 p.m. Collective taxis are also available for Chetumal, from the main square, charging about $2 per person.

Venus Bus Service operates to Belize City (from Gilharry's Bus Terminal in the town center) every hour from 3:30 a.m. to 11:30 a.m.; Batty Bus departures for Belize City are from the square every hour from 12:30 p.m. to 7:30 p.m.. Service is curtailed on Sundays, and times are approximate.

Departing By Air

Maya Airways has two flights from Corozal to San Pedro (Ambergris Caye) and Belize City, at 10:30 a.m. and 2 p.m. (daily except Sunday), **Tropic Air** at 10 a.m. and 3:30 p.m. daily. Buy tickets from Jal's Travel Agency on Fourth Avenue, one block north of the square (look for the Sahsa sign).

The airstrip is almost three miles south of town, a $3 taxi ride away. A new airstrip is scheduled to open at Consejo Shores, northeast of Corozal, in the near future.

Travel Services

• **Ma-Ian's travel service**, *13 G St. South, tel. 22744, fax 23375*, caters to guests at area hotels. They run trips to Lamanai, Chan Chich, Cerros and the Kohunlich ruins in Mexico. To any of these destinations, the price for a day outing for four persons is $300 or slightly less. They can also fetch you from the international airport ($100)or even Cancun ($250).

• **Menzies Travel and Tours**, *P. O. Box 210, Corozal, tel. 04-22725*, runs trips to the Cerros archaeological site across the bay (see below), and to Mexico.

• Travel services are available through hotels, or **Jal's Travel Agency** *on Fourth Avenue, one block north of the square*, sells air tickets.

WHERE TO STAY

Suggestion: Phone ahead for hotel reservations in Belize City or on Ambergris Caye from the BTL office, in the blue and white building a half-block from the central park.

Corozal has the best choice of accommodations in northern Belize. Most hotels are at the south end of town, about a half-mile from the center. If you arrive by bus, ask the driver to drop you in this area.

ADVENTURE INN, *in nearby Consejo Shores (see page 215)*, is your best choice if you have a car or are planning to stay a while.

TONY'S INN *(P. O. Box 12, tel. 04-22055, fax 22829)*, on the seafront off the Belize City road, consists of comfortable, Mexican-style motor-court units, built in concrete, amid nicely landscaped gardens. There is a mini-marina with a stretch of precious sandy beach, and the management is friendly, capable and helpful. The 30 rooms come in standard, moderate and deluxe category (the top of the line is with air conditioning and cable television), *and go for about $35 to $60 single/$45 to $70 double, slightly less from May to December, plus 10% service plus tax.*

POSADA MAMA, *G Street South, tel. 22107*, is a mini-motel in a residential area, executed in blue-painted concrete block. Rooms have telephones, air conditioning, and cable television. To reach Mama, turn west at the largest building along the main road through town, then right at the first cross street. *The rate is $26 single, $38 double*, and it's a bit of a walk back to anything. They get a by-the-hour trade.

The **CARIBBEAN MOTEL AND TRAILER PARK** (*tel. 04-22045*), also at the south end of town, has seen better days, but its tiny, Mayan-style thatched-roof cottages are adequate at (still only) $11 per day, with private toilet and shower, for one or two. You can hook up your camper in the large, grassy, palm-shaded parking area, at a fee that varies according to size and electrical usage.

The **MAYA HOTEL** (*tel. 04-22082*), a few blocks south of the town center, has ten clean, simple rooms in a newish building, *going for $15 single/$20 double, plus tax*, all with ceiling fans, hot water, and private bath, and some facing seaward.

The **CAPRI HOTEL**, *on the sea front about six blocks south of the square*, is mainly a cavernous pool hall, but bare rooms upstairs are available *for $8 single/$10 double*, or less without private bath.

NESTOR'S HOTEL, *123 Fifth Avenue (tel. 04-22354)*, is the choice for budget travelers. *About $10 double (or less)* for a small, clean room with fan. Weekly and monthly rates available. There are about 16 rooms altogether. Simple meals are served. Ask for Mark. At four stories, this is one of the tallest buildings in Corozal. Go up to the roof for commanding views to Cerro Maya, across the bay.

WHERE TO EAT

You'll find the best eating in the Corozal area, and a singular romantic and fun ambiance, at the seafront **ADVENTURE INN** *in Consejo Shores*, seven miles to the northeast. Pirate days are the theme in a thatch-roofed dining room set among the palms almost at the water's edge, with nothing but screening between you and the breakers, breeze, and moonlight. Tables are lit by candles, and service is fine.

A daily dinner special such as lobster goes for $10, and main courses such as seafood crepe and lobster stir fry are both worth sampling. And there are club sandwiches or burgers with fries for $5 or less.

At breakfast, the sun filters through the hardwood canopy, fan palms, mangroves and coco plums. Breakfast choices are standard eggs and waffles, as well as Mayan prixpak (eggs, tomatoes, onions and beans), for $5 or less. Portions are good-sized.

In town, the outdoor marina tables with thatched umbrellas at **TONY'S INN** are the most pleasant place for eating (and the bar-terrace is the most pleasant place for drinking). Breakfast is available for $5 to $6, including chilled, fresh orange juice, before anyone else has opened. Sandwiches, chili with cheese (excellent), nachos and tostadas at lunch run $3 to $5, and there are basic steak and fish, and lobster salad for $8 to $14, as well as house specials. The permanent breeze makes this a great place to spend an afternoon. Clean, and good service.

At the **MAYA HOTEL**, plain meals with chicken, steak or eggs are $4 to $6. The **CARIBBEAN TRAILER PARK** has a small, screened eatery, and if you can find it open, you can get a cheap burger, fish, or grilled meat. **CLUB CAMPESINO**, *on Fourth Avenue a couple of blocks north of the square*, serves chicken. Open evenings and into the wee hours.

There are also several Chinese eateries, including the **REXO**, *at No. 9 Sixth Street, northeast of the town center near the sea*; the **BUMPER**, *at the south end of Fifth Avenue*, and the **KING OF KINGS**, *Fourth Avenue just north of the square*. For basic food, **NESTOR'S HOTEL** offers one of the most inexpensive menus in Belize. Breakfasts are $3 or less, sandwiches $2 or less, fish or steak $4.

PRACTICAL INFORMATION

The **Bank of Nova Scotia** and the **Belize Bank** provide exchange services, if you haven't used the border money-changers. *Morning hours only, except Fridays.*

SANTA RITA

About a mile east and north or Corozal are the **Santa Rita** ruins, first explored by Thomas Gann, then Corozal's doctor, around the turn of the century. Gann uncovered sculptured friezes and stuccoed murals, as well as burials containing pottery of the late post-Classic period, and jade jewelry.

Fishing-net sinkers from the site show that the inhabitants exploited the waters, while copper tweezers must have been imported from some distance. Gann suggested that Santa Rita was part of a chain of coastal lookouts established when Mayan civilization centered in the Yucatan. According to his theory, fires along the coast might have served as a means of high-speed communication.

But Santa Rita flourished during an earlier period as well. Some pottery remains have been dated to two thousand years before Christ. A tomb from the Early Classic Period (about 300 A.D.) was excavated in 1985 by Diane and Arlen Chase, revealing objects made from seashells and stingray spines, and a skeleton decorated with jade and mica jewelry. Santa Rita might have been the most powerful city in the region at this time, and most certainly was again preeminent in the period just before the Spanish Conquest, to judge by the burial of a ruler of that period, with golden ear decorations of a type worn by high nobles in central Mexico.

The site, then known as Chetumal, was still occupied when the Spanish arrived in Belize. The limits of the city reached well into present-day Corozal.

To get to Santa Rita, take the road toward the border north from Corozal, and continue straight on a secondary road where the main road curves to the right. The ruins are in the area between the two roads, across from the Coca Cola depot. The site is generally not very impressive physically, compared to other Mayan cities in Belize.

Of the many original buildings, only **Structure 7**, 50 feet tall and partially restored, remains standing, with two of its four rooms intact.

CONSEJO

Consejo, seven miles northeast of Corozal, on a point of land just a couple of miles across the bay from Chetumal, has attractive vacation accommodations.

WHERE TO STAY

ADVENTURE INN, *tel. 04-22187, fax 22243 (Corozal). 20 rooms, $48 single/$55 double plus tax, lower off season (May through October). Add about $30 for three meals. Visa, Master Card, American Express. Reservations: Box 35, Corozal, or drop into the office in Corozal (open weekdays).*

The ghost of Blackbeard could well spend his vacation at this low-key, away-from-it-all yet accessible resort, in the residential development of **Consejo Shores**. The immediate environs of the Adventure Inn are a slice of seaside tropical forest that includes acacias, gumbo limbo, orchids, and palms. A canal cuts through, a dock extends outward, a wall contains a section of sand, and a bridge and walkway provide a pathway to intrigue. Shallow pools are filled by the waves. Mock cannon are sighted on hostile forces and potential prey propelled into the bay by steady onshore breeze.

Guest rooms are in attractive, well-equipped cottages, fashioned as much as possible from on-site materials — saplings, thatch roofing — with sufficient modern accretions, such as hot water and electricity, to make them perfectly comfortable. The newest units are multilevel, with plaster-on-cane walls, shower stalls or tubs, ceiling fans, hardwood floors, and screened porch. The restaurant (see above) is unusually good.

The waters off the Adventure Inn are shallow. Facilities include bicycles, kayaks, windsurfers, motorboats and sailboats for rent (windsurfing lessons are available); and the only tennis court in northern Belize. All are available for use without additional charge. Fishing, river kayaking, and naturalist and archaeological trips can be arranged, and there is a gift shop.

A taxi out this way from Corozal costs about $10, or call for transport if you'll be staying a few days. The new Corozal airstrip be almost next door to the hotel.

CERROS

Southeast of Corozal are the **Cerro Maya** (or **Cerros**) ruins, a collection of mounds on the point of land a across the bay, a few miles away. One of the temples here is 69 feet (21 meters) high, and has been partially excavated and consolidated. There are also ball courts, and remains of large facial medallions. Cerro Maya was occupied as long ago as 400 B.C. Part of the original site, which must have watched an important trade route, is now under water. Raised-field gardens might have provided provisions for traders, who reached the central area of the site by canal.

Cerro Maya can be reached by boat from Corozal, or by a long, roundabout land route during the dry season. If you try walking along the shore, you'll have to find a friendly boatman to take you across the mouth of the New River.

SARTENEJA

Almost all of northern Belize is fringed with swamp, but the widest belt is the area of waterlogged land that juts out to the east and just to the south of Corozal. Brackish pools and lagoons and entangled mangrove make excellent breeding places for a number of water-loving birds, including storks, ibis, spoonbills, herons, flamingoes and egrets, as well as for shrimp, lobster and fish.

Sarteneja is a tin-roofed settlement of fishermen and boatbuilders, huddled on a dot of dry land at the northern tip of the swamp, near Shipstern Lagoon. Picturesque and rarely visited, Sarteneja was founded by immigrants from the Yucatan in the nineteenth century.

Despite its present isolation, there is good evidence that Sarteneja was a regional metropolis for the ancient seafaring Maya. The remains of 400 Mayan structures have been identified within and near the present-day village.

One, **Structure 30**, has been partially restored. Others have been used as sources of building materials by more recent inhabitants. Locally manufactured shell jewelry has been discovered, along with gold and copper objects from elsewhere in Central America. Occupation of the site was continuous from early Classic times into the 1700s.

The remains of a nineteenth-century sugar mill are about a mile south of the village.

ARRIVALS & DEPARTURES
Arriving & Departing By Car

Roads cut into this lightly populated area from Orange Walk and a point farther to the south along the Old Northern Highway, though these are not always passable. Inquire at a service station in Orange Walk before proceeding. From Orange Walk, take the bridge east over the New River. The road for Sarteneja follows the east bank of the Progresso Lagoon.

Arriving & Departing By Boat or By Air

An alternative is to approach the area by boat from Corozal or Ambergris Caye; or to fly into Sarteneja. Maya Airways planes operating between Corozal and San Pedro sometimes touch down at Sarteneja, allowing the visitor to spend a few hours, or you can take an air taxi.

Arriving & Departing By Bus

Venus Bus Service operates to Sarteneja from Belize City (Magazine Road, *tel. 73354*) at 1 p.m., passing through Orange Walk at 3 p.m. Departure for Belize City is at 4 a.m. Confirm schedules, and whether the road is passable, at the bus office.

WHERE TO STAY

DIANA'S HOTEL, *Carlos Cruz St., tel. 04-32084*, near the sea, has ten basic rooms going for about $20 double with private bath, $15 with shared bath. To check for other accommodations, *call the community telephone, 04-22154, or speak to the Venus Bus driver.*

BLUE HERON COVE, *Lowry's Bight (P. O. Box 115, Corozal)*, is a five-room seaside guesthouse at the end of a branch of the Sarteneja road. It can also be reached by water from Corozal, six miles away. The rate is about $25 single/$30 double, and breakfast is available for an additional charge. A shed and hammocks are available for backpackers at under $10 with breakfast. Fishing can be arranged with local people. *Call the community operator in Copper Bank at 04-22950 to leave a message.*

A small excerpt from a communication from the owner:

Blue Heron Cove is my retirement property... it consists of 317 acres of forest with about four acres cleared in lawns and being planted in fruit trees. There is a cement pier for sunning and three swings . . . The breeze flows almost constantly, sometimes with a lot of force. I have kites, badminton, Ping Pong, shuffleboard, croquet, canoes, etc., and dominoes and old jigsaw puzzles for rainy days, plus a lot of entertaining tales about Belize . . . We have lots of the birds that are listed in Peterson's Field Guide, and some that the Belize Audubon Society cannot identify . . . We have a trail through the forest to Cerros ruins . . . I have seven dogs and four cats.

SHIPSTERN NATURE RESERVE

Butterflies are at home in the lowlands and marshes near Sarteneja. The **Shipstern Nature Reserve**, a private operation, breeds and exports the insects for show and sale, on a 22,000-acre tract just southwest of Sarteneja, and seriously interested entomologists will find a visit worthwhile. The area is home to as many as 200 butterfly species, some of which live in the forest canopy, and face extinction when trees are cut.

Sponsored by the International Tropical Conservation Foundation of Switzerland, the Shipstern Reserve includes Belize's only protected seasonally dry forest, as well as mangroves and salt lagoons. The forest is still growing back after being flattened by Hurricane Janet almost 40 years ago. Migrating birds from the north frequent Shipstern Lagoon. Prized visual catches include the black catbird, white-winged dove and Yucatan jay. Tapirs, white-tailed and brocket deer, ocelots and even jaguars wander the savanna.

TOURING THE RESERVE

Best viewing is on sunny days. Trails lead from the reception building through three types of hardwood forest, with trees labeled with Latin and local names. It's easiest to take a day drive out this way from Orange Walk.

Hours are 9 a.m. to noon and 1 to 4 p.m., closed on holidays. Tours cost about $5 per person.

FOUR MILE LAGOON

Just off the road to the Mexican border, is a pleasant spot for a picnic and birding. The lakeside area is privately owned, and informal arrangements may be made for camping. Despite the name, the lagoon is about seven miles from Corozal, and four miles from no particular spot.

SANTA ELENA/MEXICAN BORDER

Santa Elena, *on the Hondo River (Río Hondo),* is the Belizean customs and immigration post at the international bridge, 95 miles (144 kilometers) from Belize City. The town across the bridge, in Mexico, is Subteniente López. Border posts on both sides of the river are open around the clock.

Mexican tourist cards can usually be obtained on the other side of the bridge upon showing credible identification, preferably a passport.

Money changers give a fair rate at the border for American cash, and a slightly less favorable rate for Belizean currency.

Visitors entering Belize at Santa Elena go through formalities in a matter of minutes.

Caution for drivers: Vehicle insurance is available across the road from the immigration building on weekdays, and sometimes on Saturday mornings. Liability insurance is required, and officials will allow you to proceed at other times only with reluctance.

Aside from insurance and immigration and customs posts, there are no facilities of any kind except a couple of duty-free shops, and basic rooms and travel-trailer parking on the Mexican side.

Belizean bus companies provide onward service right into Chetumal, with a stop for immigration formalities.

MEXICO - CHETUMAL

Chetumal is not a Belizean City, but it might as well be. Since the improvement of the Northern Highway, bus connections between Chetumal and Belize have become virtually continuous, much to the dismay of Belizean economic planners, who see their countrymen take regular shopping trips across the border.

With duty-free status, Chetumal functions as the region's schlock shop, where Mexicans and Belizeans flock to pick up Taiwanese toys, Korean electronics, underwear from Singapore and Danish cookies, for much less than what they would cost in Belize or the interior of Mexico, if they were available. Belizeans are attracted as well by the comparatively low prices of basic foods and construction materials.

Chetumal lacks the fleshpots of Cancun. But if you want a break from the beaches and diving and rice and beans of Belize, and better shopping, it's an easy trip. You'll also pass this way if you travel to Belize by way of Cancun.

ORIENTATION

Not all that long ago, Chetumal was a sleepy tropical port at an end of Mexico where few people ever went. Then came designation as a development area, and with it came roads, duty-free status, and modern Mexican concrete-block commercial and residential construction, with reinforcing bars sticking out, never looking completely built or completely decayed.

Despite the peel and mold, most of what you will see in Chetumal has sprouted in the last 20 years. The old Chetumal hasn't been completely crowded out, however. The tropical port atmosphere is preserved in a number of brightly painted clapboard houses. Walk down to the lower end of the main street, and you'll end up at a lovely seaside park shaded by tall, leafy trees, opposite the colonnaded **Palacio de Gobierno**.

As a port, even with limited commerce because it is on a sea arm reached through Belizean waters, Chetumal is more cosmopolitan than many Mexican places. Most of the population is of indigenous descent, but African heritage is evident, and Lebanese and Syrian merchants have contributed to the town's growth, as you'll note from names such as Baroudi on storefronts.

Héroes, which runs south to the Bay of Chetumal, is the main shopping street of Chetumal. Major hotels are located on Héroes, and on intersecting side streets, especially **Obregón**.

ARRIVALS & DEPARTURES
Arriving By Bus
The new bus terminal in Chetumal is three kilometers northwest of the center of town. A taxi will charge well under a dollar for the ride.

Northbound Batty departures from Belize City for Chetumal from Mosul St. at Bagdad (a block from East Collet Canal, *tel. 72025*) are hourly from 4 a.m. to 11 a.m., express bus at 6 a.m. Venus bus departures (tel. 73354) are from noon to 7 p.m. from Magazine Road and Logwood St., another three blocks west of the Batty terminal.

Arriving By Taxi
Taxis from Corozal take groups of persons to downtown Chetumal for only slightly more than what buses charges.

Departing By Bus
A taxi will charge well under a dollar for the ride to the bus terminal. Venus Bus Lines departures for Belize City, passing through Corozal (air connections for Ambergris Caye) and Orange Walk, are every hour from 4 a.m. to 10 a.m..

Batty bus departures are every hour from 11 a.m. to 5 p.m., and at 6:30 p.m. The 2 p.m. bus is an express, taking three hours instead of four to Belize City. Fare is about $4.

Departing By Taxi
Belizean collective taxis bound for Corozal can sometimes be found loading passengers at the corner of Juárez (two blocks west of Héroes, the main street) and Cristóbal Colón.

MEXICAN CONNECTIONS

Buses for Cancun and Merida leave every hour or two during the day, up to about midnight. You'll often find that the next bus out is full, so buy a ticket to reserve your seat as soon as you arrive. Fare to Cancun is about $6.

WHERE TO STAY

Prices are given in U.S. dollars, but are subject to dips and jumps, with the decline of the peso and compensatory inflation. A tax of 15% applies to all hotel and restaurant bills. Most hotels are in noisy areas.

HOTEL LOS COCOS, *Av. Héroes at Chapultepec, tel. 20544. $70 single or double, tax included.*

The best hotel in Chetumal, located downtown, in low-slung buildings on grassy grounds surrounding the swimming pool. Rooms are stuccoed, air-conditioned, with television and bar-refrigerators. An assortment of shops and services includes a travel agency.

HOTEL CONTINENTAL CARIBE, *Héroes 171, tel. 20441. $60 single/$65 double with tax.*

Also on the main street, in a congested area opposite the main market. Surprisingly, the hotel is a pleasant oasis, oriented to an interior courtyard, with a swimming pool in cascading levels. Fine if you don't mind picture windows in your room facing outside passageways. Keep your curtains drawn.

HOTEL PRÍNCIPE, *Av. Héroes 326, tel. 25167. $27 single/$30 double.*

Modern, in a residential area several blocks north of downtown, set back from the street, with sufficient parking. All rooms are air-conditioned, and the value is good if you have a car, though there is nothing of interest nearby.

CARIBE PRINCESS, *Obregón 168, tel. 20900. $22 single/$27 double.*

Fully air conditioned, of recent vintage, a good value if you don't need a pool.

HOTEL REAL AZTECA, *Belice 186. $20 single/$25 double.*

A businessmen's hotel, a block west of the main street, and adjacent to the market. Air-conditioned.

HOTEL JACARANDA, *Obregón 201. $10 single/$15 double.*

Just off the main street, modest, with failing air conditioning, the kind of place that looks run down even when new. Fairly clean, with an economical restaurant.

There are several other hotels in the vicinity of Obregón and Héroes, and others near the old bus station and market, at Héroes and Colón, near the Hotel Continental Caribe, with rates as low as $5 per person.

Since Chetumal is a shopping rather than a resort center, the accommodations can seem lacking for vacationers. But there are attractive places to stay not far away, including:

Nearby Hotels

RANCHO ENCANTADO, *Laguna Bacalar, tel. and fax (52)983-80427. U.S. reservations 800-748-1756. 8 units. $120 double ($96 in low May-October) with breakfast and dinner. Visa, Master Card.*

These are cottages in a private compound on Bacalar Lagoon, about 25 miles north of Chetumal. Each is stuccoed, and finished with hardwoods and Mexican tile, and has a porch with hammock, separate living room, refrigerator and coffeemaker, and American-style bathroom. The bar-dining area is a pavilion with soaring thatched roof, and dinner is served by candlelight. The American owners have created a romantic hideaway removed from resort trappings and pressures, but within reach of archaeological sites, diving and shopping. Boats available, and windsurfing and snorkeling on the lagoon can be arranged. Children are not accommodated.

Full trailer hookups are available in **Calderitas**, *five miles northeast of Chetumal.*

WHERE TO EAT

The restaurant at the **HOTEL CONTINENTAL CARIBE** has perhaps the nicest atmosphere of any eating place in town. You can sit on a terrace overlooking the water cascading down several levels of the pool, surrounded by jungly vegetation, or in an air-conditioned dining room with wicker furniture. Enchiladas and similar Mexican specialties, hamburger platters and club sandwiches go for go for $4-$5, Tampico-style steak and larger main courses $7 and up.

The menu at the **HOTEL LOS COCOS** includes some regional specialties, such as *pibil* (Yucatecan-style chicken) enchiladas at $6 for a plate. Main courses of Veracruz-style fish, steak and shrimp run $8 to $15, and there's a daily special complete meal for $8.

SERGIO'S PIZZA, *at Obregón 182*, is more formal than most restaurants in Chetumal, aside from hotel dining rooms, and is air-conditioned, but service is exasperating, even by local standards. A small pizza or lasagne goes for $4 to $6, and the huge lemonades are refreshing.

The **SUPERMERCADO Y RESTAURANTE ARCADAS**, *at the corner of Héroes and Zaragoza*, has kebabs and sandwiches in modern coffee-shop surroundings for $4 to $6. This could well be your one stop in Chetumal. There's a complete supermarket in back, and they're open 24 hours.

If this is the only part of Mexico you'll be touching, you'll probably want to soak up some local color while you eat. *Walk down the main street toward the sea and turn left at Avenida 22 de Enero, facing the park.* Just in front of you is the **RESTAURANT PÉREZ QUINTAL**, brightly lit and plain as only a Mexican *zócalo* café can be. Sit on the terrace or inside, and watch the scenes of town life unfolding before you: lovers holding hands, vendors hawking lottery tickets, an evening marimba or mariachi concert, a patriotic ceremony. $5 will buy a large plate of enchiladas and a couple of beers to wash them down.

For roast chicken to eat in or to go, head for **POLLO BRUJO**, *on the south side of Obregón, a block west of Héroes.* About $8 for the whole bird.

And there other places for tacos and enchiladas, though fewer than you might expect downtown — squeezed out by duty-free shops.

SEEING THE SIGHTS

With or without kids, if you have some time to spare, visit the **Zoo** (**Zoológico Payo Obispo**), *along Avenida de los Insurgentes on the northern outskirts.* Take the ISSSTE bus from behind the market on Avenida Héroes, or a taxi.

Many a tropical city has a zoo that is more substantial and more fun than what we find in developed countries. This one is a jungle garden in a city of wide streets otherwise bare of needed shade, and many of the trees are labelled. Flamingoes, swans, geese, ducks and hippos are on display, but more interesting is the wildlife native to this part of Mexico and adjacent Belize: spider and howler monkeys, alligators, ocelots, jaguarundis, pacas (gibnut in Belize, or *tepezcuintle*), tapirs, peccaries, agoutis, and assorted snakes. This is one of the few places where you'll see a manatee up close, contentedly munching leaves in its pool. Who would guess that it's an endangered species?

The park is adorned with reproductions of Mayan stelae and an Olmec head, and if you've got kids, you can let 'em loose in the large play areas. Maybe the choo-choo will be back in operation.

If you're driving, load up on groceries at the huge Blanco department-and-food store, adjacent to the bus terminal on Avenida Insurgentes. Juices, beer, and all kinds of packaged foods are far more economical than in Belize.

16. WEST FROM BELIZE CITY

INTRODUCTION

Traveling west from Belize City usually means going almost all the way to the Guatemalan border. It's not that far away — about 80 miles — but there isn't much in between except the still-developing new capital at **Belmopan**.

Out toward the end of the line are the Spanish-speaking towns of **San Ignacio** and **Benque Viejo**, and the major Mayan ruins of **Xunantunich**. A branch road off the Western Highway provides access to **Mountain Pine Ridge**, a beautiful area of pine and hardwood forests in the foothills of the Maya Mountains, much of it held as a government reserve for controlled logging.

The **Western Highway** is wide and smooth-surfaced and fairly straight to past Belmopan, then paved and gently winding to San Ignacio, and onward to the border of Guatemala.

Exiting from Belize City, take Barrack Road to Freetown Road to the Northern Highway for a few miles, until reaching a major intersection lined by banks and the new Santiago Castillo shopping center. Turn left here (as soon as you see the half-sized statues of four men and a woman) and cross over the Belcan Bridge. Go straight for about 5 short blocks, where you will bear right at the traffic circle with the Shell and Texaco gasoline stations. Soon after you'll pass through the cemetery.

If you've been to New Orleans, this one will look familiar, with burial vaults rising a couple of feet from the wet ground. Afterward come tangled swamp and forest, broken here and there by clearings and landfills for commercial concerns, and garbage dumps with rusting car bodies. Nobody shows much concern about hiding the trash, which might be the best way to keep it from getting out of control.

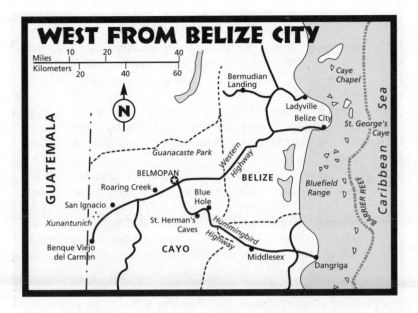

About six miles out, the mangrove swamps give way to low palmetto scrub, alternating with grasslands. The dense pine forests of other times were destroyed over the years by fires and timber cutting. Only scattered trees remain. Sixteen miles inland sprawls **Hattieville**, where refugees from the 1961 hurricane were lodged. The "temporary" settlement looked so good to the displaced that it is now a permanent town with a population of several thousand.

The Western Highway roughly follows the course of the **Sibun River** for about thirty miles. The Sibun, and the Belize River, to the north, were once major trading arteries. Great mahogany logs came floating downriver at the height of the rainy season, when they could clear the rapids, and goods had no other way to move at any other time of year than in shallow-draft boats. Early in the century, before roads were even envisioned, obstructing rock outcrops on the Belize River were dynamited, and Haulover Creek was widened and dredged to allow lumber to pass more easily.

To the west and south, lumpy foothills march into the distance over the flat baseland, toward the Maya Mountains. It's easy to imagine them as cayes, or islands, in the sea that once covered this plain.

CHARTER A HOUSEBOAT

*At **Freetown Sibun**, off the main highway from Hattieville, houseboats are available for charter from River Haven's Canadian hosts. Follow the signs to River Haven's port, three miles from the junction at Mile 16 on the Western Highway.*

These trim, 10- by 15-foot floating cottages accommodate four persons in two separate sleeping areas, and have full bathroom, 12-volt lighting system, CB and AM/FM radio, kitchenette, fresh-water tank, and four-foot-deep rear deck.

*Weigh anchor and set off for your cruise on inland waters where few visitors penetrate. Enter the **Burdon Canal**, constructed long ago to connect Belize City with the south, in response to the plaints of Sibun farmers whose produce boats were swamped at sea, since bypassed by the newer roads running inland. Onward, through the Northern and Southern lagoons, the majestic **Maya Mountains** to the west, howler monkeys and toucans and jabirus in the scrub and forest along the way. Drop anchor at whimsy and jump over the side, or troll for fish as you explore.*

But pay attention, first, at your obligatory captain's training course where you'll learn the ins and outs of being a jungle pilot.

The rate is $600 by the week, or you can get a day cruise with pilot and lunch for $200 for up to eight persons (with stops for fishing, snorkeling, swimming, birding, crocodile-watching) and shorter mid-week and weekend rentals. Housekeeping cabins in a jungle setting are also available at $250 per week or $50 per night, cabanas at $30 per night double, meals at $15 per day, and airport pickup can be arranged. Canoes can be hired as well.

*For information, write to **River Haven**, P. O. Box 78, Belize City, fax 02-32742. Visa, Master Card accepted.*

THE BELIZE ZOO

At mile 30 on the Western Highway is the turnoff; the zoo is just off the road to the north. Hours are 10 a.m. to 4:30 p.m. daily. Admission fee is $5 U.S.

A zoo this is, but one with multiple messages, and like few that you've seen.

Keel-billed toucans and king vultures and crested guans perch on trees draped in wire mesh. Pathways wind through plots of forest inhabited by a jaguar, a tapir ("mountain cow"), a puma and an ocelot, to a bridge over a turtle pond.

As much as possible, the animals reside in re-created habitats. There are black howler monkeys ("baboons"), tayras ("bush dogs"), margays and crocodiles, boa constrictors ("wowlas"), tepezcuintles (gibnuts, or pacas), coatimundis ("quash") and gray fox, great curassows and macaws.

Visitors from far away are welcome, but more than anything else, the zoo aims to heighten the awareness of Belizeans about their heritage of natural treasures. A section of a Mayan frieze shows ancient illustrations of the animals that live here. Part of the visitors' center is reserved for work with schoolchildren. Folksy signs and illustrations tell how the king vulture — King John Crow to Belizeans — prevents disease, and put in a plug for habitat preservation:

Look ya! See our eyes! We are spectacled owls–isn't that a good name for us? Know where we live in Belize? Forests by Rivers. Please remember if you clear your land – kindly leave us some trees! Thanks – Specs and Calvo.

Could *you* ignore their plea?

This menagerie was originally gathered for a wildlife film. Funds were raised to feed and keep the animals when filming ended, and the Belize Zoo is the result. The zoo moved to these new installations after years of fund-raising, consulting, design work, and site preparation, and it represents a singular ecological vision.

Animals clearly come first. While there is plenty of water to be pumped into ponds, the only toilet facilities for humans are outhouses, with no provision to wash hands (despite government warnings about cholera). Re-created habitat affords shelter from sun and from prying visitors, who peer from largely unshaded pathways. At midday, your chances of spying a jaguarundi or peccary or puma or ocelot are rather dim.

Fences and electricity, not substantial bars, are used for containment. Of course, I read to my six-year-old the warning not to touch the electric wire beyond the mesh. And of course you know what he did when his parents' backs were turned.

Myself, I felt more comfortable at the old site next door, which was something like a farm, with animals kept in enclosures of wire mesh and wood, and dirt trails winding among the pens, shaded by native trees, and overgrown here and there with un-tame vegetation. Every visitor was shown around by a guide who talked about the animals as part of his, and Belize's, family. The new zoo can be disturbing and humbling, troubling and thought-provoking. Most certainly, it's out of the ordinary.

Any Belize City-San Ignacio bus will drop you at the turnoff. Take a look at the map before you start off! Trails wind seemingly at random. Take refreshments — none are available on-site.

SHORT ROAD TO SOUTHERN BELIZE!

At mile 30 is the fork for **Democracia**, *and the new, shorter road to* **Dangriga** *and southern Belize.*

GUANACASTE PARK

Guanacaste Park is a protected section of rain forest replete with orchids, bromeliads and ferns filling the air at every level. Named for the huge guanacaste (earpod or tubroose) tree, the park is a small (52-acre) plot between the Western Highway and the confluence of Roaring Creek and the Belize River. There is a network of nature trails, and birding is excellent. Numerous mammals, including kinkajou, gibnut, agouti and deer, can also be seen.

Best of all, Guanacaste Park is readily accessible. The entrance is on the north side of the Western Highway, at the junction with the road to Belmopan. It's a pleasant locale for a picnic if you're traveling through by car or bus.

Although a few muggers once operated in this park, it is no longer particularly dangerous. It still might be a good idea to visit in a small group, or, if you're alone, consult the guards at the entrance.

BELMOPAN - THE CAPITAL CITY

Located about 50 miles from Belize City, **Belmopan** is the young capital of the new nation. Like its larger cousins, Washington, D.C., and Brasilia, the city was planned from scratch.

What a strange place for a Belizean town is Belmopan, arising from the pastures and scrub all around. It sprawls over open green spaces. Block houses are set well apart on curving drives in suburban-style designated residential sections, at least a mile from anything, in a city where many do not have cars. Long sidewalks connect the different sections — a challenge in the hot sun, or the rain. The centerpiece of the capital is a complex of two multi-windowed, low-lying, concrete-and-brick government office blocks that come to an apex at Independence Hill. The buildings are designed in an adapted Mayan style, though they could also be taken for a tropical junior college campus.

The population of Belmopan is only about 4,000, and not growing rapidly toward the projected figure of 40,000. Belmopan is not unattractive, and not unpleasant. It's just, well, bland. Most government workers prefer the tumbledown style of Belize City, and commute daily from the coast. Diplomats, too, can be seen heading back onto the Western Highway after official business or short working days.

Good housing is available, but the city has few shops, eating places, lodging houses and bars, and lacks the pulsating spirit of Belize City. The people will come when the amenities are in place; but the amenities are slow to develop without people.

The impetus for the relocation of the capital was the devastation of Belize City by a hurricane in 1961, for the second time in thirty years. The new capital, sited near the country's geographical center, sheltered from coastal storms and free of swampy surroundings, is intended to spur development of the interior.

The name of the city derives from the first syllable of Belize, and from *Mopan*, one of the original Mayan tribes of the country.

ARRIVALS & DEPARTURES
Arriving By Bus

Buses running between Belize City and San Ignacio stop in Belmopan about every hour throughout the day. Three or four buses coming from Dangriga pass through most mornings, and stop again during the afternoon on the return run.

Departing By Car

Past Belmopan, the Western Highway traverses rolling, lush country-side. Vegetation is exuberant where land remains fallow between shifting use as corn plots and pasture and orange groves. The road is narrower, and the going is slower, with curves, and occasional climbs and descents.

At mile 59 is the turnoff for **Spanish Lookout**, a Mennonite center six miles to the north. Although the community is pretty much mechanized, you'll perhaps see a few horse-drawn carts at the roadside, and straw-haired, straw-hatted kids waiting for their parents to return by bus with supplies from the city.

Three Flags, *at mile 61 on the Western Highway*, is a gas-station-general store-restaurant, and universal stopping point on the way to San Ignacio. Breakfast, sandwiches, and Chinese food are served on a pleasant shaded terrace. If there's anything you need, from children's books to cheese, check the store.

WHERE TO STAY

It's not inconceivable that you will spend a night in Belmopan, even if you don't have business with the government, as the capital is near the crossroads of the Western and Hummingbird highways.

The famous **BULL FROG INN**, *at 25 Half Moon Avenue (P. O. Box 28, 14 rooms $50 single/$62 double plus tax with air conditioning, tel. 08-22111, fax 23155, Visa and Master Card)* is your best bet, with a great bar and good restaurant.

There's also the lackluster but decent **BELMOPAN CONVENTION HOTEL**, *near the bus station and market, and within walking distance of the government center. The rate is $50 single/$60 double. Tel. 08-22130, fax 23066, or write to P. O. Box 237, Belmopan.* This hotel, government-owned (but still on the market), is modeled after a U.S. motel. All 20 rooms are air-conditioned, with large beds or twin beds, carpeting, fan, bureau, wicker sofa, television, snack table, and full bathroom. There's a good-sized pool as well.

The **CIRCLE A LODGE**, *at 37 Half Moon Avenue (P. O. Box 221, tel. 08-22296. 14 rooms, $25 single/$30 double, plus 10% service, Master Card and Visa).* Clean and airy bungalows, but, like the Bull Frog Inn, it's on the other side of town from where the bus pulls in about a mile away. Take a taxi if you have any luggage.

Near Belmopan

BANANA BANK RANCH, *P. O. Box 48, Belmopan, tel. 08-23180, fax 22366. $35 single/$45 double, or $55/$65 with private bath, $65/75 in cabanas, plus 10% service plus tax. Add $28 for three meals. No credit cards.*

Banana Bank is an American-owned beef farm where guests are more than welcome. On-site amusements, activities and attractions include horseback riding on trails through 4000 mostly jungled acres (25 saddle horses are kept), river trips, a Mayan ruin, swimming, canoeing, birding, resident artist (and co-owner), stargazing through an eight-inch telescope, lagoon with crocodile, a pet jaguar, a deer, peccary, kinkajou, coati, and spider monkey (not necessarily in order of interest). The last three are shaded by a huge tree wrapped and felled by a strangler fig. And there are assorted ornamental plantings moved from nearby forest.

A problem with many a Belizean resort is that rooms lack character. At Banana Bank, boy, do they have character. Four cottage (or cabana) units each have two bedrooms, with tile floor, wicker chairs and sofa, curving walls, canopy bed on raised platform (one has a water bed), large screened openings, and high thatched ceiling. Bathrooms in each cottage are shared. Four assorted guest rooms are available in the main ranch house, variously wicker- or wood-panelled, with lace bedspreads, screened loft, bunk or double or single beds, soaring ceilings, verandas, arches, paintings, and furniture that I can only begin to describe as idiosyncratic. Two of these rooms have private baths. Another house on the property, a wooden, domed structure on stilts, resembles a Baha'i temple.

The folks here are positively romantic about their cattle, and barbecued beef, and beef in general, are mainstays on the menu. Beer is stocked, but bring your own booze. For river fishing, bring your own rod.

Banana Bank originated to breed oxen for the logging industry. Access is via a turn eastward from the Valley of Peace road that forks north from the Western Highway near Belmopan — this takes you right onto the ranch — or you can turn in opposite the Belmopan airstrip, proceed a half-mile to the bank of the Belize River, wave and shout, and be taken across in a boat. Pickup in Belmopan can be arranged. The taxi ride costs about $10.

WARRIE HEAD LODGE, *Mile 56.5, Western Highway, Teakettle Village. 8 rooms. $45 single/$55 double, plus 10% service plus tax. Add $27 per person for three meals. Group rates available. Reservations: Belize Global Travel Services, 41 Albert St. (P. O. Box 244), Belize City, tel. 02-77363, fax 75213.*

On the site of an old logging camp, Warrie Head Lodge is a working citrus and vegetable farm. There are, as well, 500 acres of protected riverside forest and bush, with black howler monkeys, coatis, waris, toucans, orchids, and trails to allow you to see it all.

Two of the guest rooms are in the main lodge, with fans, and double beds with good mattresses, sharing a cedar-panelled bathroom. One master bedroom in the same building has a private bath. Five other large, airy rooms in a separate building have private baths, table fans, tile floors, real closets, and good beds. Meals are served on a screened porch on the second floor of the main lodge building. The bar runs on the honor system.

River swimming is available at a shingle beach along an eddy pool on the Belize River, and canoes and horses can be rented. As well, a spring-fed creek with little falls and a rock-lined swimming hole fill up in the dry season, as ground water percolates down from the hills. Excursions are also available to Mountain Pine Ridge and Xunantunich.

Though the lodge property borders the Western Highway, and is easily reached, you should contact the Belize City office if you're interested in staying here — the lodge is often filled with groups, and a cook is sent out only when it is known that there will be guests. The *warrie* (or *wari*) of the name is the white-lipped peccary, which the creek next to the lodge is supposed to resemble.

WHERE TO EAT

The **BULL FROG** is the best eating spot in town. Meals are served in a shady, open pavilion, though the menu is the usual fried chicken, steak, and rice and beans, plus Tandoori fish fillet. Try the limeade ("lime water"). Six dollars and up, $13 for lobster, a few bucks for sandwiches.

If you're out on the market square waiting for a bus, you can step into the **CALADIUM** restaurant. Burgers and sandwiches go for about $3, steak and chicken meals for $6 to $9, and the fans will help cool you off.

SEEING THE SIGHTS

The Department of Archaeology has a vault of ceramics, stone tools, carved monuments and other antiquities, *which may be visited by the public on Mondays, Wednesdays and Fridays from 1:30 to 4:30 p.m, but only with two days' advance notice.* Enter the building that is to your right, as you look up to Independence Hill, and go down to the basement. *Call first (tel. 08-22106) to make an appointment, at least two days in advance.*

The **National Museum** is scheduled to open shortly, with exhibit areas covering history, archaeology, contemporary art.

Back on the Western Highway, *just past the junction for the Hummingbird Highway and Belmopan,* is the village of **Roaring Creek**. Once a major crossroads, Roaring Creek is now overshadowed by the capital. There are about a thousand residents.

PRACTICAL INFORMATION

The **British High Commission** *is housed on Embassy Square (tel. 08-22146).* The **U. S. embassy** has an office here *(tel. 08-22617)*, but most functions are carried out in Belize City.

A few banks have branches near the market, but otherwise, there is not much in the way of commercial activity.

MOUNTAIN PINE RIDGE

At **Georgeville**, a wide spot in the road *66 miles from Belize City*, is the junction for the branch road into the **Mountain Pine Ridge Forest Reserve**, a 300-square-mile area of controlled logging, and also a concentration of spectacular scenery.

Here, on the west slope of the Maya Mountains, numerous short streams rush through granite rocks and tumble over falls, eventually to join the Belize River. The sand and gravel of the broken terrain and the cool air make for a relatively sparse growth of pine and grasses at higher altitudes that recalls scenic landscapes of more northerly latitudes.

In fact, this mountainous landscape is as unrelated to its tropical surroundings as it appears. Geologists believe that the granite ridge gradually drifted westward, and rose up over millions of years along with the limestone seabed that underlies lowland Belize. This "suspect terrane" (in the language of geologists) meets the tropical rocks below along a spectacular fault line, marked by an escarpment, creeks, falls, and breakneck changes in vegetation.

At lower altitudes, and in river valleys, are lush, dense, bromeliad- and orchid-laden hardwood forest. Numerous caves perforate the landscape. The plentiful water and lack of people, the variety of birds and butterflies and foliage, the views down warm canyons and up to the high saw-ridge of the Maya Mountains, make the Mountain Pine Ridge area ideal for leisurely exploration in a sturdy vehicle, on foot, or on horseback.

Make sure your car is full of gas before entering the area, as there are no gas stations once you leave the Western Highway. Another wise idea would be to stock up on cold beverages and light snacks.

There is no entrance fee to enter this reserve.

ARRIVALS & DEPARTURES

There's no public transport into Mountain Pine Ridge. You can arrange a tour, or rent a vehicle for an excursion, in Belize City or, more easily, in San Ignacio. A round trip guided tour through Mountain Pine Ridge by taxi from San Ignacio will cost at least $100, a one way transfer by taxi or van between the two areas will cost about $40.

The dirt roads are relatively good and often graded during the dry season, but there are a few bumpy stretches that will give you and even the sturdiest vehicle a good shaking. There is a security checkpoint manned by friendly forestry service employees who will ask you where you are visiting, and how long you will stay.

Inquire with the gatekeeper about road conditions if it's been raining, especially if you intend to drive onward to Thousand Foot Falls or Caracol. Avoid all of the logging roads in the reserve, as they are poorly marked, and there's a good chance of getting totally lost. From San Ignacio the drive takes about 40 minutes to reach the park's nearest entrance.

IDYLLIC STREAM AT MOUNTAIN PINE RIDGE

WHERE TO STAY

Though Mountain Pine Ridge is a reserve, it contains several private accommodations:

HIDDEN VALLEY INN is on the way to the falls of the same name, *some 17 miles from the Georgeville turnoff*, in the midst of an 18,000-acre private estate. There are 12 accommodations in a series of independant adobe style cottages, each with their own private bathroom, working fireplaces, extremely comfortable bedding, natural spring water running from both hot and cold taps, and plenty of fresh mountain air breezing in through large screened windows.

Upon arrival, you will be personally greeted at the inn's main lodge, a converted family home. Here guests will find the dining room, large living rooms with sofas, game room, library, screened-in sun porch, and the bar. Besides the complimentary morning coffee (grown right here on the premises) and home-style breakfast, wonderful lunches and dinners are also available. Special meals requests are no problem here.

The Hidden Valley Inn offers over 90 miles of groomed walking trails to various waterfalls and vistas (perfect for for avid hikers and birders), guided excursions to remote parts of Mountain Pine Ridge and the ancient Mayan cities of Caracol and Tikal, horseback riding, and river trips by canoe.

Rates at Hidden Valley Inn are $77.50 single/$105 double with breakfast, plus 10% service and tax, and meal plans are available. Contact the Inn at P. O. Box 170, Belmopan, tel. (08) 23320, fax (08) 23334, or in the U.S. at C.W. Maryland & Co., 1220 E. Park Ave., Tallahassee, FL 32301, tel. 800-334-7942 or 904-222-2333, fax 904-222-1992.

BLANCANEAUX LODGE *(Central Farm P.O. Box B, Cayo)* is now the lodge of choice for rich and famous visitors to Mountain Pine Ridge. This deluxe riverside cottage and villa resort, owned by movie director Francis Ford Coppola, provides a perfect setting for a romantic escape.

The 50 acres of beautifully groomed grounds surround 7 one-bedroom private cottages, and 5 two bedroom/two bathroom luxury villas. All of these outstanding thatched roof units have semi-enclosed outdoor patios with memorable views out onto the river, magnificently designed private bathrooms, furnishings and folk art from all over Central America, and plenty of charm. The larger units also contain modern kitchenettes. All sorts of tours and excursions can be enjoyed while staying here, and the recent addition of a private 9 passenger airplane will make it possible to enjoy a day trip to the Cayes and return here in time for dinner.

The property also boasts a refreshing clear water river (sight of a concealed hydroelectric plant) with great natural swimming pools. The inn's main lodge has two less impressive double rooms with a shared bathroom, as well as a fine bar featuring specialty drinks and wines from the owner's California vineyards, an outstanding Italian restaurant with the best wood burning oven pizzas and homemade pastas, and plenty of ambiance. Blancaneaux is just off the main road through Mountain Pine Ridge, some 15 miles from the Georgeville turnoff.

Rates per night including breakfast are $65 single/$90 double in the lodge rooms, $110 single/$145 double in the cottages, and $225 single/$275 double in the luxury villas. Additional persons in the same room cost $25 more each. Call them at (092) 3878 or send a fax to (092) 3919 for bookings and details.

PINE RIDGE LODGE *is about five miles into the reserve along the main access road,* on rolling, sandy-grassy grounds dotted with pines and broken by frothing streams. *Rates are from about $35 double, more in river-view units,* and will probably rise once the six cabins are more finished. These are well spread among the pines, and for now, they only have beds, louvers, screens, and bare cement bathrooms. Lighting is by kerosene lamps and candles. There are river pools for swimming, and an 85-foot waterfall on the property.

Meals are served to guests and drop-ins on a thatch-roofed terrace for $4 to $6. As the sign says, this is the last place to stop for a cold beer, and it also strikes me as a mountain biker's heaven. Things are laid-back. Guided trips into the nooks and crannies of the reserve are available.

Call 092-3310 for a radio patch to the lodge. Or write to: P.O. Box 2079, Belize City, or 2968 Somerton Rd., Cleveland Heights, OH 44118, tel. 216-781-8288 or 932-7342.

Mountain Equestrian Trails, *located three-quarters of a mile off the main road into Mountain Pine Ridge, at mile 8, just before the junction for the San Antonio-Cristo Rey road (Central Farm P.O., Cayo), tel. (092)-3310 or fax (082)-3361),* rents 4 basic 1-bedroom cabana suites, each with private bathroom, stucco interiors, mesquito netting, and no electricity. Visitors can also stay in one of 8 fully equipped Safari style tents set way back in the bush.

The four cabana units cost $75 to $100 double with breakfast, while the tents will set you back $90 to $110 for two people including all meals.

SEEING THE RESERVE
Thousand Foot Falls

The main route leads south from the Western Highway, rising from tropical hilly jungle to sandy pine barrens. Past the entrance checkpoint, the main road traverses an area of pines standing up in red dirt — pure Georgia. Follow the Baldy Beacon road westward. Out this way are the heights known as Baldy Beacon and Baldy Sibun, with some of the oldest rocks and soils known — anywhere!.

A rock-strewn spur leads back to the north, braking suddenly at the edge of a gaping canyon.

Steps lead partway down the escarpment, from which you can look across to the **Hidden Valley** (or **Thousand Foot**) **Falls**, a narrow chute of water spilling a thousand feet over rock. Below, vegetation changes over several thousand feet from pine to leafy jungle. If you had an impression of Belize as all lowlands, you will be suddenly and totally undeceived. The falls are 20 miles into the reserve.

Nature's Water Park

The main road of the reserve continues southward from the Baldy Beacon junction, crossing the **Río On** 18 miles from the Western Highway. Here the river splashes down over huge boulders and chutes and dashes through granite water slides, to and through and around pools ranging from personal solar-heated jacuzzis to Olympic-sized.

Park at the picnic area, or farther down, and scamper out over the rocks for a delightful swim in lukewarm waters, but take care. Nature's water park comes without lifeguards or first-aid stations, and accidental careens and loose footing result in bruised arms and bashed heads.

Río Frío Cave

Five miles beyond, past the government camp at Augustine, signs point the way to several caves. The largest, the **Río Frío Cave**, *is at the end of the side road, about a mile from the camp*, after a descent through lower rainforest. Trees at the parking area are handily labelled — rubber trees, mahogany, breadnut, and many other species. Walk into the forest, to the huge, arched, 65-foot-high cave mouth, and beyond.

There's no need for a flashlight here — plenty of light enters. Observe the bared strata of rock, and stalactites. There are no stalagmites, but rather, a boulder-strewn riverbed with sandy beaches where the Río Frío flows through. Continue over a rock formation that looks like rice terraces, and another that looks like a waterfall, and you'll come through to daylight again.

Two smaller caves are located on either side of the road to the Río Frío Cave.

There are many other caves in Mountain Pine Ridge, some of them spectacular. Contact a travel agency in Belize City or one of the hotels in San Ignacio to engage a guide for further exploration.

In the area of Mountain Pine Ridge are several private reserves. **Slate Creek Preserve**, *near the northern edge*, encompasses lands voluntarily protected against clearing by private landowners. The area is habitat for many resident and migratory species. Mountain Equestrian Trails (see below) operates riding trips through the area. **Society Hall Nature Reserve** is closed to the public, and used for research purposes.

CAMPING

Camping is available at the **Douglas D'Silva Forest Station** (*Augustine Village*), the administrative center about ten miles to the south of the main reserve entry. Ask permission of the forestry officer there.

HORSEBACK RIDING

Horseback trips into **Mountain Pine Ridge** are offered by *Mountain Equestrian Trails (3/4 mile off the main road into Mountain Pine Ridge, at mile 8)*. Half, full, and customized multiple day trips take visitors to many exotic sights in the area including waterfalls and canyons that just can't be seen from the roads.

Cost is $60 to $80 per person, with an excellent picnic lunch included. Call them at (092) 3310 for details. Ask about their unusual 8-day Chiclero Trail Rainforest Workshop packages.

SPELUNKING

No other cave in the area besides Rio Frio should be entered without the assistance of reputable local guides. Ask your lodge for details. Mountain Equestrian Trails also operates spelunking excursions, some by boat and raft to caves with Mayan remains.

SAN ANTONIO

An alternative way into Mountain Pine Ridge, or out, is the road from San Ignacio through the villages of **Cristo Rey** and **San Antonio**, joining the main road just north of the reserve entrance. San Antonio is a Mopan Maya village, picturesque, with many thatch-roofed houses.

Three miles to the east of San Antonio is the **Pacbitun** archaeological site, where recent excavations have unearthed a number of stelae and Mayan musical instruments. Pacbitun consists of several temples atop pyramidal bases, the largest being 50 feet tall.

A roadside handicraft store, the self-styled **Tanah Museum**, is operated near San Antonio (*Ta Nah* in the Mopan language) by the Garcías, Mayan sisters who specialize in carving reproductions of ancient Mayan glyphs in slate. Roadside stalls and shops are a common sight in neighboring Guatemala, but unique in Belize, so all organized trips make a stop here. The building is an unpretentious structure in traditional Mopan style, of limestone and thatch. An admission fee is charged. Woodcarving is also developing as a local art, with the encouragement of visitors.

San Antonio is also the home village of famed healer Eligio Pantí, and it is here that Don Eligio receives patients who come from all over Belize for herbal cures.

CARACOL

South of Mountain Pine Ridge, in the Chiquibul Forest, is the **Caracol** archaeological site, a once-densely settled area of ruins and roadbeds that flourished in the Classic Mayan era. One of the pyramids, called *Canaa*, or *Sky Place*, rises 139 feet (42 meters) above the plaza floor, two meters higher than the largest structure at Xunantunich. The ruins cover more than 30 square miles.

The siting of Caracol in a part of the Maya Mountains devoid of reliable water supply is a mystery. Specialized plants might have been harvested there, for trade to other Mayan areas. In any case, Mayan engineering ingenuity overcame natural limitations, with the design and construction of reservoirs and agricultural terraces.

Caracol was settled around 300 B.C., and occupied well into the Late Classic period of Mayan culture. Carved deities date mostly from around 600 A.D., when other Mayan sites were declining. The glyphs on one of the structures at Caracol record a war with Tikal, the major Mayan site 60 miles to the northwest, in present-day Guatemala. The wars might have yielded slaves or other profits, for Caracol went through an active construction period soon after, while Tikal itself experienced a period of stagnation. The population of Caracol and its surrounding city-state might have been as high as that of all modern Belize.

Among unusual features at Caracol is the widespread use of tombs for group burials, possibly of nobles of lower rank, and not only for rulers.

Excavations are being carried out by archaeologists from the University of Central Florida, led by Arlen and Diane Chase.

ARRIVALS & DEPARTURES

By Tour

Caracol is once again open to visitors after several years off-limits to the public. All the lodges in the Cayo district and some of the operators in San Ignacio arrange one-day tours, in cooperation with the archaeologists on the site, and in come cases in combination with sights in Mountain Pine Ridge.

Expect a long day's round trip.

EXCURSIONS

The Chiquibul

The **Chiquibul** cave system that extends to the west into Guatemala underlies much of the Maya Mountains, and could be the largest system of caverns in the Western Hemisphere. Over 100 miles of passageways have been surveyed, some with widths of over 100 yards. The Belize Chamber in the Chiquibul system is one of the five largest natural caverns in the world. Recent explorations have yielded fossils of extinct species of insects and crustaceans previously unknown.

The caves are not yet open to visitors, and permission to enter must be obtained from the Department of Archaeology in Belmopan. The best time to explore is in the dry season — the underground rivers that helped create the caves can flood them during wet periods.

SAN IGNACIO (CAYO)

San Ignacio, also known as **Cayo**, or **El Cayo de San Ignacio**, is the major town in western Belize. *Located about 72 miles from the coast*, it was once a loading point for the chicle and mahogany that came out of the surrounding forests. Both industries have now declined, and San Ignacio has become a bustling agricultural center, serving the cattle, citrus and peanut farms of the area.

ORIENTATION

With good accommodations, ruins and Mayan villages nearby, caves to the south in the Maya Mountains, and the clear, clean waters of the Macal River available for recreation, San Ignacio is a lovely place in which to spend a few days, comfortable in the midst of the tropical forest, and far away from the cares of anywhere.

The **Hawkesworth Bridge**, which connects San Ignacio with the village of Santa Elena on the east bank of the Macal River, is the only suspension bridge in the country, a substantial and unexpected engineering accomplishment in a garden setting. It is the Brooklyn Bridge of Belize, illustrated on, among other places, milk cartons.

Like many a town built on hills, San Ignacio has a certain amount of physical charm, arising in part from changing vistas available from different points, of residential neighborhoods, of the river flowing into the distance, of the hillsides all around carpeted in tropical forest.

San Ignacio has the air of an outpost of the British Empire, of the sort depicted by E. M. Forster, Paul Scott and Eric Blair, remote yet cosmopolitan. British Forces roll through the streets every now and then, along with an occasional Gurkha unit. Members of the Belize Defence Force jog double time. (Guatemala, and intermittent claims to Belize, is not far off). Horse-drawn carts of Mennonites pass by (the clapboard architecture and many second-story porches make a perfect backdrop), as do huge four-wheel-drive pickup trucks of American missionaries. And don't let me fail to mention the Lebanese, the Chinese, the Sri Lankan, the South African, and the Swede who make this their home.

In San Ignacio, the natives do not appear to be at the bottom of the pile. *Ev'rybody happy in Belize, mon.*

In the days of the mahogany and chicle trade, San Ignacio was a fairly busy port. Craft called pit-pans plied the river. The trip to Belize City took ten days. The chicle industry has died, killed by substitutes in chewing gum, and timber and people move on trucks and buses.

Nowadays, the riverside below the bridge is a gathering spot of a different sort. People wash trucks, and themselves, and clothes, and buses, and horses, and picnic along the banks. If you have some spare moments, wander down, past where horses graze near the town center, and take in the scene. It makes harried feelings seem impossible. You can join in, or, for more bucolic surroundings, walk a mile-and-a-quarter north to Branch Mouth, at the confluence of the Mopan and Macal rivers, a popular, grassy-banked bathing spot.

Most of the townspeople of San Ignacio are Mestizos and Mayan; and Spanish, with Guatemalan overtones, is the main language. But there are also storekeepers of Lebanese descent, and assorted settlers from far and wide who have found here just the right combination of pace, economic opportunity, climate, adventure, and rolling, unspoiled landscapes. San Ignacio sits in a valley, and the surrounding rolling hills, furry with vegetation, misty after a rain, are always visible from the declivities of its streets.

Across from San Ignacio is **Santa Elena**. The sister towns are connected by the substantial Hawkesworth suspension bridge, spanning the **Macal River**, a tributary of the Belize River. Together, the two towns have about 7000 inhabitants.

Cayo has the best hotels in western Belize, which makes it a good base for seeing the Mountain Pine Ridge area, the major Mayan center of Xunantunich, and smaller ruins. River trips, jungle walks, and an easy-going air will tempt the visitor to stay on. Accommodations are available both in town, and in unusual cottage resorts in the surrounding country-side.

ARRIVALS & DEPARTURES

Arriving By Bus

Batty Buses leave Belize City (Mosul St. at Bagdad, a block from East Collet Canal, *tel. 72025*) for San Ignacio at 6, 6:30, 7:30, 8, 9 and 10:15 a.m. The schedule varies slightly on Sunday. Most of these buses continue right through to the Guatemalan border.

Novelo buses leave Belize City (*19 West Collet Canal, tel. 77372*) about every hour from 11 a.m. to 7 p.m., and at 9 p.m., passing through San Ignacio about two-and-a-half hours later and continuing to Benque Viejo. Sunday departures are from noon to 5 p.m. only. There are additional Shaw buses running between Belmopan and San Ignacio.

A new service run by **Discovery Expeditions** in Belize City (*tel. 02-30748*) operares a daily door to door shuttle van (with air conditioning!) from Belize City to San Ignacio for $29 each way. Call for details.

Arriving By Air

An improved civilian airstrip off the Western Highway some 6 miles east of San Ignacio now features flights daily from Belize City. Check with **Maya Airways** for exact scheduling and pricing, but at press time the fare is $45 each way. Make sure to notify your lodge in advance to arrange a transfer from the airport.

Arriving By Taxi

Taxi trips (including waiting time, prices courtesy of the local taxi cartel) to the Guatemalan border cost about $15; to Xunantunich, $25; to Belmopan, $30; to Belize City, $75; to the airport, $88; to the Belize Zoo, $50.

To Flores, Guatemala, the fare is $150, and to Tikal, $200, or $250 if you stay the night. You can cut the price to Guatemala by more than half if you take a Belizean taxi to the border and pick up a Guatemalan taxi in Melchor de Mencos. You just have to hope that a Guatemalan taxi is available when you show up. See the next chapter for more details.

Departing By Bus

Batty and Novelo buses for Benque Viejo pass through San Ignacio about every hour during the day, less frequently on Sunday. Batty departures from San Ignacio for Belize City are hourly from noon to 5 p.m. (the trip will cost $3 each way and will take 2 1/2 hours).

In the morning, catch a bus passing through from Benque Viejo. The first few stop at the town circle, near the police station and the bridge. Others pull into the parking area off Burns Avenue in the center of town. There are additional Shaw buses running between Belmopan and San Ignacio.

WHERE TO STAY

HOTEL SAN IGNACIO, *18 Buena Vista Road (P. O. Box 33), tel. 092-2034, fax 2134. 25 rooms. $25-$65 single/$30-$75 double, no service charge. Add $28 for three meals. Visa, Master Card, American Express.*

The best in-town hotel, located uphill about a half-mile from the Hawkesworth Bridge. On the outside, the hotel looks like a farm building, but inside it's rather pleasant, basically a concrete structure softened with extensive hardwood detailing, planters, a pool, deck with white-painted wrought-iron furniture, and lovely terraces overlooking the Macal River, the town of San Ignacio, the misty plain to the east, and the surrounding mountains.

All rooms have ceiling fans, balconies, and private bath; higher rates are with air conditioning and television. The dining room is breezy and pleasant, with a menu offering a range from rice and beans to kebabs and lobster, for $4 to $10 a la carte. The bar has Formica booths with Formica tables, vinyl seats, and tropical wood panelling and screens — a typically Belizean combination of the best native materials and imported accretions. Other facilities include a travel service, gift shop, laundry service, and meeting facilities.

Just up the road from the San Ignacio is the **HOTEL PIACHE** *(tel. 092-2109)*. The owners treat you as family, and the grounds are lovely and gardened, with many plant species labelled for your edification. The 17 rooms are basic concrete units, on the small side. With shared bath, the rate is $20 single/$27 double, an air-conditioned unit costs more. Rates may be lower out of season. Meals are provided on request at the adjacent thatched, sapling-sided bar, furnished with the oddest collection of castoff furniture.

Back down in the center of San Ignacio are three economy hotels on Burns Avenue, the main street: the **CENTRAL** *(No. 24)*, the **BUDGET** *(No. 22)*, and the **JAGUAR** *(No. 19)*. There are about 60 rooms between them, all quite simple. Rates are about $8 or less single, $12 double sharing bath. The Budget has some doubles with private bath at about $15 double. Rooms at the Central are light and airy and larger than those of its neighbors, and the place is generally more pleasant.

A step above these is the **VENUS HOTEL** *(tel. 092-2186)*, also on Burns Avenue, with 25 rooms on the second and third floors above the commercial level. Everything is brand-new and clean, and the rooms have fans and even wallpaper, though many are situated along inside corridors, with no outside windows. Take a look at your room first, especially in hot weather. The rate is about $20 single/$25 double with private bath, or $12 single/$15 double sharing bath.

The **NEW BELMORAL**, *17 Burns Avenue, tel. 92-2024*, has been totally renovated, and offers rooms with television, fan, private bath and other modern conveniences for $25 single/$30 double, which includes continental breakfast. Some of the rooms are quite large and pleasant. Master Card and Visa are accepted.

The **PLAZA HOTEL**, *4A Burns Ave., tel. 092-3332*, has 12 new concrete rooms above a furniture store at $20 single/$30 double with ceiling fans, $10 more with air conditioning, Master Card accepted.

Bargain Lodgings

If these hotels are full, adequate accommodations are available at the **HI-ET**, *a block to the west, at West and Waight streets*. At $6 or so for a double, it's a Belizean budget bargain. The **HOTEL SAN JUAN** also has cheap rooms. And if absolutely everything in San Ignacio is full, cross the river to **MIKE'S GRAND HOTEL** *in Santa Elena*, where you can have a roof over your head for about $5 per person; or inquire at the Fruit-aplenty store for rooms.

Cottage Country

In the hills around San Ignacio, and westward toward Benque Viejo, are half a dozen hotels of individual cottage units. Each is not just a lodging place, but a resort in itself, with its own special characteristics and advantages. Activities for guests might include horseback riding, river swimming, visits to archaeological sites, birding, and canoe trips.

Take into account your own interests and tastes and budget when selecting one of these hotels: unless you have your own vehicle, you'll usually be relying on the hotel exclusively for meals, tours, amusements, and relaxation. These can be pricier than what's available right in town, and round-trip taxi fare from San Ignacio can add as much as $60. Check whether you're required to take your meals at the lodge, and verify any service charges.

These are **jungle lodges** (or "locales for soft adventure," as one proprietor puts it), and though they can be quite comfortable and even elegant on their own terms, and are not inexpensive, they usually lack satellite television, ice machines, superb beds, built-in closets, fluffy towels, and similar Holiday-Inn-style amenities. Food choices are limited. Screening may be inadequate, and you might share your accommodations with families of bugs until they are shooed out. Few establishments have air conditioning, and the summer months can be sweltering. And note that selected urban cares are inescapable even in the jungle. Do not leave anything of value in your room or even in the hotel safe, unless only *you* have the key.

If you arrive in San Ignacio without a reservation, call first to inquire about vacancies (from the telephone company office or Eva's Bar).

DU PLOOY'S enchanting lodge is located *about 4 miles along a dirt road from a well marked junction some 6 miles west of San Ingnacio (follow the signs!)*, and is set in hills sloping down to the Macal River.

Accommodations in the stuccoed stone buildings of the main lodge are nine large jungle view rooms, two sharing bathroom facilities. All showers are tiled, and all guestrooms have hardwood vanities, good mattresses (not the case in every lodge in the area, sorry to say), and screened porch. The property has also constructed 3 self standing private bungalows that also feature strong ceiling fans, mini-refridgerators, comfortble funishings, king side beds, additional queen size sofa beds, and hammocks on the porches. There is also a separate, six bedroom, 2 bathroom, pink guesthouse where the facilities are less epensive, but still rather impressive. The house is available for private groups, but can also be booked by the room.

Rock-paved walks lead to the common facilities. Meals are taken in a screened dining pavilion with a view to the limestone cliff tangled with vegetation on the opposite shore. For an afternoon and evening of relaxing with a drink in your hands, to the accompaniment of bird songs, continue to the tranquil bar, cantilevered from the cliff edge and 30 feet above the river and anything solid. Early each morning the bar is the sight of Ken du Plooy's infamous pre-breakfast birding activities.

Guests receive the attention of owners Ken and Judy du Plooy (from Zimbabwe and the United States, respectively). Activities include hiking, swimming at a sandy bank (one of the few such spots in western Belize), tubing and canoeing on the river, tours to Tikal and other locations such as Mountain Pine Ridge and Xunantunich, horseback rides, and optional overnight jungle trips.

If you stay here, walk through the gardens to see the pineapple, limes, papaya, hot peppers, bananas, coconuts, tamarind, mangoes, oranges, watermelons, etc., before they are removed from their natural habitat and brought to the table. Or wander down to the tangled banks of the river, watch the leaves roll by, and listen to the music of the forest.

Rates here start at $24 for a single/$32 for a double room during low season in the guesthouse, and can reach as much as $105 for a single/$140 for a double private bungalow. Credit cards accepted. Telephone # (092)-3101, Fax # (092) 3301. Guests can use the lodge's shuttle service (from San Ignacio at 9 a.m. and 4 p.m., $3 per ride, or free with three-night stay), or take a taxi from San Ignacio for $20; or, with advance notice, they can be fetched in a boat.

CHAA CREEK COTTAGES are 16 white units with Mayan-style roofs, furnished with Guatemalan blankets and weavings, but without electricity. Common facilities include a round dining pavilion with high ceiling, candlelit in the evening, and semicircular bar and lounge opening onto a deck with river view. *The rate is under $200 double with meals. Located four kilometers along a rough road from a junction eight miles west of San Ignacio. Book through travel agents, or call 2037 in San Ignacio.*

Also eight miles out of San Ignacio is the turnoff for Nabitunich (Stone House) on San Lorenzo Farm, just a half mile to the north of the Western Highway over a good gravel road. The eight simple cottages, each different, are on a slope below the farmhouse where an English-Belizean couple, Rudy and Margaret Juan, live with their seven children. Rooms are of varying sizes, some larger than others, not elegant, but neat, with basic furnishings, and naturally cool. The nicest is a sort of A-frame.

The view from the farm is commanding. Down through the meadow, across the river and up the hill are the Xunantunich ruins. You can walk to the site, fording a river on the way, or just gaze at the spectacular sunset behind them. Meals are copious, served in a lovely white dining room with great arched openings and a high thatched roof, and the menu changes every day.

There are no packaged tours, library or bar here, but you are not without diversions. Horseback rides can be arranged on trails that run through parts of the property that have been left otherwise untouched (cost is about $20 for the day), and there is a lovely swimming area down along the river. You can take off in a boat or canoe, or walk through the pasture and forest, pick allspice or a lime, go birding, or espy bromeliads and orchids overhead. Fishing for catfish can also be arranged without much ado.

The setting is genuinely homey, and the rates at Nabitunich are lower than at the other cottages: *about $65 single/$75 double with three meals, $25/$35 for room only, tax and 10% service additional. Extra beds are available at $10. Telephone 093-2309 to reach the farm.*

If you're not carrying too much luggage, you can take a Benque Viejo bus to the turnoff, and walk in.

The **WINDY HILL COTTAGES** *are located about a mile and a half west of San Ignacio. Call (092) 2017 or fax (092) 3080 for reservations and details. Rates are $70 per double cottage, plus tax and service.*

Here you can find a series of 25 independant cottages with private bathrooms, mini-bars, ceiling fans, and peaceful verandahs. Facilities here include a dining room serving 3 optional meals daily, an outdoor pool, nature trails, rental boats and canoes, horseback rides, and plenty of excursions.

MAYA MOUNTAIN LODGE, *on the road south from Cayo toward the villages of Cristo Rey and San Antonio, is a farm and mini-forest preserve, as well as a hotel. Rates are $50 to $70 double, plus 15% service, and tax. There are also two shared-bath rooms at $40 double, making a total of 14 units. Children under 12 stay for free. To reserve at Maya Mountain Lodge, phone 092-2164 (fax 2029) in Belize, or 800-344-MAYA in the United States. The mailing address is Box 46, San Ignacio.*

Cottages are set on a breezy hillside among trees laden with orchids (including the black orchid, the national flower). Each has a private bath, and hammock outside the front door, and many have a bunk bed as well as queen-sized bed. Inside, under the high thatched roof, furnishings and finishings are: screening around the eaves, linoleum floor covering, pedestal fan, hardwood doors, and pebbly, rough stuccoed walls. Creature comforts here include full-time hot water and electricity. The view from most cottages is a slope of semi-cleared jungle. In the morning, there are bird and insect calls. Meals are served family-style on a covered patio, approached at night along a lantern-lit walkway. The menu is fixed, but changes daily, even the breakfast menu. Meals range from $7 for breakfast to $12 for dinner, and superb box lunches are available for day outings, including fruit beverages in a cooler. Mixers and ice are available if you bring your own liquor (none is served at the lodge).

The lodge also has its own canoes, horses for trail rides, mountain bikes, and vans for land tours, and a swimming spot along the river. Trips are operated to Mountain Pine Ridge, the Pantí Trail by boat, Xunantunich and Tikal (see below). Package tours using the lodge as a base are available.

EK' TUN, one of Belize's most enchanting remote hideaway properties, *is situated across the Macal river off the same dirt road that passes by du Plooy's. Rates are $110 single/$140 double. The $32 per person meal plan is pretty much mandatory here, and consists of home made breakfasts, lunches, and dinners prepared by the owners. Reservations can be made by calling their US offices at tel. and fax # (303) 442-6150 in Boulder, Colorado.*

Ek'tun boasts a truly unforgettable setting on 200 acres of stunning jungle lands and lush gardens just off the northern boundry of Mountain Pine Ridge. Here you can find two duplex thatched roof independent cottages that both have an upper and lower floor bedroom, private bathrooms with stone floors, a limited electrical supply, and plenty of books. Even if you just sit down and relax on the grounds, you can't help but marvel at the awesome variety of rare birds and wildlife species that live here. A nice and cool natural spring cascades down into a natural swimming hole just a minute's walk from the cottages. The friendly owners, Ken & Phyllis, will arrange activities on their premises including guided cave tours, hikes to Mayan ceremonial caves, and light bushwhacking.

Full day trips to Xunantunich, Cahal Pech, and Mountain Pine Ridge are also offered. Since a car or jeep will not be of use to you here, ask the reservations offices to set up transfers for you in and out of either San Ignacio or Belize city. This is a great place to stay if you want to be away from it all, and are somewhat independent.

Nearby is **CAESAR'S BLACK ROCK**, *off the same road.* The last 20 minutes are by trail to a hillside clearing above a waterfall. The energy supply is plentiful: solar electricity, solar hot water, and solar pumps. Local adventures include river tubing and caving. There are six double-occupancy tents (at a daily rate of about $25 double), and a thatched pavilion eating area ($3 to $6 for meals). That's a lot of money for hiking and camping, so speak to returnees before you go out. *For information, contact Caesar Sherrard, Box 48, San Ignacio, tel. 092-2341.*

About a mile and a half north of San Ignacio, at Branch Mouth, the confluence of the Mopan and Macal rivers, is **LAS CASITAS RESORT**. This is an idyllic spot, with three high-peaked cottages on a hilltop, and grounds nicely finished with lawns and bougainvillea and hedges and concrete steps. In fact, it's suited to a higher class of accommodation than what you get: bare cubicles with cement floors. The rate is about $25 double, and meals are available for about $5 each. For just a few dollars, you can arrange to sleep in the tri-level hammock tower, or to camp out. Take the local commuter canoe (fare 50¢ Belizean) from the end of the road, along with locals, who walk through the grounds at all hours to the adjacent village. *Telephone 092-2506, fax 2475 to leave a message.*

Out on the Bullet Tree Falls road, about three miles from San Ignacio and encircled by a loop of river, is **PARROT'S NEST**. *For reservations call 092-3702, or write to them c/o General Delivery, San Ignacio, to hold your place.*

This small proprety has four thatch-roofed units going for $20 double, and the name tells all: they're tree houses with some stilts for added support, and though they ain't for the birds, they get you right up there and into nature. Swim in the river, hire horses, hang out.

COSMOS CAMPGROUND, *a half-mile north of San Ignacio along the road to Branch Mouth (look for the yellow sign),* will provide a tent, hammock space, showers, flush toilets, laundry service and cooking facilities. *Charges start at about $3 per person per night.*

MIDA'S RESORT, *also on the Branch Mouth road (tel. and fax 3172),* consists of four round thatched cottages alongside the Macal River. The owners are a British-Belizean couple, and the rate is $38 single/$44 double, slightly less with shared bath. *Campers can find space at $5 per person, and meals are served.*

THE GROVE RESORT, *in the flatter country off the Western Highway east of San Ignacio*, takes an estate-style approach to lodging, with extra creature comforts. There are six two-story pink concrete villas, with balconies, set among neat lawns dotted with plants on the edge of a citrus farm. The two suites in each villa are air-conditioned, and attractively furnished with imported wicker pieces, orthopedic beds, and small refrigerators.

A large second-floor bar-restaurant-clubhouse overlooks a good-sized pool (there is also creek swimming), and there is another pavilion bar at pool level. The kitchen equipment is serious, and even includes a pizza oven. Scuba lessons are available, and guests may use exercise equipment, rent mountain bikes, and ride horses.

The rate is $100 single/$125 double plus tax, and an additional $35 per person for three meals. More modest rooms at a lower price will eventually be added. To reserve, write to P. O. Box 1, San Ignacio, or call or fax 092-2421.

If you really want to go back to nature, head for **RANCHO LOS AMIGOS**, *a bit over a mile out of San José Succotz, just east of Benque Viejo. Turn into town from the western highway, go past the soccer field, then left at the sign. As of recently, you can even make it in by car. The rate is about $15 per person per day, less for tent space, which includes breakfast and dinner. Dial 093-2483 to let them know that you're on your way.*

Here you will find Ed and Virginia Jenkins and family, formerly of the States, who have selectively and respectfully carved a spread from 88 acres of jungle. Guest units at Rancho Los Amigos are traditional Mayan cottages, built almost entirely from materials gathered on-site: lime plastered on a framework of sticks, with a thatched roof. But do not think for a minute that "traditional" means uncomfortable. The four rooms are cool and attractive, decorated with plants and floral curtains and brushy crafts from Punta Gorda. Much of the food is local produce as well, and water comes from springs.

Meals may include fish or range beef, never pork or lard, or you can specify vegetarian. The kitchen is open-sided, and food is cooked both over an open fire and in a traditional oven. The sweetener is honey produced on-site. Trails run though the forest, where you can observe the birds and animals, and, with some advice, pick herbs. There are also some caves within hiking distance.

This is a jungle retreat. You use pit toilets (to keep the springs uncontaminated), and showers are outdoors. And yet, everything is so well thought out, and flows so naturally from the resources available, that there is little sense of roughing it.

Ed, by the way, is an acupuncturist, and claims that Virginia is the best cook in Belize.

More Countryside Lodging

Other countryside lodging/camping/roughing-it spots have been mushrooming around Cayo:

CHECHEM HA, ten miles from Benque Viejo on a poor road, is near caves, and offers hiking trips from its cottages. Call on radio frequency 905.5 from Eva's.

CRYSTAL PARADISE, *a couple of miles up the Cristo Rey road on the way to Mountain Pine Ridge. The rate is about $15 per person, or $40 double with private bath. Horseback riding and river trips are available. Call on radio frequency 147075.* This is a farm with guest rooms, operated by a Mayan family, and guests have expressed their approval.

WHERE TO EAT

EVA'S BAR, *at street level below the Hotel Imperial on Burns Avenue*, serves breakfasts, and meals of steaks, and chicken and rice and beans, sometimes tamales and mole and chicken curry. A meal costs $4 or less, and is not at all bad.

But you don't come to Eva's just for the food and the Belikin. Eva's is the hub of the Greater Cayo jungle telegraph. This is where visitors get together to plan excursions to Mountain Pine Ridge and elsewhere, where the local taxi driver can tell you about growing up in the bush and treating illness with native plants, where the Mennonite whose faith is not firm slouches over a rum and coke, where the fellow who's been here a few days longer than you will give you the total lowdown. The expatriate owner scurries among the tables and behind the bar, seeing to every need of his customers.

Scores of postcards from past patrons are tacked onto the walls. Hand-lettered posters announce new cottage colonies, tours, goods for sale. And there are NOTICES from the management. (NOTICE is a common Belizean word, you will find out.) Guatemalan handicrafts are on sale, to satisfy a market lacking in local production. I am sure Eva's will be immortalized in some novel of the Belizean jungle.

Another great spot to chat with amusing people while enjoying great food is over at the **SANDCASTLE** bar and grill *near the bus stop on Manza Plaza*. The restaurant serves up tastey local favorites (and a few internationally inspired items) in a unique open air dining room with a sandy floor. Expect to spend as little as $9 for a memorable meal.

At 27 Burns Avenue, the **SERENDIB** is a pleasant restaurant and bar. Burgers and sandwiches are served, along with beef dishes and Sri Lankan curries and seafood. Your check comes on a little tray with two hard candies. "A" for effort. *Closed on Sundays, and between 3 p.m. and 6:30 p.m.*

The **RED ROOSTER BAR & GRILL**, *2 Far West St., tel. 92-3016, fax 2057*, hosted by folks from Colorado, has an open kitchen so you can see the cooking, and serves pizza, nachos, and liquid nourishment. They cater to rafters and canoers and bikers and everyone else.

Out of town just over a mile on the road westward, the **KON TIKI RESTAURANT** offers an honest menu of hamburgers, burritos and chili con carne, all for $3 or less at lunchtime, and dinner plates for $5 to $6.

For a change of scene, try dining at one of the lodges outside San Ignacio. Most will accept outsiders for dinner, and the surroundings are certainly more refined than at any restaurant in-town. **MAYA MOUN-TAIN LODGE** has consistently good food, served on a sheltered terrace approached by a lantern-lit walkway, to the mysterious accompaniment of the calls of forest animals. *Call 2164 around to see what's for dinner (about $15 with service charge), if they have room for you, and to reserve.* Ask around among your fellow travelers as to the state of culinary affairs at the other lodges outside of San Ignacio.

MAXIM'S, a Chinese restaurant, *is on Far West Street*, which is a block over from West Street proper. There is no Farther West Street. The atmosphere is typically Chinese-Belizean — small, dark, plastic tablecloths — and so is the food — egg foo, mein, fried rice, and curries with chicken on the bone. So-so, at $4 to $7 for a meal. And there are the **ORIENTAL** and **NEW LUCKY** *on Burns Avenue*, with similar fare.

For snacks, the **FARMER'S EMPORIUM**, a general store *below the Hotel Central*, sells fresh-baked bread, granola, yogurt, and cups of the most delicious chilled, fresh-squeezed orange juice. *Across the street*, the **JAGUAR INN** serves hamburgers, and sometimes has game such as deer or gibnut.

EXCURSION TO CAHAL PECH

Surprise! In a spot of dense jungle right above San Ignacio is **Cahal Pech** *(Place of the Ticks)*, one of the most attractively and genuinely restored Mayan ceremonial center in Central America.

Unlike Mayan cities excavated years ago, Cahal Pech's center has not been denuded of shading trees, and the park-like archaeological site is alive with birds and forest mammals. Most of the structures were found standing and intact, so there has been little guesswork in the restoration. Laborers under the direction of Dr. Jennifer Taschek of the University of Oregon have simply taken structures apart, de-rooted the pieces, and put them back together, with a strong mortar topping to withstand modern foot traffic. For now, visitors have an unusual opportunity to look over the shoulders of working archaeologists.

Like most Mayan sites, Cahal Pech was occupied for centuries, during which its buildings were renewed, reconstructed, and covered over. It probably flourished in the Classic period, until about 900 A.D.; but some features, porticoes of corbeled arches, suggest a post-Classic occupation under the Toltec-influenced Maya of the Yucatan. And it could well have been an important center as early as 200 A.D.

Dr. Taschek suggests that Cahal Pech functioned more as a noble family estate, or castle, than as a political capital, and was originally occupied by Maya-related peoples as early as 850 B.C. Cahal Pech is just one of the Mayan centers that occupy virtually every hilltop in the Cayo area.

Orientation

The main constructions of Cahal Pech are situated around two principal plazas. Most of the buildings, of the type generally called palaces, are long and low-lying. The eastern side of the main plaza is lined with noble tombs, long ago violated by looters, while "official"-type structures form the other sides. Some of the surfaces have been re-covered with lime plaster in the Mayan manner. Rooms are large by Mayan standards, and corbeled archways are wider than elsewhere, perhaps due to the strength of the mortar made from local limestone.

The building known as the **Audiencia**, on the west side of the main plaza, was probably used for public ceremonies, to judge by the rise in the middle of each wide tread of its stairway, a trick of perspective to center attention on any ceremonies performed there. The outer structure dates from the ninth century, but parts of the stairway and foundation platform, dating from a century earlier, are left exposed and unplastered to show of their earlier appearance.

Climb the steps of the Audiencia, and you will look down onto a smaller plaza that once served as some sort of official reception area. The large temple on the south side, the tallest structure here, can be ascended by a stairway and path for a general view of the site. About a third of the way up is an inset that archaeologists call a throne room and seat of power.

At the northwest corner, a narrow passageway leads through the complex. A dump found below its exit suggests that this was a service passage. To the southwest of the tallest structure is yet another courtyard, possibly a private reserve for the noble family. Excavations suggest that the residents lived in increasing privation, as Classic Mayan civilization declined after 800 A.D.

To reach Cahal Pech, walk or drive past the Hotel San Ignacio, along the curve toward Benque Viejo. The ruins are on a rise off to the south. They offer spectacular views of San Ignacio (also available from the nearby disco known, as well, as Cahal Pech). Look for the red sheet-concrete roof of the new museum-visitors center, where artifacts from nearby sites are displayed. Exhibits are planned to illustrate the daily life of the Maya. The center is meant to educate Belizeans about their heritage, to encourage preservation, and to discourage looting. There is a small admission charge.

Tipu, another site in the Cayo area, is the locale of an old Spanish mission church, one of the few that were established in what is now Belize. **Pilar**, a few miles west of San Ignacio, is a Mayan ruin that has not been extensively investigated. Both sites are unrestored, with little to attract the casual visitor.

NIGHTLIFE

On any weekend night, and most nights during the week, drift along toward the sound of reggae music to find a place to unwind. The most distinguished name in dance in the Cayo area is currently the **Cahal Pech disco**. You cannot miss it, green and concrete and open-sided, with soaring thatched roof, on the hilltop south of town, next to the radio tower and microwave dish and Cahal Pech archaeological site.

Cahal-Pech-the-disco is the dancing spot with the mightiest views in all Belize. It's almost within walking distance of the Hotel San Ignacio, though you should take a taxi to your dancing date after dark.

OTHER EXCURSIONS

Easy destinations during day trips from San Ignacio are **Mountain Pine Ridge** (described above), the Mayan ruins at **Xunantunich**, and the former **Pantí Medicinal Trail** (now called the **Ix Chel Farm Trail**; see below). The **Caracol** site has just re-opened to visitors.

San Ignacio is also a good base for longer runs to the **Belize Zoo**, to several caves, the **Crooked Tree reserve**, and even to **Tikal** in Guatemala.

Tour Services to Area Excursions

The cottage and lodge hotels in the vicinity of San Ignacio offer tours to all possible attractions. These include full day adventures in the Mountain Pine Ridge, day trips to Tikal in Guatemala, boat trips upriver to the former Panti Trail, horseback rides to Xunantunich, and plenty of wildlife and birding treks. Check with your hotel for more details.

Mountain Pine Ridge is the most popular day trip from San Ignacio, and various operators put together groups, at about $18 per person. To get aboard, inquire at Eva's for Louis or for Chris Heckert. A full day tour by taxi will cost about $100, though some drivers will try to give you a shortened trip for the same price.

Red Rooster Inn (see below) takes groups into the reserve for $30 and up per person, including lunch.

SPORTS & RECREATION

Canoes

Inquire at Eva's for Toni ("Bob's brother-in-law"), *or call 2267*, to arrange to rent a canoe for a float down the Macal River. An all-day trip, unaccompanied by guide, costs $30 and up, depending on where you arrange to be retrieved, and there are hourly and half-day rates.

Canoes are also available from **Float Belize**, about a mile-and-a-half out of town on the road to Guatemala.

THE FORMER PANTÍ TRAIL IS NOW CALLED THE IX CHEL FARM TRAIL

This unusual trail, a few miles west and south of San Ignacio, is where visitors may learn about native medicinal plants. One plant is used to stop internal bleeding; another provides pure water; another cures dysentery; others are poisonous. These are more than curiosities: many modern medicines are derived from the plants of the tropical forest, and the race is on to discover the secrets of the jungles before they are destroyed by land-clearers, and before university-trained doctors totally displace traditional healers. The trail was originally named for Mayan healer Eligio Pantí, but was recently renamed. Plants, which are all growing in their natural environment, are labelled in English, Spanish, Mayan, and Latin.

The Ix Chel Farm Trail is located at Ix Chel, a farm named for a Mayan goddess and belonging to Rosita Arvigo, an American disciple of Pantí. To arrange a visit, call the Environmental Information Center at 45545 in Belize City; or dial 2188 in Cayo; or contact a travel agency. You can reach Ix Chel, which is adjacent to Chaa Creek Cottages, by taxi from San Ignacio, or by boat along the Macal River. A tour will cost about $15.

Dr. Arvigo also gives five- and seven-day seminars in herbal healing, and even dispatches herbs by mail order (in case you're strictly an armchair traveler). Write to Ix Chel Farm, San Ignacio, Cayo, for details.

Rafting

You can also arrange canoe trips, and rafting, at the **Red Rooster Inn**, *2 Far West St., tel. 092-3016, fax 2057*. A full-day float trip on the Mopan River (Class I and II rapids) costs from $30 to $50 per person, depending on the number in the group. Included are lunch, snacks and equipment. Half-day biking/rafting tours cost the same or slightly more, again depending on numbers. For more adventure, Red Rooster also has river trips extending over two, three and four days, at about $40 per day. Pickup at hotels in San Ignacio is included, and there are small additional charges to fetch passengers at country lodges.

Horseback Riding

Various of the lodges around San Ignacio will have horses brought in for guests. Or, if you wish, check in at Easy Rider stables, less than a mile up the road to Bullet Tree Falls, where you can have a full horse for half a day for $30. They can also set you up for river fishing.

PRACTICAL INFORMATION
Banks
The **Belize Bank** and **Atlantic Bank** have branches in San Ignacio. There are also money changers right at the border of Guatemala.

Telephone Office
The **telephone office** (B.T.L.) *is on Burns Avenue.*

Post Office
The **post office** *is above the police station, up near the Hawkesworth Bridge.*

General Information
For general information about the Cayo area, your best source is the bartender at **Eva's**.

BENQUE VIEJO
About 80 miles from Belize City, **Benque Viejo del Carmen** is the last settlement in Belize on the road to Guatemala. The name of the town is probably a Spanish-English corruption of *old bank*, bank being a riverside logging camp. The name bespeaks the time when the border between Belize and Guatemala existed more in theory than in fact, and English-speaking loggers and Spanish-speaking *chicleros*, or chicle gatherers, both exploited the forests. The town's population of about 3000 includes many Mopan Maya Indians.

Though Guatemala is just a short jog away, Benque is a typically Belizean-appearing village of two-story clapboard houses with tin roofs overhanging second-floor porches, set amid haze-shrouded hills. Benque sprawls, its houses set wide apart one from another.

If you're coming in from Guatemala, you'll be impressed by the rather substantial services available in a little Belizean town — a large police barracks, clean running water, even a fire station. It's also Hispanic. You won't find a city hall in Benque, but rather, a *Palacio Municipal*.

ORIENTATION
The major attraction of the area is the nearby **Xunantunich** archaeo-logical site, described below. But, as elsewhere in Belize, the human landscape is also fascinating.

Just outside of Benque is the Mopan Maya village of **San José Succotz**. The inhabitants are descendants of migrants from San José village in the Petén department of Guatemala, and the ancient Mayan customs and folklore have been more faithfully maintained in isolated Succotz than in modern San José.

Mopan is the first language, and the fiesta days of St. Joseph (March 19) and the Holy Cross (May 3) are celebrated every year.

ARRIVALS & DEPARTURES
Arriving By Bus

Batty Bus departures from Belize City (Mosul St. at Bagdad, a block from East Collet Canal, *tel. 72025*) are at 6, 7:30, and 9 a.m. Novelo's Bus Service (19 West Collet Canal, *tel. 77372*) buses depart every hour from 11 a.m. to 7 p.m., and at 9 p.m., from noon to 5 p.m. on Sundays.

For Belize City, Novelo's departures from Benque are every hour from 4 a.m. to 11 a.m., from 5 a.m. on Sundays. Batty departures from the border for Belize City are at 7 a.m. and 2 and 3:30 p.m.

Departing: Crossing the Border

The Guatemalan border post is about a mile beyond Benque Viejo. The 6 a.m. Batty Bus from Belize City goes right to Melchor de Mencos on the Guatemalan side, connecting with a bus for Flores, the main city of the Guatemalan department of El Petén. With luck, you can connect at the El Cruce junction with a bus for Tikal. If you take a later bus for Benque, you'll have to walk or take a taxi to the border.

From Flores, you can travel onward into Guatemala by bus or plane, or to Palenque, in Mexico, by a combination of bus and riverboat. See the next chapter for details.

The Guatemalan Consulate is a few miles back from the border, along the Western Highway in Succotz, near the Xunantunich ferry.

WHERE TO STAY

Benque has some simple hotels, if you have to stay here. **OKI'S**, *on George St. (the main drag)*, charges $6 per person. **THE MAYA HOTEL**, *on the same street*, charges $4 per person.

HOSPEDAJE ROXY, *at 70 St. Joseph St., on the way out of town toward Guatemala*, is really basic. For better lodgings, if you're driving, look in at **NABITUNICH COTTAGES** (mentioned above) and the other lodges on the way to San Ignacio.

XUNANTUNICH

The site of **Xunantunich** (*Maiden of the Rock*) *is just northeast of Benque Viejo, near the confluence of the Mopan and Belize rivers.*

The ruins of Xunantunich comprise the largest archaeological site in the Belize River valley. Indications from pottery and from stelae inscribed with date glyphs are that Xunantunich was occupied until about 850 A.D., somewhat later than other sites of the Classic period. The eminently defensible situation of the ceremonial center, with its commanding view of the surrounding countryside, might have had something to do with this relative longevity.

Though known to archaeologists since the late nineteenth century, Xunantunich was not excavated until 1938. A Cambridge University team explored the site extensively in 1959 and 1960, and started the work of stabilizing the structures. More recent excavations took place after looting. Only limited restoration and reconstruction has been done.

Bring a snack and something to drink, as there are no facilities for visitors.

ARRIVALS & DEPARTURES

To reach the ruins, walk or drive from Benque Viejo toward San Ignacio, about two miles, to the village of Succotz, where a hand-operated cable ferry winches cars and people across the Mopan River. Service is from 8 a.m. to 4 p.m., and there is a small charge on weekends.

Follow the dirt road from the ferry landing another mile uphill to the entrance, where an admission fee is collected.

TOURING THE RUINS

At the heart of Xunantunich are three adjacent plazas laid out roughly along a north-south line. Dominating all is **El Castillo** (structure **A-6**), the massive pyramid at the south end of the main complex. At 130 feet in height, it is the tallest building even in modern Belize, but for the recently measured Sky Palace at Caracol, to the south.

The outer shell of El Castillo is the last of a series of temples and pyramid bases superimposed one atop the last over a period of centuries. Its corbel-vaulted temples were decorated with stone and stuccoed friezes, though these have mostly been destroyed over the years by wind, rain, and penetrating jungle vegetation. One frieze on the east side, from an underlying earlier temple, shows through the damaged outer layer, and has been partially restored. Its carvings represent astronomical symbols. The temple complex was probably once covered by a roof comb, long collapsed. A wide terrace, about one-fourth of the way up, once supported lesser temples.

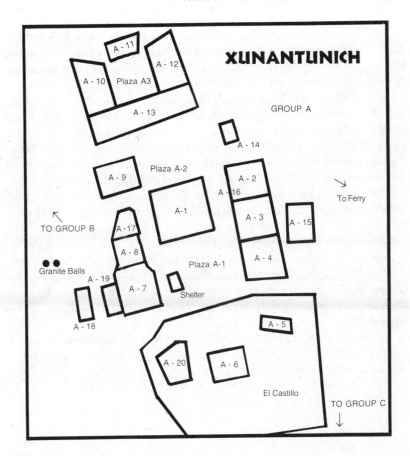

The main temple at the top of El Castillo is a typical Mayan structure. Interior rooms are capped with the corbelled, or false, arch, layers of stones protruding successively inward. This technology allowed only short spans, so Mayan interior rooms are narrow and cramped.

El Castillo can be climbed on a trail that winds back and forth across its face — certainly a less intimidating experience than going up the steep staircases of such extensively restored structures as those at Tikal. Near the top, a set of concrete steps winds diagonally up the western face, an accretion as un-genuine and atrocious as will be found in any reconstruction. On the opposite face, in a more protective approach, a wooden stairway rests above the temple and shields it from damaging foot traffic.

Whichever route you take, from the top you can see steaming, undulating rangeland and jungle, stretching away for miles to the east; the Maya Mountains to the south; and Benque Viejo, and the lowlands of the department of the Petén in Guatemala, to the west. It is one of the most impressive views in Belize.

Other structures in the central area of Xunantunich include the small **A-16**, along the trail between the two main plazas, in the plaster of which Mayan graffiti may still be seen. It is sometimes called the **stela house** for the stela that was found in its rear room. **Structure A-15** features a room with a built-in bench. Structures **A-18** and **A-19**, on the edge of group A, flank a one-time ball court. Stela A-6, which used to sit in the plaza in front of El Castillo, has been moved to a thatched pavilion at the side of the plaza. It's a good place for you to get out of the sun. An altar from Xunantunich was removed to the British Museum in the 1920s, though its carved portion was sliced off, and has been misplaced.

Excavations at Xunantunich have yielded up objects of stone and obsidian, an abundance of seashell and jade items, a spindle whorl used to make thread, and what appears to have been a jeweler's workshop, complete with flint hammers and stone chisels. These, the variety of pyramids, palaces and ball courts, and the friezes and glyphs that decorate the buildings, are indications of a complex and well-ordered society. The Cambridge University team discovered substantial damage to the site from an earthquake, which might have been the immediate cause of the city's demise.

About a mile and a half north of Xunantunich are the **Actuncan** ruins. Pottery similar to that of Xunantunich was found there, indicating that Actuncan might have been a satellite of the larger center.

17. GUATEMALA EXCURSION
- ON TO TIKAL -

INTRODUCTION

While Guatemala claims Belize, Belize has been taking over part of Guatemala, in the touristic sense. Virtually all new hotel construction in Guatemala in the last ten years has been in the part of that country accessible from Belize. More and more, visitors reach **Tikal**, the most awe-inspiring Mayan city-state currently developed for visitors, from Belize.

And it makes sense. Today's borders didn't exist in the days of Mayan ascendancy. If you have any interest in the ancient sites of Belize, the logical culmination of your visit is an excursion to Tikal. In the remote jungle of Guatemala's Petén department, removed from any significant settlement of the last several centuries, the jungle reveals temples and palaces over a hundred feet tall, the greatest monuments erected any-where in the world at the time, bespeaking a civilization intricately organized, conquering in war, yet prizing artistic expression and scien-tifically advanced.

Aside from Tikal, scattered around the Petén department of Guate-mala are the old ceremonial centers of the Maya, some of them cleared of jungle growth, but many still remaining to be explored. Flores, capital of the Petén, makes a good base for visiting not only Tikal, but some of the other archaeological sites, and is an off-beat resort center in itself.

Of course, you can travel onward from Tikal to the rest of Guatemala, with its vibrant indigenous culture, colonial monuments, spectacular volcanic scenery and unsurpassed crafts and shopping. For more details, see Open Road Publishing's *Guatemala Guide*.

Is Guatemala Safe?

Should you go to Tikal? Should you be concerned for your personal integrity? Guatemala has a long history of authoritarian and repressive governments, made bloodier by the availability of modern military technology to a virtually autonomous army and "security" apparatus.

Violence by both the government and insurgents in the 1980s forced many Guatemalans to flee to neighboring countries, including Belize. Hot spots still exist. This is a sobering background to any visit to Guatemala. In fact, it's more than just background. Overland travellers will be stopped at military checkpoints, obliged to produce identification, and sometimes searched. Though Guatemalans are unfailingly courteous, it will be obvious that they are serious about their task.

I must tell you at the same time, however, that Guatemala's well-known internal problems need not pose a problem for a visitor. Even during the worst of the troubles, tourists were not targeted. And tourism is in most of its aspects probably a positive force in Guatemala. Visitors see much of what is going on, both good and bad; they value indigenous cultures, which some Guatemalans scorn.

Of course, once you're in Belize, you'll be in an excellent position to determine whether to continue to Guatemala. No doubt, you will run into many fellow visitors who have been to Tikal, who have encountered no problems, and who will have considered the excursion one of the high points of their trip.

ARRIVALS & DEPARTURES

Transport links from Belize to Tikal have improved significantly in the last few years. Your choices for getting to Tikal and returning to Belize are listed below.

Arriving & Departing By Air

Island Air and **Tropic Air** have flying tours to Tikal from San Pedro on Ambergris Caye) and Belize City, when demand warrants. A tour bus meets the plane in Flores for the 40-mile ride to the Tikal archaeological site. Morning and afternoon visits to the ruins are included, along with lunch. Return to Belize City and San Pedro is by late afternoon. These trips operate daily with a minimum of four passengers. *Reserve at any travel agency, or call Island Air at 02-31140 or 026-2484; or Tropic Air at 02-45671 or 026-2012. The price is about $200, or more if you book through certain travel agencies.*

Aerovías, a Guatemalan airline, has flights most afternoons from Belize City to Flores. Fare is about $40 one-way. Continue on your own by bus or local tour to Tikal. Or, make your trip a circular excursion:

Travel by air or overland to Tikal, continue on the Aerovías flight to Chetumal, Mexico, on the northern border of Belize (recently once a week), and head back down.

Booking a Tour

Travel agencies in Belize City, and hotels in and near San Ignacio in Western Belize, operate one-day and longer overland excursions to Belize. From San Ignacio, a day tour to Tikal for a group of four will cost about $250, not including border fees, much more for overnight visits.

If you book an overland tour, *look for one in a four-wheel drive vehicle*. Some visitors spend a lot of time stuck in the mud on the poor roads in Guatemala.

Arriving & Departing By Taxi

A Belizean taxi from San Ignacio to Tikal and back costs $200, or $250 if the driver stays overnight (worth it!). To Flores, the fare is $150. Or, you can take a Belizean taxi to the border ($15), and look for a Guatemalan taxi to take you onward to Tikal for another $50 or so round-trip.

Arriving & Departing By Bus

By bus, the total fare to Tikal is less than $10 from Belize City. If you catch the early Batty bus, you can even make it to Tikal one day, though it's a jouncing trip. If you're returning to Belize, you'll have to allow at least three days for the round trip. Read ahead for more details.

TRAVEL PLANNING FOR GUATEMALA

Visas

U. S. citizens require either a visa or a tourist card to visit Guatemala. Currently, tourist cards are issued at the border for a fee of about $5, though policy changes from time to time without any advance notice. If you are thinking of visiting Guatemala, it is prudent to obtain a visa in advance.

No visa is currently required of citizens of Austria, Belize and other Central American nations, Belgium, Canada, Denmark, Finland, Germany, Holland, Italy, Israel, Japan, Luxembourg, Liechtenstein, Norway, Spain, Sweden, and Switzerland. Visa regulations can change, however. If you are a citizen of one of these countries, check with a Guatemalan consulate before you leave home, if possible.

Citizens of other countries need a visa, which they should try to obtain in their home countries. To stay more than 30 days in Guatemala, you'll need to apply to the immigration office in Guatemala City.

Currency

Currency in Guatemala is the **quetzal**, currently worth about 17¢ US. Belizean currency is not accepted anywhere in Guatemala, but may be traded with border money-changers. The rate is usually better on the Guatemalan side. Credit cards and travelers checks are accepted at higher-priced hotels, and U.S. cash may be used for minor expenses until you can get to a bank. Again, prices in this book are quoted in U.S. dollars.

Language

The people in northern Guatemala speak Spanish, along with Mayan. English will be understood only at hotels and tourist facilities in Tikal and Flores.

Roads

Roads are generally unpaved and in poor condition. The exception is the paved road from Flores to Tikal.

Telephone

Phone service for international calls from northern Guatemala is available only from the Flores area.

Health standards

Health standards are generally lower than in Belize, and cholera is a threat. Eat only fully cooked foods that are still warm, fruits with a peel; drink only hot beverages or bottled beverages. Safe food is available on the tourist circuit.

Climate

The weather in northern Guatemala is similar to that in western Belize. Nights can be cool the farther you go inland, especially in December, January and February.

Measures

Weights and measures in Guatemala are a mixture of English (pounds, or *libras*, for weight), American (gasoline is sold by the U.S. gallon) and metric (road distances are expressed in kilometers).

OVER THE BORDER

The border crossing between Belize and Guatemala is a jungle outpost about a mile west of **Benque Viejo**, isolated but for the presence of a couple of automobile insurance shops nearby. The pavement ends on the Belizean side. Coming into Belize, procedures are minimal. Entering Guatemala, you'll face some paperwork. You'll pick up a tourist card for $5, if you're a U.S. citizen. Subject to changing regulations, you may also be able to enter on a tourist card if you're British or Mexican.

There are small fees to pay when entering Guatemala, which rise significantly if you cross before 8 a.m., at lunch time, or after 6 p.m., or on a weekend or holiday; or if you have a vehicle; or if there is anything about your documentation that can be construed as out of order.

And, according to who's on duty, there are unofficial service charges (tips, or bribes, depending on how you look at the matter).

THE PETÉN

Guatemala's last frontier was the **Petén**, the vast and sparsely settled department covering the northern third of the country. Thousands of years ago, the Maya settled the area. They burned away jungle to plant patches of corn, traded by way of rivers and laboriously constructed roads, and built great ceremonial cities that endured for centuries. They abandoned the Petén for unknown reasons, though a later group of Toltec-Maya immigrants from the Yucatán settled near Lake Petén Itzá and remained unconquered by the Spanish until 1697. After the Petén was nominally brought under Spanish control, only a few scattered settlements were established in the wilderness.

The Petén is an area of dense hardwood forests and dry jungle, of grassy savannas and small hills and valleys, dotted with lakes and seasonal swamps, cut here and there by rivers draining into the Gulf of Mexico and the Caribbean. In the southeast, the Maya Mountains rise to 500 meters, but most of the land is much lower. Thick layers of underlying sedimentary rock give evidence that much of the Petén was covered by the sea 200 million years ago, then slowly emerged and eroded into its present form.

Until relatively recently, about the only product that came out of the Petén was chicle, the raw material for chewing gum, bled from sapodilla (*chicozapote*) trees in the forests of the north by a rough-and-tumble breed of workers, and shipped out by plane. There were no roads running into the area from the rest of Guatemala, and so the forests remained unspoiled refuges for birds, wild boars and dogs, jaguars, and other animals that had disappeared long ago from the settled parts of the country.

Today, the face of the Petén has changed. Thousands of people from the crowded and overworked lands of the south have moved to the virgin lands of the north. Forests are cut and burned off to create new farmland, simple pole-and-thatch houses are quickly erected, and whole communities spring up where maps still show empty land. A flight over the Petén will reveal that some of the land remains untouched. But wide swaths run across the landscape wherever a road has been built, and the land cleared for farming to either side.

MELCHOR DE MENCOS

Situated on the boundary with Belize, 70 miles (112 kilometers) from Flores, **Melchor de Mencos** is named for a Guatemalan sergeant who once battled English pirates. Traditionally a base for chicle workers, Melchor de Mencos, like other towns in the Petén, is now a storage and shipping point for corn, sprawling and disordered, with a population of about 4000. The town center of Melchor is off to the north side of the main road.

ARRIVALS & DEPARTURES

Arriving & Departing By Bus

Buses for Melchor de Mencos leave from Santa Elena/Flores starting at 5 a.m. Buses for Flores leave from Melchor de Mencos at 3, 4, 5, 8 and 11 a.m., and, subject to changing schedules, at 1 and 4 p.m. If you arrive after all buses have left, look for a taxi to take a group of passengers on to Tikal or Flores for $50 or less.

Arriving & Departing By Taxi

Collective taxis to the border from town charge less than $1.

Departing By Car

The road from Melchor de Mencos westward is unpaved and bumpy for 56 miles (90 kilometers) to the junction with the paved road from Flores to Tikal. Near the boundary with Belize, vegetation is lush, the countryside rolling. Farther on are mixed farms, corn plots and pasture and scrub, all hill-fringed.

WHERE TO STAY

Low-end accommodations, not too different from those in Benque Viejo, can also be found in Melchor de Mencos.

The **HOTEL MAYAB**, with 29 rooms, charges about $5 per person. Better and smaller, the **HOTEL PALACE**, with just a few rooms, charges $12 single/$20 double.

LAKE YAXJA

At kilometer 61 on the road from Flores (17 miles or 29 kilometers from Belize), a branch road leads north for five miles to the twin lakes called **Yaxjá** and **Sacnab**. On the north shore of Lake Yaxjá are the Yaxjá ruins, unusual among Mayan sites in that small sections appear to have a grid street pattern. Other ruins, on Topoxte Island near the south shore of the lake, show elements of the Yucatán Maya style, indicating that a migration from the north to this area might have taken place after Classic civilization in the Petén had come to an end.

A jeep trail, passable in the dry season, leads from the end of the branch road to the Yaxjá ruins. Alternatively, you can try to hire a boat at the village at the end of the branch road in order to reach Yaxjá and Topoxte Island. The lake is a pleasant place to stop if you're traveling in a camper.

EL CRUCE & EL REMATE

Back along the east-west road, you continue through a land of lush, rolling hills, disordered farms, and houses of adobe and *bajareque* (mud on a stick frame), scattered Catholic and evangelical churches, white Mayan huts, cattle, and egrets congregating in low spots filled with water. *At kilometer 27 from Flores is* **El Cruce** (*the crossroads*), or **Ixlu**. *A kilometer to the north,* at **El Remate**, at the eastern edge of Lake Petén-Itzá, is a pretty lakeside area, where locals drop in their fishing lines and do their laundry. By all means, take a break here for a rest on the tree-dotted grass, a swim, or a meal at the thatched eatery.

If you're coming overland from Belize, you'll face a traveler's dilemma at this point: turn northward directly to Tikal; stay in one of the accommodations in the immediate area; or continue to Flores, where there are many hotels.

WHERE TO STAY

A bluff rises across the road from Lake Petén-Itzá at El Remate, and atop the bluff is **LA MANSIÓN DEL PÁJARO SERPIENTE** (*Mansion of the Plumed Serpent*), a set of double-level, thatch-roofed stone cottages that issue from the slope like treehouses. The four guest rooms open so far have wood and wicker furnishings, large screened openings, and tiled baths; and the most sublime views available from any sleeping place in the Petén. *The rate here is $80 per person, including two meals, and pickup at the airport in Santa Elena, near Flores. Contact tel. and fax 501514 in Santa Elena.*

HOTEL CAMINO REAL, *U.S. tel. 500204, 800-327-3573 in the U.S. 72 rooms. $140 single/$153 double.*

On a hillside at the northeast corner of Lake Peten-Itzá, about three miles from El Remate, the Camino Real is the Petén's premier resort. There are no pretensions to roughing it — the rooms, in proto-Mayan buildings capped with thatched roofs have cable t.v., balcony and lake view. Windsurfers, mountain bikes, canoes and sailboats are all available to guests, and there is a pool. The emphasis is on fitting in with the environment. A treatment plant keeps the lake water clean, and kitchen waste is recycled into an experimental farm and greenhouse where some of the hotel's produce is grown.

Camping

The excellent **GRINGO PERDIDO** (*Lost Gringo*) campground (*tel. 02-327683 in Guatemala City*) stretches several hundred yards along a jungly lakeside slope studded with palms and buttress-trunked forest giants. There are eight *palapas* (thatched shelters) where you can hang your hammock or pitch your leaky tent, in grassy clearings. But "campground" is somewhat of a misnomer — there are bunkrooms and cabins as well, accommodating a total of 28 persons at $14 each, and a couple of board-and-batten family bungalows near the water with four beds, going for $18 per person. For camping, with use of showers and latrines, the rate is $4 per person. Meals in the thatched lakeside dining area cost $5 for breakfast (juice, cereal, fruit, pancakes, beans, honey, etc.), $8 for lunch or dinner.

The location is ideal for swimming and fishing, (though there are no boats available to guests), and the Cerro Cahuí reserve nearby affords limited hiking. The site can be sticky in the rainy season, away from the concrete walkways.

Turn left off the Tikal road at kilometer 33 to reach Gringo Perdido. A sign points the way – Gringo Perdido is two miles onward. You need your own transport, or have to be willing to walk the last few kilometers from the main road.

CERRO CAHUI RESERVE

At the northeast end of Lake Petén Itzá is the **Biotopo Cerro Cahuí** (Cahuí Hill reserve), established to protect the Petén turkey and other wildlife of the region, and as a start in preserving the watershed of an increasingly populated region. Among common wildlife at Cerro Cahuí are parrots, toucans, woodpeckers, hawks, kingfishers, ducks, and herons; dozens of species of butterflies; crocodiles, turtles, snakes, ocelots, peccaries, white-tailed deer, raccoons, armadillos, *tepezcuintles* (gibnuts, or pacas) and howler and spider monkeys.

And there are numerous tropical hardwood trees, including the breadnut (*ramón*), mahogany, and cedars; and jungly ferns, palms, orchids and bromeliads. The reserve covers a relatively small area — 1600 acres of forest, marshy lowland (*bajos*) and hills, ranging from 300 to 1200 feet above sea level.

ARRIVALS & DEPARTURES

You'll see a sign pointing the way to Cerro Cahuí along the Tikal road, about 28 kilometers from Flores, at El Remate. The easiest way to reach the reserve by public transportation is to take a bus toward Tikal and walk from El Remate junction.

Otherwise, you can take a taxi, hire a boat from Flores (expensive), or check at the terminal in Santa Elena for an occasional bus going past the reserve to Jobompiche. Hours are from 7 a.m. to 5 p.m. The nearest place to stay is the Gringo Perdido campground and lodge.

TOURING THE RESERVE

One section with a trail is directly opposite the Gringo Perdido campground and lodge. There are two well-marked gravel-and-clay paths, one 1,400 meters long, the other taking you more then three kilometers up through broad-leafed forest. The grade is mild, there are steps at the sections that are in the least challenging; but the heat and humidity can be enervating, and you are well advised to take advantage of the rest areas, provided with benches fashioned from saplings. If you take the long way around, fully or partly, you'll climb high enough to obtain panoramic lake vistas. Some of the trees are marked with their Spanish names.

The rainiest months here are between May and October. Average temperature is about 75 degrees Fahrenheit (24 Centigrade). The humidity, the damp, and the limestone all let you know that you are in the jungle; the smells, the animal sounds and the sensations are much the same as at Tikal. This will not be your priority stop if your time is limited, though it's worth the detour if you have your own transportation.

TIKAL

Tikal, greatest of all Classic Mayan cities, towers above a dense jungle in a part of the Petén still little-inhabited. In this remote area, one of the greatest civilizations of its time established a city that endured for centuries.

Tikal is a place for wondering, not only at the engineering accomplishments of the Maya, but at the splendors of the jungle. The site of Tikal is a national park, one of the few accessible areas of the Petén that has not been taken over by agriculture, and where the native flora and fauna still flourish relatively undisturbed.

The site and its surroundings are dense with mahogany, *chicozapote*, cedar, ceiba and palm trees, and intertwining vines. Howler and spider monkeys swing in the treetops, snakes prowl, and foxes, coatimundis, pumas and wild turkeys roam the ground. The hundreds of bird species include toucans and macaws, easily visible for their size and bright colors, the harpy eagle, curassows, egrets, vultures, road runners, motmots, Montezuma's oropendolas, and tinamous.

ARRIVALS & DEPARTURES

Tikal lies 62 miles (100 kilometers) by road from the border of Belize.
Restoration efforts at Tikal started in the 1960s, but easy access to the site only came years later.

Arriving & Departing By Air

While many companies advertise air tours to the ruins, the actual landing spot is near Flores, 40 miles (64 kilometers) to the southwest. (The airstrip right at Tikal is no longer used, to prevent possible damage to the site).

A bus from the Jungle Lodge meets all planes and charges about $5 per person for the trip to Tikal, or more if there are few passengers. You can also take a taxi for about $25, rent a car at the airport, or take local buses from Flores.

For flight schedules and details, see "Arrivals & Departures" at the beginning of this chapter.

To return to Belize by air, you'll have to stay overnight, unless you've come on a tour flight.

Arriving & Departing By Bus

There are daily buses and express microbuses from Flores to Tikal . Buses leave Tikal for Flores promptly at 6 a.m. and 1 p.m. The microbus leaves at about 3 p.m., and you're assured of a seat only if you've booked from Flores. If traveling directly from Belize, you'll take a bus from Melchor de Mencos, and transfer at either El Cruce or Flores.

To return to Belize, take the Flores bus from Tikal as far as El Cruce, and wait there for a bus to Melchor de Mencos.

Arriving & Departing By Car

The road from Belize is quite rough to the junction with the highway from Flores to Tikal, though it is passable in a passenger sedan throughout the year, with caution. If you're driving a vehicle rented in Belize, ask for permission to take the vehicle to Tikal.

Jeeps can be rented in Flores for travel to Tikal and other parts of the Petén, at rates much lower than those in Belize.

THE DEVELOPMENT OF TIKAL

As is the case with all Mayan sites, the origins of Tikal are only barely discernible. Findings of pottery dating from a few hundred years before Christ give evidence that Tikal was inhabited at that time, perhaps by people who were attracted by the height of the site above surrounding swamps, and by deposits of flint, useful for making tools. No intact buildings have been found from the earliest periods of Tikal settlement, since the Maya were in the habit of destroying old structures in order to use the materials for new buildings.

By the time of Christ, the Great Plaza had already taken its basic form, with platforms and stairways constructed on the north side. Over the next few hundred years, the city grew in extent and height, as old buildings were razed or covered over with new ones, and tombs set into the plaza floor. The corbeled arch came into use, as did new-style pottery vessels painted in three or more colors. Similarities in artistic styles, tools and materials suggest that the pre-Classic Maya of Tikal were in contact with other peoples of Mesoamerica.

Tikal's Golden Age

The Classic era of the flourishing of Tikal lasted from about 300 to 900 A.D., more or less the time when Copán and Palenque were also at their heights (written dates on stelae at Tikal range from the fourth century A.D. to 869 A.D., which is thought to have been the period during which civilization in the city reached its greatest development). In addition to raising their temples to ever greater heights, the Maya of Tikal worked changes on the landscape. Ravines were dammed to form reservoirs for seasonal rains. Causeways were built to connect different parts of the city, and to provide trade routes to other Mayan centers. Trade developed with far-away peoples who could provide jadeite, obsidian and other useful raw materials.

Some sort of residential city grew around Tikal, though its nature is a matter of debate. The great buildings in the center are assumed to have been temples and palaces for religious purposes, though they might also have been residences for the noble classes. Scattered for more than three miles in every direction from the center of Tikal are thousands of platforms that might have been the foundations of houses of stone and wood.

As many as 50,000 people lived in Tikal and its hinterland, perhaps many, many more. Estimates of the population depend on interpretations of how many people would have lived in one house, whether all houses were occupied at one time, and, perhaps most importantly, on how much food could have been produced in the surrounding area.

The most visible evidence of a large population, a bountiful agriculture, and a highly developed social organization, is, of course, the very magnitude of Tikal. Many laborers had to work over long years to carry the rock and rubble needed to fill the bases of temples. While the fill was being set in place, masons had to build retaining walls, and later to face structures with carefully cut blocks. Meanwhile, lime mortar had to be made by burning limestone, a process that required the cutting of immense quantities of wood. All this had to be done with brute human labor, for the Maya did not know the use of the wheel, nor of iron, nor did they have beasts of burden.

While all this hard labor was going on, artisans were at work scraping away at limestone to form the low-relief sculptures of stelae, and incising

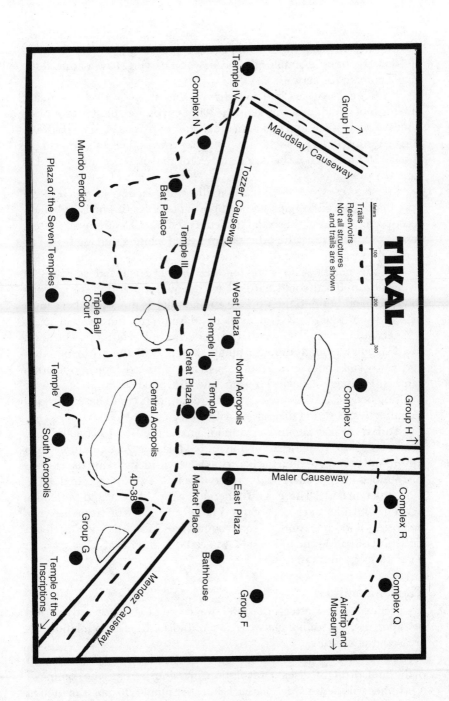

TIKAL

Meters

Trails
Reservoirs
Not all structures
and trails are shown

100

200

300

Temple IV

Complex N

Group H →

Maudslay Causeway

Mundo Perdido

Bat Palace

Tozzer Causeway

Plaza of the Seven Temples

Temple III

West Plaza

Triple Ball Court

Temple II

North Acropolis

Temple V

Central Acropolis

Great Plaza

Temple I

Complex O

Group H →

South Acropolis

4D-38

Market Place

East Plaza

Maler Causeway

Complex R

Group G

Bathhouse

Group F

Airstrip and Museum →

Complex Q

Temple of the Inscriptions

Mendez Causeway

designs into beams of *chicozapote*. This wood, carved when fresh and soft, takes on an iron hardness when exposed to air. The original temple lintels of Tikal, the finest examples of Mayan wood carving, have endured the jungle climate for centuries.

Additional workers had to patch up fallen bits of plaster, replace missing blocks of limestone, keep the temples painted, plaster over plaza floors worn with use, and maintain the reservoirs. Artisans created jewelry and beautiful pottery vessels with painted scenes of daily life, and jadeite jewelry and mosaics of shells and stones for personal decoration and as funerary offerings.

Priests presided over human sacrifices, the victims of which might have been secured in raids on neighboring peoples (if one is to believe recent interpretations of scenes depicted on some Classic Mayan pottery vessels). Other priests and officials supervised matters ranging from ball games to the administration of justice to the calculation of the calendar.

All the people who were tending to the organized activities of civilization in Tikal could hardly have devoted much time to growing food. So in addition to the workers and nobility of the town, there must have existed a large class of farmers. Mayan agronomy was in many respects more advanced than that of modern tropical farmers. The Maya of Tikal took seemingly dreadful jungle swamps, with their store of water, and reworked them into resources that supported large population centers. Drainage canals were dug, and dirt piled up to create raised planting beds. Cassava, yams, corn and ramón nuts could have provided a complete and varied diet, along with wild game.

Today, one can sit atop a pyramid, gaze at the Great Plaza and roof combs rising up from the sea of jungle, and imagine the times more than a thousand years ago when the plaza was alive with activity and the city was surrounded by cultivated fields dotted with houses. But one can do little more than imagine. There is no coherent history of Tikal and there may never be one. Bits and pieces of information are picked up from drawings on pottery and bone, finds of tools, similarities in artistic styles between Tikal and other Mayan and non-Mayan centers, and the glyphs that have been deciphered up to now.

Tikal's Decline

Some short time after the last stela was erected, Tikal entered a period of rapid decline. Buildings were left unfinished, and population decreased dramatically.

A number of possible explanations have been proposed: exhaustion of the land, drought, disease, revolution, invasion, perhaps the coming of a prophet who led his people back into the jungle. It's all a matter of speculation. Whatever happened at Tikal might have occurred at Copán (in present-day Honduras) and Palenque (in Mexico) as well, for those cities began to decline at the same time.

After the fall of civilization at Tikal, the city was inhabited intermittently, but there was never the kind of highly organized social system that characterized Tikal at its height. Tombs were occasionally looted, monuments were moved, and buildings were left to decay. Trees took root among the temples, their roots holding the stone and plaster together, and the stelae were covered over with moss.

Archaeological Excavations

The first systematic exploration of Tikal was carried out by Modesto Méndez and Ambrosio Tut, officials of the government of the Petén, in 1848. The report of Méndez awakened European interest in Tikal. A Swiss scientist showed up and carried off some of the temple lintels, and Alfred Maudslay arrived from England in 1881 to start clearing and photographing the ruins. Over the next fifty years, exploration was carried out by archaeologists sponsored by the Peabody Museum of Harvard University and the Carnegie Institution of Washington. From 1956 to 1969, the University Museum of the University of Pennsylvania undertook a massive excavation and reconstruction project in cooperation with the government of Guatemala. Work at the site is now supervised by the Institute of Anthropology and History of Guatemala.

Tikal consists of thousands of constructions ranging from temples on pyramid bases to palaces to ball courts to tombs and burial chambers to stelae. Many of the structures remain in the form of mounds into which they collapsed during centuries of abandonment of the site, and many others lie buried under later buildings. Most of the restored and partially restored structures date from the Late Classic Period, which lasted from about 550 A.D. to 900 A.D. The major monuments are in clusters, some in the vicinity of the Great Plaza, others in outlying areas reached by following causeways built by the Maya.

WHERE TO STAY
How Long Should You Stay?

The ruins of Tikal are extensive, and you should allow two days to see them, if you have the time. Since flights are scheduled *from* Belize in the afternoon and *back to* Belize the next day or the day after, Tikal can eat up four days of your itinerary if you rely on air travel, other than tour flights.

For example, you might want to take a taxi from San Ignacio to Tikal, and return to Belize City by air from Flores.

Hotel Orientation

Hotels, restaurants, the museum, and campground are all grouped around the airstrip, which is about a twenty-minute walk from the ruins. Since the total number of rooms at Tikal is limited, and there are few facilities, most visitors stay in Flores, and go to Tikal on day outings.

There has been talk for years about closing down the hotels at Tikal, and accommodating visitors at a new center. Just in case this comes to pass, go and stay at Tikal now! Despite less-than-luxurious conditions, spending a night, listening to jungle noises, and waking to the squawking of parrots and monkeys, is memorable.

A long-standing favorite lodging place at Tikal is the **JAGUAR INN**. Unfortunately, there are only two double rooms, which go for about $35 double with meals, and two safari-style tents with night tables, mattresses, and electric lights, available at about $15 double. *Write well in advance if you'd like to stay (to Jaguar Inn, Tikal, Guatemala), or call 500002 in Santa Elena (Flores), and send a deposit and your phone number.* You'll be met at the airport in Flores.

JUNGLE LODGE, *32 rooms, tel. 501519. $70 single, $82 double, less with shared bath. In Guatemala City: 29 Calle 18-01, Zona 12, tel. 768775, fax 760294.*

Tour leaders used to describe the Jungle Lodge apologetically to their clients, but no more. The rustic abodes of yesteryear have all been totally rebuilt. Modern cottage rooms now are airy and light, whitewashed inside, each with two double beds, tiled shower, marble vanities, closet, pastel bedspreads, ceiling fan, porch . . . all in all, quite unexpected. The large lobby-dining room, screened and open to jungle sounds, is a pleasant gathering area, though food offerings are quite limited. Electricity is available only a few hours a day.

The **TIKAL INN**, also much improved, charges $100 double with dinner and breakfast, or $75 for two without meals in hotel rooms; or $35 per person with two meals, $25 per person without meals in bungalows. The hotel is concrete and airy, and a thatched roof and wicker furnishings provide a pleasant environment. The best feature is the swimming pool.

Camping

There's an ample grassy campsite right at the entrance to the visitors' reception area, with running water, shower and toilets, open thatched shelters, and plenty of room for vehicle parking. The charge is about $6 per night (an unofficial and variable arrangement). The diners nearby rent hammocks and mosquito nets for a couple of dollars a night, with a deposit required. A blanket will be useful in the dry season (December through May) since it can get surprisingly cold at night. Mosquito repellent will come in handy in the rainy season. There are fireplaces for cooking, and plenty of firewood is available for gathering. Campers should note that dogs are not allowed into the national park.

Try to choose your spot as soon as you arrive. Conditions at the campsite are a great improvement over those just a few years ago, when you had to fetch water from a crocodile-infested pond. The crocodiles are gone now, but so, unfortunately, are a couple of workers.

WHERE TO EAT

At the **JAGUAR INN**, *on the north side of the airstrip*, meals are served in a pleasant and cool thatch-roofed pavilion. The food is as good as you'll find in Tikal. Breakfast costs about $3, lunch or dinner $5, and there are sandwiches, vegetarian dishes, and an a la carte menu more varied than you'd expect way out here. They'll also pack a picnic. The **JUNGLE LODGE** serves meals, at slightly higher prices in its cool and pleasant dining area, but offerings are limited.

The restaurant at the **visitors' center** has an ambitious menu, with a few non-jungle main courses, such as pepper steak and fettucine, at $6 and up, though you should not expect the food to live up to its description.

South of the airstrip are a couple of inexpensive diners.

OTHER FACILITIES

Facilities at the Tikal reception area include a temple-style visitors' center, holding a mock-up of the ruins, an exhibit of some stelae, and a restaurant (see above). There's also a post office, the museum, and a jungle nature trail. That's all.

TOURING THE RUINS

An admission fee of about $6 is collected when you arrive at the park entrance, about 17 kilometers (10 miles) from the visitors' center of Tikal.

Before You Start Out

Wear light cotton clothing and a hat when you go out to the ruins. The sun is usually strong, though you can escape it for a while by ducking under a tree or into a temple. Carry some fruit or a canteen of water, or both. Bottled sodas are sold at various sites in the ruins, but no food. The Jaguar Inn will pack a box lunch if you've come without a hamper.

Wear shoes with non-slip soles for climbing temples. Getting up the long flights of steps is no problem, but if you've got a fear of heights, getting down can be hairy. A flashlight will be useful for looking into temples and underground chambers.

Hours

On foot, follow the road from the airstrip (vehicular traffic is prohibited). It's twenty minutes to the main plaza. *The site is open from 6 a.m. to 6 p.m., though the guards start to clear visitors out at 5 p.m.* You can get into the ruins during the full moon if you request permission at the *inspectoría*, a little building beside the trail from the airstrip.

THE ANCIENT CITY

The **Great Plaza**, dominated by Temples I and II, sits on an artificially leveled tongue of land between two ravines, at the center of Tikal. The grassy plaza was originally covered over with lime mortar, which was renewed every few centuries.

Temple I

Temple I, also called the **Temple of the Giant Jaguar**, rises 145 feet (44.2 meters) over the east side of the plaza. The base is formed of nine terraces with sloping sides, supporting a platform on which sits a three-room temple building. The crowning roof comb appears to have been mainly decorative. Roof combs were hollowed out to lighten their weight, and faced with carved limestone blocks. The eroded figure of a seated person can barely be made out on the comb of Temple I. The stairway now visible was used during construction. It was once covered over by a more formal set of steps.

The Maya built temples by creating mountains and placing molehills on top. At the base of Temple I (and under most of the other temples) is a great burial vault, a reconstruction of which may be seen in the Tikal Museum. The body of a noble was placed on a masonry bench in the chamber, along with offerings of ceramics and pieces of jewelry. Inscriptions indicate that the noble was called Ah Cacau (Lord Cacao), and that he ascended to power in 682 A.D. and ruled for almost fifty years. A corbeled arch was built above his chamber and capped with wooden beams, after which began the laborious process of building retaining walls, filling the spaces with rubble to form the first layer of the pyramid base, then building successive layers to the desired height. After the artificial mountain had been raised, a temple building was constructed at the top. The corbeled arch used by the Maya consisted of layers of stone successively protruding inward, until they could be capped by a single block. This arch could span only a narrow width, so massive Mayan structures contain claustrophobically small amounts of interior space.

Inside Temple I, some of the original carved wooden beams are still in place. Lintels at the entrances to temples were left undecorated. A secondary burial, dating from after the completion of Temple I, was found beneath the floor of the rear room.

Temple II

Temple II, known as the **Temple of the Masks** for the decorations on its stairway, reaches a height of 125 feet (38.1 meters) over the west side of the plaza. With its roof comb intact, it might have stood almost as high as Temple I. The walls of the inside rooms are scribbled with ancient graffiti. No tomb has yet been found under the base, but the temple is thought by some to honor the wife of the ruler buried in Temple I. It may be her portrait that decorates an interior wooden lintel.

Both Temple I and Temple II date from relatively late in the life of Tikal, about 700 A.D.

Placed around the plaza are stelae and associated altars, some plain, others carved in low relief. Many appear to have been moved after the fall of Classic civilization at Tikal. Later stelae (the date glyphs can be read) were larger and sculptured more skillfully out of harder rock than the limestone of the earlier stelae, on which many of the inscriptions have worn away. The portraits on the stelae might have represented nobles to whom they were dedicated. Faces on some of the stelae appear to have been smashed intentionally, perhaps when the portrayed figure died or was succeeded in office.

The North Acropolis

The **North Acropolis**, fronting on the north side of the Great Plaza, is one of the most heavily constructed areas of Tikal. Hidden under the visible structures are many superimposed earlier buildings.

Excavations in **Structure 5D-34** revealed a tomb cut into the bedrock deep below, containing the skeletons of a noble and his retainers, along with turtles, a crocodile, and pottery. In **Structure 5D-33**, facing the plaza, a number of layers of construction are visible. Here, the outer layer has been removed on the left side, revealing a great *mask* (large facial medallion) decorating one of the earlier buildings. On the right side, a matching mask may be seen by entering an excavation in the intact outer structure. Still another temple base covered the outer structure seen today, but was so badly eroded that most of it was stripped away during the reconstruction of the North Acropolis.

Stela 31, now in the Tikal museum, was found buried in the second-layer building. One of the most beautiful of the early stelae at Tikal, it was defaced prior to the building of the now-destroyed outermost temple. Paradoxically, burial in rubble preserved it from further damage. Pictured on it is a ruling noble whose name glyph has been read as *Stormy Sky*.

This may be the person whose mutilated skeleton was found in a tomb under the structure. Some archaeologists now believe that the Sky family were hereditary rulers of Tikal. Glyphs on another tomb in the North Acropolis identify an earlier ruler of Tikal called *Curl Nose*, who might have come from Kaminaljuyú.

South of Temple I is a small ball court. Scenes painted on pottery suggest that players hit the ball with padded knees and hips. South of Temple II, another pyramid contains no ruins on top, suggesting that it might have been capped with a perishable thatched structure. Excavations in the plaza floor southeast of the stairway of Temple II have revealed *chultuns*, chambers carved in bedrock and filled with what appears to be trash. Many of these chambers have been found, though their original use remains unknown.

The Central Acropolis

Adjoining the south side of the Great Plaza is the complex of buildings known as the **Central Acropolis**. The buildings here are called palaces, not because they were royal residences — nobody knows what they were used for — but to distinguish them from the temples and pyramids elsewhere around the Great Plaza. The palaces are relatively long, low buildings surrounding small plazas, or courts, on different levels. Many are unrestored.

The palaces were constructed at different times, sometimes on top of older buildings. Alterations went on after construction was completed, with the addition of doorways, second stories, and outside stairways. The interior rooms have benches, which might have been used for seating or as sleeping platforms. The palaces are multi-story structures only in a primitive sense, since the upper floors are set back and supported mainly by a layer of rubble fill behind the rooms of the lower floors. Only one of the palaces, fronting on Court 6, has an interior staircase. Many of the palace facades were decorated with low-relief friezes, only a few of which survive intact.

The Palace Reservoir

The **Palace Reservoir**, just south of the Central Acropolis, was created by damming a ravine and sealing the porous limestone with clay. Nearby terraces were sloped so that water would drain into the reservoir.

Along the eastern end of the northern base of the Central Acropolis is the Late Classic **Structure 5D-43**, a platform supporting a two-room building. The rectangular molding on the base, and the sections jutting out above and below the molding, are similar to architectural features at Teotihuacán in Central Mexico, indicating a possible flow of architectural influence from that site, or from Kaminaljuyú, a Teotihuacán outpost in present-day Guatemala City.

North of Structure 5D-43 is the open area known as the **East Plaza**. On its east side is a ball court, beside which is a quadrangle of buildings called the Market Place. Farther to the east is a large, rubble-filled platform which might be the foundation of a temple left uncompleted. On the east rim of the platform is a building believed to have been a steam bath, with a low doorway and an inside firepit. **Temple 4D-38**, to the southeast of the plaza at the entrance to the Méndez Causeway, is notable for the cache of human skulls discovered under the base of a stairway, which suggests that human sacrifice was practiced at Tikal.

West Plaza & Tozzer Causeway

The **West Plaza**, to the northwest of Temple II, includes a large palace on the north side, an unfinished temple covering a tomb on the west side, and a number of stelae, which might have been moved from their original positions after the fall of Classic civilization at Tikal.

Leading west from the West Plaza is the **Tozzer Causeway**. The causeways at Tikal were wide, raised roads paved with mortar. Most are now named for archaeologists. A foot trail winds among the buildings to the south of the Tozzer Causeway.

Temple III & Complex N

Temple III, 54.9 meters (180 feet) high, is also known as the **Temple of the Jaguar Priest**, after the figure on an interior lintel of a fat man in a jaguar skin. A stela at the base of the stairway contains a date glyph equivalent to 810 A.D., indicating that Temple III was probably built in Late Classic times. Near Temple III is the **Bat Palace**, or **Window Palace** (so called for the unusual window openings on one side), another Late Classic structure, the second story of which fell down long ago.

Beyond Temple III is **Twin-Pyramid Complex N**, a set of structures of a kind peculiar to Tikal and Yaxjá. Two identical flat-topped pyramids with stairways on each side face each other across a plaza. A row of uncarved stelae and altars stands in front of the east pyramid. Off to the side is an enclosure containing a stela and altar. In the case of Complex N, these are among the finest examples of stone sculpture at Tikal. Complex N is dated 711 A.D. Dates on stelae in similar complexes elsewhere in Tikal indicate that they were erected every twenty years.

Temple IV

Temple IV, at the end of the Tozzer Causeway, is the tallest known structure in the Mayan world, with a height of 64.6 meters (212 feet). It might also have been the tallest structure in pre-Columbian America, depending on whether one takes into account the base platform.

The top is reached by a difficult trail (the stairway is gone), and affords spectacular views of the other temples. The three-room temple at the top contained two exquisite lintels, which were carried off to Switzerland. Impressions of the carvings on the top sides of the beams may be seen in the interior doorways. Glyphs on the lintels date Temple IV at 741 A.D.

Other Sites Near Temple IV

From Temple IV, a trail follows the **Maudslay Causeway** through the jungle to the northeast, ending at **Group H**, which includes two twin-pyramid complexes. The first, Complex M, was partially destroyed, possibly when the causeway was built. Complex P includes some relatively large rooms, the walls of which are covered with ancient Mayan graffiti.

The **Maler Causeway**, with a footpath down its center, runs from Group H back to the East Plaza. Midway is a set of twin-pyramid complexes. Complex Q, the easternmost of the group, is the only twin-pyramid complex to have been partially restored.

Back to the center of Tikal. From the East Plaza, the **Méndez Causeway** runs to the southeast, passing **Group G**, a complex of palace-type buildings, the walls of which are scribbled with graffiti. At the end of the causeway, about a twenty-minute walk from the East Plaza, is the **Temple of the Inscriptions**, named for the many glyphs on the roof comb and on the temple trim.

South of the Central Acropolis lies the **Plaza of the Seven Temples**, reached most easily by a trail running south from Temple III. This group is named for a series of temples in a north-south row. The central one features decorations of crossed bones and a skull. On the north side of the plaza is the **Triple Ball Court**, an unusual series of parallel playing areas.

To the west of the Plaza of the Seven Temples is the area recently re-christened **Mundo Perdido** (*Lost World*), which is only now being explored intensively by archaeologists. The **Great Pyramid** (Structure 5C-54) rises 105 feet (32 meters) above the Lower Plaza. It consists of five superimposed pyramids constructed between 700 B.C. and 250 A.D., the last at the end of the pre-Classic period. Stairways ascend on each side of the outermost, visible layer. Two *mascarones* (masks, or facial sculptures), of the original 16, survive on the western side of the pyramid, and are sheltered by thatched roofs.

Temple V

Beyond the Plaza of the Seven Temples, to the east, is **Temple V**, last of the great pyramid temples of Tikal, 190 feet (57.9 meters) high. Unusual features include a stairway finished with moldings along the edges, rounded corners on the base and superstructure, and an interior room small even for a Mayan structure.

After a look at Temple V, you can continue with explorations of the outskirts of Tikal, if you wish. From the southwest corner of the Mundo Perdido complex, follow a trail down steps and over a stick bridge, and 300 yards onward to a recent excavation site. You can enter a thatch-covered trench to inspect several large stone sculptures of faces.

The trail continues back to Group G. If you search around, you may find other such little-visited areas on the periphery of Tikal where you can see restoration work in progress.

THE MAYA BIOSPHERE RESERVE

Formed in 1990, the **Maya Biosphere Reserve** *is one of 273 such conservation areas around the world, intended as a storehouse of natural wealth for all mankind. Covering about 1.5 million acres, the Maya Biosphere includes:*

- *Tikal National Park, Río Azul National Park, Laguna National Park in the northwestern corner of Petén, Sierra del Lacandón National Park along the Usumacinta River, and El Mirador National Park.*
- *The protected areas, or biotopos of the Petén: Laguna del Tigre, Dos Lagunas, and El Zotz.*
- *A multiple-use area of sparsely settled lands. Sustainable use of the land is encouraged. Examples: gathering of nuts, spices and ferns.*
- *A buffer zone fifteen kilometers wide on the edge of the biosphere. Cutting of forest and settlement in parks and biotopes is prohibited or limited, at least in law and theory. In practice, logging and farming continue out of view or beyond the control of responsible authorities.*

The Tikal Museum

The **Tikal Museum**, located just north of the airstrip, contains a collection of some of the artifacts discovered during excavations at the ruins. Most interesting is a reconstructed tomb complete with skeleton and offerings of jadeite jewelry and pottery. A number of rubbings on rice paper show the designs of stelae more clearly than does a direct glance at the sculpture in daylight.

Other items include stone tools and grinding stones, pieces of jewelry formed of mosaics of jadeite and shell, flint tools, and the remains of Stela 29, one of the oldest pieces of Mayan carved stone yet discovered, dating from about 292 A.D. Photographs show the process of excavating and restoring the ruins.

The museum is open from 9 a.m. to 5 p.m., weekends to 4 p.m. Other stelae are housed in the visitors' center. An additional entrance fee is collected, higher for foreigners, but nominal nevertheless.

Nature Trail

The **Camino Interpretativo El Caoba** ("Mahogany Interpretive Trail"), which starts by the Jaguar Inn, is still being developed. It passes through a chicle-gatherers' camp. This is a chapter of the Petén's history that has just recently closed, with the substitution of ingredients in the manufacture of chewing gum. Take a walk of an hour or two, depending on your interest and condition.

UAXACTÚN RUINS

Uaxactún ("wa-shak-TOON"), *about 25 kilometers north of Tikal,* is in many ways a primitive, miniature version of Tikal. Like the larger site, Uaxactún consists of groups of temple and palace structures. But at Uaxactún, the highest temple rises to only slightly over 27 feet (eight meters).

Excavations at Uaxactún have given some clues to the evolution of the Classic Mayan temple. Post holes in one of the earlier levels of construction indicate that temple bases might once have been capped with wooden houses. Explorations have also turned up painted murals.

The eight groups of structures at Uaxactún are located on either side of the airstrip of an old chicle camp. **Group E**, east of the airstrip, is noted for a set of three temples, oriented so that an observer standing opposite would see the sun rising over the northernmost temple on the day of the summer solstice, and over the southernmost temple on the day of the winter solstice. Two large stucco faces flank the stairway on the facing temple base, which is one of the oldest visible Mayan structures in the Petén.

Uaxactún was discovered by Sylvanus Morley, who coined its name from the words meaning "eight" and "stone" in the modern Mayan language, after finding a stela bearing a date from the eighth cycle of the Mayan calendar, equivalent to 68 A.D. Other stelae at the site bear dates up to the equivalent of 639 A.D.

A jeep trail, passable in the dry season, leads from Tikal to Uaxactún. Buses may operate along it — inquire at the **Hotel San Juan** in Santa Elena.

On foot, the walk from Tikal takes about six hours. The village of Uaxactún, with a population of about 400, was originally a chicle shipping center. Beans and tortillas are available, but not much else. If you walk from Tikal, plan on camping out at Uaxactún. The ruins remain almost totally unrestored.

RIO AZUL

This isolated site, *80 kilometers northeast of Tikal,* near the border with Belize, includes a 155-foot-high (47-meter) temple. The Maya reworked the landscape extensively around **Río Azul**, constructing dams, canals, and fortifications. An intact burial chamber from about 400 A.D. was discovered here by archaeologist R. E. W. Adams, amid dozens of other tombs that had been looted. Also unusual is a pot with a screw-top lid. Río Azul is still inaccessible to casual visitors.

FLORES, SANTA ELENA, SAN BENITO

The island city of **Flores**, founded in 1700, is the successor to the last stronghold of the Maya. Centuries after Tikal and other cities of the Petén had been abandoned, some of the inhabitants of Chichén-Itzá in the Yucatán migrated southward and founded **Tayasal** on an island in Lake Petén Itzá. The Spaniards were aware of the existence of Tayasal. Hernán Cortés, conqueror of Mexico, spent three days there in 1525 while on a march to Honduras, and a statue of one of Cortés' wounded horses became one of the principal idols of the town.

But for almost 200 years, the Spaniards were occupied with conquering and administering a continent, and paid little attention to the city in the jungle. Some friars visited Tayasal in about 1618, but they only managed to earn the hatred of the people by destroying their equine idol. A military expedition led by Martín de Ursúa finally managed to subjugate Tayasal in 1697.

By the time the Spaniards moved into the area, the old Mayan causeways had long been covered with jungle growth. Though the building of a road through the Petén to Belize remained a dream for many years, nothing was done about it, and Flores and the towns of the area remained isolated outposts, subsisting on corn-and-bean agriculture, and sending workers out to bleed chicle trees in the jungle.

With the opening of the Petén, first by airplane and later by highway, the area around Flores has boomed. Most of the growth has been in **Santa Elena** (population 6,500) and **San Benito** (population 9,600), opposite Flores on the mainland. Flores itself (population 1,500) sits on a small island, with no room for expansion. It remains a charming and quiet old place, with only a bit of dust kicked up now and then by vehicles traveling the road around its rim.

FLORES ORIENTATION

Even if there were no spectacular ruins accessible from the town, Flores would be a pleasant place in which to spend a vacation. The *cayucos* (dugouts with sides built up of planks) plying the surface of Lake Petén Itzá, the thickly forested surrounding hills, the tropical bird life, and a sense of remoteness all give the place a unique atmosphere.

Flores is located at a bend in the southwest corner of **Lake Petén-Itzá**, which covers 38 square miles (99 square kilometers) and is dotted with a number of smaller islands. The lake is a large depression filled with ground water, fed by small streams and emptied by underground seepage. The name Petén was applied by the Itzá Maya to the island where Tayasal was located. It was later used as a name for the lake and finally for the whole region.

For swimming, you can jump in the lake anywhere, though the water around Flores is encrusted with vegetation and is not too appetizing. Head for a spot away from the settled area, either on foot or in a canoe.

For the best views from Flores, walk up to the town square (in this case a circle) at the crest of the island. You'll be able to look down on the western end of the lake, and over to the low surrounding hills.

Until the causeway connecting Flores with Santa Elena was built, the only way to get to the island was in small cayucos. A commuter service of motorized cayucos still operates between Flores and San Benito. The fare is a few cents.

As accommodations at Tikal are limited, you might want to spend your nights in Flores, and take buses or tours to Tikal during the day.

ARRIVALS & DEPARTURES

Arriving By Bus

Buses from the border with Belize terminate in Santa Elena, on the south side of the lake.

Arriving By Air

The airport for the Flores area is located about two kilometers east of the center of Santa Elena. Taxis run to town, or you can walk to one of the nearby hotels, or board a waiting bus for Tikal. (And it waits . . . until all flights have landed.)

All scheduled service to Flores is somewhat theoretical, subject to delay and cancellation. Plan accordingly — visit Tikal and the Petén early in your trip, rather than at the very end, when a delay might cause you to miss your flight home.

Island Air and **Tropic Air** run day-long tours to Tikal. Passengers land at Flores in the morning, continue by bus to Tikal, and return to Belize City or San Pedro in the evening.

One afternoon flight operates between Belize City and Flores most days of the week, on either **Aerovías** or **Aviateca**. One-way fare is about $60.

Currently, one weekly flight operates between Flores/Santa Elena and Chetumal, Mexico, and other connections to Mexico are planned.

Aerovías, and **Aviones Comerciales** have daily flights in small planes, departing from Guatemala City at 6:30 or 7 a.m., and returning in the afternoon. Fare is about $60 each way.

Aviateca flies larger planes to Flores, usually Boeing 737s, at 7 a.m. and 3 p.m. *The Aviateca schedule can be confirmed in the United States or Canada by phoning 800-327-9832.*

Departing By Bus To Guatemala City

One *"directo."* bus (making fewer stops than others) departs at 9 p.m. from the terminal in Santa Elena, others, taking at least 13 hours, leave at 10 and 11 p.m. and 5 and 11 a.m. Book your seat the day before you travel, if possible. Buses to Poptún leave Santa Elena at 6 and 10 a.m., and 1 and 4 p.m.

Departing By Bus to Melchor de Mencos/Belize border

Five buses depart daily, starting at 5 a.m.

WHERE TO STAY

In Santa Elena

HOTEL TZIQUINAHA, *Tel. 501359 (20258 in Guatemala City). $55 single/$65 double.*

Within walking distance of the airport (if you don't have much luggage), and a couple of kilometers from the center of Flores. There's no noise problem, since only a few planes land during the day. Air conditioning, pool, cable TV, restaurant. Food not great.

JAGUAR INN, *Calzada Rodríguez Macal 879, tel. 500002. 18 rooms. $18 single/ $25 double.*

A haven for travelers, new, cheery, built around a gardened courtyard. Comfortable rooms have ceiling fans and attractive woodwork, and are decorated with locally woven crafts. One of the owners speaks English, the other is English. Restaurant. Turn left just before the Texaco station as you approach from the airport. Under the same management as the Jaguar Inn at Tikal

HOTEL MAYA INTERNACIONAL, *tel. 501276 (348136 in Guatemala City). 22 thatched cottages. $59 single/$66 double.*

Near the causeway to Flores — look for the large thatched dining pavilion. The units are currently reached by rickety walkways over the watery grounds. Well maintained. Jeep tours arranged.

HOTEL EL PATIO, *tel. 501229 (371963 in Guatemala City, 800-327-3573 in the). 22 rooms. $75 single/$82 double.*

Located back from the lake, near the Maya Internacional, on the road in from the airport. A substantial two-story colonial-style structure with archways around a relatively cool central courtyard. The neat, modern rooms have overhead fans and cable television, and the bar and restaurant are air-conditioned.

HOTEL COSTA DEL SOL, *Calzada Rodríguez Macal, tel. 500336. 29 rooms. $28 single/$35 double.*

A motel built around a large swimming pool along one of the main streets in Santa Elena — lots of dust can blow in, but the rooms are air-conditioned and have cable television, the management is friendly, and the restaurant isn't bad. A good buy.

HOTEL DON QUIJOTE, *20 rooms. $6 per person with shared bath.*

Simple rooms in a modern building, a half-block from the causeway to Flores. Inexpensive restaurant. The area is often dusty because of heavy traffic (or muddy if it's been raining).

HOTEL JADE, *10 rooms. $4 per person, sharing bath.*

The green-painted building, just before the causeway to Flores. Rooms are basic but acceptable.

HOTEL SAN JUAN, *On the main street of Santa Elena, tel. 500041. $10 single/$12 double.*

Bare rooms with shared bath. So-so, but a good travel base, as buses for Tikal leave from the hotel.

In Flores

Hotels on the west side of the island, with a view to San Benito and some open water, are preferable to those on the south side, where you'll only see the causeway, and traffic kicking up dust in Santa Elena.

HOTEL PETÉN, *tel. 501392. 21 rooms. $23 single/$28double (less with private bath).*

West side, in two buildings. The main building of this hotel is more pleasant than it appears from the street. Rooms are in tiers, some with good lake views.

HOTEL LA JUNGLA, *11 rooms. $12 single/$15 double.*

LA MESA DE LOS MAYAS, *tel. 501240, $23 single/$29 double*, one of Flores' old-line restaurants, has recently made several guest rooms available.t

HOTEL CASONA DE LA ISLA, *north side, tel. 500692, 27 rooms. $24 single/$36 double.* The newest hotel in Flores, with air-conditioned rooms, restaurant, parking. A good buy. The **HOTEL ITZÁ**, *on the south side,* is a dive: no soap, no towel, no customers, unless everything else is full.

In San Benito

San Benito, the red-light district of metropolitan Flores, is a hodge-podge of buildings strewn around a market. It's not the most pleasant place in which to stay, but there are a couple of dreary hotels with rooms for about $3 per person.

Outside Flores

HOTEL VILLA MAYA, *tel. 500086. 28 rooms. In Guatemala City: 8 Calle 1-75, Zona 10, tel. 348136, fax 348134. $90 single/$98.*

Located beside little Lake Petenchel, surrounded by jungle and palms and forest and swamp eight kilometers east of Santa Elena on the way to Tikal, then another four kilometers north on a rough road. Villa Maya is currently in only partial operation. Rooms, in hillside jungle houses, have red-tiled floor, hardwood bed and built-in furniture, prints of toucans, and a small terrace facing the lake, as well as odd and interesting shapes. There are fans only to cool you off.

The restaurant serves a basic menu of fish and beef dishes, and usually has *tepezcuintle*, and sometimes other game.

Monkeys, pheasants, and assorted other wildlife are on the grounds, both caged and roaming free, or, in the case of multiple macaws, sitting on perches and watching you; and everything is as well manicured as it can be in a land of exuberance. All structures are roughly Mayan in design, but unmistakably modern — a metal *palapa* (pavilion), stone terraces, and a pool on several levels. Most of the advertised facilities, such as tennis courts and a miniature golf course, are still to be installed. Boats are available at no charge to guests, and small Jeep-type vehicles are available for rent.

In El Remate

Several more accommodations are available east of Flores, where the road for Tikal branches from the road to Belize.

WHERE TO EAT

Elegant cooking is nearly unknown in the Petén, which is still largely a frontier area. Chicken is invariably rubbery, and your filet mignon will be something tough and unrecognizable. Don't let yourself in for disappointment by ordering something that local hands aren't up to preparing.

On the other hand, the Petén is now settled enough to have its own *moyenne cuisine*, based largely on such native game as *tepezcuintle* (paca, or gibnut in Belize), wild boar and turkey, and deer. I wouldn't pass up the chance to try these.

At the **MESA DE LOS MAYAS** in Flores, you can enjoy a meal with local game that is not elegant, but wholesome, well-cooked, and reasonably priced at about $5. You're also safe with fish, beef on skewers, and Guatemalan-style steak in onions and tomatoes. This is an unpretentious place, with reed mats decorating the walls. There are simpler menus, without game, at the less attractive **RESTAURANT GRAN JAGUAR** and **LA JUNGLA**, both nearby in the center of Flores.

Almost all of the hotels, as well as these restaurants serve reasonably priced breakfasts. The cafeteria at the **HOTEL SAN JUAN**, the base for buses to Tikal, is open at 6 a.m.

EXCURSIONS

You can arrange with one of the boat owners for an excursion to several points of interest near Flores. A trip that costs under $10, and takes about two hours, starts with a ride across to the temple mounds that are the remains of part of **Tayasal**, the last Mayan stronghold, *on the shore to the north*. At the dock where you land, Mayan women do their laundry and bathe bare-breasted.

A trail leads up one of the mounds, covered with trees and brush. Is it worth it to ascend 136 steps in the jungle heat, to the top of the **Mirador Rey Canek** (a viewing platform in a jabín, or quebracho tree), and look down over a peninsula to the villages of San Andrés and San José nestled at the base of the long rise along the far northern shore, onto the islet of Santa Bárbara with its radio tower, to Flores and Santa Elena and the airport and the forest-bordered lake stretching beyond under a haze? Only you can answer.

Next stop on most excursions is **Ramonal**, *the island nearest Flores*, which has been left as a park and picnicking area, with treehouses, a rickety diving tower, and *la garrucha*, a cable and pulley. You can climb onto a platform, take hold of triangular bars, swing out, and ride a hundred feet or so down and over the water lilies to the peninsula to the north, then return on the companion cable. Fun, but perhaps a bit too reminiscent of commando training movies.

Farther on is **Petencito** (*Little Petén*), a municipal park and zoo *on an island and adjoining mainland, 20 minutes from Flores by boat*. All the animals — pheasants, parrots, boas, wild Petén turkeys, ocelots, pumas, jaguars, spider monkeys, white-tailed deer, tepezcuintles, crocodiles, foxes, margays, marmosets, and alligators — are native to the Petén. The mainland part of the zoo is reached by a footbridge several hundred meters long.

Also in this section are the main amusements: concrete water slides 30, 60 and 90 meters long. Wet yourself at the trough, turn on the water tap on the slide, hand your personal belongings to your boat driver, perhaps write down a last wish, then launch yourself as a human bobsled on the 90-meter slide — legs in, arms together, bombs away! Down, down you go, taking the curve at 70 miles an hour, rising slightly on the last stretch before being propelled through the air and crashing into the lake.

The 60-meter slide, curved and mogulled, is only worse. You don't find devices like these in the first or second world, at least not in concrete, but here, liability insurance is not known. Once was enough for me (I have to think about my children).

Hours at Petencito are 7 a.m. to 6 p.m., and there's a small admission charge.

Spelunking

For spelunking, the **Actun Kan caves** are south of town. *Follow the road right off the Flores causeway through Santa Elena, take the left fork at the edge of town, then go right. The caves are about three kilometers from the lake.*

Actun Kan (*Serpent Cave*) is illuminated, and for a small fee, a boy will escort you and point out natural formations that look like a sheep, a marimba, a mammoth, and a waterfall.

There are bats, and dripping water, and stalactites and stalagmites, but, except for an ancient carved face of *Chac*, the Mayan rain god, it's all minor league as caves go.

For more adventurous exploration on your own, the **Jobitzinaj caves** are the western outlet of the same underground system. Go right at the fork at the edge of Flores, then left and around the hill to reach the entrance. Take a flashlight and spare batteries, or candles.

PRACTICAL INFORMATION

A **post office** and a branch of the **Banco de Guatemala** (national bank) are located *in the center of Flores.*

The **tourist office** *is at the airport in Santa Elena.*

Guatel, the telephone company, *is on the mainland in Santa Elena, about three blocks west of the causeway.* Look for the microwave tower.

The **Hotel San Juan** *in Santa Elena* is a good place to get recent travel information. Several bus lines are headquartered there, and air tickets are sold.

TOURING TIKAL FROM THE FLORES AREA

From the Airport

A bus operated by the **Jungle Lodge** in Tikal meets flights and takes passengers to Tikal for about $5 each way. The fare will be higher if there are not many people on board.

Taxis are also available for individual or shared trips, and there are several car-rental counters where Jeeps and similar four-wheel drive vehicles are available. The car-rental operators are willing to bargain when business is slow.

Jeeps are rented by Koka Rentauto, *Calzada Rodríguez Macal at 1 Avenida B (tel. 501233), and at the airport (tel. 501526);* and by Enrique

Garrido, at the airport. Rates are about $50 daily for a Jeep, subject to bargaining when things are slow. It's often a better bet to hire a taxi for the day. $35 to $40 will get a group of four a round trip to Tikal.

From Flores and Santa Elena

Buses usually leave the terminal in Santa Elena at 6 a.m. and noon, make many stops, and take at least 90 minutes to reach Tikal. Buses depart Tikal promptly at 6 a.m. and 1 p.m. Fare is about $1.

To give yourself more time at the ruins, take the express microbus that leaves from the **Hotel San Juan** in Santa Elena at 7 a.m. This gets you to Tikal in an hour, and departs for Flores at 3 p.m., or whenever the passengers can be rounded up. Fare is about $5 round trip.

There's also a later microbus departure if demand warrants. Sign up at the Hotel San Juan the day before you travel, and you'll be picked up at your hotel. Daily tours to Tikal are offered by hotels in Flores. Or you can simply fly in and pick up a tour at the airport.

If you're going to camp out at Tikal for a night or two, and plan to do your own cooking, stock up on food in Flores. Oranges, grapefruits and other fruits make good snacks in the ruins. Leave what you can at your hotel in Flores, since there's no safe place to stow belongings at the Tikal campsite.

By Bus

For recent schedules and information about new routes, inquire at the **Hotel San Juan** on the main street in Santa Elena. The terminal for the Flores area is in Santa Elena, a couple of blocks south and east of the causeway.

ONWARD FROM FLORES

Aside from Tikal, it's difficult to get to many of the Mayan sites in the Petén by public transportation. **Uaxactún** can be reached in a day on foot from Tikal. **Sayaxché**, reached by bus, is the starting point for river trips to **El Ceibal** and a few sites near Lake Petexbatún. **El Ceibal** can also be reached by a jeep road from Sayaxché. **Yaxjá** and **Nakum**, east of Tikal, are accessible by jeep during the dry season. **Piedras Negras**, **Altar de los Sacrificios** and other sites along the Usumacinta River are reached by motorized canoe from Sayaxché. **Yaxchilán**, on the Mexican side of the Usumacinta River, can also be reached by chartered plane from Guatemala City or by road to a point on the river opposite the ruins.

One of the greatest Mayan sites, **El Mirador**, near the Mexican border in the north of the Petén, is reached by a two-day hike from Carmelita, a settlement that is accessible by bus from Flores. Tours to the more remote sites, as well as river and fishing trips, are offered by several travel agencies in Guatemala City, and by some hotels in the Flores area.

Bus service is available to some remote border regions with few facilities for the conventional traveller. Take the daily **Calzada Mopán** bus, and you can continue overland into the jungle of Campeche. I don't guarantee that you'll get there quickly. Or take the bus at 5 a.m. or 1 p.m. to **Naranjo**, northwest of Flores, (where basic accommodations are available), a ride of five hours or more. Catch a boat on the San Pedro River, and continue to La Palma, on the border (there's an immigration post, so it's all legal), and onward to **Tenosique** in the Mexican state of Chiapas, on the rail line to Mérida. There is a surer chance of getting through on this route.

ECO-SPANISH

By the time you've read or traveled this far, there's a fair chance that you've become interested in ecology and in learning some Spanish to ease your travels beyond Belize.

*In San Andrés, on the northwest shore of Lake Petén-Itzá, the **Eco-Escuela de Español** is pioneering a combination of language study with immersion in the effort to save the rain forest. Beyond one-on-one Spanish instruction, lectures and field trips emphasize forest ecology. Students go off the usual tourist track, network with local residents instead of with tour guides, and stay with villagers. Costs for room, board, and language lessons runs only about $100 weekly.*

*For information on this pioneering program, contact **ProPetén Eco-Escuela**, Casa Ing. Asturias, Flores, Petén, Guatemala, fax 502-9-501370, or **Conservation International Eco-Escuela**, 1015 18th St. NW, Washington, DC 20036, tel. 202-429-5660, fax 202-887-5188.*

Southwest of Flores
SAYAXCHÉ

Sayaxché (population 2,500), *44 miles from Flores*, is a jungle port of stilt houses and huts, not far from a number of archaeological sites. The town was founded late in the nineteenth century by monks who set up missions in order to assert Guatemalan sovereignty in lands claimed by Mexico.

The area around Sayaxché is rich in mahogany, cedar, rubber and balsam, which are exploited mainly along the rivers. The town sits on the south bank of the Río de la Pasión, a tributary of the Usumacinta that borders Mexico. Some of the corn grown in the township is shipped by canoe upriver to Sebol, far to the south.

ARRIVALS & DEPARTURES
By Bus
Buses leave Santa Elena (near Flores) for Sayaxché twice daily (recent schedule: departures at 6 a.m. and 12:30 p.m.). The trip takes two hours. The bus drops you on the north bank of the river, where you can catch a cayuco or the car ferry to the other side, for a small fare.

WHERE TO STAY & EAT
The **GUAYACÁN**, *to the left of the ferry landing as you cross over*, is a well-kept building. *Rooms are about $25 single/$35 double*, and meals are available, sometimes including wild game.

And there is another hotel, the **MAYAPÁN**. Several small diners in town serve meals. There is also a fishing lodge on Lake Petexbatún (see below).

EXCURSIONS
Several archaeological sites are accessible from Sayaxché by water. The **Tamarindito ruins** sit on a north-facing rock outcrop about four kilometers west of Lake Petexbatún, which lies south of Sayaxché. **Aguateca**, with large stelae, is above a creek that runs into the south side of the lake. **Dos Pilas** is about 12 kilometers west of the river flowing out of Lake Petexbatún to the Río de la Pasión. There are also some sulfur springs along the shore of the lake.

Don't attempt to reach the ruins without a guide. The settings are spectacular, as is the jungle scenery. But the sites are relatively small, and are unrestored.

MOTORIZED CAYUCO
A trip by motorized cayuco can be expensive unless you've got a few people to share expenses. To Lake Petexbatún, Aguateca or Dos Pilas, the cost will be at least $60. The long trip to Yaxchilán, on the Mexican side of the Usumacinta, will cost as much as $300. Negotiate prices with the boat owners.

Most cayucos will safely hold up to four people, including the operator. Large cargo cayucos heading for Sebol will sometimes take on passengers. Be ready to go immediately, or to wait a week or more until a boat leaves.

Fishing
Fishing in Lake Petexbatún for snook, peacock bass and smaller species, and for tarpon in July and August, is said to be excellent. A lodge on the lake has operated from time to time for fishing parties, and as a base for groups visiting archaeological sites.

EL CEIBAL

The ruins of **El Ceibal**, *up the Río de la Pasión from Sayaxché*, can be reached by jeep (tours from hotels in Flores are available) as well as by boat. Features of the site include a stairway decorated with many glyphs, and numerous stelae. The later ones show Mexican clothing, faces, and design motifs, suggesting that the decline of the Classic Maya, at least at El Ceibal, was associated with domination by peoples from the north. Structures at El Ceibal are relatively low and, strangely, most do not use the corbeled arch typical of the Maya. The finely carved stelae, depicting priests, ball players and other personages, are well preserved. The last inscribed date is equivalent to 889 A.D.

The ruins of El Ceibal are threatened by plans to develop an oil well on the site.

ALTAR DE LOS SACRIFICIOS

The ruins of **Altar de los Sacrificios** *are downriver from Sayaxché, at the point where the Río de la Pasión joins the Chixoy River to form the Usumacinta.* The site was discovered in 1895 by Teobert Maler, who named it for its great stone altars. Altar de los Sacrificios, like El Ceibal, lacks arches.

YAXCHILAN

Farther north, **Yaxchilán** *stretches for several miles on the Mexican side of the Usumacinta, at a sharp bend.* Considerable clearing has been carried out among the structures, which follow the contours of the land instead of being set on artificial platforms, as at other Mayan sites. Figures are carved on stelae and elsewhere in unusually deep relief. Interpreters of Mayan glyphs believe that Yaxchilán was ruled by the Jaguar dynasty. Dated structures were erected until the equivalent of 840 A.D.

Yaxchilán and several other sites on the Usumacinta are threatened by plans for hydroelectric development.

PIEDRAS NEGRAS

Downriver from Yaxchilán on the Guatemalan bank is **Piedras Negras**, named for rocks of blackish limestone in the river sand. The site is thought to have flourished in Early Classic times, and is known for the carved stone lintels in its structures, and for its rather numerous stelae. Many of the important structures were roofed with straw or some other perishable material.

Most of the stelae, which were erected every five years, have been removed to museums, leaving the site relatively bare. The large number of stelae with obviously interrelated inscriptions enabled modern-day cryptographers to interpret Mayan glyphs indicating dynasties and city names.

The Usumacinta was an ancient trade route of the Maya, who are thought to have used it for commerce with coastal regions along the Gulf of Mexico. But strangely, few artifacts from the coast or from the Guatemalan highlands have been found at Piedras Negras. Access is by boat or by chartered plane.

FURTHER EXPLORATION IN GUATEMALA

While the archaeological sites of the Petén are a logical extension of a trip to Belize, travel onward in Guatemala is another book; consult my *Guatemala Guide*, Open Road Publishing.

18. SOUTHERN BELIZE

INTRODUCTION

The overland route to southern Belize is less than straightforward. Vehicles must follow the Western Highway from Belize City to Belmopan, then double back to the southeast along the Hummingbird Highway; or take a newer cutoff to the south at **Democracia**, 31 miles west of Belize City. The road distance to **Dangriga**, the biggest southern town, is 107 miles by the first route, 77 by the second, while the sea route is 36 miles long. The waterlogged terrain directly south of Belize City accounts for the switchback.

Public transportation in the south is poor. On most days, four buses run up from Dangriga to Belize City in the morning, and return in the afternoon. Two buses a day leave from Dangriga for Punta Gorda, and one for Mango Creek. Service to Placencia is less than daily. Confirm schedules before you head south, especially if coming from the west and changing buses in Belmopan.

From Belmopan, the Hummingbird Highway is paved for about twelve miles through flat country of low bush, much of it once forest that has been logged out, to Caves Branch. The road then rises and runs along the northeastern skirt of the Maya Mountains, through an area of eroded limestone hills. Here the earth is honeycombed with caves — many of which still contain ancient Mayan altars and offerings — and underground streams, and topped with misty tropical hardwood forest dense with orchids, bromeliads and ferns.

ST. HERMAN'S CAVE & BLUE HOLE

Off the road, *in the vicinity of mile 13*, is **St. Herman's Cave**. To reach it, take the unmarked road leading to the west, about a mile south of the roads department depot at mile 12. A thousand yards in, take the path up and then the steps down into the cave. It's an enchanting area, with mist and sunlight filtering through ferns and trees, and jungle vegetation tumbling down the limestone face.

You'll need a powerful flashlight and extra batteries to go any distance in. There are extensive passageways, and a small river. Knowledgeable speleologists downgrade this cave. But at least it's accessible, and for the less-than-knowledgeable, it's quite impressive. Mayan Pottery found here is kept in the vaults of the Archaeology Department in Belmopan.

About two miles farther south along the highway is the **Blue Hole**. Once the sight of occaisional thefts, the zone is now guarded over by full-time park rangers and is safer now than in the past. I still suggest locking your vehicle here.

From the roadside, take the steps down, to where water flows up from underground. The hole is, indeed, blue and deep and lovely, with vines and plants cascading down the enclosing little canyon. The waters flow off in a clear stream, then into a cave and back into the earth. Bye-bye. Dye tracings show that the waters that emerge at the Blue Hole come from St. Herman's Cave, and ends up in the Sibun River. Take a refreshing swim, if you're not too worried about your car.

A nature trail, about 1.5 miles long, connects the Blue Hole and the entry to St. Herman's cave, through the forest and away from the highway. *Do not walk it alone.*

Notable bird species at Blue Hole, according to the Belize Audubon Society, include the slaty-breasted tinamou, spotted wood quail, black hawk eagle, white hawk, keel-billed toucan and nightingale wren.

SPORTS & RECREATION
Spelunking
Adventurous Belize, *tel. (08) 22800* operated by Ian Anderson, offers caving, among many available capers, on a 60,000-acre leased plot near Belmopan, perforated by hundreds of caves. Underground run the waters of the inland Blue Hole, which re-surface on the site, and disappear into yet another cavern.

Mr. Anderson is not your typical tour operator. When you accompany him into the jungle and down into caves, you go *his* way, which is to leave sites as if you had never been there. Cigarettes are bagged and removed. Footprints are washed off crystal.

Some caves are of the walk-in type, others require a rappel down ropes from surface openings. Some are considered archaeologically sensitive, with fossilized Mayan footprints, ancient sculptures, and crystallized skeletons in place. Some caves hold waterfalls.

Camping and day trips range from "soft" to "hard" in difficulty. An underground river tubing trip, suitable even for timid folk, runs from

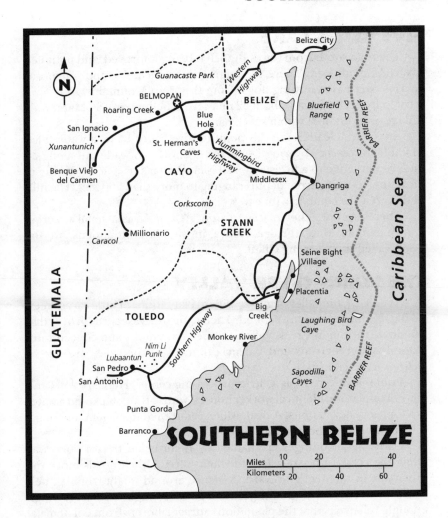

light shaft to light shaft, up to the surface and down under again, around pillars several feet thick carved with Mayan images, with breaks to walk through the jungle where logs have floated through and jammed the thoroughfare. Trips to remote sites last as long as a week.

Adventurous Belize has a few bedrooms available in a couple of farm houses off the Hummingbird Highway, south of Belmopan, a sort of hostel, with bed and meals for $60 per day, less if you stay in a tent, plus $25 to $30 for each day's outing (more if you're staying elsewhere). There is no electricity and no running water but for a basic cold shower.

There are also walking trails lined with identified native flora transplanted from the vicinity. Observation decks are being constructed at canopy level.

FIVE BLUES LAKE

The road south from Caves Branch is being improved, and potholed stretches eliminated. There are many dips and climbs, and numerous bridges over rivers flowing down from the Maya Mountains. *At mile 32* (posted from Dangriga — about 22 miles from Belmopan), **St. Margaret's Village**, is a rest area with a snack bar.

A Jeep trail leads from this point to **Five Blues Lake**, a water-filled sinkhole, or *cenote*, covering five acres. Visitors can wade out along an underwater ledge to a forest-covered island. That's five *shades* of blue in the name, resulting from depths ranging to more than 200 feet. The hills in this area are combed with caves.

There are few other places to stop. *At mile 26* is a small waterfall known as **Poor Man's Fridge**. Above, in the Maya Mountains, are the peaks called the **Sleeping Giant**.

THE STANN CREEK VALLEY

At mile 24, the valley begins to widen. Plantations of little cacao trees, no bigger than a man, are sighted. Then come the vast citrus groves that dominate the Stann Creek Valley. Canned fruit juices and concentrates made from grapefruits and Valencia oranges of the valley are one of Belize's main exports.

Pomona, *at mile 13*, is a citrus processing center. Here are rows and rows of miniature, identical worker houses, with rotting steps, and a water tap for every dozen units. A neat, white, red-roofed management bungalow sits atop a manicured hill.

Cartloads of oranges are hauled by Belorussian tractors one way along the road, to be squashed for their juice, and cartloads move the other way to the peel graveyard. A glance around might trouble one's social conscience. But conditions are good enough, and wages high enough, relatively, that the plantations attract laborers from Guatemala, El Salvador, and Honduras.

The agriculture of the Stann Creek valley was dominated once by sugar, and later by bananas. A railroad was built in 1908 to take bananas to the coast, where they were picked up by vessels of the United Fruit Company. Panama disease wiped out the plantations in the 1920s, and the railroad tracks were removed to serve a logging operation in the north. A disease-resistant variety of banana is now being grown in the valley, and exports are on the rise once again.

GALES POINT

At about mile 9 off the Hummingbird Highway southbound, turn left onto the Coastal Road (also known as the Manatee Road) on to a 2 1/2 mile long sandbar peninsula that extends into the Southern Lagoon. Great volumes of water flow down from the Maya Mountains and move through the lagoon and out to sea, and plenty of fish inhabit the waters.

At the tip of this small landmass is **Gales Point Manatee**, a charming Creole fishing village of 500 souls. Dozens of simple wooden houses built on stilts line the waterfront, and are inhabited by the descendants of the loggers that arrived here over 200 years ago. These are some of the friendliest Creole in the country, and often can be found playing all night domino games at **Gentles's Cool Spot**, the town's only watering hole (cool beers and home-made cashew wine served).

Although the villagers still hunt the deer, gibnut, armadillo, and peccary, a few are starting to get involved in the area's expanding tourism and hotel industry. The recent addition of dirt roads, a community telephone, and limited electrical service (only at night) have thus far not changed the laid-back quality of this sleepy town. While not on the typical tourist schedule, it's certainly worth the side trip to visit here, or perhaps spend a day or more in peaceful relaxation.

ARRIVALS & DEPARTURES
By Bus
A Z-Line bus runs here from Belize City on weekdays at 1pm, weekends at 10am and 5pm. The ride takes 95 minutes and costs only $3. Buses from Dangriga to Gales Point leave daily 6am and 10am and costs about $2. If the heavy rains occur, the roads may be closed, thus the busses will not operate.

Call (02)73977 in Belize City or (05) 22702 in Dangriga to check the schedule.

By Boat
A gentleman named Michael Usher runs day boat trips to the Manatee Sanctuary from Belize City, when demand warrants, at about $50 per person. These include trolling along the way, and a stop at a cashew grove. Look for a notice on bulletin boards at smaller guest houses in Belize City.

WHERE TO STAY
MANATEE LODGE, *Gales Point Road, Gales Point, tel. & fax # (021) 2040. US reservations at (800) 334-7942 at C.W. Maryland. 8 double rooms. $77.50/single, $105.00/ double with breakfast. Meal plans are additional.*

This former fishing lodge at the tip of Gales Point has been beautifully converted into one of the most tranquil waterfront inns imaginable. The large rooms in the two main structures all have private bathrooms, ceiling fans, mahogany furnishings, several screened in windows, and either one or two beds. The lodge is managed by Debbie Callender, who can also be found rolling up her sleaves to work in the kitchen or gardens. Surrounded by the Southern Lagoon on three sides, this casual property is a great spot to fish, watch for manatees, view a huge assortment of tropical birds, or just simply lay back on a hammock and forget about your worries. Nearby excursions can be arranged to take guests out on scuba dives and land-based excursions. The lodge's central dining room serves 3 meals a day that feature local ingredients, and lots of fresh fruits.

At press time, **THE SHORES** oceanfront lodge is just about ready to open with 6 nice rooms that all have private bathrooms, ceiling fans, and great views. *For rates and information, give David Morris a call at (021) 2023.*

A co-operative community-based **bed-and-breakfast service** can offer ten rooms at the moment for $10 per person plus meals, without indoor plumbing and sometimes without running water. *Call the Gales Point community telephone, 05-22087, or inquire at the Seaside Guest House in Belize City.*

SEEING THE SIGHTS

An inland waterway approach to Gales Point is possible from Belize City in small craft, by the Burdon Canal from Haulover Creek, and the Jones, Northern, and Manatee lagoons. There are some caves a couple of miles from town, but these are subject to flooding, and should be visited only with a locally-hired guide.

Farther back from the sea and inland are the **Ben Lomond** and **Manatee** caves. These can be reached by boat from Manatee (or from Belize City). The caves are a hike of several miles from the nearest landing point.

The **Gales Point Manatee Community Sanctuary** is currently being developed with the cooperation and participation of the local community. In addition to the marine mammal that gives its name to the lagoon, the rivers and hills and mangroves around the village are home to crocodiles, hawksbill turtles, jabirus, ibis and egrets, some of them rare in other locations.

DANGRIGA

Known until recently as Stann Creek, **Dangriga** is one of the principal settlements of the Black Caribs (*Garífunas*, or *Garinagu*), the people of mixed African and American Indian origin who live along much of the Caribbean coast of Central America. The Caribs trace their arrival in Dangriga to 1823, when their ancestors fled Honduras in the wake of a failed rebellion. The anniversary of their landing is celebrated on November 19 every year.

The old name of Dangriga owed its origin to the trading post, or stand (which became Stann), established in the seventeenth century by Puritans from the island of New Providence. The Puritans also farmed some of the offshore islets, now called the **Tobacco Cayes** after their major crop, and settled in numbers at Placencia, farther south, though they left no permanent marks on the country. The new name, Dangriga, means *standing waters* in Garifuna.

Although only 36 miles apart in a straight line, Dangriga and Belize City have little in common beside their seaside locations and a preponderance of wooden buildings. Belize City is in a swamp; but in southern Belize, the rivers rushing down from the Maya Mountains have, over the many centuries, deposited a wide and thick layer of soil, making the coastal belt agriculturally rich and eminently habitable.

With a population of about 8,000, Dangriga is almost a metropolis in people-scarce Belize, clean, bustling with the commerce associated with the citrus industry.

ORIENTATION

The sea views from Dangriga are lovely. Two rivers that flow through, **North Stann Creek** and **Havana Creek**, are populated at most times of the day by fish, people, and boats of every size, in equal numbers. Dangriga is jolly, cheery, lively. The church is usually packed. But Dangriga is flat, and physically not too interesting or attractive. It's not to everyone's taste. If you're spending the night anyway, and want a change of scene, take a walk north along the water, via the narrow beach, past the cemetery, over a rotting footbridge, to and past the Pelican Beach resort. Nobody much is around. A low escarpment marks the coast to the north.

The Garifuna culture, about which much has been said and written, is not easily penetrable unless you stay in town for a while, get to know a few people, and are yourself an open person. You might be offered coconut bread by a street vendor, but other traditional Garifuna food, such as cassava, is usually eaten at home. Garifuna dancers are most evident on Garifuna Settlement Day. But the celebrations continue off and on until the end of the year. Masked John-Canoe (or *Yankunu*) dancers perform in the streets before Christmas for gifts of money, rum or candy. Conch shells are blown at midnight on Christmas Eve. Other ceremonies are rarely seen by outsiders. One is the *dugu*, a healing ritual in which a priestess communicates with the dead while in a trance. The dugu takes place over the course of a week, to the accompaniment of drumming and dancing, and sacrifices of chickens and pigs.

You'll see the studios of several Garifuna artists in the area below North Stann Creek. The most noted is Mr. Pen Cayetano. Hours are whimsical. Garifunas are also known for their home-made instruments, especially drums.

ARRIVALS & DEPARTURES

Arriving By Bus From Belize City

Z-Line buses (Magazine Road, *tel. 73937, 22211 in Dangriga*) leave at 8 and 10 a.m. and 2, 3 and 4 p.m., Monday through Friday, with more limited service on weekends. The fare is about about $4 and they run along the Hummingbird Highway with a one hour stop and change of buses in Belmopan.

The James bus (Pound Yard Bridge on West Collet Canal, *tel. 07-2056*) leaves Monday, Wednesday, Friday and Saturday at 9 a.m. Another Z line bus service is a time saving daily express twice daily bus along the Coastal Road between Belize City and Dangriga without the usual stop off in Belompan, and it costs $5.

Arriving By Air

Maya Airways flights leave Belize City for Dangriga daily at 6:30 a.m. (except Sunday), 9 a.m., 10:55 a.m., 12:30p.m., 2:30 p.m., and 4:40 p.m. from Monday through Saturday. On Sundays the 10:30 a.m. and 12:30 p.m. flights do not usually run. These same planes usually continue to Placencia and Punta Gorda. Northbound flights from Big Creek and Punta Gorda also touch down here. Fare is about $26 from Belize City to Dangriga. *Telephone Maya at (02) 44234 in Belize City for the latest information.*

The airstrip in Dangriga is in the Pelican Beach Resort's back yard.

Departing By Bus

Promised Land buses, *tel. (05) 23012*, to and from Placencia park in Dangriga Riverside, on the south end of the bridge over North Stann Creek. Z-Line buses, tel. # (05) 22160, also have a depot on the outskirts of town near the corner of St. Vincent Street. The are almost hourly Z line departures (less on Sundays) for Belize City via Belmopan; James bus Tuesday and Friday at 1 p.m., Sunday and Thursday at 6 a.m. These are the schedules via the Hummingbird Highway. The Z Line express bus leaves twice a day with direct service to Belize City via the Coastal Road.

Every day but Sunday, buses leave Dangriga for Punta Gorda at 12:30 and 7:30 p.m., for Mango Creek at 3:30 p.m.

Z-Line and Promised Land buses leave for Placencia three times daily from Monday through Saturday (once on Sundays) The James Bus from Belize City also continues to Punta Gorda on the four days when it's running. And that's all the southbound bus transport there is.

Departing By Air

Maya Airways flights leave for Belize City at 7:20am, 8:00 a.m. (except Sunday), 10:40 a.m., noon (except Sunday), 2:00 p.m. (except Sunday) and 4:50 p.m. Southbound flights continue to Big Creek and Punta Gorda. Buy tickets at the Maya Airways ticket agent next to the airstrip, the Pelican Beach Resort, or at any shop on Dangriga's main street with a Maya Airways sign.

GETTING AROUND TOWN

Vans are available for rent, with driver, at the **Pelican Beach Hotel**, for about $150 per day. You can also try **Rosado's Tours**, *35 Lemon St., tel. 22119*, for inland and fishing tours, or **Lester Eiley**, *25 Oak St., tel. 22113*, for boats. All of the above will also arrange fishing trips and transport to the cayes.

WHERE TO STAY

Telephone dialing code for Dangriga is 05 from Belize, 011-501-5 from the U.S.A.

PELICAN BEACH RESORT, *P. O. Box 14, tel. 05-22044, fax 22570). 20 rooms. $57 to 70 single/$75 to 85 double, plus 10% service plus tax, slightly lower March through October. Add $25 for three meals. Visa, Master Card, American Express.*

Pelican Beach is located at **Scotchman Town**, a mile north of Dangriga, next to the airstrip. Rooms are upstairs in the main lodge, and in an annex. About half face the water. They're plywood-panelled with hardwood floors, ceiling fan, vinyl easy chair, large night table — typical of no-frills rooms in the cayes, but much larger, and with a real tub in the bathroom. The dining room is pleasant, with sea views through louvers, and the goofy combination of elements that you will have come to expect in Belize: Star Trek table lamps, formica counters, bamboo accessories, a stuffed sailfish, overhead fans, and sagging ceiling panel — altogether perfect. A large common area has table tennis.

The best feature, though, is the lovely, wide, palm- and pine-shaded beach, fringed with sea grapes, that extends to the veranda of the hotel. There are plenty of chairs under the second-floor overhang, where you can sit and watch the fleets of pelicans.

Boats, fishing excursions, cottages on **South Water Caye** ($115 for the trip out, $100 for the cottage per day) and jaguar reserve tours ($150 for five persons), windsurfers and snorkeling equipment are all available at a price.

As the only resort, there are some slight extra charges built in to staying here — a less advantageous exchange rate than at the bank, and the fact that taxis charge a relatively steep tab *per person* for the one-mile trip from town.

JUNGLE HUTS MOTEL, *Ecumenical Dr., tel. 05-23166. 6 units. $30 single/$35 double, or $43/$50 with air conditioning.*

You will know them when you see them: four little square cottages, with either zinc or thatched roofs, by the bridge that carries the highway into Dangriga. For those who prefer not to be right in the center, these are a good choice.

Dangriga's in-town hotels are more modest and have fewer amenities. The **HUB GUEST HOUSE** (*573A South Riverside, P. O. Box 56, tel. 05-22397*), just south of the bridge at North Stann Creek, is a clean concrete bungalow, with seven rooms going for $18 single, $25 double with private toilet and shower. Meals are served with fresh orange juice, which you won't always find in Dangriga (rice and beans with chicken, or breakfast, for $4), and the owner is generally eager to please. Ask here about boat rentals, and excursions. Credit cards are accepted with a surcharge.

The **RIVERSIDE**, *in the center of Dangriga at 135 Commerce St., has small rooms at $10 per person with shared bath*. Homey atmosphere. The owners also have a lodge on one of the cayes offshore, where the daily rate is $125 per person with all meals. It's another $125 to get out there.

Rooms at the **CAMELEON CENTRAL**, *119 Commerce St.*, are barer than at the Riverside. The rate is about $8 per person. The **RÍO MAR INN**, *977 Waight Street (Southern Foreshore), tel. 22201*, has just a few rooms at less than $10 per person. Down at the south end of town by Havana Creek, **PAL'S GUEST HOUSE** *(tel. 22095)* has sea views from some of its ten clean, bare concrete rooms. The rate is $15 single/$20 double with private bath and fan, or $10 per person sharing bath.

The **BONEFISH HOTEL** (*15 Mahogany Rd., P. O. Box 21, tel. 05-22165, fax 22296, 10 rooms, $45 single/$60 double), on the seafront*, does, indeed, have the air conditioning and cable television that it advertises, but the rooms are concrete with musty carpeting and the barest of furnishings, though it's clean. An all-day fishing trip (for bonefish, naturally) can be arranged for $150. Located two blocks south of the bus park, then two blocks east to the sea.

In the U.S., call 800-798-1558 to reserve – ask for Byron.

WHERE TO EAT

Restaurants are generally open in Dangriga at meal times only, i.e., 7 to 10 a.m., noon to 3 p.m., and from 7 p.m.

Two Chinese restaurants *on the main street*, the **SUNRISE** and the **STARLIGHT**, serve sandwiches, rice and beans, and assorted chow meins. **THE BURGER KING** (no relation to anything else by that name) serves rice and beans, fried chicken, conch soup, and burgers, too. The tab runs to $2 for a sandwich at any of these eateries, $5 to $6 for a main course. For more predictable fare, the dining room of the **PELICAN BEACH HOTEL** is open to non-guests at regular meal hours. Breakfast or a light lunch about $6, dinner $10 to $14.

SOUTH WATER CAYE & TOBACCO CAYE

If you're in the mood to go offshore for a bit while you're in the Dangriga area, try either of these two laid-back cayes.

ARRIVALS & DEPARTURES
By Boat

Boats for Tobacco Caye usually leave from Riverside at about 2 p.m., or when the 10 a.m. bus from Belize City arrives. Fare is about $15 per person.

Otherwise, call 22171 in Dangriga (the number for Reef's End) to hook up with a scheduled departure, or hire a boat at Riverside for a special run.

WHERE TO STAY

If you're interested in accommodations at South Water Caye, off Dangriga, speak to the folks at **PELICAN BEACH RESORT** or at the **BONEFISH HOTEL**. Mr. Eiley, *tel. 22113*, can arrange boat transportation for about $120 for a group, and has a good reputation.

For Tobacco Caye accommodations, inquire at the **RÍO MAR INN**.

Southward

The Southern Highway forks from the Hummingbird Highway six miles inland from Dangriga. The road is unpaved all the way, and the few vehicles that ply it kick up generous amounts of dust, or churn it into mud. If you don't have your own vehicle, you're at the mercy of a limited bus schedule. But farmers, Gurkhas, British soldiers, and anyone else going this way are usually pretty good about giving rides. Good luck!

Depending on soil conditions, the vegetation along the road is palmetto and pine in red dirt, or leafy tropical forest. Along the way are numerous short streams that rush down as torrents after heavy rains, and trickle among boulders when it's been dry, crossed by plank or newer steel bridges. Inland, beyond the bush, occasional orange groves and pasture, and a stray village, is the ridge of the Maya Mountains.

HOPKINS

A side road from the Southern Highway leads to the Garifuna fishing village of Hopkins, with no bars and no organized attractions, just wooden houses on stilts scattered for several miles along what could well be the widest, clearest, and sandiest beach in Belize.

ARRIVALS & DEPARTURES

By Bus, Truck or Taxi

A bus leaves Hopkins for Dangriga at 7 a.m. on Monday, Wednesday, Friday and Saturday, and departs Hopkins for the return trip at noon. Trucks also make the trip — the lottery sellers seem to know if a truck will be running on any particular day. A taxi from Dangriga costs $25 or more.

By Boat

Ask at Riverside in Dangriga about boats for Hopkins.

WHERE TO STAY

A brand new beachfront property called the **JAGUAR REEF LODGE** has opened its doors to the public. They feature 14 beautiful thatched-roof cabanas with private bathrooms. The resort offers lots of nature, wildlife, scuba, and snorkeling excursions.

Rates are $65 to $85 single, and $85 to $100 double, and meal plans are available. Call for information at tel. # (092) 3452.

Besides that, Hopkins has several no-frills lodging places:

At the south end of town is the **SANDY BEACH LODGE**, run by the Sandy Beach Women's Cooperative, with 15 basic rooms in two cottages on stilts. Meals feature such Garifuna specialties as *hudut* (fish soup), cassava bread, and *hiyu* (a cassava beverage). *The rate is about $10 per person.* The **CARIBBEAN VIEW**, privately owned by people from Hopkins, *has eight rooms at about $9 per person.*

To reserve a place at either hotel, *call the Hopkins community phone at 05-22033.* The operator can arrange for you to be called back if you're in Belize.

Miss Timothea serves meals of renown at a large table in her kitchen, by candlelight after dark — beans, rice, salads, fresh-caught fish, maybe fresh-killed gibnut. You will find her at the northwest corner of the only intersection in town. She also has a couple of rooms for rent.

SITTEE RIVER

At **Sittee River Village**, on another turn from the Southern Highway, *about 20 miles from Dangriga*, is a guest house operated by the folks from **Glover's Atoll Resort**, where bunk beds are available at $5 a night to outgoing passengers, as well as drop-ins. There should be room on any weeknight. Private rooms are available nearby at Prospect Guest House for about $10 per person. *Call the community operator, 05-22006, to inquire.*

Another facility, **SITTEE RIVER LODGE**, is available only to groups booked through travel agents.

Glover's can arrange for excursions in the area, among them: visit with an herbalist, $10; river ride to rapids, $15; dugout rental, $3 per hour.

COCKSCOMB BASIN WILDLIFE SANCTUARY

The world's first and only jaguar reserve, the **Cockscomb Basin Wildlife Sanctuary**, *is located off the Southern Highway south of Dangriga.* Just a few years ago, jaguars were hunted as big game, and were in danger of disappearing from Belize, as they have from most other countries in the Americas. Now they're a protected species.

Largest of the hemisphere's cats, jaguars (*panthera onca*) grow up to six feet in length and weigh up to 350 pounds. Armadillos and gibnuts (pacas) are among their favorite foods, though they'll eat animals of all sizes, from deer and peccaries to rats and birds. Despite local tales, there's no evidence that they have a special taste for humans. Jaguars use old roads and trails to get around the reserve, which includes several abandoned logging camps.

The Cockscomb basin is an area of moist tropical forest bounded on three sides by ridges of the Maya Mountains, crossed by two large rivers and numerous creeks. The forest reserve was established in 1984; the wildlife sanctuary within it in 1986, with the support of public and private organizations, including the Jaguar car company.

The wildlife sanctuary takes in the habitats not only of the jaguar, but also of Belize's other cats: pumas, jaguarundi, margays and ocelots. Local wildlife also includes brocket deer, paca (*gibnut*), and peccary; Baird's tapir (*mountain cow*), and kinkajou (*nightwalker*), boas, iguanas, tree frogs, and much else. Common bird species are toucans (*billbirds*), king vultures (*King John Crow*), curassows, and scarlet macaws.

The 100,000-acre reserve also includes at least one Mayan site, Kuchil Balam, chanced upon only a few years ago by scientist Alan Rabinowitz. *A small fee of $5 will soon be imposed on all visitors to the sanctury.*

ARRIVALS & DEPARTURES

To reach the sanctuary, take a bus or drive to Maya Center, at mile 14 on the Southern Highway. The reserve is seven miles westward.

WHERE TO STAY

Bunk beds are available in dormitories, at a fee of less than $10 per person, and camping is permitted, also at a charge. Bring your own food. There are also several nature trails, and exhibits illustrating local species.

TOURING THE RESERVE

Before going, inquire about facilities and seasonal conditions at the **Audubon Society**, *12 Cork St., Belize City, tel. 77369*. Or call at the Pelican Beach Resort in Dangriga, which is in radio contact with the reserve.

Have no fear if you plan to walk in — jaguars don't frequent the entry road. In fact, though you might sight jaguar tracks, your chances of seeing a live jaguar are better even at the Belize Zoo than here. What you'll espy is evidence of the jaguar's nocturnal presence: tracks and droppings. Expect mainly to enjoy the nature trails, in a rain forest that has been little altered even by loggers.

It takes about two hours to reach the camp on foot from the Southern Highway. Remember that the rainy season in this area runs from June through January, and that with from 100 to 180 inches of precipitation per year, it is *wet*.

PLACENCIA

About a hundred miles south of Belize City is the idyllic **Placencia Peninsula** (also spelled **Placentia**), a skinny, 16-mile long finger of beach and coconut palms that points southward from the mainland.

Placencia village, at the southern tip, is home to about four hundred Creole fishermen and their families. Most of the locals are also becoming involved in the area's blossoming tourism industry. The principal means of transport are the wheelbarrows that ply the village's mile-long narrow sidewalk.

The center of Placencia is everybody's back yard. There's no hustle and bustle, just open sand, wooden houses scattered under the coconut palms, and the concrete sidewalk. The point of arrival, and the point of departure for orientation, is the fishing co-op's dock at Placencia Point. This is located at the end of the peninsula's only road, and is the center for all communications and transportation in Placencia. Here you can find the village's post office, telephone office, gas station, bus stop, charter fishing operation, taxi stand, and air line ticket agency.

For cheese, potatoes, ballpoint pens, mustard, wine, ketchup and other general and specialized merchandise, the best-stocked source in this part of Belize is **Wallen's Market**, on the vehicle road by the soccer field near the bottom of the peninsula. Assorted other shops and services include a book exchange, acupuncturist, and a bakery.

The advent of all-year road connections have begun to change the sleepy character of Placencia. Already, chartered buses arrive on some weekends, filling most hotels with vacationers from Belize City. Plan to go in the middle of the week, but do go now, before the yacht harbor, air terminal, travel agency, "in" bars, and glass-bottomed-boat sightseeing tours are in place.

From the top of the peninsula, there's water to both sides: the reef-protected Caribbean to the east, and the mangrove-lined Placencia lagoon to the west, with the Maya Mountains towering in the distance. Being on the Placencia Peninsula is just like being on a sleepy tropic isle, with most locals being quite friendly, except perhaps for those in the village of Placencia itself.

ARRIVALS & DEPARTURES

A recently constructed road provides all-year access to Placencia from a turnoff at mile 23 on the Southern Highway. From this point, it's seven miles to the sea and the beginning of the peninsula; 16 miles to Maya Beach; 19 miles to the Garifuna village of Seine Bight; and 22 miles to the end of the road at Placencia.

Arriving By Bus

Three buses leave Dangriga for Placencia daily, except on Sundays when there is only 1 bus. The ride takes about three hours and costs about $4. If coming from Belize City, confirm connections by calling the Z-Line bus company *(02-73937)*.

A Z-Line bus departs Dangriga at 3:30 p.m. daily for Mango Creek for $6, where you can hire a boat to Placencia (see below).

Arriving By Air

Flights land at the new Placencia airstrip 2 miles north of town. Taxis are available upon arrival, and will charge about $5 to most in town hotels. **Maya Air** has several departures daily from Belize City in both directions, with some of them also servicing Dangriga and Punta Gorda. *Telephone (02) 45968 in Belize City for the latest information.*

Three **Tropic Air** flights, *tel. (026) 2012,* also land here daily. Northbound flights from Punta Gorda also touch down at Big Creek.

Arriving By Boat

If you have a reservation at one of the resorts, you'll be picked up. Otherwise, you'll have to find a boat that's going over, either from Big Creek or nearby Mango Creek. Charter runs can also be arranges by checking with your hotel.

Departing By Bus

Three buses daily (only one on Sunday) leave Placencia for Dangriga. Inquire at hotels for exact schedules.

Departing By Air

Flights between Belize City and Punta Gorda touch down several times daily at the Placencia airstrip. Reserve through **Maya Airways** or any of the two dozen area ticket agents displaying the Maya logo on their storefront.

WHERE TO STAY

A small number of resorts located between Placencia and Seine Bight villages provide exclusive accommodations, each with its own stretch of coconut palm-shaded private beach. You should make reservations before heading to any of these, especially if you don't have your own transportation — they're spread out, and it can be a hot or rain-soaked walk to find there's no room. Most of the budget lodging places are located right in Placencia village.

Telephone dialing code for Placencia is 06 from Belize, 011-501-6 from the U.S.

RUM POINT INN, *tel. (06) 23239, fax (06) 23240. 10 self standing private cabanas. $175 single/$224 double (with 3 meals Placencia airstrip. Special off season and holiday rates available upon request. American Express, Visa, Master Card, Discover. Reservations: Toucan Turs, 32 Traminer Dr., Kenner, LA 70065, tel. 800-747-1381, fax 504-464-0325.*

A couple of miles up the coast from Placencia Point, Rum Point Inn offers its guests a choice of one of 10 large uniquely sculpted ferro-cement cabanas. Each beach view unit can accommodate between one and four people, and contains a private bathroom, ceiling fan, locally hand-made hardwood furnishings, purified water, and plenty of interior space. The inn features a main building where clients can enjoy 3 delicious meals in an open air dining room, indulge in a few cold drinks in a rustic bar, relax on plush sofas while reading from the extensive library, or just kick back in one of the verandah's colorful hammocks.

Rum Point also offers many of the area's best fishing expeditions, excursions, and nature treks guided by the most experienced local experts. In addition, optional scuba and snorkeling programs aboard their own fleet of boats (including their 42-foot jet boat Auriga) are offered daily to interested guests of all skill levels. This is truly a great place to stay!

SERENITY RESORT, *tel. (06) 23232, fax (06) 23231. $75 single/$85 double. $25 per extra adult, $10 for children. Add $30 for three meals. Off-season rates available.*

The most substantial resort in the Placencia area, the new Serenity consists of 12 private beach side cabanas, and an additional 10 double air conditioned rooms. All accommodations here have private bathrooms, comfortable furnishings, ceiling fans, daily maid service, mini-refrigerators, coffee makers, and verandahs. The grounds are large, with 1000 feet of white sandy beach frontage. Guests can bring their own alcohol. All meals are individually prepared and served in the new sea view restaurant by local Creole, Mayan, and Garifuna staff.

A large variety of sea and land excursions with expert guides can be easily arranged. There are also special conference and business meeting facilities available on the premises. This is the perfect place to soothe your mind, body, and soul in a tropical paradise.

THE NAUTICAL INN, *Seine Bight Village, Placencia, tel. & fax (06) 22310. 12 double cabana rooms. $75 to $89 single/$85 to $99 double. Add $30 for 3 meals daily. Multiple day dive packages available. US Reservations: (800) 225-6732.*

The spacious modern rooms at the inn are situated inside three duplex octagonal cabanas on a beautiful private beach. All of the sun drenched rooms here have either air conditioning or ceiling fans, deluxe private bathrooms, hotel quality bedding, and mahogany furnishings. The main Oar House contains the inn's bar (with a satellite television system) and a dining room featuring three meals a day. Besides the beach and adjacent volleyball court, guests can rent a Hobie Cat, motorized scooters, and a canoe. The Nautical Inn also provides daily tours to scuba and snorkeling sights along the Cayes, boats rides to Monkey River, and trips by air conditioned van to Mayan temples.

The smiling staff here all come from the traditional Garifuna village of Seine Bight. If you want a great seaside hotel with all the services, facilities, and standards of a 4 star hotel, this is the place to go!

KITTY'S PLACE, *tel. 06-22017. 3 units. A small apartment upstairs in a beach tower, with butane refrigerator, cooktop, two beds and full bath, goes for $70 per day; the two rooms downstairs, sharing bath, for $30 single/$40 double, plus 10% service plus tax. Another apartment with separate bedroom goes for $90 plus service charge, rooms with private both for $50 single/$60 double.*

The extensive grounds include coconut palms and cashew trees, and assorted chickens, ducks and rabbits, not to mention the ante-bellum sports bar.

The new **WESTWINDS HOTEL** *on the beach just steps away from the heart of town, tel. (06) 23255*, offers an assortment of nice rooms with plenty of atmosphere.

TURTLE INN, *tel. 062-3244. 6 cottages. $45/$50, plus $30 for three meals, no service charge. Visa and Master Card. Rates are slightly lower June through September. U.S. reservations: 2190 Bluebell, Boulder, CO 80302, tel. 303-444-2555.*

Talk about low-key — there's not even a sign to identify the Turtle Inn. The guest units are thatch-roofed bamboo structures lined with reed mats, raised to catch the breeze. Each has an RV-type toilet. All electricity is from solar panels, so the background generator hum found at many Belizean resorts is missing. Meals are mainly seafood. A two-bedroom beach house is available by the week. The American owners specialize in land, sea and river float trips, and rainforest treks and overnight stays.

MOTHER OCEAN'S TROPICAL ENVIRONMENT AND RE-SEARCH STATION, formerly The Cove, *P. O. Box 007, tel. 06-22024, fax 22305. 6 rooms. $75 per person daily, plus 10% service plus tax, with three meals, or $65 per person from May through October. American Express, Visa, Master Card. U.S. reservations: 800-662-3091.*

These are clapboard cottages on stilts, all with private bath and ceiling fans, about a mile north of Placencia. Each has two queen-sized beds. The screened porches have hammocks, and there's a tennis court. Scuba, snorkeling and fly fishing and trolling are available, along with hosting of fishery and oceanic research.

SONNY'S RESORT, *12 units. Reservations: tel. 06-22103 (Placencia) or 13 and F streets, King's Park, Belize City, tel. 02-44975.*

Right in Placencia Village, and only in Belize: house trailers pulled up onto the sand, with screened porches added on. More attractive are six cabanas. Each is panelled inside, has a ceiling fan, tiled bathroom with tub, mini-refrigerator and coffee pot. The rate is $50 for up to four people. Trailer rooms are $30 single/$40 double.

TRADE WINDS CABANAS, *near the Placencia Co-op dock, has five units, two individual cabanas at $50 per night accommodating up to four persons, and three rooms at $20 for two to three persons.*

All have private bath and hot water.

RANGUANA LODGE, *tel. and manual fax 06-23112*, has the fanciest cabana units in Placencia, each with one double and one single bed, a bathroom with tub, refrigerator, coffee pot, porch, and genuine wood panelling, though the beds could be better. *The rate is $70 double with tax. Visa and Master Card accepted.*

Budget Lodging & Camping

Several establishments in the center of Placencia Village charge $10 to $15 double – not a bad price, but don't expect luxury. **RAN'S** is a cool house shaded by palms, *back from the sea*. The **HOTEL HELLO** has simple rooms, some with private bath, *right on the beach*. Pleasant. Look for the white house with blue trim.

The **SEASPRAY**, *also on the seafront*, is comparable. **MISS LUCILLE'S**, *the yellow house behind the Galley eatery*, has several clean cubicles with fans, sharing toilet facilities. Other rooms are available next to the Seaspray. **MISS LYDIA'S**, *100 yards north of Jene's restaurant (tel. 06-23117)*, has clean little rooms with fans, sharing toilet and shower facilities. The proprietor will also make coco bread on order.

More substantial (though still unluxurious) are the rooms at the **PARADISE VACATION HOTEL** (formerly Dalton's E-lee), *the clapboard building 200 yards west of the co-op's pier at the southern tip of Placencia, next to the Tentacles bar.* Airy rooms upstairs go for $10 per person with sea view, balcony, and shared bath. Less breezy rooms downstairs, with private baths, are $25 double.

Seine Bight, *three miles north of Placencia*, is a quiet Garifuna village of unpainted stilt houses. Basic seafront accommodations are available.

Parking for camping vehicles is available at **KITTY'S PLACE**, *a mile and a half north of Placencia Point (tel. 06-22027), for $5 per night*. There are other places where you can pitch your tent for $1 per person, but you're on your own as to washing and the like.

WHERE TO EAT

JENE'S restaurant and bar, *opposite the Seaspray hotel*, is a comfortable, dark-wood-panelled room that suits Placencia to a "t." Meals run from $4 for rice and beans to $10 for lobster, with chow mein, conch, shrimp and steak in between. Also sandwiches and breakfasts. Try the turtle steak. Good food, attractively served. They also have an assortment of wine, as well as hard liquor and beer, and sea weed, a milk shake made with marine flora, and liquor if you wish. A *notice* advises that British Forces are excluded, due to consistently rowdy behavior.

Other, tourist-style bars have arrived, and more no doubt will come. The **KINGFISHER** is a large thatched pavilion *facing the sea*, serving fish, pork chops, t-bone steak, shrimp and lobster for from $6 to $15. **TENTACLES** is a bar and steak house that extends over the water, *at the very south of the peninsula*. You can get fish fried, poached, or broiled, or shrimp sauteed in butter — something more elegant than the usual back-country food.

The **GALLEY**, *along the sidewalk south of downtown Placencia*, serves burgers, fries, fish and juices at all hours during the day. (Most eateries are open from 7:30 or 8 a.m. to 2 p.m., and from 7 to 11 p.m.)

North of town by more than a mile, **FRANCO'S RESTAURANT** is the sportsman's bar and restaurant, in a balconied plantation-style house, a great second-story area open to the sea, with fans overhead, extensive nautical decoration, loads of books and tapes, and television usually showing the most important football, baseball or basketball game from somewhere in the world. The set meal for $12.50, served upon reservation, usually includes seafood; breakfast and sandwiches are available as well.

Call a few hours ahead to reserve a table at one of the many fine resort dining rooms. Meals in these places are much better than average, and contain several home-made entrees that can be found nowhere else. A typical dinner at a seaside hotel should average $14 to $18 including hearty soup, fresh salads, a seafood or meat entree, seasonal vegetables, and tempting desserts.

NIGHTLIFE

What little action available here during weekend nights takes place over at either the **Cozy Corner** disco just off the beach, or the **Dockside** bar near the pier. Don't even think about showing up before 11pm if you want to see other people there.

EXCURSIONS

The barrier reef offshore is still little visited, and, in some places, unexplored. Small cayes are protected by the reef. Diving and picnicking trips can be arranged at the **Placencia Dive Shop** in the village next to the fishing co-op pier, *tel. (06)-23313*. **Rum Point Inn**, **Nautical Inn**, and the **Turtle Inn** also have new dive boats from which visitors can either scuba or snorkel. Other resort hotels can make arrangements as well.

Typical rates for a day's excursion with two dives is $70 to $80, depending on how far you go; certification courses run around $350, day snorkeling trips with lunch at about $40 and up.

SPORTS & RECREATION

Serenity Resort, *tel. (06) 23232*, offers several inland tours to the Jaguar reserve and Mayan ruins. Dave Dial has full day and overnight trips by boat available to Monkey River, a fishing village down the coast. Most resorts also rent canoes, windsurfers, bicycles, and assorted gear for diving and snorkeling.

A small boat for fishing can be rented for $100 to $150 per day, depending on who you're dealing with and how far out you're going and the time of year (rates are lower in July and August, when things are slow).

Charlie Leslie (Kingfisher Sports), among others, can drop you at Tobacco Caye to camp out or stay in basic accommodations, or set you up for fishing in the flats for bonefish, permit, snook and tarpon. He has a new camp at Punta Negra, down the coast. The weekly rate is about $1,500, and if you're really into fishing, it could be worth it. *Contact Charlie Leslie at 062-3104, or, in the States, Robert Hardy, 107 Lafayette, San Antonio, TX 78209, tel. 512-822-6415.*

And you will find signs posted by Captain Joel, Conrad, at Miss Lydia's rooms *(tel. 06-23117)* and many others offering fishing and snorkeling.

On the Mainland

Mango Creek and **Big Creek**, on the mainland opposite Placencia, are settlements of sun-weathered clapboard houses that have turned into beehives of activity in the last couple of years. Newly constructed deep-water docking and container facilities at Big Creek serve citrus and banana exports from southern Belize, and Texans and Louisianans take refuge in the air-conditioned hotel in Big Creek between bouts of oil exploration.

A branch road leads from Mango Creek and Big Creek to the Southern Highway. For access information, see Placencia, above.

WHERE TO STAY IN BIG CREEK & MANGO CREEK

The recently renovated **HELLO HOTEL** *in Mango Creek (tel. 06-22011)*, with a dozen rooms with private bath and air conditioning, is your best bet, going for about $40 double.

Another good choice would be over at the **PLACENCIA LAGOON RESORT**, *tel. (06) 22363*, where you will find mid priced comfortable guestrooms located right off Malacate Beach in Big Creek. They also offer meals.

NIM LI PUNIT

Located about a half mile off the west side of the Southern Highway, in the vicinity of mile 75, is the **Nim Li Punit** archaeological site. No restoration work has been done, and the site is only partially cleared; but it makes for a nice picnic spot if you're driving through.

Nim Li Punit (*Big Hat*, from the head gear shown on one of the stelae) was discovered in 1974 during exploration for oil, and, as often happens to Mayan ruins, was soon looted. A tomb of a noble, overlooked by the robbers, was uncovered by archaeologist Richard Leventhal in 1986.

Nim Li Punit includes several groups of buildings set on plazas, and a ball court. Only the southmost group can be visited. Twenty-five stelae have been found. One, 31 feet high, is the tallest carved stela in Belize. Or it would have been, had it ever been erected. It appears to have been unused because of an error in carving.

Stelae at Nim Li Punit bear dates, in the western equivalent, between 700 and 800 A.D. As many as 5000 people might have lived at the site in that period. Similarities in architecture, and proximity, suggest a connection with the larger site of Lubaantun, to the southwest.

Access to the site is by a trail from the Southern Highway. A sign points the way. If you're heading south and see the Whitney lumber mill on the east side of the road, you'll know you've gone too far.

BIG FALLS

Just to the south of Nim Li Punit is **Big Falls**, *where the Southern Highway crosses the Rio Grande*. Nearby are the only known warm springs in Belize, on the Peter Alaman farm. Mr. Alaman runs a general store, and can direct you to the springs. Ask for permission if you're interested in camping. Big Falls is a popular weekend bathing and picnicking spot.

PUNTA GORDA

Nearly two hundred miles by road from Belize City, or half that distance by sea or air, **Punta Gorda** (population 3000) is the last town of any size in southern Belize. Predominantly a Carib settlement, Punta Gorda also includes assorted Creoles, Mopan Maya, Kekchi, Chinese, Lebanese and East Indians in its ethnic quilt. Once exclusively a fishing village, Punta Gorda has been converted into an agricultural market town by the construction of roads to the interior and to Belize City. Beans and rice, produced by Carib and Indian farmers, are the major food crops.

ORIENTATION

Punta Gorda is airy, breezy, open, hill-fringed, and quiet and affable. The center of town is more or less the area by the pier, where there is a lovely verandahed post office-governmental services building, and a pole on which a signal beacon is run up at night. The market is at Queen and Front streets, but there's generally not much activity.

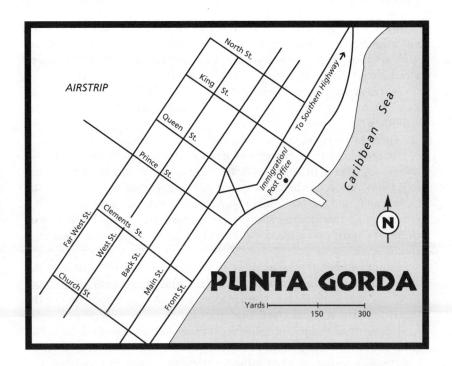

The seafront in town is not for swimming — sewer pipes run into the water, for one — but the narrow, long beach to the north is attractive. The main highway runs along it for a couple of miles before turning inland. Punta Gorda is near the end of Belize, but not at the end of the world. The Voice of America has an antenna complex on the outskirts, and is a major local employer. Texans are occasionally present to look for oil, and missionaries and foreign "experts" are here on assignments.

Then there are the Gurkha and British troops stationed nearby to make sure that the Guatemalans don't take their claims to Belize too seriously. Harrier jets from Belize City roar down along the coast and perform impossible turns in full view of the residents of Punta Gorda, and, more importantly, of the Guatemalans. Helicopters ferry soldiers to hilltop jungle observation posts, from which, unofficially, they saunter down to shops over the line to buy packs of cigs, watched, but not stopped, by their Guatemalan opposite numbers.

Nightlife consists of the **Dreamlight Disco**, *on Main St. opposite Mahung's Hotel*; and walking under the glow of stars, and of the lights atop the Voice of America radio towers.

In many Belizean towns, much of the local activity consists of children going back and forth to and from school; but more so in Punta Gorda, where educating children from villages of the hinterland is something of a cottage industry. The kids arrive every morning by bus. One of the educational institutions, on Front St., is a collection of long, multistory clapboard buildings with rows of shutters; they look like nothing so much as outsize chicken coops.

If you are not continuing into Guatemala, the **Maya Indita** store *on Middle St.* has one of the best selections in Belize of Guatemalan weaving and other craft items.

To be taken as an old hand, always refer to Punta Gorda as "P.G."

Across the Bay of Honduras from Punta Gorda is **Livingston**, *in Guatemala*, also a mainly Carib settlement. A regular boat service is maintained between the two towns. Offshore, the southern end of the barrier reef, and the Sapodilla and Ranguana Cayes — little frequented picnicking and swimming spots — are accessible by boat. Punta Gorda itself is the most rain-soaked spot in Belize, and vegetation in the area is suitably exuberant.

Punta Gorda has seen its share of adventurers and outcasts over the years. Caribs were the first to find refuge. Later, in 1866, emigrants from the Confederacy, which had been in loose alliance with Britain during the American Civil War, received land grants.

Just north of Punta Gorda are the remains of their Toledo settlement, where sugar cane was planted. The settlement slowly disintegrated, as the descendants of the original refugees tried their luck in other parts of Belize, or returned to the United States.

Later years brought laborers deported from India, Creoles from up north, and Indians from Guatemala.

ARRIVALS & DEPARTURES

Arriving By Ferry

A ferry leaves from Puerto Barrios, Guatemala, on Tuesdays and Fridays at 7:30 a.m. for Punta Gorda. Fare is about $6.

Arriving By Bus

Z-Line buses leave Belize City (Magazine Rd. west of Collet Canal, *tel. 73937*) for Punta Gorda daily via Dangriga. Fare is about $8, and the trip can take up to eight hours, depending on road conditions.

Arriving By Air

Flights on **Maya Airways** *(tel. 02-77215)* operate from the Belize City airstrip for Punta Gorda at 8:30 a.m., 2:30 p.m., and 4:30 p.m. via Dangriga and Placencia. One daily **Tropic Air** flight operates to Punta Gorda. Fare is about $63.

Departing By Ferry

A ferry leaves for Puerto Barrios, Guatemala, on Tuesdays and Fridays at 2 p.m. Fare is about $8. Get your ticket as early as possible in the two-story brick building on Middle St., next to the Maya Indita store. *Call 07-22065 to verify the current schedule.* Check out with immigration before boarding, with your Guatemalan visa or tourist card in hand.

If you miss the boat, a charter trip can be arranged in a skiff for something like $100.

Departing By Bus

Z-Line buses leave for Belize City several times daily, less frequently on Sundays.

Departing By Air

Maya Airways flights operate northbound multiple flights each day (less often on Sundays). One daily **Tropic Air** flight operates northbound connecting with flights at the Belize international airport.

Tickets on both airlines are sold at Bob Pennell's hardware store/ insurance agency on Main Street in Punta Gorda. Reserve as far in advance as possible. Fare is about $63 to Belize City.

WHERE TO STAY

Telephone dialing code for Punta Gorda is 07 from Belize, 011-501-7 from the U.S.A.

The clean and airy seafront **NATURE'S WAY GUEST HOUSE**, *at 65 Front St., at the south end of town (tel. 07-22119, P. O. Box 75)*, is an off-beat place, a wooden house with odd corners and nooks. There are only eight rooms, each with one large bed and a small upper bunk. Access to local ways is facilitated if you stay here, as the owners are an American-Belizean couple. They keep a collection of books and source material on the peoples and places of southern Belize. *About $15 single/$20 double, no service charge, no credit cards. Most of the rooms are with shared bath.*

The **MIRA MAR HOTEL**, *a concrete building near the center of town at 95 Front Street (tel. 07-22033)*, has rooms in several tiers with private bath and fans, above the Chinese restaurant. *Rates range from $19 to $55 single/ $30 to $74 double, including tax. The surprising top rate gets you air conditioning, cable television, and mini-refrigerator.*

Away from the water, the **SAINT CHARLES INN**, *23 King St. (tel. 07-22149, 15 rooms, $16 single/$25 double)*, is a substantial house with fair-sized rooms, all with fans, most with private bath with hot water, and cable television. If nobody is visible to serve you, inquire at the general store next door. **G & G'S INN**, *49 Main Middle St., tel. 22086*, has rooms in the same price range.

Your basic lodging houses, at $10 per person or less, include **PALLAVI'S HOTEL**, *19 Main St.*; the **ISABEL**, *on Front St. near the town center*; and **MAHUNG'S HOTEL**, *11 Main St. (tel. 22044).* Mahung's is probably the best bet for cleanliness, though the late hours bar across the street might not be an asset. The **WAHIMA HOTEL**, also with cheap rooms, *is along the seafront just north of the Texaco gasoline station.*

STAY IN A MAYAN VILLAGE

There's an unusual program afoot in Punta Gorda to spread the benefits of tourism by arranging for visitors to stay with families in the interior. This involves spending hundreds of dollars for your ticket, taking time off from work, and ending up somewhere in the bush to sleep on a hard bed or in a hammock in a thatch-roofed hut with a dirt floor, stumble in the dark through the scratching chickens to an outhouse, eat rice and beans, and wash with cold water, and if you see it strictly in these terms, skip to the next section, please.

So what's in it for you? Meeting local people as people, who go about their daily business to survive and enjoy life, not as servants to outsiders. Learning how corn is soaked in lime water and prepared for making tortillas; how wild herbs are used in cooking, and to cure illness; how local materials are harvested from the forest to build houses; how crops are grown with a minimum of chemicals.

Tilling corn and beans, splitting firewood, beating clothes on rocks in a river. Hiking to caves and visiting ancient cities with native guides. Seeing how it's possible to live without cars and piped gas and electricity, and also how radios and satellite TV have made their way to some of the more remote places on earth. And giving indigenous peoples the assurance that they have something to contribute to the west of the world, as well as some of the cash that normally flows to more go-getter types in the tourist trade.

*If you're interested, contact the **Toledo Visitors Information Center** at the wharf. Most of the families speak English and Spanish, as well as their native tongue. In strictly monetary terms, the price of lodging is under $15 per person per night, and meals are less than $5 each, and there is a registration fee of about $10 with the Toledo Visitors Information Center.*

More formal guest houses are being organized in participating villages, with western-style toilets. And it's possible to stay as a paying house guest by making your own inquiries in villages in the bush. One reader has recommended the house of the José and Amillia Oh family, near San Pedro Columbia, as "the cleanest place I stayed in Belize." She had a room in the family sleeping house with a private entry, explored for medicinal herbs, and visited the ruins and caves of the area in the company of Mr. Oh. The Ohs can be reached through a neighbor's phone at 07-22303 – call in the evening, and tell when you will call back.

Hotels North of Punta Gorda

SAFE HAVEN LODGE, *Office at 2 Prince St., Punta Gorda, tel. 07-22113. $100 single/$140 double with meals.*

A fishing and diving lodge, located on the Rio Grande, a few miles north of Punta Gorda, and just off the sea. Packages include meals, lodging, and transport from Punta Gorda. Fishing packages do not include tackle. Non-sportsmen ("eco-guests") are allowed use of a boat. Currently, there are five cabanas with two rooms each, and a few rooms in the fishing lodge, which is a large house with beamed ceiling and veranda. Food is mostly seafood, with some local and Chinese plates, and special requests honored.

ACCESS BELIZE, *adjacent to Safe Haven,* is in development as a lodge free of barriers to the disabled and elderly. *For information, contact Alda M. Lyons, 95 Washington St. no. 217, Weymouth, MA 02188, tel. 617-843-0404, fax 617-331-1785.*

WHERE TO EAT

This is not one of the high points of Punta Gorda, but things are gradually improving.

NATURE'S WAY GUEST HOUSE, in continuing evolution, serves meals on an airy, garden-bordered porch. $3 gets you a breakfast of eggs and beans and huge slabs of home-baked bread. Lunch or dinner, with rice and beans, and chicken or beef or fish and salad, runs $4 to $5. Ask to sample Mayan and Carib dishes. For just sitting and watching the palms and the sea, this is the place.

The **MORNING GLORY CAFÉ,** *59 Front Street,* is clean, open for breakfast, reasonably priced, and affords a sea view.

The **KOWLOON,** *opposite the Maya Indita store on Middle St.,* has a real menu, with hamburgers and other sandwiches for $2 or less, and meals with fried fish, chow mein and assorted Chinese and non-Chinese main courses for $4 and up. They can modify something to order if it's not too much trouble. A plain and simple place, with video parlor in the front room, but clean.

The **MIRAMAR HOTEL** *on Front St.* has a Chinese restaurant, the hours of which are a well-kept secret. $6 and up for a meal. **GOYO's,** *up on the triangular town square,* serves home-style (inelegant) meals of fried chicken, stewed pork or eggs for $4. There's no sign on the concrete building.

And there are various other cook shops around, among them **BOBBY'S** restaurant and bar, *next to the Dreamlight disco, across from Mahung's hotel;* and **LUCILLE'S** kitchen, *around the corner.* And the airstrip at Punta Gorda has a snack bar.

EXCURSIONS

The **Nature's Way Guesthouse**, *65 Front St.*, runs trips in a van to sites near Punta Gorda. For six persons, a trip to Blue Creek or Lubaantun costs $75; slightly more if you stop at both sites. They'll also arrange boat trips: $75 to Moho Caye, $150 to Hunting Caye, or $225 to the Río Dulce in Guatemala — and back. And they have camping equipment and a sleep-aboard trimaran available for rent, a sailboat, inflatables and windsurfers, and can help with arrangements for fishing.

Julio Requeña, *12 Front St., tel. 07-22070*, also offers boat charters and van trips.

The **Toledo Visitors Information Center** *(P. O. Box 73, Punta Gorda, tel. 07-22470)*, a private operation, located at the wharf, specializes in low-impact tourism, village stays with Kekchi and Mopan families (see below), and river, fishing and caye trips.

There are also a few taxis — the rate is about $120 for a day-long excursion — but otherwise, not much in the way of an organized tourism industry. A few roads poke back into the hinterland of Punta Gorda, over flat ranch and rice land, and into pocket canyons in the jungled foothills of the Maya Mountains. A route taking in the Indian villages of San Pedro Columbia and San Antonio, the Mayan site of Lubaantun, and the cave at Blue Creek, is described below.

Traders regularly go on foot from San Antonio village inland over a good trail to the border, but the route isn't recommended for outsiders, who need entry stamps and visas. Passable agricultural roads also go to the southern border, at the Sarstoon River, and to Barranco, the southern-most coastal settlement.

Inland from Punta Gorda

Two Indian villages in the back country are interesting for the old ways maintained by their inhabitants. Nearby are some important archaeological sites. A day trip is most feasible if you have your own means of transport.

SAN PEDRO COLUMBIA

San Pedro Columbia is a settlement of Kekchi Indians whose forebears came to Belize to escape forced labor on coffee plantations in the Verapaz region of Guatemala. Traditionally isolated and self-suffi-cient, the Indians of San Pedro and nearby San Antonio have recently added the market crops of red beans and rice to their corn and black bean agriculture.

Many houses in San Pedro are thatched pole structures built entirely of local forest materials. Often, a piece of corrugated sheet metal at the ridge of the roof is the only hint that the inhabitants live in the machine age. San Pedro's women dress in distinctively long wraparound skirts similar to those worn by Indians in Guatemala, but the material is now often cut from machine-woven bolts of cloth, rather than being hand-loomed. Grinding corn with stone querns, cooking over wood fires, and laboriously tilling the earth with only a hoe are a few of the daily activities of the inhabitants of San Pedro that seem to belong to another era.

On the way into San Pedro is **Dem Dat's Doin'**, a self-styled "resource center for self-sufficiency and microenterprises," with plant nursery, fruit trees, biogas digester, solar electric panels, and, for any visitors who drop in and pay the entrance fee, a souvenir shop.

LUBAANTUN

Located on the outskirts of San Pedro Columbia, **Lubaantun** (*Fallen Stones*) is the major Mayan archaeological site in southern Belize. The ruins were first reported to the outside world by refugee Southerners of the Toledo settlement, in 1875, and have been explored at various times by archaeologists and adventurers, among them Thomas Gann. Recent excavations were carried out by Norman Hammond.

The ceremonial center of Lubaantun, like that of Xunantunich, to the northwest, is atop a ridge that dominates the countryside. A series of plazas, each surrounded by stone temples and palaces, ascends from south to north, conforming with the rising ridge line. The structures are mostly terraced, and overlie earlier buildings. Around the ceremonial center are hillsides that show signs of also having been terraced, and faced with masonry, either as an esthetic continuation of the plaza architecture, or for agricultural purposes.

The major structure at Lubaantun is 40 feet high and 100 feet in length, and the plazas are relatively long and wide. But the natural hills that Lubaantun's temples cap give the impression that structures are taller. On a clear day, an observer atop the temples can see to Punta Gorda.

Unusually, temples and palaces at Lubaantun were constructed of precision-cut stones, fitted together without mortar. The corners of some structures are rounded, a characteristic also of some sites along the Usumacinta River to the north. Sides of structures are formed of two-stone courses, with the upper stones protruding. Superstructures atop the temples were probably made of perishable materials, such as wood and thatch, for nothing remains.

Some of the original lime-mortar facing and flooring can still be seen. A ball court indicates that some kind of game was played, either for recreation or as part of a religious or political ritual. Three ball-court markers, removed for safekeeping, are the only carved monuments discovered so far at the site.

Life in Lubaantun

Excavations at Lubaantun have yielded a wealth of materials that reflect the way of life of the ancient inhabitants. The most interesting discoveries are molded whistle figurines, an art form uncommon among the Classic Maya. Found in burials, the figurines, as well as bespeaking an interest in music, illustrate Mayan styles of dress, and show that weaving techniques included tapestry and tie-dying, still used by Maya-related peoples in Guatemala. Black and red and green powders might have been used as facial makeup and body paint, applied using iron pyrite mirrors.

Grinding stones indicate that corn was prepared for tortillas just as it is today. One grinding stone showed traces of flint, which was ground and added to clay to make pottery. Conch shells and fish bones might have come from **Wild Cane Caye**, a Mayan maritime outpost. Jade beads, obsidian knives and turquoise came from a considerable distance away. The inhabitants of Lubaantun probably traded with the highlands of present-day Guatemala, using cacao beans as their currency. The figure of a skull made from a transparent, glass-like quartz (the so-called "crystal skull") is of uncertain origin—it might have come from Brazil as late as the sixteenth century, though the daughter of Mitchell Hedges, the archaeologist who discovered it, claims an ancient Mayan origin for the piece.

The materials found at Lubaantun indicate that the city reached its peak toward the end of the eighth century A.D. All building of ceremonial structures came to an end soon after.

The little-visited Lubaantun site is open from 8 a.m. to 5 p.m.

The temples are overgrown with trees, not prettified by modern reconstruction, but beautiful in their existing state. The caretaker will show you where various items — caches of mollusk shells, a human jawbone — were discovered, point out what might have been a prison for captives, and indicate where native religious rituals have been performed even in recent times. Bring your own refreshments.

ARRIVALS & DEPARTURES
By Car

To reach Lubaantun from Punta Gorda, drive west to a mile and a half past the Shell gasoline station at the junction of the Southern Highway, then turn right — currently, there's no sign. Two miles ahead is San Pedro Columbia. Continue to the left around the church, then right and downhill, over a concrete bridge, for about a mile. To the left is the trail to the site, passable in vehicle in the dry season for part of the way. Park at the turnout before the rotted plank bridge.

There are Mayan hilltop structures stretching all over the area beyond the excavated part of Lubaantun. About three miles to the northwest, along the Columbia Branch of the Rio Grande, is **Uxbentun** (*Ancient Stones*), also on a leveled hilltop, and largely unexcavated. The related site of Nim Li Punit is to the northeast, just off the Southern Highway.

SAN ANTONIO

The Mopan Maya who settled **San Antonio**, *a hilltop village west of San Pedro Columbia*, fled military service and taxes in San Luis, about 30 miles to the west in Guatemala, at the end of the nineteenth century. At first, the crops they planted in forest clearings did poorly, and disease and sickness afflicted the migrants. Analyzing the situation clearly, the Indians marched back to San Luis, raided the church, and carried off the statues of their saints to their new village. Thereafter, people and crops prospered, though the authorities of San Luis pressed unsuccessfully for years for the return of the religious figures.

San Antonio has a substantial stone church and mission house. Thatch and pole and plank dwellings made from local materials are still seen; but these are giving way to standard Belizean clapboard houses. Most men are farmers of corn and vegetables. Women wear long skirts, and loose blouses. The village is close-knit, and cooperative ways still flourish. Villagers assist each other in burning off their corn fields, or milpas. Dances are performed at fiesta times — particularly June 13 — by young men in masks and costumes. These are Indian traditions carried from Guatemala, though, unusually, girls participate in the ceremonies.

ARRIVALS & DEPARTURES

By Car

To reach San Antonio from Lubaantun, drive back to the road from Punta Gorda, go westward for just over two miles, then go right at the fork for another two miles.

About a mile west of San Antonio is a waterfall. Another two miles onward, near Santa Cruz, is the **Uxbenka** (*Old Place*) archaeological site with twenty stelae, seven of them carved, and one dating from the Early Classic period, a time period corresponding to few of the glyphs on Mayan structures in southern Belize.

WHERE TO STAY

There's one lodging place in San Antonio, the simple, pleasant, **BOL'S HILLTOP**. It is, indeed, *at the top of the hill*, a concrete-block structure with balconies. Rooms are quite small and bare, but clean, with shared bathroom, and the location affords a breeze. *The rate is about $5* *per person, and meals can be ordered.* By all means stay here if you have a vehicle and don't want to hurry back to Punta Gorda.

BLUE CREEK

Southeast of San Antonio are the caves at **Blue Creek**. From San Antonio, drive back to the junction, and follow the sign to Aguacate. Blue Creek is five miles onward, past Blue Creek village, at a narrow concrete bridge where bare-breasted Maya women beat their laundry on the rocks, and bathe themselves. Park alongside the road, and drop in at the attendant's hut to sign the register. You'll note that somebody turns up to visit only every few days; sometimes every few weeks.

Follow the clearly marked trail inland, along the stream, over dirt and then rocks. Less than half a mile from the road is an open-sided camp building.

What an enchanting spot. Trees arch 100 feet overhead, bromeliad-laden, canopying the stream. Vines hang down into the lazy blue-green waters. It's worth it to come to Belize just to have a picnic and swim here. But there's more.

From the camp house, keep to the path that follows the water (not the one farther north), then continues along a seasonally dry creek. If you lose your way, don't try to blaze a trail in the jungle — some of the plants are unfriendly. Retrace your steps until you find the trail again. The trail cuts across the smaller creek, and through a boulder-strewn area. After about 15 minutes, you'll scramble over rocks, up to where water gushes out into the open at the base of a box canyon laden with luxuriant vegetation, several hundred feet high; and tumbles through pools and over boulders.

Adjacent, to the north, is a large cave entrance; be careful in exploring. The water is cool, not frigid, perfect after your scamper. Go skinny dipping if nobody is around, which is usually the case.

PUSILHA

The **Pusilha ruins**, *just a mile east of the Guatemalan border*, are accessible only by boat. The ceremonial center characteristically sits on a hilltop, with terraced limestone hills nearby. There are many caves in the area, some of which were used by the ancient Maya.

Like Lubaantun, Pusilha was a low-lying city. Arches and stone superstructures are lacking. The longest building measures 400 feet by 130 feet wide, but is only 16 feet high. More than 20 carved monuments have been found in one plaza, including stelae and carved stones in the forms of jaguars and ocelots. An unusual feature is a pair of abutments from a bridge that once spanned the Pusilha River, a branch of the Moho River that enters the Caribbean south of Punta Gorda. Also unusual is a walled-in ball-court. Another of this type is found at Nim Li Punit. Pusilha carved monuments include zoomorphs — animal-like sculptures — similar to those of Quiriguá, in Guatemala. Stelae bear date glyphs ranging from the equivalent of 573 A.D. to 731 A.D.

Archaeological sites abound along the rivers of southern Belize. Wherever a mound appears that doesn't quite belong in the natural landscape, chances are that an ancient Mayan structure lies just underneath the surface. It might once have been excavated, and then again, it might have been untouched for centuries.

INDEX

FROM THE PUBLISHER

Our goal is to provide you with a guide book that is second to none. Please remember, however, that things do change: phone numbers, prices, addresses, quality of food served, value, etc. Should you come across any new information, we'd appreciate hearing from you. No item is too small, so if you have any recommendations or suggested changes, please write to us.

Have a great trip!

Open Road Publishing
P.O. Box 20226
Columbus Circle Station
New York, NY 10023

TRAVEL NOTES

YOUR PASSPORT TO GREAT TRAVEL!
FROM OPEN ROAD PUBLISHING

THE CLASSIC CENTRAL AMERICA GUIDES - ALL NEW!

COSTA RICA GUIDE by Paul Glassman, 6th Ed. This classic travel guide to Costa Rica remains the standard against which all others are judged. Discover great accommodations, reliable restaurants, pristine beaches, and incredible diving, fishing, and other water sports. Revised and updated. **$16.95**

BELIZE GUIDE by Paul Glassman, 7th Ed. This guide has quickly become the book of choice for Belize travelers. Perhaps the finest spot for Caribbean scuba diving and sport fishing, Belize's picture-perfect palm trees, Mayan ruins, tropical forests, uncrowded beaches, and fantastic water sports have made it one of the most popular Caribbean travel destinations. Revised and updated. **$14.95**

HONDURAS & BAY ISLANDS GUIDE by J.P. Panet with Leah Hart and Paul Glassman, 3rd Ed. Open Road's superior series of Central America travel guides continues with the revised look at this beautiful land. **$14.95**

GUATEMALA GUIDE by Paul Glassman, 9th Ed. Glassman's treatment of colorful Guatemala remains the single best source in print. **$16.95**

CENTRAL AMERICA GUIDE by Paul Glassman, 1st Ed. If you're planning on visiting several countries in the region, you've got to get Open Road's new guide to all of Central America's top spots – 768 pages of great coverage to Costa Rica, Belize, Honduras, Guatemala, Panama, Nicaragua and El Salvador! **$17.95**

OTHER TITLES OF INTEREST

BERMUDA GUIDE by Ron Charles, 1st Ed. Discover fun-filled Bermuda and revel in a perfect vacation escape. Ron Charles leads you to world-class lodging, elegant restaurants, beautiful pink sand beaches, terrific shopping, and all the water sports you can think of! **$14.95**

SOUTHERN MEXICO & YUCATAN GUIDE by Eric Hamovitch. Complete coverage of beautiful southern Mexico and the Yucatan peninsula. Discover terrific beaches, majestic Mayan ruins, great water sports, and the latest on hotels, restaurants, activities, nightlife, sports and more! **$14.95**

PLEASE USE ORDER FORM ON NEXT PAGE

ORDER FORM

Name and Address: _____

_____

_____

_____ Zip Code: _____

Quantity	Title	Price

Total Before Shipping _____

Shipping/Handling _____

TOTAL _____

Orders must include price of book <u>plus</u> shipping and handling. For shipping and handling, please add $3.00 for the first book, and $1.00 for each book thereafter.

Ask about our discounts for special order bulk purchases.

Order from:
OPEN ROAD PUBLISHING
P.O. Box 20226, Columbus Circle Station, New York, NY 10023